PRISONER
AT WAR

PRISONER AT WAR

The Survival of
Commander Richard A. Stratton

Scott Blakey

ANCHOR PRESS/DOUBLEDAY
GARDEN CITY, NEW YORK
1978

ACKNOWLEDGMENTS

The author gratefully acknowledges the permission to reprint copyrighted material from the following:

Quotations from *To Kill a Mockingbird* by Harper Lee, copyright © 1960 by Harper Lee, reprinted by permission of J. B. Lippincott Company. Quotations from Michael Miner from an article in the *Chicago Journalism Review,* May 1973. Quotations from Harrison Salisbury's introduction to *The Prison Diary of Ho Chi Minh,* published by Bantam Books, Inc., 1971. Quotations from the New York *Times* issue of February 13, 1973, © 1973 by The New York Times Company; reprinted by permission. Quotations from "Soldiers," Part I, by Ward Just, published in *The Atlantic Monthly,* October 1970, reprinted with permission of International Creative Management, © 1970 by Ward Just. Quotations from the April 7, 1967, issue of *Life:* copyright © 1967 by Time Inc.; reprinted with permission. Excerpts from a *Life* article and interviews by *Life* assistant editor Margery Byers with the families of U.S. prisoners in North Vietnam: copyright © 1967 by Time Inc.; reprinted with permission. Quotations from interviews, with Douglas B. Hegdahl, reprinted with permission. Quotations from interviews with Mrs. Ellen Todd Cooper, reprinted with permission. Quotations from interviews with Captain Richard D. Mullen, USN, reprinted with permission. Quotations from Neil Sheehan in *The Pentagon Papers,* reprinted with permission from Times Books, Inc. Permission to use "Tell Brave Deeds of War" from *Poems of Stephen Crane* by Stephen Crane, published by Alfred A. Knopf, Inc. Quotations from *The Survivor* by Terrence Des Pres, Oxford University Press, © 1976 by Terrence Des Pres, reprinted with permission. Quotations from interview with Lee Lockwood: reprinted with permission. Quotations from *P.O.W.: A Definitive History of the American Prisoner-of-War Experience in Vietnam, 1964–1973,* by John G. Hubbell: copyright © 1976 by the Reader's Digest Association, Inc. Reprinted by permission from *P.O.W.: A Definitive History of the American Prisoner-of-War Experience in Vietnam, 1964–1973* by John G. Hubbell. Copyright © 1976 by the Reader's Digest Association, Inc.

ISBN: 0-385-12905-x
Library of Congress Catalog Card Number 77-92208

To
Lone, my wife,

and Yong Lūdvig Aksel Edwin Erting,
Royal Life Guard; Danish Resistance;
in memory

Author's Note

This book descended, after a fashion, from a documentary film entitled *2251 Days,* which I co-produced (along with Cynthia Samuels, whose original idea it was; the late Blair Stapp, and Joseph M. Russin) in 1973 for KQED television in San Francisco. A shorter version was broadcast the following year by PBS.

The evolution of PRISONER AT WAR, however, came about through my own research and interviews, though some passages from the original film have been included; the book was begun early in 1974 and completed in the fall of 1977.

It has not been my intention to write a political tract or an apologia for Vietnam. I have tried to give a detached rendering of the American involvement in Indochina. I also believe the despair and doubt the war engendered should not prevent the acknowledgment of its lessons or the recognition of examples of human courage such as the Strattons represent.

There are some things I should like to note briefly, in no particular order of importance:

In the majority of interviews, I defied my old-school newspaper training and used a tape recorder; also, in some instances, interviewees were allowed to review their remarks with the understanding that I reserved for myself final editorial control. All of my tapes, documents, transcripts, notes, and other research materials have been sent to the Hoover Institution at Stanford for inclusion in their Stratton archive.

PRISONER AT WAR was written, I am unhappy to say, without the benefit of interviews with any of the North Vietnamese participants. All my attempts, through colleagues, correspondence, or personal contacts, to travel to Vietnam and interview there were, perhaps understandably, rebuffed.

The United States Department of Defense has not participated in the research, writing, editing, or printing of any portion of this book. A copy of the final manuscript was sent to the Naval Recruiting Command as a courtesy.

Finally, some of the persons I interviewed for this book decided to speak for background purposes only, or wished for personal reasons that their comments be used without attribution. I complied with those requests.

I could not have written this book without the help or advice of a number of persons, and I should like to acknowledge them here:

First, to all participants, and particularly the Stratton family, I am beholden for the book itself.

Second, I am deeply grateful to Rob Haesler of the San Francisco *Chronicle*, a friend and colleague of many years, who read and edited, advised and encouraged through each page of each revision of the text; and to Michael D. Brennan, a former Marine Corps officer and a Vietnam veteran who gave freely of his time, expertise, and friendship.

I am grateful, too, to Edward Radenzel, former foreign affairs analyst of KQED, who advised me on the historical passages of the book, and Jack D. Hubbard of CBS News, who always produced (and in the nick of time) the missing fact, the long-lost source, the precise amount of encouragement. By the same token, I am indebted for the assistance of Ames Nelson and the Honorable François Simon de Quirielle in France, and Nicholas and Lynn Wiseman in Great Britain; also Jon Margolis, and Philip Menzies and William Berg, formerly of the Naval Health Research Center at San Diego.

My father-in-law, Aksel Erting, imprisoned by the Gestapo for his World War II resistance activities, shared with me the insights and sometimes painful recollections of his experiences that I might better understand Richard Stratton's; and my uncle, Lieutenant Colonel Stewart L. Chaloner, USAF (Ret.) lent invaluable advice on matters pertaining to the American military.

The initiators of this book and its constant supporters were Edward MacGuire and Lee Peterson.

Some of the persons who have also been constant supporters are Tom Dahlgren, Eugene Gartland, Mel Wax, Pat Boonazian, John and Margo Patterson Doss, Janet Erting, John L. Wasserman, John and Karen Dell, W. V. Moody, and Marty and Ann Heredia. Included here should be my ever-ebullient editor at Doubleday, Elizabeth Knappman, and my agent, Phyllis Seidel.

The yeoman work of bringing order out of the chaos of notes, revisions, corrections, and the like, was done by typists Gloria Choi and Marie Zane and translator Annegret Fortenberry.

Finally, my greatest thanks must go to my wife, Lone, who sometimes wondered if this book would ever be completed or if she had, in fact, wed a lunatic, but nonetheless sustained the family, beat off the bill collectors, and waited just to see, I suspect, how it all would end.

SCOTT BLAKEY

San Francisco
March 1978

CONTENTS

PART I YANKEE STATION   1

PART II BEGINNINGS   43

PART III PRISONERS   89

PART IV DOG DAYS   139

PART V DIGRESSIONS *1967–1969*   201

PART VI CRUSADES *1969–1973*   243

PART VII RENAISSANCE   297

PART VIII A POSTSCRIPT   363

APPENDIXES   369

NOTES   377

SELECTED BIBLIOGRAPHY   385

INDEX   389

PART I

YANKEE STATION

. . . Why are we in South Vietnam? We are there because we have a promise to keep. Ever since 1954 every American President has offered support to the people of South Vietnam. We have helped to build, and we have helped to defend. Thus, over many years, we have made a national pledge to help South Vietnam defend its independence. And I intend to keep our promise.

—Lyndon B. Johnson:
Remarks at Johns Hopkins
University, April 7, 1965

CHAPTER 1

There was no wind that January morning in early 1967 as the U.S.S. *Ticonderoga* steamed west toward the coast of North Vietnam.

The blackness and the cold would later be replaced by sweat-raising heat, a peculiarity now and then of those latitudes in winter. But now many of the 3,630 men keeping President Lyndon Baines Johnson's promise were bundled up as they went about duties necessary for the six o'clock launch. The *Ticonderoga,* like her sister ships *Intrepid, Lexington, Hancock, Bon Homme Richard, Oriskany,* and *Shangri La,* had been built during World War II and designated Essex-class carriers; modernization after the war brought with it a new classification: Hancock.

The *Ticonderoga* was an awesome sight: 894½ feet long, she rose out of the water like a warehouse. She was home to eighty aircraft and capable of moving her 44,700 tons through the water at thirty-three knots. Her complement of 3,000-plus men, including the air crew, was a population that far exceeded those of some of the smaller communities that rubbed up against her home port of San Diego in southern California. On that morning, the fifth day of the new year, the U.S.S. *Ticonderoga* was rubbing up against the Democratic Republic of Vietnam; the waters through which her four Westinghouse turbine engines thrust her were not the rippled blues of San Diego harbor but the flat black-grays of the Gulf of Tonkin.

It was in these waters, only a few short years before, that a covey of North Vietnamese Navy patrol-torpedo boats with their 21-inch torpedo tubes and 25 mm ack-ack guns bearded the American destroyers *Maddox* and *C. Turner Joy* on August 4, 1964; it was the second such reported harassment in two days. One week later, with patriotically wrapped jingoism rampant in Congress, Lyndon Baines Johnson signed into history Public Law 88-0408 and dubbed it the Tonkin Gulf resolution. The United States had a major war on its hands and did not even know it. Not then. Now, three years later, it surely did. The fighting was still going strong, getting more intense, and the U.S.S. *Ticonderoga* was making its own wind in the Gulf of Tonkin, carrying the American war to the enemy.

The junior maintenance officer aboard the *Ticonderoga* that black and cold January morning was Lieutenant Commander Richard Allen Stratton, a native of Massachusetts, an Irish-American, and a staunch Roman Catholic. He was thirty-five years old. It was his first cruise on the Yankee Station (the staging area for the U. S. Seventh Fleet along the seventeenth parallel, south of Hainan Island) and he readied for his twentieth mission over the Democratic Republic of Vietnam, which in truth he considered, when he considered it at all, neither democratic nor a republic.

So it was that at 5:50 A.M. that day Lieutenant Commander Stratton sat strapped and tubed and wired into his aircraft, an A-4E attack plane, on the flat flight deck of the *Ticonderoga,* awaiting a steam catapult launch into the ship-made wind toward the coast of North Vietnam. It was to be, he would later remark, a day when nothing went right.

But now, in the cockpit, the aircraft's J-52 jet engine (unconverted) whirring slowly underneath him, his eyes and ears and hands and feet simultaneously performing the routine ballet of final pre-flight check, he did not know the future.

He had risen shortly before 5 A.M., dressed in skivvie shorts and a yellow T shirt, U. S. Marine Corps fatigues—which were nonregulation—had breakfasted, been briefed, and donned G suit, torso harness, and the other equipage of modern single-seat warplane flight. He physically checked out his aircraft. Stratton was up and about early that morning by virtue of his position in the

4

pecking order of the *Ticonderoga*'s officer country. The ship's top brass wanted their department heads—and Stratton, being a maintenance officer, classified as a department head—to be in attendance during the *Ticonderoga*'s air operations. That meant airborne, as well. And because Stratton was the *junior* maintenance officer (which in naval hierarchy, and on the *Ticonderoga*'s organization chart, meant there were plenty of peckers above him and precious few below) he pulled the early morning duty.

The sky washed to gray. Dawn in those waters does, indeed, come up like thunder: first the night black, then the gray, then day, just like that. The carrier's turbines were turning at a fierce rate now and the huge ship, vibrating, prow pointed toward the unseen mainland, sliced through the water at better than twenty-two knots to create the precious wind needed to help lift the aircraft off the flight deck and keep them from dipping too close to the sea after take-off. There were two A-4 squadrons to be launched this morning, six planes each (four for the air and two in reserve) and the rest of the little winged armada: an air tanker, the photo-reconnaissance aircraft, an early-warning plane, and an electronic-countermeasures plane. They were all gathered on that sprawling deck and the steam from the catapults swept back over them. The *Ticonderoga* crewmen on deck worked swiftly, their colorful clothing denoting the job sections to which each belonged.

The launch was routine. The service planes went to their assigned sectors and the A-4s whirred to the Vietnamese coast—a group of men and their machines on their way to work, albeit not your everyday office job; they would be back soon enough to the ship, to good food, clean bunks, and the masculine camaraderie of its green-tabled wardrooms.

A smart navy pampers its fliers, feeds them and maintains them like prize stud bulls—a simile to which many of the *Ticonderoga* pilots would gladly accede. It was an easier way to fight a war if you had to fight a war, flying to work each morning, shooting up an unseen but identified enemy, dropping little lethal gifts without having to sustain the gritty necessity of hanging around to see how the populace received them, then home again to your big gray house in the suburbs of the Gulf of Tonkin. Surely it was better than shore duty, doing the job you had been trained to do, better than running the PX at Great Lakes, better than instructing at North Island. And flying is fun, and if you are a flying warrior, then it follows, to some degree, that war is fun.

This is not to say there weren't problems. There were. As in any suburb, well, things could be better even in the best of times.

There was the water problem.

A converted carrier like the *Ticonderoga* had water problems: specifically, not enough, and when the weather warmed up at mid-day, water hours and rationing went into effect.

There was the smoke problem.

The best way for a layman who is even marginally interested to tell the difference between an A-4 and an A-4E aircraft is to observe that the A-4Es are the ones that shoot down the easiest. They shoot down the easiest because of the smoke. The smoke is made by the engine, a J-52 jet ("one of the marvels of modern American engineering," Stratton called it). The Navy could not afford the fuel additive needed to cut the smoke. The smoke made these particular planes easy to track in the sights of an anti-aircraft gun.

There was the ordnance problem.

Stratton's smoky A-4E that morning was carrying under its wings two pods of 2.75-inch rockets, which blow neat little holes in things that fly in front of you; they are air-to-air rockets and reasonably effective when used that way. The Navy, in 1967, was using them as air-to-ground rockets and in that capacity they were, Stratton groused, "useless as a wooden tit on a boar." The 2.75s were in abundance, overbought mementos of the Korean conflict and in need of being used up. If you wanted the more effective 5-inch rockets from the *Ticonderoga*'s magazines, you took some 2.75s, too. Two for the price of one. It helped keep the magazines from the clutter of extra ordnance.

(There was one other thing about those 2.75 babies, too: their stabilizing fins folded into the tail end of the rocket; upon firing they were snapped out and into position by springs. They had a habit, now and then, of malfunctioning when springs did not work and fins did not come out and rockets went catawampus in front of the plane that had fired them.)

And there was the armchair admiral problem.

Here were all these highly trained, highly educated men trans-

6

ported with their airplanes half a world away from their homes and loved ones and forced to fight a war under some very strange restrictions. You couldn't bomb this. You couldn't strafe that. Certain areas were off limits to bombing but not to jettisoning ordnance. You couldn't shoot at a ship unless it was sailing in a certain direction and had visible cargo aboard. It was frustrating and in some cases dangerous. The rules of this game were not being made at the Pentagon, either, but by a bunch of civilians, politicians, and diplomats who knew nothing about the day-to-day business of war, only the paper niceties of it. If they wanted the goddamn war fought and won, why the hell didn't they let the men they had sent over to Vietnam do it, do it right, use the armament and the ordnance, get the frigging thing over with so everybody, gob and gook, could go home?

So much for suburbia.

Stratton was not dwelling on much of that as he rocketed along smoking up the morning sky, his plane's nose pointed toward the coast and the *Ticonderoga* postage-stamp-small fast disappearing behind him. But it would all come home to roost in one hell of a hurry.

He had now, at 0605 hours, forty minutes of freedom left.

* * *

Lieutenant Commander Richard Allen Stratton, USN, banked his aircraft steeply to the right and headed up on a northward bearing. Behind the cockpit, the A-4E's engine whined its might. The ceiling was 5,000 feet, the minimum required for combat flight. Beneath him, the coastline wandered lazily along. Villages flashed by: Tinh Gia, Nhu Xuan, Thanh Hoa, Sam Son, Phat Diem. The villagers could hear the planes. Hopefully, coastal radar would not be turned on. One hundred and fifty kilometers north and west, Hanoi was at work. Behind Stratton, 500 feet behind him, and 500 feet up and to the left of him, was his wingman, Lieutenant John Parks. They were old comrades. Parks had been Stratton's wingman all through training. Like Stratton, Parks was aggressive and tough and a fine pilot. He was, too, all Navy; a man's man. He had seen it all before: this was his second cruise.

The planes continued north.

Underneath the G suit and the fatigues, the harness and helmet, the wires and tubes, Richard A. Stratton, late of Massachusetts, was not necessarily a thing of beauty. On that January morning he was, by his own description, a "hot jet ace," a loudmouthed male aviator.

He could be petulant and domineering. Blessed with an Irish wit and a sharp tongue, he could be cutting and cruel. Backed with Jesuit training and armed with degrees from Georgetown and Stanford, he was well read and highly educated, though not necessarily a scholar. And somewhere along the line, whether it was a conflict between the relatively strict Catholic education and the liberalizing influence of Palo Alto—or something else altogether —he had developed a rather narrow and conservative point of view. He was something less than tolerant of points of view that did not square with his. With his education and his honed tongue, he was a good debater, and failing that, a good ridiculer, and failing that, he could use his Irish temper.

His fuse, so to speak, was as short as his black hair, which was worn cropped close to his skull: a necessity as much as anything, because this was a man whose hair was as independent as he and no amount of combing, teasing, training, or anything else short of liberal doses of Vaseline hair oil would make it stay down if worn long. He was a hair under six feet in his stocking feet, tall for a pilot, and his 185 pounds sloped downward and outward from his shoulders. While he was not exactly paunchy, something about his figure gave the illusion of a pear-shaped man whose hips were somewhat wider than his shoulders—an illusion eliminated when he wore dress uniforms with their flat shoulder boards denoting the two full and one half stripes of his rank. Unlike some of his fellow Navy aviators, he was no athlete, an oddity in that jock-strap-populated arm of the fleet. His lack of athletic prowess was due in part to the poverty of his youth, a certain lack of co-ordination, and a dislike of that kind of competition.

His most distinguishing feature was his nose, a combination Roman–Irish–Semitic–drugstore Indian all hybridized onto what for want of it would have been an otherwise undistinguished face. But the nose gave it character; it was his calling card and his identity. He had been dubbed "the Beak" by the wags in the wardroom and the nose was, in itself, a badge of acceptance and he

8

wore the nickname threaded in gold in his squadron cap. He had, in short, as the Irish say, a good handle to his face.

The smile, when friendly, was warm and open, as were the eyes. Not that he was open, not with outsiders, anyway, and most people were outsiders. His non-service friends were few and those few that were close to him were men, not women. Within his family circle, he was kind and warm, though not necessarily open in the true sense of the term, and the same was true for those few close friends who, because they loved him or admired him for one reason or another, chose to overlook his priggishness.

He had secrets. Closely guarded was the fact that he had studied for the priesthood but it had gone awry and he had quit it before ordination. The training was still there in his head, a discipline stricter than anything the Navy had to offer.

He bore the traditional New England traits of independence and privacy and the traditional Irish ones of pride and family loyalty. Away from the political arena, he was known for his sense of humor. He could be delightful or earthy depending upon the circumstances, and with some of his fellow fliers he was a hail fellow and boon companion with a taste for ribaldry and Irish whiskey.

He was also a narrow-minded, conservative, loudmouthed son of a bitch, an opinionated boor with an excellent education but who eschewed it to bend politics or history or anything else, for that matter, to support his own rather stilted point of view: an intellectual bully with a fly-boy ego. A very complicated man.

He was a family man, a close man, a very private man. He had married his wife, Alice, in 1959 in the traditional Navy ceremony and she had, within the past year, borne him a son, Charles; two other sons, Patrick and Michael, were adopted. He was a strict father but a loving one, for he liked children and young people and hoped that one day, when the Navy was behind him, he might teach.

It was Alice to whom he was closest, with a love, an affection that bordered on worship. She was his counterpoint: bright, witty, sometimes shy, attractive, proof of his eye for a fine-looking woman; she could handle him deftly, love him deliberately, bend under his maleness when she chose to. There was a bond between them that neither could break and few outsiders understood. Like

9

himself, she was well educated. She was a social worker with a master's degree hanging on her office wall and she was almost as poor Scots as he was poor Irish.

Stratton was not thinking about Alice as he put the A-4E into a steep bank. But he would. In twenty minutes. She would save his life.

* * *

The mission that morning was water reconnaissance, water-recky in carrier slang. Many of the *Ticonderoga* pilots considered it a farce under the contemporary rules of warfare; business had been slow of late. The planes would run up the coast, probably as far as the mouths of the Red River near Thai Binh, then come about and retrace the route south to the Thanh Hoa area, a stretch of coast approximately 175 kilometers long. They looked for water traffic, hopefully, junks or other ships carrying men or material that had unwittingly or unwillingly not put into port or hidden in one of the coastal river outlets for the day, safe from the prying eyes and rockets of the Americans. The rules of engagement at that time prohibited *Ticonderoga* pilots from attacking "normal" traffic moving to offshore fishing grounds from the coast. In truth, because of the increased bombing in recent months, few fishermen ventured out of port, an indication that perhaps the rules were not being observed by all of the pilots all of the time. But for Stratton and Parks it was easy decision-making: the peaceful, "normal" traffic, the fishermen, would be sailing —when they sailed—on an east-west course; "anything north-south had to be contraband traffic, as far as we were concerned." What was not so easy was the required fly-by to make sure the north-south target was carrying contraband. Stratton was uncomfortable about it:

"Now, if you are in an airplane leaving a smoke trail behind it and you spy a suspicious ship and you have to go down and fly along beside her to see if she has deck cargo and then go up again to your perch to make a [bombing] run, you're just giving the enemy one hell of an advantage. You announce your arrival, you allow him to track you up to your perch, you allow him to track you down and have a shot at you."

10

Added to this was the fact that often the aircraft would be using air-to-air rockets, which for air-to-ground use meant they had to come in close, putting plane and pilot within range of the small-arms firepower of North Vietnamese sailors, who had a tendency to try to give as good as they were about to receive.

The *Ticonderoga* pilots had developed a habit that Stratton and Parks were following that day. The planes in twos or fours would sweep north up the coast, trying not to alert all the North Vietnamese radar and shore batteries, to see if there were ships moving in the north-south pattern. The planes stayed well off the coast. If no potential targets were spotted (as none had been this morning), then the next run would be made close to the shore at a speed best described as "balls to the wall" to see if anything might be hiding close in.

They were over Thanh Hoa now, at about one thousand feet, just as always, coming up on a river that empties into the gulf. The river is named Song Coa and it has a distinctive hairpin pattern. Stratton's headset came alive: Parks had spotted a target inland. Barges, he said, on the river. It was about 6:40 A.M. The details are still clear in Richard Stratton's mind, even today.

"Parks said he saw a barge in there. Or course, I didn't see it, but I was perfectly willing to admit that I was getting old. I'd flown with him enough, though, and it was his second cruise, so I just gave him the lead and said, 'Go ahead and I'll follow you in.'

"So he went in, which meant a little bit over land into the river area. He went low and I assumed the wing position and I still didn't see what he had but I suddenly saw a junk and I said, 'I still don't have what you have and I'm going to check this junk out. You start making your run and I'll make a sweep over the junk and I'll come back.'

"Well, the junk was under full sail and it had stacks of crap halfway up the mast; it was quite obvious.

"Now, I don't believe in this second-run business. I just go in and press it in close and fire; if I can visually acquire it, I'm ready to fire at that point, which is dangerous with a five-inch rocket because it has a fragmentation pattern of up over one thousand feet. And if you do what I did, that means you're going to pull up through your own frag pattern. But, you know, what the hell: if

11

you fly by and take a look and come back you're going to fly through his frag pattern. You might as well fly through your own as his, that was my point of view.

"So I was willing to take the chance. I went in and squeezed off a couple at him and, unfortunately, I never got to see what I did to him. (The fact that John Parks never reported the junk in his battle report makes me feel I got it, which makes me feel better. It makes me feel I blew him right the hell out of the water, which I should have done with the five-inch rockets.)

"So I came back and joined John and saw where he fired, but all I could see was that there was an island in that river and I saw that he was firing at something down there. I have always had the nagging doubt he may have been looking at that island thinking it was a barge; he may have been blinder than me.

"I went in behind him and I thought I saw some bridge sections sitting alongside the river—which made sense. That was the logical place to bring a pontoon bridge. So I just homed in. I could have cared less what he had. I thought *I* had some bridge sections. So I went in and fired off the 2.75-inch rockets. There are nineteen of those to a pod and I was carrying two pods."

With that squeeze of the trigger, Lieutenant Commander Richard Allen Stratton's day fell apart: he had just managed to shoot himself down.

"Two of the rockets—at least two—came out and malfunctioned. They'll do this if the fins don't open. There was an impact and an explosion and the debris. Immediately! Instantaneously! Just like that. And the crap came back through the air intakes into the engine and it began to chug: chu chu chu. Well, modern engines aren't supposed to chug, so, obviously, something went in the engine. I was still heading inland and just pulling off the target and I told John, 'John, I've ingested something. I'm heading back to the water.' So I turned back on basically 040 degrees and the engine chugged out and I reset it and babied it along.

"Things settled down for a while to a nice, quiet vibration. I was losing altitude steadily.

"And—I remember it quite distinctly—at 2,200 feet at 220 knots, the airplane exploded.

"The tail blew off and the rudder pedals just went flip-flop, flip-

12

flop. The nose went straight down. There was a sheet of flame. And there I was.

" 'Oh, shit!'

"And then I thought, should I pull the curtain or should I not pull the curtain [a special device used to protect the pilot during automatic ejection]? And I remembered Alice's comment to me as I left her at Lemoore: 'Don't you dare die and leave me with these three little kids.'

"I'm sitting there, really spinning and winding up real tight, I have no idea how many turns. And I have in mind the Hanoi March of 1966 and the fact that Ted Kopfman, a friend of mine, had been shot down and all that, having no illusions about what they might do to me. The temptation was not to pull the curtain.

"There's a fine point in Roman Catholic theology where one is not required to take extraordinary means to save his life, a fine difference between suicide and the inevitable. But I decided, for the old lady, I'd pull the curtain.

"By that time, I'd pissed away so many microseconds there wasn't any time left. By now, centrifugal force is so much that I can't reach the curtain. My hand just went out and stayed there. So, with my other hand, with my fingers, I just crept down my clothes to my crotch where, under the seat, there's an alternate ejection handle. I get a hold on it and then, whoosh, I pulled it and out.

"Head down and everything up. You're not supposed to make it that way—bust your neck or sprain your back or something like that. But everything worked perfectly even without the curtain and all those little automatic doohickey things happened and the chute deployed. And I began thinking of things.

"Like I finally had managed to get a haircut appointment for later that day and I was going to miss the haircut. The flashing is amazing. How quickly the thoughts go by.

"Like, oh shit, I'm going to miss a haircut appointment and, thank God, at least I had a chance to get a steak this week.

"Now they were firing at me from the ground. I was really discouraged.

"I can hear them shooting because it's real quiet. I can feel the heat from the burning aircraft. The tail has liquid oxygen in it, which makes it burn real nice.

"I pulled out my survival radio and broadcast—John never heard it—I said, 'No chance, no chance, they're waiting for me on the ground,' and then I broke off the antenna and threw the thing in a rice paddy.

"I remember trying to maneuver the chute. There was just one house down there and I was trying to land on the seaward side of it. When the plane exploded, it looked like I could reach out and touch the sea. I was that close. I'm willing to bet I wasn't three miles from the water. A minute and a half by air from the water. I could have touched it. I could smell it.

"There was only one tree down there, too; one tree in a whole twelve-square-mile area and I landed in it. Not a mark on me. There were two persons waiting for me that I could see, a very old guy and a younger one probably anywhere from 18 to 22; the old guy, jeez, he was 102.

"Jesus Christ, the old guy had a gun that big. I could look right down the muzzle and see his teeth, look right into his belly button.

"The young guy had a machete. I got out of the chute sling; they didn't say anything and I didn't have anything to say. I was scared shitless. They were scared shitless, too. All of us standing there scared shitless.

"I started to get my helmet off, and just at that point John came across the rice paddies and all of us just went diving into a ditch. You have to be pretty low with a non-air afterburner aircraft to go across a rice paddy and leave a rooster tail. You've got to be pretty goddamn low. It sure was impressive.

"So there we were all in the ditch together. What I hadn't known was that there was another guy there, in uniform, behind me when I came down, with an AK 47 [a semiautomatic Czech-Russian assault rifle]. I hadn't seen him. Had I made any overt action when I came up off the ground after getting out of the chute, I would have been had.[1]

"I stood up in the ditch, hands up, and out of nowhere comes another one, a kid, and in an instant he had my watch. I still don't know how he got it off. The last I saw of him, he was hightailing it toward Hanoi, I guess.

"The kid with the machete stripped me with that knife: whoosh, whoosh—even the boots. Sliced all the laces and never marked

14

the tongues. They piled up the clothing and I stood there in my skivvie shorts."

Stratton was bound with manila hemp around his bicepses, his hands and forearms left free. Rope leashes were attached front and rear to his bonds. And all four men, the three Vietnamese and the barefoot giant American in his underwear, began walking away in the ditch.

There was a measure of pride in the young man's step. He was, recalled Stratton, "the so-called conquering hero."

Richard A. Stratton, USN, had suddenly become Richard A. Stratton, POW.

CHAPTER 2

Fate is sometimes lenient in matters of destiny. For example, no one precisely knows when one sperm and one egg set up housekeeping in an unoccupied womb and thereby perpetuate the mystery of life itself. Nor, again, do two persons driving toward each other on a highway anticipate, until those final moments of blessedly brief terror, that they are about to do one another in. As with a practiced poker player, the hand is rarely tipped until the pot is closed.

Now here is Richard Allen Stratton, only a few minutes ago free as a bird and flying like it, slogging along in a rice paddy in Thanh Hoa Province, stripped of his clothes, tied, tethered, at the mercy of captors he understands neither verbally nor psychologically and who do not understand him. A few catawampus rockets and bingo: captivity.

Stratton's wingman, John Parks, having made his rather dramatic pass over the rice paddy, was streaking back to the *Ticonderoga* radioing the news of the shoot-down. The ponderous Navy machinery for dealing with such matters was already in motion, though it would still be a matter of several hours before the chaplain's official black automobile would stop in front of Stratton's home in Hanford, California.

But Stratton at this point, his adrenalin barely keeping his nakedness warm in the forty-five-degree temperature of that January morning, wasn't thinking about Hanford but trying to sort out the

16

events of the last thirty minutes. The mission was blown. The aircraft was lost, and he was lost. He wondered giddily if the Navy might bill him for the plane.[2]

With Parks's departure, the scene suddenly crowded with people: men, women, children came out of ditches, out of the earth, out of nowhere, a curious brown gaggle of Vietnamese Lilliputians gazing in awe at a groggy American Gulliver. They kept their distance. Little talk. Just looks. Eyes. A great, sudden sea of wide, staring brown eyes. When Stratton, prodded by the AK 47 and tugged by his leash, began walking away with his captors the sea followed along on top of the paddy ditch, quiet, sometimes pointing. Save for a bit of whiplash in his neck and his dented ego, Stratton was unhurt. Neither his captors nor his wondering public had assailed him.

By means unknown, word of the American spread quickly. By the time Stratton and his captors passed through a small hamlet not far from the scene of the crash, the crowd following had increased by perhaps a quarter to a third. Eyes found tongues and there was no longer a silent sea. It was loud and angry. As the official quartet passed through a second hamlet, an old man took off one of his sandals and threw it at Stratton. Then the other. It probably was his only pair. More sandals were flung, and lumps of dirt and angry words, and by the third hamlet Stratton and his captors were moving quickly, pushing and pulling each other through the ditches, over hillocks, along the paths. The crowd pursued and the air filled with sandals and clods and words and stones and cooking pots, some of them complete with contents and hot off cooking fires. The barrage was so heavy many of the missiles missed their target and struck other Vietnamese. There were yells and thumps with hands and shaking fists. The crowd grew larger, kept following. It was something Stratton understood.

"They were understandably angry. One of the fields in the second hamlet had been hit with what looked like either a five-inch or a Bullpup rocket. One thing I was told as a cadet was to be sure never to land in an area where you have been bombing or strafing because the reception committee is not going to be too friendly. I have never heard of any guy ever bitching about the reception of the general populace, because that's the breaks of naval air. If you can't take a joke, you shouldn't be flying around there."

17

The last mile of this initial journey was thus covered at a dead run and they had gone a little more than two miles in all when they came out of a ditch into a tiny village—the place, apparently, where the young man with the machete either lived or worked or both.

The central attraction in this community was a well-made, well-maintained thatch house that fronted on a brick-walled courtyard. There were outbuildings, too, of similar but lesser construction and without the convenient wall restricting the local chickens and goats who often enjoyed a standard of living on a par with that of their keepers.

It had been the youth's intention to bring his prize into this walled house for temporary safekeeping. He was thwarted by an angry matriarch whose house this obviously was. Heated words were exchanged and they changed nothing. There were no chickens in that house, no ducks, no pigs, and there were going to be no Yankee fliers, either. Patriotism is one thing; a woman's castle is another. A final wave of the old woman's hand sent captors and captive off to one of the smaller outbuildings.

Stratton's first jail was a small thatched hut with woven walls and a dirt floor. The ridge beam was supported by two posts that rose from the floor, and the end rafters by posts in each of the hut's four corners. On the packed dirt floor was a mound of dirt that kept a fire and around the base of the hut was more dirt piled to keep out rain water. The resident of this rude home was a man as aged as the one who had helped capture Stratton. Terrified by the unexpected arrival of guests and the noisy crowd, he quickly gathered up his tin cup, teapot, blanket, mosquito net, and cook pot, rolled them in his straw sleeping mat, and fled.

Stratton was tied to a center post and a primitive interrogation began, using a method known in the service as "pointie-talkie." This utilizes a book of phrases in the native language with English equivalents on the opposite page, like a Berlitz book for travelers. His captors would ask their questions in Vietnamese, point to the Vietnamese phrase in the book, and then, putting it under Stratton's nose, trace with a finger across the page to the English phrase. The questions, of course, differed somewhat from usual Berlitz fare. Instead of "When's the first/last/next train to . . . ?" or "Excuse me, can you tell me the time?" fingers pointed to

"What kind of plane do you fly?" or "Where is your concealed gun?" Few words were spoken. Fingers pointed; Stratton's head shook in the negative, over and over.

Outside the hut, additional rubberneckers joined those who had followed captors and captive along the way. Inside the hut, captors had been joined by a motley group of area dignitaries. Interrogation pressed on. And it pressed on until noon, about four and a half hours from the time they had first arrived in the village. With the passing hours, the heat had come up (in inverse proportion to Stratton's adrenalin going down). The shock of the shootdown and the trauma of ejection were wearing off. He was, by now, mentally exhausted, physically weary, and numb to the army of fingers wig-waggling under his nose. He was very thirsty.

Finally, very softly, he croaked, "Je vous aime de l'eau." Those crowded into the stifling hut didn't understand it, but they knew it was a linguistic potsherd from the colonial past. It stirred things up. There was a lot of chatter and one of the interrogation team was sent scampering away. He returned shortly, not with water, but a schoolmaster, an old man who carried seriously the dignity of his station. His black beret was pulled over his right ear. The schoolmaster was not a terribly tall man and he looked all but shrouded in a well-worn, double-breasted pin-stripe coat, similar to one well worn by Stratton himself in his Georgetown days, a relic handed down by a second cousin who had purchased it new in the thirties.

The schoolmaster had been around when the French had been around in their halcyon days, had probably fought against them, and knew their strange tongue. Briefed by members of the interrogation team, he began the questioning again in French. Stratton still played dumb but pressed again his desire for water. With a free finger, he scratched into the dirt floor the words "water" and "eau." The message was received, transmitted, and some minion sent scampering away to return, eventually, with newly made tea. The interrogation continued, in French, while the schoolmaster's pique rose. Stratton's brand of French, a combination of emigrated Canadian and nasal Bostonian, had been pronounced hopeless even at Georgetown where he practiced it. It had not improved with age.

The schoolmaster would no longer bother with this farce. He

straightened his coat, reset his beret, squared his shoulders, shot a withering glance at the failed French student tied to the post and at his captors, turned on his heel, and strode from the hut without a backward glance. Stratton got his tea; interrogators studied their books.

Outside the hut the crowd seethed, working itself into a frenzy. More dignitaries arrived, some in uniform. Their status allowed them inside the hut to look at the prisoner. They chatted briefly and departed. The crowd did not and, as the afternoon wore on, became more agitated and finally got out of hand. Fists hit the sides of the frail hut; knives and sticks and hands poked through the woven siding. Eyes peeked through the gaps. The tumult increased. Stratton's captors apparently had not counted on this and they became frightened, as did the captive. Two of the interrogators went out and returned quickly. They carried a stretcher and a blanket. The crowd hooted at them.

Stratton was untied from the post and rebound. Someone motioned to him to lie down on the stretcher. He obeyed. The blanket was unfolded and he was covered from his toes to the top of his head. Then the young man with the machete uncovered the pilot's face, put forefinger to lips signaling silence, and then recovered him. The stretcher was heaved up and Stratton felt himself being carried out of the hut and through the screaming mob. The stretcher bearers began to run. When they paused to rest, someone, probably a child, lifted the foot of the blanket. Stratton did not cry out when teeth sank into his big toe; he was impressed with the precariousness of his situation. The bearers ran again, rested, ran again; new bearers took over, were relieved and relieved again. He did not know how long they ran or in what direction, but he thought he smelled the sea. The stretcher was set down finally, tilted, on an incline.

There *was* a salt smell and a faint sound of surf. An onshore breeze rustled through pines—New England smells and sounds; yes, he knew them well. There was another smell that, like the others, he recognized from his youth. It was fresh-turned earth. He worked the blanket aside a bit and managed to see that he was lying beside a freshly dug hole with the dirt thrown on the far side away from him. He could hear and sense rather than see that the hole was being lengthened at his head by two men working furiously with spades. It took him, tired and frightened as he was, but a millisecond to realize it was a grave.

His grave.

Now he sweated with the last liquids left in him. This was it. Why had he bailed out at all? Alice? No priest. No last rites. No friends. No family. God, why? Nobody. Jesus. Suffering Jesus.

He sensed the footsteps coming. He closed his eyes.

He felt the muzzle against his head. His chest was exploding and he felt the pain down into his bowels. It was over. Perhaps the questions one more time and then it was done. They would throw him in the earth and cover him over.

It was that simple, dying?

There were no questions.

The muzzle never moved. It was as if he could see it: the finger on the trigger tightening. Tightening. Snap! Release. The spring inside the bolt uncoils. The firing pin slashes forward. Strikes the brass cartridge. Ignites the powder.

The explosion was deafening.

CHAPTER 3

One hundred and seventy kilometers northwest of where Richard Stratton lay next to his grave, the citizens of Hanoi were finishing their workday.

Many afoot, many riding bicycles, they headed toward the residential sections of the capital or streamed north out of the city across the still undamaged Paul Doumer (Long Bien) Bridge to residential areas near Gia Lam and Yen Vien on Highway 1 or east on 11A to Tho Khoi or south or west to Van Dien or Yen Thai.

In the old Hotel Metropole, known officially now as Reunification House, the kitchen crew prepared supper for the guests. One of those guests on January 5, 1967, was Harrison E. Salisbury, an associate managing editor of the New York *Times*. His visit was unprecedented and his dispatches from Hanoi had kicked off an international ruckus.[3] The shouting was loudest in Washington, D.C. There were other Americans in Hanoi, too, less visible, perhaps, than Salisbury, and on different missions: a group of women pacifists; David Schoenbrun and Charles Collingwood of CBS News; William C. Baggs, editor of the Miami *News,* and his associate, Pulitzer Prize–winning journalist Harry S. Ashmore, traveling under secret documents and charged by the U. S. State Department to explore possible avenues for cease-fire discussions between the United States and the Democratic Republic of Vietnam.[4] (About 140 other Americans without passports or portfo-

22

lios were locked up in Hoa Lo prison and unavailable for interviews.)

Hanoi was a city of about 500,000 persons with an area population of a little more than one million. It was a besieged, wartime capital and the grays and winter blacks and browns of the landscape and the damp, cold weather of the previous week did little to brighten the bomb-pocked metropolis. Sections of Hanoi proper had been bombed for the first time on December 2 and again on December 4, 13, and 14. The North Vietnamese were in a foul mood over it and the substantial list of civilian casualties sustained in the raids had angered people in the streets as well as the government officials touring the Americans through the bomb damage. Salisbury and some members of the diplomatic corps in Hanoi believed the damage was inflicted accidentally. Other notable tourists, ones with grim faces taking notes and plenty of photographs, were investigators for Lord Bertrand Russell, the British philosopher. Lord Russell had planned a war crimes trial to be held in Sweden. The defendant was the United States and the prosecutor's bird dogs were picking up evidence right and left.

There was, too, in the city an assortment of other nationalities: Cubans, French, Poles, Czechs, Rumanians, Russians, and a pride of stone-faced Chinese who neither spoke to nor saw any of the others.

The bombings had affected them, too—more precisely, all of them diplomatically and some of them physically. In the raid on the city of December 14 a rocket from one of the visiting American aircraft had landed in Hanoi's diplomatic quarter, hit a tree, and exploded with a terrifying roar. A piece of metal, red-hot, whipped through the window of the Rumanian Embassy. Other high-flying pieces damaged a wall and part of the roof of the Chinese Embassy. The Polish Embassy had been hit as well. Several of the embassies' employees had been tossed about by the concussion. No one was injured seriously.

Parts of the rocket also struck the Canadian mission to the International Control Commission. One of the Canadians gathered some of the rocket's fragments and sent them in one of the mission's red diplomatic pouches by courier to American friends in Saigon with a waggish rejoinder that bombing was bombing, but this was carrying things a bit too far.

Things undoubtedly would have been carried a great deal further had any embassy personnel been severely injured or killed.

The damage to sections of Hanoi proper occurred during simultaneous attacks on the thirteenth and follow-up raids on the fourteenth by Navy and Air Force planes on a truck repair facility at Van Dien south of the city and the rail yards in the Gia Lam quarter to the north. In the Van Dien raid on the thirteenth the Vietnam-Poland Friendship School was bombed a second time (the first was on December 2), and on the fourteenth, destroyed. According to Vietnamese sources, more than one hundred civilians in all were killed or wounded; twelve American aircraft were downed.

Bombing had become the single most discussed and debated issue by 1967, not only at the Presidential Palace in Hanoi, but in numerous foreign capitals in Asia and Europe and in the United States. The anti-war movement was gaining strength in America and was spilling off the campuses and out of the teach-ins into the streets. True, a majority of Americans still supported the war effort, but the number was lessening. Even certain Administration officials were beginning to cave in.

The bombing of North Vietnam began in earnest on the morning of February 13, 1965, and was dubbed "Operation Rolling Thunder." It had a solid ring to it. Operation Rolling Thunder had been ordered by the President himself. It was something the American Joint Chiefs had sought for a long time; it was a fulsome victory.

(About two and one half months later, the President would decide, also, to use American ground troops for offensive actions in South Vietnam after observers correctly noted that Operation Rolling Thunder and its rain of bombs was neither staving off collapse in the South nor slowing the flow of war material from the North. Typically, the President would order the decision kept secret.)

The bombing of the North inched up the map past the eighteenth parallel and the nineteenth and the twentieth and the twenty-first; daily sorties were in the hundreds. The supplies kept rolling south. By January 1966 Washington was desperate: by the spring another long-sought plan, this one to eliminate North Vietnam's petroleum storage tanks, was recommended by Defense

24

Secretary Robert McNamara and approved by Lyndon Baines Johnson.

There were large fuel tank farms near Haiphong, Hanoi's and North Vietnam's major port, and near Hanoi itself. In fact, about 95 per cent of North Vietnam's petroleum and oil storage capacity was concentrated in but thirteen sites, four of which had already been hit.

The bombing campaign began June 29: the Hanoi facility was destroyed, and Haiphong's nearly so. One American aircraft was lost to ground fire. The mission was pronounced a success. Washington now awaited the results.

They never came.

With a resilience and a resourcefulness yet to be fully appreciated in Washington, Hanoi ordered petroleum and petroleum products stored in fifty-five-gallon drums and the drums scattered through the fields and rice paddies of the nation. Other supplies were similarly dispersed. American correspondents visiting the North in late 1966 and early 1967 took special note of the North Vietnamese countryside abundant with war material: fields full of fuel drums, bridge repair supplies, bamboo poles, pontoon boats, food supplies, railroad ties, track, and tools. The railroad kept rolling and the trucks kept rolling and supplies kept rolling south. And the bombs kept falling.

Civilian areas had been hit. There was no doubt of that. Whether they had been bombed intentionally or unwittingly was moot. The Vietnamese had truth on their side and Richard Stratton comments, "[The Vietnamese] have a very strict morality and they have to have a grain of truth in everything they say. Now, you have to look kind of hard through that pile of manure to find the pony, but it's in there someplace. . . ."

It should be noted that "legitimate" military targets in North Vietnam routinely lay next to civilian areas; willingly or no, the slightest miscalculation on the part of an American pilot, whether in an attack plane close to the ground or a B-52 miles in the sky, was guaranteed to drop lethal steel on noncombatants or nonmilitary buildings.

The Vietnamese were quick to seize on the results. There was, for example, the inevitable photo of a dead baby, a fried fetus dug from the rubble of its equally fried mother and demolished home.

25

Every bombing of a civilian area seemed to produce such a grisly piece of "evidence." In the December 13 raid the fetus was found in the Phuc Tan quarter; the mother, a Mrs. Lien, was killed, said the caption on the back of the photo.[5]

There were the survivors, too: innumerable Mother Suots, the "old ferrywoman who defies U.S. bombs on the Nhat Le River." Or Mai Xuan Diens, a motorboat driver on the ferryboat *April 3*, who, hit by rocket fragments and dying, spent his last breaths helping his assistant "to drive the motorboat under bombs and shells and imparted to him his fighting experiences."

"Even the cattle and the poultry are trained to find trenches for themselves" when under attack.[6]

Pragmatic and shrewd, Hanoi spread the story around the world, through the Socialist brotherhood, and then to the United States itself. Washington vigorously denied the claims, labeling them propaganda (or when some nonmilitary target was struck and the effects proven beyond doubt, accidents). Hanoi would not let Washington have it both ways: Johnson could not brag about the accuracy of his bombardiers, the sophistication of his equipment, and in the same breath claim accidental striking of nonmilitary targets or unintentional killing of civilians. There were no accidents, said North Vietnam, just cold, calculated destruction and terror bombing.

And into this schism stepped Harrison E. Salisbury and the New York *Times*. Salisbury's dispatches from Hanoi in December of 1966 and January of 1967 were shocking for many Americans. He had carefully documented and photographed the extent of casualties and the extent of damage produced by the saturation bombing of certain North Vietnamese cities and towns and the capital.

Salisbury found Vietnam's Guernica and Monte Cassino: they were Nam Dinh and Phu Ly. His articles (later confirmed for accuracy by Ashmore and Baggs and by secret CIA reports) refuted claims by the Administration that the air war against North Vietnam was restricted to the pinpoint bombing of "concrete and steel" targets of military value only. In response to the Salisbury blockbuster, the Administration, which had committed itself to (and from the American public concealed) military resolution of the war, challenged first Salisbury's veracity and later his loyalty.

One thing Salisbury made clear: North Vietnam had dug in for the duration and Hanoi was an embattled capital.

A wartime capital, and yet the city each night was freckled with lights in that cold December; its airfield, north of the city, was pockmarked but the ICC aircraft landed and took off with something approaching regularity, though only at night. The port city, Haiphong, was forever jammed with foreign shipping, some of it from the West, and the quays were piled high with supplies. There were few frills in Hanoi. But couples still strolled on Sunday under the city's ubiquitous sou trees and among the thousands of air raid shelters that lined every street and path. And children, those that had not been evacuated or wounded or killed, played along the sides of the delightful little lakes that dot the eastern part of the city. The municipal traffic system still worked, though its trolleys were badly in need of paint and spare parts; a majority of the city's workers commuted from outlying districts by foot, bike, and oxcart pool. Food and clothing were rationed, but the city's bars were regularly filled by six in the evening. The birth rate had leveled and the draft had taken a frightful toll of the males; couples met and courted, loved and birthed.

Hanoi, like the nation, had been deliberately conditioned to expect bombing of the city, to expect more and more raids from the Americans. By July the bombs had finally reached the city limits of Hanoi and Haiphong and now, in January, every province in the nation had been hit at least once. There were plans in the archives at Government House for full evacuation of the city should it be necessary, and for a new capital to be built near Hanoi after the war should the old city, where Malraux once discussed philosophy with Maugham over cool drinks from the zinc bar at the Metropole, be leveled. Many of Hanoi's shops were closed and more should have been, for there was precious little to offer. Those stores that continued in business opened only in the early morning and late afternoon. Even the shop where the diplomatic community did its buying had more empty shelves than anything else. Food for the populace was distributed mostly by the factories. There was still rice, though those days 10 per cent of the individual allotment was in maize. The meat ration, meager, was often given in lard or fat. Vegetables could be purchased in open market, but prices made them dear. Salt and cigarettes and paper and soap and matches often disappeared for weeks at a time. Bicycles were abundant and reasonably inexpensive, probably as much for national defense as for morale. The citizens dressed shabbily because cloth was in short supply and, with the exception of the Christmas celebration just past with its finery and decorations, the dominant clothing theme was black, white, and faded, padded blue, well mended. The Opera House, the city's jewel, was closed, as were other halls, because the government was fearful of large numbers of citizens gathering in a building that could be bombed without warning. Masses at the city's dozen Catholic churches were held only twice a day, at 6 A.M. and 6 P.M. Preparations were already under way for the lunar new year holiday, Tet,[7] as if there was no war at all; the first flowers were blooming and on Tet the streets of Hanoi would be waist-deep with them for fleeting moments of joy and forgetfulness of the terrible days of sorrow.

There was no forgetfulness at the Presidential Palace and the government ministries. War was ever present. Paper work and planning never ceased, not that for the war in the field and not that for manning the home front. The flow of publicity (or propaganda, if you choose) was endless. American bombs had ravaged the city's famed leprosarium, churches, homes; bombs had flattened workers' homes in Phuc Tan and Pho Nguyen Thiep streets, both of which abutted the landfalls of the Paul Doumer Bridge, which was undamaged.

Photographs of the damage and of some of the victims, dead and alive, were dropped quickly into the international publicity mill, their captions written in English and French on onionskin paper pasted to the backs of the prints. The Foreign Languages Publishing House produced paperback after paperback in English describing the travail and providing sometimes surprisingly accurate information on the state of the hostilities (rebutted in Washington publicly and substantiated by the CIA privately). Hoang Tung, the witty and sophisticated editor of the major Party newspaper, *Nhan Dan,* entertained visiting Western journalists in a lakeside office, its main window blown out in a raid. He had refused to replace it. Interviews and business were conducted during winter months in overcoats and with an abundance of steaming China tea and sweet native cherry liqueur.

On a regional basis, the bombing had wreaked devastation. The town of Phu Ly, south of the city, had been leveled in two days by eleven raids. The military objective had been a railroad siding. Nam Dinh, the third largest city in the nation, was crumbling: fifty-one raids since the summer. Dikes, schools, cloth and thread factories, more than 10 per cent of its houses, churches, and businesses bombed and bombed and bombed. To date, 89 citizens had been killed, 405 wounded,[8] a figure kept low by the evacuation of 80 per cent of the population. The military objectives were a small railroad yard and a cargo transfer dock. Raids like these probably (and honestly) convinced the North Vietnamese that there were no accidents, that the bombing of nonmilitary targets was to set an example of what might lie in store for Hanoi and every other city, town, village, hamlet, and dike in the nation. And even if the authorities were not convinced, they were not about to let go unexploited a ready-made public relations campaign.

Civilian deaths had passed the 20,000 mark.

They fought back, of course, with the regular army and the citizens' defense corps and with their guerrilla colleagues in the National Liberation Front, their anti-aircraft and SAM missile units. The *Hanoi Courier* had bannerlined on December 16 the downing of the 1,600th American aircraft and Hanoi was threatening to try captured United States fliers as war criminals.[9]

It was an angry nation, an outraged nation, that had won freedom by force of arms at Dien Bien Phu only to see it snatched away by the Americans. Hanoi would fight on—five, eight, ten, twenty years, however long it took to drive the Americans into the sea and reunify the nation under Ho Chi Minh, or be destroyed trying.

CHAPTER 4

The rifle discharged just once, a flat, compressed "thwack." The sound rolled away into the trees.

What confused Richard Stratton was that he could still hear ringing in his ears. His body was cold with evaporating sweat, but he could feel it. His mouth was dry and his swollen tongue filled it, but he could feel them.

He was alive.

His mind raced to assemble some detail, some order, out of it. He realized now the rifle that had fired was another a short distance away, not the one pressed against his forehead. It was a ruse. Why? The blanket snapped back from his face and he squinted up into the sudden light. Looking down on him was the face of the young man who had helped capture him. The face was smiling. It winked at him and said, "Shhh . . ." and his face was covered again. He felt the stretcher lifted and lowered and the light dimmed; they had placed him in his grave swaddled in a gray blanket sopped with his fear. Away from the grave, his ringing ears picked up faint new sounds. A man shouting and a response, many voices shouting in unison over and over something that sounded like "Yah, yah, yah." And then it was quiet. After a while he heard the wind again in the pines. His body shivered under the blanket.

Later they came back, his protectors, his captors, and peeled off the blanket. The light was fading. And there was a momentary passing of ideology, unexpectedly a male bridge over the cultural gap, a bond joined by fear: Richard Stratton stood up, a man among men, and pissed over the corner of his grave. When his bladder was empty he lay down again and stayed that way for more than an hour and it was dusk. About 5 P.M. a man on a bicycle pedaled up, balancing a stack of little tin dishes filled with rice and pieces of sweet, bony fish; they ate together and there were "ahhhs" of approval when Stratton passed up a tin spoon for chopsticks.

While he was eating, sitting in his grave, some boys sneaked in close, then backed off and threw clods of earth at him. His first thought was to protect the food, while some of the men moved to his rescue, shooing the boys away and for good measure giving them a lecture.

"Yah, yah, yah!"

It was quiet again except for the wind and the chopsticks tapping on the tin plates. It was finally dark.

Perhaps two more hours passed; he had lost all track of time. They raised him up out of the grave into the cold night: the blanket fell away and the shock of sudden cold nearly drove the breath from him. They checked his biceps bonds, then pulled his hands behind him and cinched his wrists tightly. It hurt and the skin ruptured and he could feel an itchy sensation as the blood oozed and dried on the top of his right hand. He was blindfolded. The small party moved out of the graveyard, walking in the darkness along the edges of rice paddies.

It was a busy night. Millenniums of war, first among themselves and then with the Chinese and Thais, then the French and the Japanese, the French again, and now the Americans, had created among the Northerners of that battered nation a system of transit that moved only after dark: men and material, bullets and broadsheets, field guns and flannel, rice, rags, animals, soldiers, civilians, bicycles, and bullock carts moved along paths and trails and roads safe from the eyes of an enemy that ruled the sky by day. To a Vietnamese it was as natural as breathing and even missions that had nothing to do with the war were carried out under cover of darkness. In some areas, particularly near the Laotian border where the bombs rained nearly twenty-four hours a day, planting, too, was done at night. Stratton's guards knew the paths

31

and in the dark were as sure-footed and comprehending as goats on a peak.

Streams of people like ants. Streams of people going somewhere to do something. Often Stratton and his guards would have to stand aside—despite an obvious priority—to let this or that human convoy pass by. Where they were going, what they carried, he could not see and did not know. He really did not care. His mind was on his own welfare and, at that, only sporadically, for he was very cold and near a point of total exhaustion.

They walked for a long time and came finally to a farmhouse where they removed his blindfold and sat him down in the itchy comfort of a haymow. One of the guards went inside the house and shortly Stratton smelled freshly steeped tea.

He realized, slowly, that the man in charge was not a soldier but a middle-aged Vietnamese civilian dressed in shabby gentility. He was undoubtedly the political commissar for the area. This was a guess; Stratton never would know. It was a moot point: he was a kindly man. He checked the prisoner and noticed the wounded and bleeding wrists. Over the protests of some of the uniformed guards, he untied them and massaged Stratton's hands and forearms to restore circulation and feeling. He offered the pilot a cigarette; Stratton, a nonsmoker, refused and a shadow of anger crossed the older man's face. But it passed, and they silently shared tea together, and that done, the older man rose, patted Stratton on the head, and moved off.

Somebody else brought clothing. He was dressed, then retrussed about the bicepses as before. The clothing was Vietnamese and barely covered his large frame; the pants were impossibly small and reached only to his calves. The jacket was tight and ended well above midriff and at midarm. It felt like well-washed denim. It was better than nothing.

They walked again and finally stopped at some central location; it was a well-used area with many trails issuing from it and there was a truck. He guessed it was some kind of a small weapons carrier, about three-quarter-ton with a canvas top. He was put in the back. With him were one armed guard and a large pile that contained his flight suit and equipment, his parachute, and other paraphernalia gathered at the crash site. Two other guards climbed into the front. The truck's engine started, the gears sounded, and they drove away slowly into the night.

The truck stopped (or so it seemed) at every bridge, every hamlet, every village or railroad track crossing, every creek and ferry crossing. When the truck stopped, its horn started and his guards would call out into the night and people, God knows from where, would come running and the guards would open up the back of the truck and shine their flashlights on him. People would thump away at him and berate him. The blows were not vicious. They were mostly openhanded whacks of frustration and fear and pent-up anger. The guards themselves never touched him.

Between Thanh Hoa in the south and Hanoi in the Red River delta is a low range of mountains. And it was into these mountains that the truck crawled and arrived, finally, at some military installation. Stratton was sore, cold, and bone-weary. The truck pulled off the main road and rattled a short distance down to a stream. Over the stream, a short distance away, was a small bridge. A North Vietnamese officer and four uniformed, armed soldiers were waiting. Two men in civilian clothes waited with them. Behind them, pulled up side by side, were two vehicles: a two-and-a-half-ton truck with military markings and camouflage and a 1941 Packard sedan. It was a welcoming committee of sorts.

Stratton was ordered out of his truck. His Marine Corps fatigue jacket was fished out of the pile of clothing in the back of the truck and draped about his shoulders. He was marched to the middle of the bridge and motioned to sit down. He sat. The men in civilian clothes turned out to be photographers, and though his picture had been taken before, shortly after he was captured, this appeared to be some official effort. The vehicles were backed and filled with much shouting and directions until as much light as the masked headlights allowed shone on the flier. The photographers snapped their pictures, then packed their gear, clambered into the Packard, and drove away. Stratton was taken to a bunker, where the officer went through the pile of clothing and other things that had been in the back of the truck. In the process of rummaging, the officer discovered two small bottles among the contents of Stratton's survival gear. After some sniffing and a little conversation, the contents of the bottles were poured out onto the ground. Stratton was horrified as any frugal Irishman would have been, fatigued or not. The bottles held scotch and Bourbon. This concluded, the flier's gear was repacked. The bundle, Stratton, and two soldiers climbed into the rear of the truck. The others got into the front. The truck headed north, down the mountainside toward Hanoi. There was one other item in the back of the truck: a fifty-five-gallon drum in which the truck's reserve gasoline supply was carried. Stratton had caught a glimpse of it as they blindfolded him.

The truck whined its way up a long incline. It reached the top, shifted gears, and began a speedier descent. The drum moved and one of the guards kicked out suddenly with one of his feet, sending it skidding toward Stratton, who sat with his back against the rear of the cab. Stratton could see a bit under the blindfold. He heard the drum coming and knew what it was. He tried to fend it off with his foot, but his timing was poor and the drum caromed by his foot, spraining it and peeling back one of the toenails. When the truck started up another incline and before its forward momentum had been slowed, Stratton managed to send the drum skidding back toward the guards. On the next decline it came sliding back, and as the truck leveled, he kicked it back at them. It was quite a deadly little game. Back and forth the drum went. The soldiers giggled in delight; Stratton sweated and cursed his injured ankle and throbbing toe. Finally they reached the delta flatlands and turned onto National Route No. 1 and the game petered out. Stratton dozed fitfully.

The truck sped on; dawn was an hour away. Stratton could hear voices instructing in what he guessed were morning exercises. The voices came over loudspeakers attached to telephone poles. The loudspeakers were shared by the national radio station (which was now broadcasting the exercise routine) and the air raid warning network of the defense ministry. The sound rattled him and the Vietnamese voices grated. He had been, at this point, at least twenty-four hours without real sleep; the shock of the ejection over Thanh Hoa had worn off, leaving him drained. He was hungry and thirsty. His foot throbbed in dull, persistent pain and his wrists ached where the lacings had cut. Now there was this Orwellian madness of voices. He was panicky and fearful. If he could only somehow get to a military installation, he thought, a formal military installation, then he would be safe; he would have it made.

It was the Party that was going to do him in, it was the natives that were going to get him. But once he was in the hands of the military—his peers—they might play war crimes trials and all that crap, but he would be home free. They might slap the piss out of him a couple of times, but they would find out he really didn't know anything (and he really didn't know much) and would leave him alone. He would be safe. Because military men share an understanding. The brotherhood.

The truck stopped. Its engine idled for a moment and the gears shifted. Slowly it backed into a long tunnel. He could see more from beneath the blindfold now. It was getting gray again. A new day. The tunnel was very narrow and he had a wild surge of fancy, a fleeting impression of the Dallas police station garage he had seen on television where crazy Jack Ruby had blown a hole in Lee Harvey Oswald that insane week in Texas four years before. And then his brain flashed awry again and it was the garage of the NKVD or something he had seen in a movie long ago.

The truck stopped. The engine stopped.

They came and got him out of the truck and walked him across the corner of an interior courtyard and through another shorter, wider tunnel and through doors. He limped on bare feet and the sounds of footfalls echoed up the high walls on either side of him. It smelled musty, damp, like the cellar back home in Quincy. It was cold.

They sat him down on a tile floor. The tile was red and cold. They left him. It was quiet. He dozed intermittently. Afraid. What next, he wondered. Perhaps two hours went by, he couldn't really tell. He fretted.

He would not know where he was, of course, until later. But they had brought him to Hoa Lo, which in Vietnamese translates out roughly to "fiery furnace." Some of its residents, American fliers like himself, had dubbed it the "Hanoi Hilton." It was a prison.

He waited.

They came for him.

CHAPTER 5

Stratton had heard footsteps and occasional snatches of gibberish earlier in what he assumed was a corridor outside the room in which he was sitting and it was purely by instinct, some sixth sense, that he knew they were coming for him. He was both apprehensive and relieved: now they all could get on with it, the questions, the slapping around (he was prepared for that, expected it), and maybe the black box number and all the rest of the survival school lessons he had learned. But that would be the end of it. It would soon be obvious to his captors that they had an American James Bond here, a tough, shrewd, clever chap impervious to insults, threats, or slaps.

Certainly, *they* expected it. They would ask, he would refuse to answer, they would trash him a bit, he would roll with the punches, and, that done, he would be shipped off to a tough-guy camp, a stalag. These were the rules of the game. Hanoi, after all, had signed the Geneva pacts regarding treatment of prisoners of war. Despite the legendary cruelty of Orientals, the survival school instructors had impressed on them there had been no real torture in Korea. And there was the American Code of Conduct governing the actions of captured Americans; Hanoi certainly knew about that, what with 140 airmen already bagged and imprisoned. There was respect beween fliers, and between military peers. He would be able to honor his oath as officer; he would bring no

36

shame on his nation or his commander in chief or his service. He would bring no shame on his family name. That was as important as all the others.

Stratton felt fumbling hands loosening the knots of his bonds. His arms ached as blood flowed unimpeded through the vessels. His blindfold whipped away and light splashed into his eyes. He was pushed forward, blinking like an owl in the sun. He came to attention and saluted. It was returned, one military man to another. Hands pushed him down onto a stool barely eight inches off the floor. There was a moment of silence, a tableau older than the Inquisition: Stratton faced a table covered with a cloth dyed royal blue. It was filthy. There was a small table lamp. Seated behind and at the ends of the table were six men, all in uniform.

"What is your name?"

"Stratton. Richard Allen."

"Your ranking?"

"Lieutenant Commander, United States Navy."

"Number?"

"Six-oh-two-oh-eight-seven-slash-one-three-one-oh."

"You were born when?"

"Fourteen October nineteen thirty-one."

Pause.

"Now, Stratton, what is the name of your ship?"

"I am not required under the terms of the Geneva Convention to answer that question, nor am I permitted by my government to answer that question. I am required only to give you my name, rank, serial number, and date of birth, and this I have done."

"Stratton," the interrogator persisted softly, "what is your squadron?"

The Geneva Convention.

"What aircraft do you fly?"

The Geneva Convention. Geneva Convention, Geneva Convention; we know all about the Geneva Convention.

The interrogator's hands pressed calmly together, resting on the blue cloth. Two miniature table lamps reflected off the lenses of his rimless spectacles.

"Stratton, you do not seem to be aware of your situation. You are a military man and you obeyed the orders of your superior

37

officers. Now you are here, and you must obey our orders because you are subject to our military laws. Now, what is the name of your ship?"

It was all quite civil, this required joust. All of the information that Stratton refused to divulge was painted clearly in precise block letters on the sides of his aircraft and had been dutifully copied off the undamaged portions of the fuselage and forwarded to military intelligence in Hanoi, along with the report on the American's capture.

"I am not required under the terms of the Geneva Convention . . ."

The inquisitor stared at him without expression. Staring back, Stratton studied a distinguished-looking, gray-haired man perhaps fifty-five years old. To Stratton, whose exposure to the Orient was limited, this man looked to be "obviously of mixed blood. The eyes, the color of the skin were oriental, but the rest of it, the cut of his face, appeared to me to be Germanic. His haircut was like one my father wore in his time.

"He did all the talking. And he was obviously military—the cut of his uniform (which was immaculate and well tailored, but without rank or insignia) and his bearing. He was professional military, not somebody just brought in for the war. And the trend of his interrogation was that of a military man well indoctrinated by his political peers."

It is impossible to know the contrary impressions of the interrogator, a scrubbed, barbered, grandfatherly man in the well-tailored, unadorned tunic favored by upper-caste military and civilian figures of his nation. What he saw, of course, through the glasses that artfully caught the lamplight, was a dirty, unshaven enemy ridiculous in a peasant's coat and britches several sizes too small for him. He saw smudges of fatigue under the eyes of the beaked, beetle-browed head; and in the eyes, what?

He knew his name, his rank, his date of birth, serial number, his ship, squadron, aircraft, and, from captured papers, the ordnance it carried; when the flight had begun, where it ended. He knew this Stratton to be uninjured, his size, that he had been unarmed and had not resisted capture, knew that he had arrived at Hoa Lo at 5:30 A.M., knew he could be broken like a dry twig. Knew all of that, and maybe more. The interrogator waited for Stratton to finish and shifted the conversation.

38

"Morality dictates, Stratton, that you answer our questions, that you make up for your past sins and offenses against the Vietnamese people."

He continued his monologue, describing an illegal, unjust, and immoral war perpetrated against the Vietnamese Fatherland, against innocents, by U.S. aggressors. He punctuated with ritual words: escalation, perfidy, criminals, murder, sacrifice, determination. He explained, with some care, a brief, bloody history of four thousand years of Vietnamese resistance against other aggressors, their crimes, their errors, their arrogance, their demise.

Again he asked for the name of the ship, the number of the squadron, the type of aircraft. Again Stratton held to his name, his rank, his serial number, his date of birth. Stratton had been on the stool for nearly two hours. His hams were on fire, his legs cold and numb. His back and neck ached. He felt woozy, assailed by the room's rancid smell of stale urine.

Still civil but with a new hardness in his voice, the Vietnamese said, "Stratton, we can harm you. We can hurt you. We can kill you, and we shall not hesitate to do this. We can harm your family; this we can do, too. You are dependent upon us for your survival.

"You shall have no water, no food, no clothes, nothing, unless you reconsider!"

Stratton nodded from his perch. All that was true, but he still could not answer, would not.

They gave it up.

The interrogator stood, gathering his papers. The others stood, too, scraping back their chairs, shaking kinks out of their legs. The guard heaved Stratton to his feet and the strained leg muscles barely held him upright. The interrogator's mouth was tight.

"Now I give you two hours to think this all over. Then, if you do not agree that you are subject to us and answer all our questions, then you shall be severely punished."

He turned and left. Stratton never saw him again.

The others left with him. The guard collected the blue cloth and the lamp, motioned Stratton to a corner and for him to sit, and then he, too, was gone. The door was closed and bolted.

He slouched down in the corner, glad to be alone. His ankle ached. It was going down by the book, but it was as nerve-racking as pulling time in a dentist's chair. What a pesthole this place was:

it stunk. It was cold, and he was tired and hungry. How long without sleep? By his reckoning, at least twenty-eight or thirty hours,
and no food since his "wake." He was dehydrated, but perhaps
that wasn't so bad: there was no place to take a leak in this room.
No wonder it stunk. Did it in a corner or your pants.

Smelly and strange: with the table lamp gone, the only light
came from a small, underweight, fly-specked bulb dangling from a
black cord that hung down from the ceiling. There were no windows and only the one door, with grimy, translucent panes, a broken one replaced with wood. The floor was red tile, and not
smooth, as he had imagined, but badly chipped. The walls were
acned with fist-sized bumps of cement or plaster; its once-upon-
a-time whitewash was yellow, stained with smears and dark
splotches. Two rusted angle irons protruded from the center and
one corner of the ceiling. A third sprouted from the floor. He
shivered and tried to think of something. He heard sounds and
smiled as he recognized the tick-thunk, tick-thunk of a Ping-Pong
game. Hey, no shit, Dick Tracy! It was the stalag boys, American
James Bonds enjoying a leisurely luncheon game—must be noon.
Another day and a half, he'd take a turn himself.

On the balcony overlooking the inner quadrangle, a guard
stepped away from the green, hard table, handing the paddle to
his replacement. He walked to the end of the balcony and went
quickly down the wooden stairs to ground level and turned right
through the passageway that led to the inner courtyard where the
head was. He stopped in front of Room 18, flipped open the
wooden panel and looked in. Whistling, he motioned the criminal
back to its proper place.

*　*　*

The door swung open smartly. There were three of them, one of
the officers who had sat in before and two others that he assumed,
for some reason, were noncoms. The officer was short, with a
square face as empty of intelligence as Stratton's stomach was of
food. One of the noncoms wore a jaunty pith helmet garlanded
with a camouflage covering of dried leaves and twigs.

"You, Stratton, have you understood what you are told?"

"Yes, I understood."

40

"Have you changed your thinking? Will you answer our questions?"

"No way."

They left, closing and bolting the door behind them.

In a matter of minutes, the officer and the noncom with the bonnet returned. The officer seated himself casually on a chair. The man with the hat, known to other prisoners as Vegetable Vic, dumped a load of nylon cargo straps on the floor and produced a pair of steel manacles. He moved behind Stratton, pushing him away from the wall, pulling his hands behind his back, slipping the manacles around his wrists. These devices were opened and shut by means of a key wrench—they did not stop closing just because flesh got in the way, only when the wrench stopped turning or bone interfered.

The wrench kept turning and the steel vices slowly chewed through skin and subcutaneous tissues and blood vessels and tendons, stopped finally by bone barring the hinge. The pain was so terrifying, he nearly fainted; his eyes watered and he swallowed a scream of shock. He felt the blood, warm and sticky, just before his hands went numb.

A length of nylon strap was knotted tightly around his left arm, just above the elbow, and the bight end passed over and around his right. He was rolled onto his side and Vegetable Vic, in his leafy hat, stood on his arms as he drew the elbows close together.

"Now, Stratton," the officer said casually, "you must be severely punished."

PART II

BEGINNINGS

Freedom and justice have for centuries been the goals of the Irishman's fighting nature. Sean O'Faolin has written, "I do not myself believe that anything will ever completely kill that ancient, almost wild passion for personal freedom that is in the marrow of the Irishman's nature." . . .

In America, Irish pride and ferocity and what Yeats labeled "fanaticism" caused the Irish to maintain, and even exaggerate, their natural characteristics.

—Stephen Birmingham:
Real Lace: America's Irish Rich

CHAPTER 6

For more generations than is comfortable to remember, the Irish were Boston's niggers; no more degrading term comes readily to mind. The Brahmins of Boston who found in their hearts and pocketbooks compassion and cash to ease the plights of black southern slaves or pogromed Jews regarded a burgeoning Irish population in the mid-nineteenth century as something less than vermin. (Even today, more than one hundred years later, upper-crust Boston refuses to extend equality to the descendants of those early immigrants.) While there is no easy explanation of proper Boston's view of the Irish, part of it must be laid to the Irish religion and part to the so-called Irish personality, an irritating combination of stubbornness, fiery temper, chip-on-the-shoulder aggressiveness, and an inability to be humble.

The Irish of Boston were dependent upon only themselves for survival. That struggle marked them indelibly.

They overcame violent prejudice, physical abuse, malnutrition, strikes, depressions, lockouts, poverty to gain their niche, and respectability, even if total acceptance escaped their grasp. They labored equally to maintain their Old World ethic and morality and, against overwhelming Puritanism, their Latin church and its dogma. It was a victory hard won, not to be frittered away by laxity.

Irish fathers passed on to Irish sons family pride and virtues: love of country, love of family, respect for tradition and authority, loyalty and piety, frugality, moderation, self-confidence and self-reliance, values that were not to be taken lightly by Irish-American, Roman Catholic boys of Boston. There was a pattern to life. Boys followed it. It was natural and necessary.

These were the lessons impressed upon Charles Arthur Stratton during his childhood in his parents' traditional Irish home in South Boston in the early 1900s. Charles Stratton matured into a large, squarish, conservative man with a sense of blarney and an easy smile that tempered a rather formidable countenance. His formal education ended in high school and he learned the clerk's trade—more precisely, the shipping clerk's trade, which he was to follow all his working life. He met, courted, and wed Mary Louise Hoare, an Irish girl from Somerville, and they set up housekeeping in the city of Medford. Finally, they scraped together a down payment and purchased a home in Quincy. This was in the late 1920s.

Quincy is eight miles south of Boston across the Neponset River, which flows into Boston Harbor at the Squantum peninsula. Charles Stratton commuted daily to Boston, spending his days at Slattery Brothers, which kept offices at 210 South Street.

The young couple took pride in their home, witness to their labor and frugality. It is still the family home: a two-story, wood-frame structure of typical Greater Boston architecture sitting on a small, grassy lot. It has long since been repainted, but in those days it was fashionable cream and brown. On Sundays, after mass, they sometimes entertained at home members of their small clan. Charles Stratton had three sisters, one of whom was a spinster and another of whom would remain childless. Mary Stratton had one sister and a brother who was regarded as something of a rake.

The Charles Strattons increased the clan by one in June of 1929 when their first son, Charles, was born. Their second son, Richard, was born two years later. The third child, a girl christened Ellen, was born in 1937, not to them, but to Mary's sister and brother-in-law; the baby's natural mother died in childbirth and Charles and Mary brought Ellen home to Quincy and raised her as their own despite the fact the baby's natural father was alive and well. Problems occasionally arose over this arrangement. They were never discussed outside the family or with the children.

Raising a family during the Great Depression on a shipping clerk's wages was difficult. But at least there was income, if no automobile, Richard Stratton recalls. There were food and shelter and love.

Given the time and culture the Strattons were a "typical" family, if such a thing truly exists. Charles Arthur Stratton ruled the family; his wife ran it, not in her place, but from it. She was a warm woman who cared for her children, but stern and forbidding when provoked. Richard Stratton's memories of those days are of a tight family unit.

"My father was head of the household. When my father said something, that's all there was to it. It was something that was instilled in us.

"We ate supper at 5:50 P.M. every day that my father worked. We sat there and awaited his arrival. The radio would be turned off. He was the head of the household. He would come home and go upstairs to the bathroom to wash his hands, then come down and usually sit in his vest at the head of the table. And we would sit around the dining room table and, as only the Irish can do, eat the evening meal in state. My father would be served first. My father would be served the best of everything—and my mother would eat last. His salary was never very rewarding and we ate a lot of bread and potatoes at times. I wonder, sometimes, how they fed three hungry hounds, but they did. We were never hungry and we lived in a nice home."

That evening meal, in state, was also a training table.

"My parents gave us examples. Now, at that dinner table little words of advice would come out indirectly, never in lecture form; there was an exchange of ideas and information; we didn't realize it at the time. We were there to fill our bellies, and I don't know whether they actually planned it or not, but we filled our minds as well. Around the table, too, you learned manners. I remember if I reached out for something across the table, my mother with her fork would reach out and go 'chink' and dent my arm with the tines. It didn't take too many times or dents to realize you didn't reach for food across the table or in front of somebody. And they taught us their code of ethics, their Catholicism, by example, too. It was never preached.

"My father never understood my affinity for books in lieu of

47

baseball. But my father himself read every newspaper that was published in the city of Boston—from front page to back—and he read the local Quincy paper and the Sunday papers. It was a horrendous task! This example of reading and his calling our attention to things stimulated us, I think . . . to a point where we came to a love of periodicals and journalism and of the necessity of comparing one newspaper story to another and refusing to take things at face value from one source."

There was never any need for extraordinary discipline.

"My father (to my knowledge) never laid a hand on us. I never recall any physical, corporal punishment. I do remember a couple of times he'd get right to that stage. He'd be so furious with us for doing something, he'd say, 'I'm gonna lay this belt on ya!' and he'd unbuckle his belt like he was really going to take it off. Charlie and me, we'd scream, 'My God, he's really going to do it!' and we'd be crying. He never did it."

There appears no consensus on exactly when young Richard Allen Stratton began to demonstrate his independent ways. But some combination of upbringing, environment, and genes produced a guarded, sometimes spiteful, tough-minded child; ever after there was a private side, unbreachable, revealed to very few, that endures to this day. Where his brother, Charles, was warm and outgoing, with a gaggle of friends, Richard tended toward aloofness, with few friends though many acquaintances. Charles was competitive and tested himself in athletics. Richard hated sports, and his own competitive spirit tended toward solo efforts and the relatively controlled sport of politics: he became president of his high school junior class. His delight appeared more in the chase than the victory. He admits to being a poor class officer because he was working a fairly heavy schedule.

At times his single-mindedness was impressive in one so young. There was one summer, his sister, Ellen, recalls, when she and other children in the neighborhood passed sleepy vacation days playing or doing nothing. Richard taught himself to type.

"I have one particular, personal memory of that age when I was in nursery school," Ellen says. "Dick had to come every lunch from his grade school to my nursery school to ride me home in a buggy. I think it really irritated him. In retaliation he took me home over the only, I swear, unpaved road in Quincy. I had this bumpy ride all the way home."

As Ellen grew older, she, too, began to read and a favorite character was Nancy Drew, the young female sleuth of children's fiction. Brother Richard gave her a volume by Nathaniel Hawthorne.

His own reading, of course, far exceeded that of any other member of the family; he also preferred occasional operas and classics on the radio, and later on, when television became popular and the Strattons could finally afford a set, his tastes included the "Voice of Firestone" hour, a program of classical music.

He was, his sister recalls, too, an excellent student, a boy who did what was expected of him, did it well, easily, and without being told. Good grades were not always then the mark of masculinity, but it never seemed to bother him: he appeared above or unimpressed with peer group standards.

Ellen played "more with Charlie, even though he was older, because we were more like [equals]. We had more in common. Dick, on the other hand, was always more of a mentor. My early recollections were . . . of his trying to guide me. Charlie was more accepting of me as I was and we would play ball together and things like that. The two boys didn't do too much together because they were very competitive.

"I do remember that the boys had to take me to Boston [to a dentist] when I was seven or eight years old. When Charlie went with me it was sort of an adventure. We always got lost and we had fun. When Dick took me it was different. It was a chore for him. My boots were too big and they slapped when I walked. I also had a habit of staring at people on the trolley. I think I embarrassed him."

However moody he was, and private, there was a selflessness at some personal expense. He went to work when he was eight years old, in the third grade of school, caddying at the local golf club, and kept at it until he entered high school, when he shifted to an indoor job at one of the local First National stores. Part of his earnings went for clothing and pocket change, the rest into the family coffer. Working builds character, Richard Stratton says, but there is a price to be paid.

49

"I was junior class president, but I was a lousy one because I was working in the grocery store all the time. I wasn't able to do the things I was supposed to have done. Fortunately the other kids who were class officers with me were fine people and were not working and were able to do what *I* should have done; *they* made it a successful class year.

"Now, if my boys want to get a job Saturday afternoon doing something, cleaning up a store, say, sure, that's fine. But you can't do your homework and you can't learn in school and you can't contribute to your school society and have the whole experience that's intended for you if you are going to run off to work every afternoon at the grocery store. The same goes for college. I believe that."

But if tight finances were a constant in the Stratton home, so were they in other homes. Charles and Mary Stratton were religious people, impressing early on their children their "practical Catholicism" and the need to share their financial income, no matter how meager, with the Church.

Stratton recalls: "My parents insisted that we give, too. Give part of what we were earning caddying, that we give our share. But it was explained to us that it was not something we *had* to do, but an idea of practical application. The pastor had to eat, the pastor had to heat the church and his house. He had expenses and where was he going to get the money to pay them unless we gave him a share of what we had? If you could spend nine cents to go to a movie on Saturday, you could at least give nine cents to the greatest show on earth Sunday."

* * *

Richard Stratton celebrated his tenth birthday in 1941, the same year the United States entered World War II. Europe had been at war more than two years, since Germany's invasion of Poland in 1939. For New Englanders there were inconveniences and constant reminders of the war their inland countrymen never knew. There were aircraft overhead, coast watches below. Houses of a certain type and location built on the bluffs of the South Shore and Cape Cod were commandeered by the Coast Guard. Armed Coast Guardsmen, accompanied by fierce dogs, patrolled

50

the beaches after dark. Civilians were barred from using them from six at night until six in the morning.

In the early days, German U-boats hung off the coast torpedoing tankers and freighters with aplomb; sometimes the beaches would be covered with bunker or fuel oil, the blood of the dead ships sunk along the Atlantic lanes. The harbor at Boston and the naval shipyard at Portsmouth, New Hampshire, interested the Germans and there were worries about invasion or shelling. There were memories of the first war, too, when things like that happened. One U-boat had actually surfaced to fire on the tugboat *Perth Amboy*. A window frame from its pilot house, shattered by the gunfire, was on display in the maritime museum at Provincetown.

Sometime in the early forties the Navy towed a Hog Island liberty ship named the *General Longstreet* into Cape Cod Bay, filled her with drums of cement, and grounded her forever on a muddy shoal about four miles off the coast. The planes from Squantum and Weymouth used her to practice bombing, strafing, and rocketry. On dull, quiet days the Cape natives gathered along the bluffs to watch the show. The aircraft were painted Navy gray or left silver and flew in formation. They had huge letters like *Y* or *Z* painted on their fuselages. The bombs went "thud, thud" when they exploded and there were great clouds of dirty white and yellow smoke.

The Strattons' home on Bowdin Street in Quincy was under one of the flight patterns of the Naval Air Station at Squantum. Overhead in daily procession roared the Grummans and the Curtisses, the North Americans and the Chance Voughts, fast deadly bomber and pursuit aircraft of the naval air arm.

Richard Stratton was like many boys growing up during the war: feet on the ground and head in the cockpit (or greenhouse, as it was called then) of a high-flying Avenger. He made model airplanes when he had the time and studied the silhouette aircraft identification books issued by the Civil Defense. Massachusetts boys were ever watchful, too, should one of the German or Italian prisoners of war escape from the compounds in Barnstable. The POWs wore blue denims with large white *P*'s or *PW*'s painted on them, and waited out the war weeding turnip and cabbage fields on the Cape.

51

He wanted to fly and he wanted to join the Navy, maybe go to college. He was sure he did not want to remain in Quincy, not forever. He knew from his readings there was a bigger world. He wanted to see it. That he knew. A friend of one of his cousins had made an impression on him: the man had been a fighter pilot with the Navy in the Pacific. He had bagged two Zeros and had sent Richard war mementos. The Navy, that was it.

But there were problems. Money was one of them, or rather the lack of it:

"My father said that unless I wanted to go to one of the service academies, I was probably not going to go to college. So perhaps I had better think in terms of going to work, maybe for the gas company because my Uncle Freddie had pull and I could get a job reading meters and work my way up to some big-deal position. And marry Marie Culhaine down the street and raise a lot of kids."

But in that teen-age head was a touch of the wanderlust and down the street was not a port of call he fancied, not that Marie Culhaine was anything but perfectly charming. The gas company was out, too. He sent for a syllabus that would offer him the key to unlocking the doors of Annapolis, the Naval Academy. He was a good student, sixteen years old, president of his class and a crackerjack stock boy at the First National. The brochure unnerved him: he read that one had to take a lot of tests, that athletics loomed large, that one needed a measure of political influence to get congressional sponsorship into the place. He was uncharacteristically discouraged. Annapolis was beyond him. He made a new and startling decision about his life. His reasoning is sometimes vague.

A child from a neighboring community with pyromaniacal tendencies and, unfortunately, a pack of matches set fire to the Strattons' parish church. It was destroyed. Richard saw it burn. Gradually, after that incident, he says, his mind "was directed more and more toward the Church." He started reviewing again what people could do with their lives and he thought about it very deeply.

"And I, Richard Stratton, age sixteen, decided the best thing a man could do with his life, rightly or wrongly, was to become a priest, and by God, I was going to become a priest."

His parents argued against his decision in vain. So did two

priests called for reinforcement. His decision was irrevocable. His parents gave in. He left school at the end of his junior year to enter seminary with the Oblates of Mary Immaculate at Newburgh, New York. He was off to see the world.

* * *

There were to be six long years of seminary, of chastity and obedience, of study and meditation, and short summers working to earn tuition. Richard Stratton liked his life in those early days; he wanted to be happy and accepted and to great degree he was. Pictures of him at Newburgh show him standing in a long, black cassock with his fellows and a marvelously bearded, ancient mentor. He appears relaxed but somber with hair uncustomarily long. Crew cuts were forbidden in seminary.

He has described his fellow seminarians as "gentle people," a term he would never apply to himself and a condition that would cause him grief and, finally, his apostasy. They were, however, "men's men" and in that he was comfortable. They were down to earth, "not effeminate," but it was inevitable that his own personality would find itself in conflict with monkish piety. Its outward manifestations seem innocent enough, at least to laymen:

"It was not nice to say 'Hell' or 'Damn' and yet I found myself saying them (and I was saying them after five years in seminary); I would drop something and say 'Damn!' and my associates would look at me aghast. This is not good self-discipline and, to that extent, we were not compatible.

"But everything went pretty well in minor seminary [at Newburgh] and then I hit the novitiate at the end of my fifth year."

The novitiate was situated on the north shore of Massachusetts at Ipswich, about twenty-five miles from Boston. Life at Ipswich was something less than idyllic for Stratton, now twenty-one. He was, of course, grown to manhood. He had the booming voice and dark beard of the Stratton men. He was tall and he was tough. He clashed frightfully with the resident novice master, a firm Irish priest named Charles Costello, in a personality conflict of some moment in not the easiest year of his life. He made it through and took priestly vows for his first year of major seminary in Washington, D.C.

But he knew by then, had perhaps suspected for a time, that his dream had gone a-glimmering, that if he did become a priest—which he could do—he would be an unhappy priest. He had seen old priests, ailing, lonely men. One he knew died alone and it disturbed him deeply. He had always been a family man in his way. He was used to poverty and obedience. There was enough self-discipline to handle chastity, but he realized he had no calling and therefore no vocation. To continue in those circumstances would be cheating his Church. That he would not countenance.

He telephoned Ellen in Quincy. She was now a senior in high school. Could she join him for the upcoming Easter weekend? Indeed she could, hitching a ride with the parents of one of her brother's fellow seminarians.

"It was Easter vacation and it was to be his last spring there. He told me of his decision, and I was given the job of telling several people that he was leaving, including the family of the seminarian who had driven me down there and who were taking me back home.

"He seemed pretty relaxed about leaving, having made the decision and everything. I remember he said, too, that he wasn't coming home right away. As I recall, he remained away all that summer in Washington and went right to work because he seemed to feel, well, besides the financial pressure, I guess, a stigma. Not that he felt it himself, but that people back home might see his leaving as a failure."

* * *

He had little time to worry about stigmas—no time, in fact. Richard Stratton in spring of 1954 was nearly twenty-three years old, his education suspended, his vocation gone, bank account bare, far from home, and 1-A with the secretary of the local draft board in Newburgh, New York. It is no secret that he relished this least of all.

"The draft board in Newburgh, where I had to register because I was going to school there, was rather hot and heavy on my heels. And (to regain draft-deferred status) I had to get a degree, which required a year's residence at some university. So for the present and the future I had to quickly prepare, basically, a bunch of contingency plans.

"First of all, what could I now do in the service of my country

54

and fellow man? I thought, very grandiosely, in terms of the Foreign Service. It would be a good field in which to serve and also one in which I could gain something for myself, a sort of a mutual-scratching-of-the-back routine. I could travel around the world, go to exotic places, meet a lot of different people, educate myself more fully, and also be serving the country. Georgetown University was noted for its Foreign Service School." He selected Georgetown and began the paper work necessary for entrance into the summer school. But his planning of "contingencies" had only begun. He faced what in the 1950s was blandly called one's "military obligation" and there was the matter, further, of career alternatives.

"I realized, looking ahead, that college degrees were becoming quite a normal thing in America, that in ten or fifteen years the college degree would be what the high school degree used to be. It appeared to me that undergraduate work was just leading up to some kind of graduate work and that a master's degree was the logical capping of any liberal-arts-type education. And then my physical condition dictated certain kinds of activities as to how I approached going into the service. Now, in one year's time, I have to cover all these contingencies."

Simultaneously, Stratton applied for the Army Reserve, which would allow him to continue on to graduate school while satisfying his military obligation; he got a commitment from Catholic University to admit him to graduate work in geography upon successful completion of undergraduate work at Georgetown; he applied and was accepted for the July 1955 class of the Officer Candidate School at Newport, Rhode Island, and, after treatment for weak eyes, applied for naval aviation cadet training.

But the one "contingency" he had begun with, the Foreign Service, escaped him, and in hindsight he said:

"Of course, I had to go into Georgetown's College of Arts and Sciences instead of the Foreign Service School because the seminary matrix most closely resembled Jesuit liberal arts undergraduate work. So that was most easily convertible into a degree. But I did take courses over at the Foreign Service School and I took a look around Washington, visited embassies when they had open houses, hung around the State Department's outer offices and met people, just sort of what I call 'rooting around.'

"And it appeared to me that I was not compatible with the type personalities that were then in the Foreign Service. . . . In other words, I was not disillusioned by the type of work they were doing, the long years of apprenticeship that a man had to put in, the difficulty of the Foreign Service exam or the language requirements; by no means do I feel that the Foreign Service is a second-rate profession. It was just that at that time, in 1954–55, the people I saw—I did not think my personality was compatible with theirs and that I could be happy with my fellow associates. As a result, I decided foreign service was not for me. Now, recall also, I had been in Washington and attending many of the McCarthy hearings and I may have subconsciously been influenced by some of the nasty things that were said about our State Department in those hearings. I don't think so. I think it was an honest, rational decision on my part."

In addition to his schooling, and his planning, and his rooting around, Stratton worked six to eight hours a day. Briefly he tried dishwashing and quickly got wiser. Washington is a city where, if one has the energy, one can be a full-time student and a full-time worker. There are, with proper application of political yank, patronage jobs on Capitol Hill: jobs as elevator operators, security police, a wide variety of gophers, things like that. Politically yank-less but equally enterprising young students like Richard Stratton work as watchmen, or as night operators of quiet switchboards, as night attendants at hotel parking garages, or, the crème de la crème, as bouncer-in-residence of a girls' dormitory that locks its doors at ten each night.

It was during this year that Stratton was taken under the wing of a Navy commander named Paul Durup. Contingencies were fine but they were still paper wishes; night work was convertible into currency, but not so much that you didn't skip a meal now and then. Stratton, for all his self-reliance, needed guidance and it was Durup who gave it. Durup had known Stratton a good part of his life and was the Navy pilot who, during the war against the Japanese, had sent the young Stratton war souvenirs and perhaps had first fired his hopes of flying; whatever that early impression, Durup's Washington influence altered Stratton's whole life.

"He was in Washington at a time when I was extremely hungry. He opened his house to me and I believe I literally ate him out of house and home. He fed me, and upon his largesse, I think, I physically survived. And he suggested that since I was having trouble with my eyes and that my age had now advanced to nearly twenty-five—and twenty-seven was the limit for flight training—perhaps it would be wise for me to hop into the Navy immediately while the eyes were still good and then count on the Navy to help me get along on my graduate work.

"It was a very difficult decision to make. I was very happy in my school environment. I also was very happy with the accumulation of girl friends I was managing to acquire." Durup's reasoning won out.

Stratton graduated from Georgetown in 1955. He canceled out the Army Reserve, geography at Catholic, and Officer Candidate School and cashed in his chit for aviation cadet training. It damn near killed him.

He recalled the following interview with a screening officer for the cadet training program:

"What letters do you have?"

"I don't have any letters, sir."

"What sports did you play?"

"I didn't play any sports, sir."

Interviewer gave the terrified cadet the "where's your purse?" look and the "maybe you should come back and see us another time" look.

"Well, tell me, why didn't you play any sports?"

"Well, sir, I was always working, sir."

"In grammar school?"

"Yes, sir."

"High school?"

"Yes, sir."

"College?"

"Yes, sir."

"Ohhhh. Okay."

Well, not quite okay. There was the small matter of aviation cadet training. One third of the program is athletics and physical training:

"You are only twenty-four and a half years old. You go in as a cadet competing with kids who are eighteen and nineteen years old. I was a thing of rare beauty!

57

"I was on the sub–physical training squad from the day I checked in, and I did not graduate with my class. They kept me for an extra month on sub-PT, eight hours a day, five days a week, and four hours on Saturday. I smelled like a billy goat. I had to run the big obstacle course *twice* a week, once with the regular class and once with the sub-PT class, and push-ups, pull-ups, the whole nine yards.

"I'd run the hurdles, knock 'em all down. I'd go to leap the small barrier, run right into it. You needed forty-four points to pass; the most I could ever get was forty-two. Oh, it was horrible. Finally, I think some [instructor] took pity on me. He found out I was serious, that I wanted this awful bad, so he started teaching me the tricks of hurdles and barriers, which no one had ever taught me before, and I finally passed."

Despite his physical agony to stay in the program, Stratton was not sure a naval career was for him. He was not sure the Navy was all it appeared to be and, of course, he had never in his life been inside an airplane.

"I didn't know whether I could hack it or not, to tell you the truth. . . . It was an experiment: did I enjoy flying? What was the mission of the Navy and was it compatible with what I thought it was, and how about my fellow associates? Could I live with them on an even par? Of course, the Navy had to take a look at me, to see if it wanted me or not. That was equally important. Because you have to be wanted. That was another thing I discovered: there's no sense hanging around places where you're not wanted. You might as well move on, go someplace else. Life is too short not to be happy in it, and if you're unhappy, you can't do your best work."

It turned out he was compatible. He liked flying, and he was comfortable with his shipmates. He applied for a commission in the regular Navy and was accepted. He trained as an attack pilot and was good at it. He also discovered, perhaps because the Navy insisted, leadership abilities. Richard Allen Stratton, like his Irish forebears in Boston, had found his niche.

In 1958 the hotshot naval aviator found himself posted to Alameda Naval Air Station on San Francisco Bay.

During the Christmas season of that year, one of his shipmates fixed him up with a blind date. His shipmate was dating a social worker from Michigan, and she had a couple of roommates, also social workers, also from Michigan. The girls were going to throw a Christmas party and would Stratton be interested in coming along as the date of one of the roommates? Yes, he would, thank you.

Stratton's date was Alice Marie Robertson.

Four months later they were married.

CHAPTER 7

She arrived in San Francisco, bag and baggage, with two old friends and heaven knows what hopes, in 1958, in July. One of the reasons for the trek, they all agreed, was professional. No reason to doubt that; nobody (or hardly anybody) comes to California, to San Francisco, because it is better back home.

Alice Robertson, Mary Zaio, and Jeanne Crawford were three very bright, qualified, and eager social workers who met with no difficulty getting jobs within California's social aids program, which then, as now, barely coped with a vast disarray of human folly and problems. They settled in a large, airy flat in San Francisco's north-shore Marina District, sharing the joy of being "San Franciscans" and a rent none could afford individually. Their only serious problem, it appears, was a paucity of "interesting" men with whom to share their leisure time, an indication that the trio had not boned up on or refused to adopt the city's lifestyle, which is considerably looser than that of Detroit or Grand Rapids.

For this reason, during the Christmas season of 1958 Robertson, Zaio, and Crawford decided a large holiday party was in order and a blind date was established for Alice. That was, of course, Richard Stratton. After they were married, he occasionally ribbed her about coming to California "husband-hunting." Well, there was some truth in that, she wryly admits.

"Dick seemed to me to be right out front right away. That is the kind of person I was attracted to, I think. That's the kind I was attracted to before I left Michigan, [at least] with another guy I was going with, and it was going nowhere. That was one of the reasons I left. It was one of those wonderful relationships but it was not going to end up as anything other than a wonderful relationship —for the rest of my life—and no marriage. I could see that. So . . ."

So on the appointed evening there he was, sure of himself, witty, gentlemanly after a fashion, funny and not quite like any man she had ever met, a self-described "big noise."

"It was, really, the old love at first sight, almost. He told me he was a pilot and I thought he was an airlines pilot. I did not know the Navy had pilots, not then. And I remember I took him back to the bedroom to show him my family pictures, of which there were many; he got out his wallet to show me a picture of his mom and dad (which he had taken) at Mount Vernon. Well, I didn't recognize Mount Vernon and I thought, 'My God, this guy lives in a lovely house!' Wasn't that a dirty trick? Then I found out he was almost as poor Irish as I was Scots. We went right out after that and we got engaged in January—didn't take long—and got married in April."

On the day of her marriage, a traditional Navy ceremony, crossed sabers and all, Alice Marie Robertson was just twenty-five years old. No shrinking violet but rather a shy one, she was tall with long, slim legs and a good figure. Dark hair framed an attractive square-jawed, open face, a farm girl's face with an innocence about it. She could be blunt, but without the cruelty candor often inflicts. She had a self-deprecating humor but not always an accurate sense of who and what she was. She was, however, one of the few persons who could needle the sometimes imperious or stuffy Mr. Stratton, and she had at her command, though there is no recorded instance of its use, a mucker's vernacular:

"My first working experience was at the University of Michigan's Fresh Air Camp, working with disturbed children. I was little Miss Middle-class. There I was standing with the other [counselors] on the opening day of camp and the first bus pulls up. A kid at a window shouts, 'Fuck you, counselors!' and gives us the finger.

"My heart froze.

61

"Dick sometimes worried about his sailor's language, but the words I learned at summer camp were better than those of most sailors. I also learned a lot about human behavior."

So she was on the one hand a shrewd, liberal, hard-working and qualified social worker, well educated, with a master's degree, well read and traveled; and on the other, a little Miss Middle-class, as she called it, with Michigan sod under the heels of her sensible shoes, a staunch, conservative Roman Catholic, wide-eyed and wondering as a child at its first circus. It was a curious combination and, as it turned out, a very practical one.

"All I have is what I came from, which is really the farm—with my mother's farm virtues."

Margaret Jeanne Lobban, Alice's mother, was the daughter of Scots-Canadians. She was born in a cabin on the family farm in London, Ontario. The family was Catholic. She left the farm for the first time to take her nurse's training and finally when she married Martin Rindlaub Robertson in 1927, moving with him to Howell, Michigan, about fifty-five miles northwest of Detroit. Martin Robertson was a chemical engineer. He was also a Scot, the son of a watchmaker, and a Protestant. There is a certain coolness between Scots Catholics and Protestants and when, some years later, Martin Robertson converted to his wife's religion, his family was not told.

The Robertsons' first child was a girl who was born in 1928 and died in 1933, a year before Alice was born. Their second child, a son, Philip, was born in 1929, and their fourth child, named John after his paternal grandfather, was born in 1938. The children were raised in the Catholic faith. In 1939, when Alice was five, Robertson moved his family into a "dream house" in Grosse Pointe, that pastoral hideaway on the shores of Lake St. Clair, just north of Detroit. Such a house: within its well-made walls were a darkroom that served Robertson's passion for photography, adequate space for his large library, a miniature theatrical stage and dressing rooms, and in the basement an indoor play area with swings.

Martin Robertson was a deep, complex man; the full "depth of his personality" escaped his daughter until she herself was an adult. He was laconic, talented, bookish, with a gifted, retentive mind, occasional twinkling humor, and an abhorrence of braggadocio, and cursed with weak lungs. He was, too, a man of income but not means, and generous with his money. The Robertsons made annual trips back to the Lobban farm in London, never without gifts for the relatives. One year the gift was a refrigerator. Even after his children were working, he always checked to make sure they had cash in their pockets. None of this is to imply that Robertson was a spendthrift; there was still a streak of Scots frugality. Alice recalls that "even though he was well employed, things were tight [in the depression years]. It wasn't a good salary, but it was adequate. It covered the bills. I didn't ever feel worried that we were going under, but I never felt we could squander our money away, either. We were comfortable, that was my feeling."

And never more than comfortable, for Martin Robertson was a man "quietly overlooked because he was quiet." And to the little girl there was something a little frightening about that kind, quiet man with the bookish mind.

"I worried about my father and his quietness. . . . So when Dick [Stratton] didn't have that quietness, I think I was attracted to that. I saw that as a strength, as good mental health. I think the quietness was scary to me, a little, that I couldn't get to [understand] it."

It was from the mother that Alice drew strength and comfort and independence.

"She was always there when I needed her. When I got home from school she sat and listened to me, to the day's recital. She was always there.

"One of the things she prided herself on was that she always got up to make breakfast for my dad. He never went off to work without breakfast, and of course she was always up with us kids, too.

"Now, she didn't drive, and in a sense she never changed from her farm upbringing. You get married, you stay at home; and they were quiet people. They didn't go out very much. I don't ever remember a baby-sitter at home. They might have had one when I was very young, but they really didn't go out much—maybe a couple of times a year, or they would have friends in a couple of times a year, though occasionally, later on, they would go off on vacation once in a while without us kids.

"In general I really feel it was a steady family that was always

63

there and life was predictable. There was no question whether I was loved or not. I knew I was, although my parents did not do a lot with us kids. We went out with our friends and we had a really good time growing up. We went on bike rides and did a lot of things that I don't even see my own kids doing now. We had fun.

"We all did what we were supposed to and I think it was part of the atmosphere of those times. Nobody sassed back, and if there was a problem, I guess it was us three kids fighting sometimes. But basically I was a very quiet child up until I got into junior high and the juices started to flow. I remember a teacher writing home, 'Alice talks too much in class.' 'Hooray!' said my mother. I was almost an introvert up till then.

"One thing they allowed me was the freedom to be whatever I wanted to be. One thing that helped was my mother being a nurse. She understood my need to be something and encouraged that. . . ."

It was about this time, with her juices starting to flow and tongue starting to wag, that the household was imperiled by a sudden illness of Martin Robertson. It was for Alice a traumatic and significant period, as clear in its telling today as in its occurrence in 1946.

"One time, just before I was thirteen, my father caught pneumonia. He was given penicillin and he was allergic to it. He almost died. And he got quite depressed after that, I remember, he really went into a slump. They gave him shock treatments. They helped, and he came out of it well.

"But I remember my mother's concern and the whole family's worry—none of them quite knowing how to deal with it. Yet *I* knew for sure it *would* be dealt with by my mother in her steady way. It would be handled. He *would* get better! *She* would handle it! She was a very stong person—a tough, gutsy lady—and when it came to a crisis like that, what you felt from my mother was 'We shall overcome.' She might have low periods and she might slump for a while, but, by God, you never worried that she wouldn't pick herself up and march on. Yes, I remember one day in that period [her] being really low, [me] being scared. Then, boom! there she was back at the tiller sailing on. No question.

"That's when we moved. I guess they were concerned that maybe [the 'dream house'] was too big or too much a financial

64

burden. We moved into a nice, adequate, brick middle-class family home in Grosse Pointe Farms."

It was during this period, after his illness and recovery, that Martin Robertson converted to Catholicism.

"I think their lives came together stronger after that," says Alice, "because they had a religion in common now. It had been one of the differences between them that I am sure my mother found difficult. My mother's faith . . . was such a natural, taken-for-granted faith that as a kid I never really questioned whether or not there was a God. A lot of persons go through that questioning period, especially as teen-agers. It just never happened to me. I think it was just my mother's constant, quiet, simple faith in God. It was part of her whole being and such an important part of her.

"[Religion] was the one thing my parents argued about. I would say three times in my life I remember the voices rising, my father saying, 'These damn Catholics!' When *he* converted to Catholicism, he became a better Catholic than any of us."

Martin Robertson's illness, recovery, and conversion had a profound effect on his young daughter. These incidents propelled her, she says, into a career of helping others as a social worker. At seventeen, reasonably ebullient, she arrived in Ann Arbor to begin undergraduate work at the University of Michigan.

"Oh, I loved it. I just loved it. In high school I had had a lot of fun with my girl friends but I did not date very much. (My mother would say a prayer Alice would get a date for the prom and I would get one—some turkey would show up.) Then I went to college. Now, the University of Michigan at that time [1951] had about seven men to one woman and even the turkeys got all kinds of dates, and I had a ball! Wheee! I remember thinking, 'Isn't this fun?' And it was too, you know? And I joined a sorority and it was just a lot of fun. I really enjoyed college days."

Her blossoming as a Michigan co-ed did not distract from the more serious business at hand and in 1955 she was awarded her baccalaureate in sociology. And after a summer's work at the fresh-air camp she returned to Ann Arbor in the fall. She was awarded her master's degree in social work in 1957. During her two years' study she had gained experience as a social worker in the Grosse Pointe school system and in one of Michigan's state hospitals. Her academic and field work was highly regarded and, upon completion of her master's, she joined the staff of Hawthorne, a psychiatric hospital for children, and worked closely with Dr. Ralph Rabinowitz.

"He gave me so much, it colored my whole social work experience from then on. [The children at the hospital] were disturbed kids who could not live at home because their problems were so severe. Some were schizophrenic, some psychotic or severely damaged children that often had bounced from foster home to foster home and just had to be locked within the walls of this psychiatric hospital.

"But it was a very good residential treatment center with a super staff and a large ratio of adults to children and many conferences and you just learned. Like the camp situation, which was so good, [Hawthorne] was a place where you learned about human beings right on the spot. It was such a good experience, and Dr. Rabinowitz gave me so much theory that I felt was important and valuable, and which I could fall back on."

She worked at Hawthorne for a year, leaving in 1958, with her two co-workers, for San Francisco. Almost immediately, she began counseling at the child guidance clinic in San Mateo, a few miles south of the City.

* * *

The bride wore white, the bridegroom dress blues, and they honeymooned at Highlands Inn, an expensive and woodsy hideaway on the cliffs overlooking the Pacific just beyond Carmel. Matrimonial rituals behind them, Richard and Alice Stratton settled in the city of San Lorenzo, one of the myriad carbon-copy communities ringing the more famous cities of the San Francisco Bay Area. San Lorenzo was a compromise. It was nearly equidistant from where they worked, he at the air station at Alameda, she at the clinic in San Mateo. They would stay three years before moving to Palo Alto for his graduate work, then on to Omaha, where he would be assigned as aide to the admiral attached as naval liaison to the headquarters of the Strategic Air Command.

It used to be, and perhaps it is so today, that there were not a whole lot of things in life more pleasurable than the beginning years of marriage for a well-paired man and woman, a time for laying down foundations for a joint venture, discovery of physical joy, planning for the future, deciding about family.

That she was suddenly a military wife had small effect on Alice Stratton, a circumstance created by her own innocence and a no-nonsense attitude on the part of her blunt-spoken husband.

"I really didn't have any thoughts, one way or the other, about being 'in the military.' I had my parents' conservative, middle-American attitude about the military, which was that it was good and we needed it. Dick, too, has always been kind of a common-sense guy about some of [its] restrictions: things he felt were amenities to people he observed, the 'Mickey Mouse' stuff he [ignored], so I didn't have to put up with it either.

"My mother's farm virtues did not fit in with social teas and this and that. I did have some of that in college and at the sorority—polishes you up a bit, right? At least I had it to fall back on. But I did not like all that brass, the reception-type things. Jeez, I hate it, and I say it every time we go, even now.

"Once I got hold of somebody to talk to, it was okay, but I hate to stand there talking chitchat to some strangers over and over. I can't think anybody would like that, it's so superficial and something you have to do. There are a lot of things in the military that are there for courtesy, if you are dumb enough not to know how to be courteous. When you come into a new place [for example], you call up your new boss and say, 'I'm here,' and maybe go over for a drink. The military puts a fancy name on it, 'calls paid and received,' but it is just common courtesy.

"But I was not uncomfortable. I have always been out in the community, too, like with my work. So I haven't been restricted by [the military] and it has not been my whole life. And until we got to Omaha there was not a whole lot of it.

"Before he left in 1966 for the cruise, he was a junior officer, very junior, and you know you don't get a lot of it when you are a junior, not as much, anyway. You get together with your peers, your drinking buddies, more. And you are young and you are talking about babies and you are all starting your families, and to me it was fun in those first squadrons. Oh, we had fun! It was almost like an extension of college, all these dumb pilots. They are wild, you know? Drink a lot, getting out: they would start out at one house and go from house to house until by two in the morning you'd have gotten up to the skipper's house. Don't do that any more. But we had fun those first years and we hung in there when the men went on cruises . . . and it was peacetime.

67

"But then we got to Omaha—that was my first real contact with 'the Military,' the teas and the la-di-da. But Dick protected me from a lot of the functions an aide's wife performs that I felt unequipped to do, and luckily I got pregnant with Charlie."

Whatever luck had drawn them together, there was no denying it was a fortunate match for both of them; the mutual chemistry worked. Alice readily acknowledged, though somewhat tongue in cheek, that many of her new husband's qualities, his bookishness and knowledge, reminded her of her father. But he was not a quiet man, and occasionally his bluster and intimidating manners reached outrageous limits, not that much of it was ever directed at her.

"He was different with me than he was with other people and I could kid him and tease him about his harshness—not harshness, but severity—and he'd take it from me. So it was an easy, quickly easy, comfortable relationship with him. I just felt he was an easy man to be around, up front and open. I know other people didn't see that, or so they tell me. God, when we were in Hanford, somebody told me how the bank clerks were afraid of him. . . . Well, I was never afraid of him, ever."

When they did have arguments, these were loud—and brief. Neither was given to sulkiness. On the other hand, their disagreements were decidedly few because Alice would defer to her husband, if she could not budge him from his point of view. It was something they had negotiated early on, that they would follow an earlier tradition that the husband was the head of the household, that the Stratton ship could have but one captain, and when they reached an impasse, the decision would be made by Richard Stratton.

"I think I was basically shy and quiet and I had to work hard to get over that because both my parents were shy and quiet. I saw Dick so easily open and outgoing, and that was good and I thought he could help me out. And he did, really. He had high expectations of himself and of people and the one thing I worried about at times was not wanting to let him down, maybe not being what he wanted me to be. He always saw more in me than was there; always felt I could teach, right from the beginning. Ho, I couldn't teach ten years ago, just didn't have it in me, but he saw it there (and you know, now I think I can and would like to). So that was good."

Whatever it was, shyness or a certain lack of confidence in herself, Alice Stratton tended in those first years of marriage to hang on to her husband's coattails and she near-idolized him, as he did her. That in itself was not a bad thing, but it also meant, in her eyes, she admits, that she had to be just like him, "as good as I thought he was." And it caused her grave concern. Her husband, for example, made decisions quickly, if not always correctly. She could not. He could cut through to the essence of a problem in a wink. She could not. She couldn't be like him; it was an unrealistic view, but that apparently escaped her.

"No, I never was afraid of him, nor even really [of] not living up to his expectations. Back in college, I was pretty pip-pip-pip. My friends would say to me, 'Oh, Alice, you are so normal, you don't have any problems.' I do tend to present an image, I think, that everything's under control, which obviously it isn't, but Dick was always warm and accepting, all the hugs, you know, but he is, too, a private man."

It was one of his few soft spots. He was a self-described "cheap screw"—parsimonious to a fault. He was intolerant of human weaknesses in others, though, thanks to his seminary training and what rough edges the Navy managed to chip off his tongue, he did not voice his feelings too often. And he was afflicted, or so he claims, with a dose of machismo.

"I was not all that demonstrative with Alice: 'You know I love you, why do I have to tell you? I come home every night, I bring home the bacon, I'm not running around, so what the hell?'"

What the hell, indeed.

"I can see [now] how people can be a little awed by him, but he is easier on me than on anyone. He's really got a soft spot for his old lady."

They wanted children and had gradually raised the ante to six by the time they were ready to bring forth the first. They tried, but nature betrayed them. Disappointment arrived regularly each month. The doctor had no answer. There were no medical reasons. Perhaps it was psychological, pressure. She quit work and relaxed at home; took more tests; gulped birth control pills, hoping, when she quit them, some kind of bounce-back effect would lure her unsuspecting body into motherhood. Nothing.

In 1962, the same year they moved to Palo Alto, where Richard Stratton began work at Stanford on his graduate degree in International Relations, under Navy auspices, they adopted a son and named him Patrick Thomas. The following year a second baby was adopted and called Michael Francis. The names were carefully selected by Richard Stratton, a ritual admittedly "usurped" from his wife.

"I tried to give the boys names with meaning. For example, Patrick was named for St. Patrick, not only because he was Irish, but also because he was an orphan, had undergone some trials, and grew to be a man of great strength; and Thomas was for St. Thomas Aquinas. I wanted [Patrick] to have this example of this Dominican who was both a learned man and actually a very humorous man.

"And for Michael, of course, Michael the Archangel, giving the idea of competence and strength, and Francis for St. Francis of Assisi because St. Francis was noted for his good humor, but I cannot take credit for having guessed that Michael would be our gentle one."

Her husband insisted Alice go back to work, if for no other reason than to get out of the house for a few hours each day. Like other student couples, they shared the housework and baby-caring chores, learning those mysterious moods, whims, and sounds by which infants control the adult world around them. Richard Stratton completed his degree in 1964. The Navy posted him to Omaha and attached to his uniform the sparkling gold aiguillette of an admiral's aide.

". . . And I got pregnant. I don't know why, after six years of marriage. And so Charlie was born [and named for his paternal grandfather and uncle] and then I got pregnant again right away —Charlie was just three months old—but I had a miscarriage. So I guess the plug got pulled or something. Who knows why?"

With three small children, Alice Stratton was spared the fate of many aides' wives, which is, in essence, lady in waiting to the admiral's wife, which can be heaven or hell, depending upon the personalities, insecurities, or whims of the aide's wife and the admiral's lady.

As she had found in her husband an ideal mate, so, too, she discovered a doting father.

"Dick really did spend a lot of time with the kids when they were little, but he was only there for, for almost five years of Patrick's life and consequently only three of Michael's and one year of Charlie's. But those years, I think, he spent an inordinate amount of time with them for a father, much, much time with Patrick. There's only so much time, of course, that he could give, and Michael got less, and Charlie: I don't think but one or two times he changed Charlie's diapers where with Patrick he changed them all the time. Patrick was the oldest and Dick was with him when he was at Stanford and he had the time then; took him to the park, sat on tractors with him looking silly.

"And it was good for me [because] Dick, unlike many fathers, spent enough time with them to know what [little children] can do to your emotions when you are with them long term—the boredom and disinterest sometimes as well as the joy, the annoyances, the difficulty in just having a bunch of little kids around. So he was much more empathetic than another father might have been, who could have been but just hadn't experienced it."

Ironically, perhaps, parenthood raised unexpected problems for the Strattons (who, in a period of just over two years, were halfway toward their six-child-family goal) and those problems were the increasing amounts of time the Navy required of him, and the financial demands of a household of five persons.

"It was fine as long as we didn't have children. And once we had the children, it was fine until we were separated and then I found that difficult, because it was really hard on the kids, I feel, to have a dad that came and went. He had to work extra, overtime, and you could do it—and a lot of people have done it beautifully—but Dick and I had begun to talk seriously about whether it was worth it, you know, before he left. Many families do it well, but we were not sure we wanted the extra burden for the kids."

It was a discussion they were never to finish.

In early 1966 the now Lieutenant Commander Richard Stratton was transferred back to California, to Lemoore Naval Air Station, where the distant war in Vietnam was much in evidence. He began preparing for combat duty. They settled in a home in Hanford, about five miles north of the base, and Alice went to work part-time in Hanford's child guidance clinic. A baby-sitter filled in for Dick Stratton, whose leisure time was at a premium. Preparation for a wartime cruise on a military base is, as one might imagine, quite serious business. What Alice Stratton calls the "Mickey

71

Mouse" routine of peacetime all but vanishes: "People are sort of hanging in there with their families, trying to get things sorted out."

The Strattons were no different from the others. It is an inescapable truth for fliers and their families that airplanes crash on occasion. For combat pilots, natural risks are increased by man-made ones, and even should a pilot escape his shattered ship, he runs the risk of severe maiming, or burns, or capture. All this Richard Stratton carefully re-emphasized to his wife, and to his credit, she heard all he was saying. To her dismay, she comprehended hardly a word. Never discussed was time: the cruise that began in October of 1966 was to end nine months later, in June 1967. He left it at that, never told her he suspected the war would last ten years.

They had debated endlessly over his going, and she had shed more than a few tears over it, but he was firm and finally she deferred to his judgment, even came to see his logic, though, God knows, she found little joy in it.

"He was a very patriotic man and he was in the service because he saw the Navy as an extension of our foreign policy, and once the war came along, it was his obligation and duty to go. He didn't want to go to war, as we certainly didn't want him to go. . . .

"We discussed it at great length, at great length. But he felt . . . that he was doing this so, hopefully, his sons wouldn't have to do it. He felt he was doing it for freedom's sake, too, and he was very idealistic in his way. He felt that if his contribution made some men a little more free, then it was worthwhile."

They made a pact that in the unlikely event he was shot down and survived, she would move the family back to Palo Alto, where they had lived while he was at Stanford. They had liked that community with its rich, suburban life; there was a studied elegance about Palo Alto they both admired; a family of close friends lived there, too, the Foys, expatriate Yankees. And he would know where she was.

That tied up about all the loose ends.

As with all the other cruises he had left on, she said good-by at the front door; no quayside displays for the Strattons.

It was a light parting, with the children present; they had shed their tears and said their private good-bys the evening before.

"Now, Richard," she called after him in the comic voice she affected to mask misgivings, "don't you *dare* go get yourself killed and leave me with these three little kids!"

He laughed and waved.

Lord, it was going to be a long nine months, she thought.

Yes, indeed.

CHAPTER 8

Richard Allen Stratton was a teen-age novice in seminary at Newburgh, New York, on December 30, 1949, when the Truman administration approved a National Security Council study on the Far East, setting the "course of United States policy . . . to block further Communist expansion in Asia."

Events and men had conspired to change America's perceptions of Indochina radically: the hardening of the cold war, increasing tensions in Europe, the ascension of Mao Tse-tung in China, the conflict in Korea, the infection spread by Senator Joseph McCarthy of Wisconsin, all hamstrung the nation's ability to sort out the complexities of the communist world. Gone were Franklin Roosevelt's thoughts of aligning American might and prestige with postwar anticolonial movements. France had slipped back into Indochina to reclaim its former colonies with United States approval —however grudging. In Indochina, the leader of the anticolonial forces, the Vietminh, was Ho Chi Minh, an ardent nationalist and dedicated communist. He had for a time entertained hopes of postwar American aid. He had, after all, fought with the American OSS against the Japanese. His pleas for Washington to halt reimposition of French hegemony over his nation failed to reach President Harry S. Truman.

It was only a matter of time before Ho and his troops took up arms against the French in a war the latter were ill equipped to fight.

The United States urged France to win not only the land by force of arms but the hearts of the Vietnamese with political largesse: namely, more independence for the natives to blunt the popularity of the Vietminh cause and gain support for the alternative, the newly installed (by the French) Emperor Bao Dai. France finally agreed to allow Vietnam independence within the shrunken French commonwealth.

Then China went to Mao.

Washington now saw France's lengthening struggle in Indochina as less and less a colonial war and more and more a last-ditch crusade against Communist Conspiracy in Asia; Administration policy makers were unconvinced by reports from State Department intelligence operatives that there was no direct evidence supporting a theory that Ho Chi Minh took orders from the Kremlin.

In January 1950 Moscow and Peking (Peiping) recognized Ho Chi Minh and the Democratic Republic of Vietnam. In February Washington recognized the rival and French-backed regime of Emperor Bao Dai, and for the first time announced that economic aid—in the amount of $10 million—would be given France to help her in her war effort.[1]

(The United States also found itself at war, in the brown bleakness of Korea, in a United Nations "police action" against combined Chinese and North Korean troops. That bloodletting was brought to a strained conclusion in 1952 by the newly elected Eisenhower administration. Whatever bitterness there was between Harry Truman and Dwight Eisenhower, they shared the contemporary American view of Asia. The French-Indochinese war went on for another two years. It was a doomed effort.)

France's glory, its quest for the old order, died in the mud of an outpost called Dien Bien Phu at 5:50 P.M. on May 7, 1954. It was a set-piece battle and the French were slaughtered. They had violated two of warfare's cardinal rules: know your enemy, and never, ever let him hold the high ground of a battlefield.

* * *

A conclave of major international import was already under way in Geneva, Switzerland, when the word came of Dien Bien Phu's collapse. The Geneva Conference of 1954 had been convened in an attempt to iron out Asian problems resulting from the Korean and the Indochina conflict.

Washington, stunned by the turn of events in Indochina and fearful of a mass communist takeover, viewed Geneva as a sellout to the communist and socialist forces, another Munich. In the end, the United States refused even to endorse the work of the conference (though pledging not to undermine the accords signed there) and two months later produced its own "accord," the Southeast Asia Treaty Organization (SEATO), a solid extension of not only the Truman Doctrine of 1947 but the Monroe Doctrine of 1823 as well.

Given Europe, given China, given Korea, given Dien Bien Phu, given McCarthyism, there was little room in America for "accommodation"; the National Security Council concluded that the Geneva Conference was indeed "a disaster" that "completed a major forward stride of Communism which may lead to the loss of Southeast Asia."[2]

Thus the so-called domino theory was christened.

Documents that much later would come to be known as the Pentagon Papers indicate that it was at this juncture that the United States decided to give economic aid directly to the Vietnamese through the Saigon administration. That regime was now headed by Ngo Dinh Diem, a cherubic Vietnamese Roman Catholic who was a particular favorite of Washington; Bao Dai had gone into exile. The United States further decided to work with Diem, to broaden his government and help establish more democratic ways for it. There was no mention in the official policy papers cited of the other Vietnamese who had won independence by force of arms at Dien Bien Phu.

The Pentagon Papers accounts indicate that the decision for direct American involvement came in August of 1954 but that the Eisenhower administration had already sent a team of Americans to Vietnam in June to begin secret operations against the Vietminh even before the Geneva Conference had ended.

In 1955 Diem organized a referendum so South Vietnamese voters could choose between himself and the exiled Bao Dai. Winning more than 98 per cent of the vote (under questionable circumstances) he proclaimed himself President. National elections scheduled for the following year, ordered by the Geneva accords, never came to pass. The two Vietnams, divided by the seventeenth parallel according to the Geneva architects, remained. The nation polarized into two nations with two capitals. In Hanoi, thought turned to rebuilding a war-tattered economy, reunification, and undermining Saigon. In Saigon, thought turned to building an economy, containing the communists, and undermining Hanoi. Action to these ends was covert.

In 1959 North Vietnam had picked up its rifles again and a fledgling National Liberation Front was plugging away in the South. In Saigon the American mission reported publicly and to the United States Congress growing support for President Diem and his administration. It also reported, contrary to intelligence reports, that (1) South Vietnam was in no serious danger from North Vietnam, and (2) Diem's strength, popularity, and well-trained forces would permit American personnel to depart the nation by early 1961. Private communiqués reported the opposite; this was the situation, the Pentagon Papers would later report, that greeted an incoming Kennedy administration.[3]

* * *

The essence of good foreign policy, suggests Pulitzer prize–winning journalist David Halberstam, is constant re-examination. If this is correct, it appears that this essence was absent in great degree in those hopeful, early days of 1961 when Camelot settled on Washington. The Kennedy administration failed to reassess or re-evaluate a Vietnam legacy passed on to it by the Eisenhower administration, which had received it from the Truman administration. Instead, the Kennedy people studied the old policies and upgraded them to New Frontier standards. When these new policies went sour, as they eventually did, the blame was laid, not on those who had studied them and upgraded them, but on the American mission in Saigon and American journalists reporting the action from the field and sitting behind editorial desks in the United States.[4]

The commitment to Vietnam was there, habit-forming but not irrevocable. It is conjecture to wonder if American involvement in Vietnam might have changed had John Kennedy lived out his

77

term and been re-elected to a second one. Vice-President Lyndon B. Johnson, the man to whom the office passed in 1963, had made up his mind by 1961:

"The battle against Communism must be joined in Southeast Asia with strength and determination to achieve success there—or the United States, inevitably, must surrender the Pacific and take up our defenses on our own shores. Asian Communism is compromised and contained by the maintenance of free nations on the subcontinent. Without this inhibitory influence, the island outposts —Philippines, Japan, Taiwan—have no security and the vast Pacific becomes a Red Sea. . . .

"There is no alternative to United States leadership in Southeast Asia. Leadership in individual countries . . . rests on knowledge and faith in United States power, will and understanding. . . ."[5]

It is not known whether Johnson's stirring report had any influence on the President; what is known is that the Kennedy administration transformed Eisenhower's "limited risk" gambit into a broad commitment to prevent communist domination of Southeast Asia.

In the spring of 1961 Kennedy authorized sending 400 Special Forces troops (Green Berets) and 100 other advisers to Vietnam. There was no publicity. The numbers were not large by later standards. But it indicated for the first time a willingness by the United States to exceed a 685-man limit on the size of its military mission in Vietnam. Had it been done openly, something would have happened; the authorization of the 500 men was a violation of the Geneva agreements, which limited the nation to 685 men and no more—and they were already there.[6]

* * *

The Pentagon dates commencement of the American Indochinese War to 1961. The role of Kennedy's 500 men was clandestine, deadly, and provocative. The mission was to form networks of resistance, to establish bases and teams for sabotage and light harassment of "the enemy," and to train and advise South Vietnamese Rangers for raids into North Vietnam and Laos.

The North Vietnamese were not long in realizing what was happening and began a flurry of protest to the Geneva-established International Control Commission (ICC) and to Great Britain and the Soviet Union, the two nations that had chaired the conference at Geneva. The protests did little to deter a determined America. In November the President agreed to expand the role of United States military advisers and for the first time put American GIs in combat-support roles that increasingly found them in actual fighting. During Kennedy's thirty-four months in office, American manpower in Vietnam increased from 685 to more than 15,000. American casualties went up tenfold. Through a series of secret meetings, the President was urged to commit upwards of 200,000 men and Navy and Air Force units to break the communist drive in Vietnam. In a secret dispatch to the President from General Maxwell Taylor, returning from a fact-finding mission in Saigon, the military viewpoint was made clear:

"The risks of backing into a major Asian war by way of South Vietnam are present, but not impressive. North Vietnam is extremely vulnerable to conventional bombing, a weakness which should be exploited diplomatically in convincing Hanoi to lay off South Vietnam. . . . There is no case for fearing a mass onslaught of Communist manpower into South Vietnam and its neighboring states, particularly if air power is allowed a free hand against logistical targets."[7]

Increasingly, through 1962 and 1963, the military and political situations in South Vietnam and Laos worsened from the American point of view. The beginning of the end for Diem and his administration and the final steps for the United States toward total involvement in Vietnam began in May of 1963, with a series of violent and violently opposed Buddhist demonstrations against the South Vietnamese President. In November a coup d'état overthrew Diem.

Kennedy was assassinated some days later in Dallas. The Presidency passed to Johnson. So did Vietnam.

* * *

Richard and Alice Stratton and their two young sons had been in Omaha barely three months when the so-called Tonkin Gulf incidents occurred on August 2–4, 1964.

Operation 34A was the code name for further clandestine operations against the Democratic Republic of Vietnam authorized in February 1964 by President Lyndon B. Johnson. Neither the

Congress nor the public was informed of Operation 34A, but it would lead to a final Americanization of the war and forever alter the lives of hundreds of Americans, Richard and Alice Stratton's among them.

The President was increasingly preoccupied in the spring and summer of 1964 with his election campaign. His popularity was at high-water mark and his success in obtaining passage of domestic legislation begun by his predecessor outstanding. But Vietnam was a sore spot and he determined to keep it out of public sight as much as possible. In no way must it be mishandled and thereby used by his opponents, the Republicans and their standard bearer, Senator Barry Goldwater of Arizona.

"I'd drop a low-yield atomic bomb on the Chinese supply lines in North Vietnam," Goldwater told a *Look* reporter in April; one month later he told a reporter in an interview in Washington, D.C., "We are just down there as advisors, we are down there with our boys and our boys are getting shot. Defoliation of the forests by low-yield atomic weapons could well be done."[8]

It scared a lot of people, this kind of talk. The public knew there was shooting going on in Southeast Asia but atomic warfare, even with low-yield bombs, was another matter. What the public didn't know, of course, was how much shooting (or bombing) was going on and by whom; it didn't know about the clandestine raids or the border assaults by American troops or American-trained troops using American weapons, didn't know about 34A, didn't know about a quasi declaration of war, already researched and typed, waiting on LBJ's desk for the right moment, didn't know about the Pentagon's prepared plans for large-scale bombing of North Vietnam.

"In the long run," Johnson assured his nation, "there can be no military solution to the problems of Vietnam." That was in May 1965. In August in New York the year before, he had said, "Some others are eager to enlarge the conflict. They call upon us to supply American boys to do the job that Asian boys should do."[9]

But the rhetoric didn't alleviate the insiders' problem with Vietnam, didn't neutralize it in the event the Republicans took hold of and ran with it. Something was needed to tie it up, to bind the President, the people, and the Congress to a matter of national honor and patriotism.

That something came in July.

Stepped-up activity in Operation 34A was putting the pressure on the North Vietnamese high command: South Vietnamese and American pilots in American aircraft based in Cambodia or Thailand were strafing North Vietnamese villages along the Vietnam-Laos border; South Vietnamese commandos were parachuting into the North (and were being captured almost before they hit the ground—and interrogated); South Vietnamese PT boats made hit-and-run raids on North Vietnamese naval installations.

On July 30 or 31, 1964 (the dates differ in different reports), South Vietnamese torpedo boats raided the North Vietnamese islands of Hon Me and Hon Ngu in the Gulf of Tonkin. The boats, under command of the United States mission, made the raid as part of Operation 34A. At the same time, the U.S.S. *Maddox,* a destroyer attached to the Seventh Fleet, was cruising on a northward heading on a reconnaissance and surveillance operation code-named DeSoto. The mission was to play games with the North Vietnamese and Chinese radar defense systems: certain gear aboard the *Maddox* could simulate an air attack and this it did; other equipment was capable of pinpointing and charting radar installations (which had gone into operation under the impetus of the fake attack). Should a real attack be necessary, the first strike would be against the now pinpointed radar installations, literally blinding the enemy's defense capabilities.

The *Maddox* passed the South Vietnamese PT boats streaking south from their island attacks. The two islands were 120 to 130 miles north of where the *Maddox* cruised that day. It is not known if the destroyer's captain knew the raids had occurred.

On August 2 the *Maddox* reported two changes in course to avoid North Vietnamese PT boats and a fleet of junks. The *Maddox* had reached the northernmost point of her assigned course, had come about, and was steaming southward approximately twenty-three miles off the North Vietnamese coast when North Vietnamese PT boats attacked her, perhaps mistaking her for a South Vietnamese raider escort vessel. The fray was short and brutally one-sided: one of the PT boats was stopped dead in the water and sunk with a direct hit from one of the *Maddox*'s five-inch guns; two others were badly damaged by aircraft launched to assist the destroyer from the U.S.S. *Ticonderoga,* cruising in nearby waters. When news of the attack reached Washington on August 3, the President ordered the *Maddox* reinforced by a second destroyer, the U.S.S. *C. Turner Joy.* The *Maddox,* with the *Turner Joy,* was sent back to its DeSoto mission but ordered to stay at least eleven miles offshore. That night, August 3, two 34A raids were conducted by South Vietnamese PT boats against the radar installation at Vinh Son and a naval detachment in the Ron River estuary. The captains of the *Maddox* and *Turner Joy* were notified of the raids.

Twenty-four hours later came the controversial attack against the two destroyers by another fleet of North Vietnamese PT boats. Within six hours of notification of the incident, the President ordered bombing reprisals, the targets being selected from a pre-drafted Pentagon list of ninety-four possible sites. Twelve hours later, the avenging aircraft were launched. A resolution, also drafted months earlier, was carried from the White House to Capitol Hill.

The Senate passed the Tonkin Gulf Resolution 88–2, the two being Senators Morse and Gruening: the floor management of the bill was handled by Senator William Fulbright. The House followed suit: the vote was 416–0.

Neither Fulbright nor any of his colleagues knew about 34A, and they were not told. There was no backing away now; the President was going in for the kill and the Congress was going in with him. The Vietnam situation was under control. It had become a matter of patriotism.

Johnson was understandably relieved and allegedly quipped to a favored reporter, "I didn't just screw Ho Chi Minh, I cut his pecker off."

Vietnam did not become a pivotal issue in the campaign. In November, Lyndon Baines Johnson was elected President in a landslide remarkable in the nation's history.

In the following weeks a campaign of aerial warfare against the Democratic Republic of Vietnam and the Vietcong strongholds in the South was planned, debated, written, and rewritten. The President moved forward, then hung back, moved forward, hung back. Christmas passed, and New Year.

In February 1965 Vietcong troops attacked the United States military advisers' camp at Pleiku; a retaliatory strike was swift.

Guerrillas next attacked an American installation at Qui Nhon on the central coast and the President ordered a second, heavier retaliatory raid. Two days later, on February 13, 1965, the President ordered Operation Rolling Thunder, the sustained air war against the North.

Johnson had gone in.

CHAPTER 9

There are women who experience a twinge of anxiety or sudden, unexplained chills about the heart when calamity befalls an absent loved one. Alice Stratton was not one of them. So it was that calamity caught her by surprise.

She had spent that January Thursday working with her young and troubled patients at the child guidance clinic in Hanford. Dick had been gone since October, and she and the boys had received a Christmas tape recording from the Philippines, where the *Ticonderoga* crew had spent a brief respite from the war. His voice, measured and calm, with an almost forced gentleness, talked to them from the large, black cassette recorder. The *Ticonderoga* had stood down on December 20 and would go back up on the line on December 31. The weather in the Gulf of Tonkin had been lousy. He had had a couple of missions in Laos, which he preferred, he told the boys, because there was a minimum of heavy anti-aircraft fire, mostly small-arms stuff.

On one mission he and his flight had destroyed a truck column. On another they had nailed hundreds of VC in a box canyon. He described the rescue of a shipmate who had crashed and (with some disgust) the hysteria among the fleet over the discovery of a Chinese fishing fleet working the banks off Hainan Island:

". . . acting like a bunch of children," the voice said. "We think Tonkin is our preserve. They have as much right to be here as we do. I know why the Europeans and the Asians look at us with a jaundiced eye, but we're not going to change it much here now."

He closed quickly, telling the boys he missed them, and gave them brief messages for other members of the family.

They missed him, too, and it was going to be a damn long six months until June. Thank heaven she had the boys and, more so, her work. It took her out of herself, and out of the house.

She was preoccupied as she swung onto Earl Drive, took no more than passing notice of the black sedan parked a house up the street as she wheeled the big station wagon into the driveway. She turned off the engine and set the hand brake.

They were on their feet even before her hand was off the door latch: a chaplain and another officer from the base, wearing long, serious faces appropriate for their distasteful chore.

She knew. Instantly. Terrible, sudden fear smashed her flat in the chest.

"Is he dead?"

She managed that much before her throat closed. Anguish buckled her into a chair.

They were both talking and their words slid and tumbled by her, but they didn't say, "No, he is not dead," at least not like that, not right out, and she began to fade away, the sounds from their throats small in her ears, the room, their gestures, time, feeling, everything in slow motion.

Her face was slick and pasty in color by the time they got it out, or at least by the time it penetrated into her numbed brain. He was alive and presumed captured. Information was still scanty.

They were sorry, and they were gentle with her, and they left. There was a doctor sometime—take one of these, it will help you sleep—and she managed to get her senses unraveled enough to collect the boys and tell them, somehow, something they could understand. She clutched the youngest, Charlie, in her lap; Charlie, who was coming down with something, vomited sour and foul. Through the clouds she remembered thinking, "You said it well, Charlie."

Then the house was full, other wives cooking, soothing mother and children alike, mopping vomit, changing diapers, cleaning dishes, bedding children, talking, stroking, supporting. Some stayed the night.

The sleeping pills dulled neither her horror nor her grief. She cried through most of the night. She was as alone as she had ever been in her whole life, since she had been a young girl and her father lay near death.

An official telegram came the next day, and her world ended. It was no nightmare, no flight of senses; they were not coming back to admit their dreadful mistake, to tell her it was some other Alice's husband:

JANUARY 6, 1967 AM 8:23
CT WA 089xv GOVERNMENT PAID FAX WASHINGTON DC
6 10 29 AEST
MRS. ALICE MARIE STRATTON, REPORT DELIVERY, DO NOT PHONE
2021 EARL DRIVE
HANFORD, CA

"I deeply regret to confirm on behalf of the United States Navy that your husband, LtCdr Richard Allen Stratton 602087/1310, USN, was reported missing in action on 5 January 1967 on a combat mission over North Vietnam. During this mission your husband reported that his engine was running rough and he turned his aircraft toward the coast. Smoke and flames were seen coming from the tailpipe after which the aircraft was observed to explode.

"Your husband was not observed to eject from the aircraft but a good parachute was seen by one of the pilots following the explosion. Another member of the flight observed the parachute caught in some trees and heard an emergency radio signal. Your husband was not sighted on the ground and voice contact with him was not established. It was also noted that the parachute was pulled out of the trees within minutes.

"In view of the above information your husband will be carried in a captured status pending receipt and review of a full report of the circumstances. You may be certain that you will be informed of any information received regarding your husband or any action taken regarding his status. Your great anxiety in this situation is understood and I wish to assure you of every possible assistance together with the heartfelt sympathy of myself and your good husband's shipmates at this time of heartache and uncertainty.

"If I can assist you please write or telegraph Chief of Naval Personnel, Department of the Navy, Washington, DC 20370. My personal representative can be reached by telephone at OXford 4-2746 during working hours and OXford 4-2768 after working hours. In as much as your husband is presently being carried in a captured status it is suggested, for his safety, that you reveal only his name, rank, file number and date of birth to inquiries from sources outside your immediate family. Vice Admiral B. J. Sims, Jr., Chief of Naval Personnel."

It was not to be denied.

"Other wives . . . were there for a couple of days getting meals, in and out, wouldn't let you alone, wouldn't let you be, but it was good. You wanted to be alone but you didn't, and in those early days, I would be talking and I would have to walk around the corner. The tears would come. I didn't want to cry all the time but it was there. All the time.

"You never think it is going to happen to you. After the initial shock, you get to the feeling, why me? That questioning—why, God? why me?—it is the feeling you wake up with in the middle of the night and look out in the dark. You know there is no answer to it, so what do you do? You torture yourself with that question and [finally] you stop asking it and then pretty soon you have the answer: rain. It falls on everybody, the rain, and I just happened to be in the way. You have to accept it. It did happen to you.

"It takes about three months until you accept it and then, quickly, the adjustment period begins."

What made acceptance and adjustment so difficult for Alice Stratton was her innocence or, more cruelly, her naïveté. The staggering depth of her unawareness surprised her:

". . . The whole war thing was not an issue in my life until Dick got shot down, frankly. I hate to say that. I was so uninvolved with it, it just hadn't hit me. In fact, I didn't even think of him as going to a war, to tell the truth. I just thought of him as going on another [training] cruise. He knew what he was going to but I really didn't."

She was assigned by the Navy a casualty assistance officer who would keep her abreast of whatever development affected her or her prisoner husband, who could serve as an adviser for all manner of things, should she require it, and as a friend whom she could call day or night if she was in trouble.

Following the plan the Strattons had agreed upon, she would now move with the boys to Palo Alto as soon as possible. The Strattons' close friends the Foys, who also lived in Palo Alto, would smooth the way for her, as well as help find a suitable house (Foy was a realtor).

Still and all, it was the blackest of times. She could not shake the sadness; to make matters worse, the Navy had advised her not to talk about anything, and she kept most of her fears to herself. She reached a point of paranoia "where I would look out the window and maybe there would be a little man with slanty eyes looking at me, taking notes. I just didn't know."

She could not know it would get worse. She could not know a whole different life would open for her. One thing was certain: Richard Stratton was a memory.

PART III

PRISONERS

Life in extremity reveals in its movement a definite rhythm of decline and renewal. The state of wakefulness is essential, but in actual experience it is less an unwavering hardness of spirit than a tenuous achievement with periods of weakness and strength.

—Terrence Des Pres:
The Survivor

CHAPTER 10

"Now, Stratton," the officer said casually, "you must be severely punished."

A length of nylon cargo strap was knotted tightly around his left arm, just above the elbow, and the bight end passed over and around his right. He was rolled onto his side and the man in the leafy hat stood on his arms as he slowly drew the elbows together. The pain began instantly, as if someone had thrown a switch. He felt his shoulders trying to roll out of their sockets. He gasped, inhaling violently at the intensity of hurt. He no longer felt any discomfort from his shredded wrists. More lengths of strapping bound his legs below the knee and at his ankles.

The man with the leafy hat, Vegetable Vic, seized the end of the strap binding his arms and heaved upward. His whole upper body exploded and his eyes flooded. The pain increased. Indescribable. Pectoral muscles tore against their anchor points and his sternum pushed outward as the rib ends tried to pull away from it. He clenched his teeth so tightly they near cracked in their sockets.

The elbows moved higher.

Don't scream. Don't give the cocksucker the pleasure of knowing it hurts. Give nothing. Tough it out. You can tough it out. You can take this, James Bond. You can take anything. They're trying you out. It will be over in a few minutes. Hang in. Tough it out. You can tough it out. Remember Charlie Costello?

Remember Charlie Costello.

Ipswich. Good old Charlie Costello was the novice master, the drill instructor for a clerical Parris Island. Stratton had arrived at the novitiate at Ipswich after his fifth year in seminary. There had come, suddenly, a great personality clash between himself and the iron-willed novice master, Charles Costello. Somehow he had gotten it into his rough-tongued Stratton head that Charlie Costello had placed himself between Richard Stratton and Richard Stratton's goal.

Charlie Costello was an enemy and now he must do battle with him.

The forces joined and the battle went on for a year and a day, the requisite time the novitiate required of its young men before they took their first priestly vows and moved up to the major seminary.

And there he was, taking the vows of poverty, chastity, and obedience, kneeling in front of good old Charlie Costello, looking up at him, saying to himself, "You son of a bitch. I made it!"

But he wasn't making it.

Ipswich was away and gone. He thrashed about the floor, trying to move away from the pain. His muscles were simply being torn apart, slowly, jerking, slowly, jerking.

He screamed and screamed.

His torturer wearied. He took the bight end of the arm straps and looped it around Stratton's neck; the bight end from the legs he pulled up, drawing the heels against the buttocks, and tied the two together, forcing the body into an even more painful *U:* if Stratton dropped his arms or kicked out in a spasm, he would strangle himself. The pain grew even more intense. Why he couldn't pass out, he didn't know. Vegetable Vic sat down and lighted a cigarette, puffing it slowly, dragging the smoke deep into his lungs, taking full advantage of his rest break.

The officer got up and left.

Stratton gagged, his mouth filled with whatever was left in his stomach. Vic reached over, tenderly cleaning out his mouth so he would not suffocate on his own puke.

He began drifting in and out of reality. He heard screams issuing from his own throat. They did little to relieve the hurt. The room filled up with a foul odor. He realized in a moment of lucidity his bowels and his bladder had betrayed him; whatever shame he might have felt was blotted away by the pain. Dear God, it never went away. Intense, suffocating pain. Try as he might, he could not make his mind dissociate. He could not stop screaming.

The straps and handcuffs had long since cut off the circulation in his arms. This was going on too long:

"I'm going to lose my arms. There is no blood going through there. How long before gangrene sets in?"

Terror and pain played in his head.

"Hey, you dumb bastards, I'm really going to lose my arms. You don't want to do this. This isn't in the script. You are really not supposed to be doing this."

He was worked over again like a piece of dough being readied for the bread pan. The face of the man in the hat was impassive. There was no flicker of emotion, not at the piercing screams, the gurgling pleas of his victim, not at the blackening limbs, not at the slicks of urine or feces. Nothing.

"I can't take it any longer. Wait! You have a tolerance. Think! In survival school, they said if you think you have reached your tolerance, you are not there yet. Tough it out, wait."

He waited, screaming. Finally, no more.

"I'll talk. I'll talk."

The guard, impassive, left the room and returned shortly with the officer.

"Are you ready to talk now?"

"Yes. I'll talk."

There was a nod, a flash of triumph, and they sauntered out, leaving him where he was, trussed like a filthy chicken.

They left him there for he didn't know how long. He had lasted maybe two hours.

"I learned something very rapidly: you will cry in spite of yourself. And after they have broken you, they will jab it to you just a little bit more.

"Well, [finally] an officer came in carrying a pad of paper and a guard undid the straps from around my feet and took the straps off my elbows. You talk about the excruciating pleasure of pain. Well, I'll tell you, when the blood goes back into you, it's agony, but it's a mixed blessing. There's something there—I thought I had lost them from the elbows down."

The manacles were left in place. He was dragged onto the small stool, sat down in his own filth, facing the officer with the pad and the dull face, and it started all over again.

What was his name, his rank, his serial number? What was his date of birth? He repeated them all.

What was his ship? He gave it.

What type of aircraft was he flying? He told them.

What was his squadron, his air wing? He told them.

"Now, it didn't bother me too much to talk in this fashion. First of all, which I think is interesting, this is what made it difficult to withstand torture. I knew that the name of my ship was painted on the side of my aircraft; it had my squadron, my air wing, my ship painted on its sides, and I knew my aircraft was not totally consumed by flames because I could see it coming down in the chute. Also, it was somewhere in the papers they had captured with me. So I didn't feel that I had done anything terrible, but was just making it tough for them.

"[But after I had given them that], then I said, 'I can't talk any more with the handcuffs on,' because the pain was still there from them. He said, okay, fine, took those off, and once again, boy, the pain when the blood goes into those fingers. Then I told him I couldn't say anything without water. They put a cup of water down there [beside me]. I found I had lost the use of my hands and could barely get my arms up."

The interrogation resumed:

"Stratton, tell me about your crimes."

"I did not commit any crimes."

"Tell me about your raids."

"I didn't commit any raids."

"Tell us how you bombed Hanoi."

"Bombed Hanoi? I didn't bomb Hanoi. I've never been to Hanoi."

The last question surprised him. But it was a hint, a first glimmer, of what they were really after from Richard Stratton. Only later would he realize how much they were really after it.

"So the guy says I have a bad attitude, which is always their statement when they are pissed off at you. I went back into the Geneva Convention stuff, back and forth and like that. And he said fine, but since you have decided to talk, we will feed you. So now I was a good man, I was talking. I still had a bad attitude, but they would feed me and give me something to drink to show me that they were, indeed, very humane. And I would be expected to talk with them further in the evening.

"They gave me a cup of water and they brought in some rice with what looked like brussels sprouts; God knows what was in the soup. That was the meal. I stuffed every bit of it into me, figuring it was going to be a while before I ate again.

"After that, the interrogator returned and said to me—this is the essence of it—are you ready to admit that you bombed Hanoi? And I said, 'I did not bomb Hanoi!'"

"You will be severely punished."

Vegetable Vic moved him off the stool and onto the floor. The manacles would not fit this time. He pushed and twisted, but they would not fit. He was puzzled, exasperated. Stratton looked around, looked into the bewildered face, and started to laugh. The man in the hat, at first startled, began to giggle, too. Still giggling, shaking his head, he left the room and returned with the other North Vietnamese noncom Stratton had seen earlier, a man known as Straps and Bars. He was the chief torturer of Hoa Lo, and he saw nothing humorous in this situation.

Straps and Bars looked at the manacles, looked at Stratton's shredded, blackened wrists, and instantly hit upon the solution to the problem.

"[Straps and Bars] had Vic hold the arms and the cuffs—I'm catching this through my armpit—and lays them down on the floor. Then Straps and Bars stomps on my wrists with his heel until they fit into the manacles and then they locked them down to the last notch. Boy, that hurt. Whew. No two ways about that. Then they tied up my elbows again and I found out [Vic] hadn't done it right the first time, didn't *really* make it hurt the first time because [he] really never got the elbows to touch. But this time, with me laying on my side and both of them standing on my arms, they got my elbows to touch and finally locked together. Boy, were they together."

The pain switch was thrown again. The agony was so intense, and his struggles to try to move away from the pain so frenzied, that the fist that smashed his nose startled more than hurt. Sometime, a cuff on the ear ruptured the eardrum.[1] He started screaming, and a slapping fist on the head could not stop his cries. His

95

nose was bleeding badly. He puked his supper; no one cleaned his mouth. He was cuffed again, and again. He screamed.

He was rolled into a sitting position and they worked the straps on him, straps soiled the time before with his own wastes, straps cinched tight into open wounds.

Vegetable Vic, already wearied, lighted a cigarette; through a haze of pain and blood Stratton saw Vic move behind him, out of sight. Next he felt intense little needles of pain in already super-sensitive arms. At another point, both men worked behind him ". . . and there was pain in various parts of my hand and all I know is when I finished coming out, when I came out of it, both my thumbnails were bent back from the quick, one about sixty degrees, one about forty-five degrees, roughly. My presumption is that they yanked those things back from the quick while they were working behind me."

In a desperate, perhaps instinctive, effort he attempted to harm himself as he had been instructed in survival school. He tried to dash his head against the floor, and to hyperventilate. He was stopped immediately. He had nothing left.

He was through.

He lasted perhaps twenty minutes. They simply walked away from him, leaving him cinched up in the terrible, tormenting U-shape. How long? He did not know—a minute was as good as an hour. But he was convinced, later, anyway, that he had given it a good go, even though James Bond died in that ugly room.

He was unbound and the manacles removed once again. He was in terrible shape and hardly conscious. The fury of the beating had taken a terrible toll. He had not slept for nearly forty hours. But he would walk, sing songs, recite poetry, anything to stave off another beating for the moment, anything to buy some time to clear his head and gather whatever wits he had left.

An officer sat across from him, and began talking to him, lecturing him on the immorality, the illegality, the unjustness of the war. The officer, who was called Dum Dum by Americans already at Hoa Lo, was the one who had ordered the torture earlier in the day. He described the wantonness of the American pilots, their killing of innocents, women and children. The lecture went on for nearly two hours before Stratton's promise to talk was tested.

Did he have a family? Was he married? What part of the United States was he from? And Stratton answered the questions.

"So as I'm going through this ritual with him, I'm reassessing my situation. Obviously, there is such a thing as torture in Vietnam. Obviously, I am not James Bond and I am not going off on a sexual orgy in downtown Hanoi right after this adventure, as James is capable of doing. Obviously, I had better figure out where the hell I am going. . . .

"I made a basic decision at that point that I was going to have to depend upon brains rather than brawn to get me through whatever they were going to put me through. . . . They were not going to use anything but basic brutality on me and I had two strikes to prove it. God gave me a head. Why take a third strike and then give up something I had no control over? This was the thing that was going through my mind: why don't I try to keep as much control over the situation as I can and try to outwit them? Which I think was a basic mistake.

"(At the time I did not think it was. In fact, for a couple of years, I never thought that it was. But looking back on it, it was a basic mistake because, obviously, there was a certain superiority complex here. Here's a bunch of dumb bastards and I can outwit them, you know? I am smarter than they are, better educated than they are, traveled farther than they had, and no one is going to believe their crap on the outside anyway. So I decided I would go into a different mode [of resistance].)"

The conversation ended. Stratton slid into nothingness. Friday slid into Saturday, January 7.

* * *

Interrogation resumed at 7:30 the next morning.

Stratton conceded they had him in a difficult position: he was in pain from the beatings and tortures of the previous day; his arms would lift no higher, and then only with great effort, than his shoulders. His hands would not retract. His body and the peasant clothing he still wore were caked with dirt and blood, stained and soggy with his body wastes.

Who were the members of his squadron? they wanted to know. What were the *Ticonderoga* pilots' air tactics; roll-in altitudes, dive angles, air speeds? What defensive altitudes were used to avoid North Vietnamese MiGs or surface-to-air defensive missiles? What were offensive maneuvers for attacking them?

He responded as best he could, trying to concede nothing while

97

making it sound legitimate enough to stave off further beatings. Several former (and dead) American Presidents, for example, were shanghaied into the carrier's wardroom. He babbled out approximate figures on air speed, altitude, and the like.

"It made sense, their asking all this. This was the first time they had had somebody from our ship who was new on the line and they wanted to know if we were following the same basic tactics as the others. . . . And I was making up anything, anything that was *not* what we did, close enough to appear reasonable, but not close enough to help any of their gunners or anything else.

"Then the big play for the rest of the morning was 'your next targets.' They knew our targets were released from the White House on a basis of three targets per ship per line period. By that I mean lucrative targets that hurt them. (The rest were reconnaissance targets or targets of opportunity—trivial Mickey Mouse.)"

Stratton, like the rest of the *Ticonderoga*'s airmen, had not the foggiest notion what the future targets were; Edward McKeller, their skipper, announced major targets only on the night before actual attacks were to occur. While this saved Stratton from revealing critical military information, it also put him in a bit of a bind: he had to come up with something to demonstrate his willingness to keep on talking.

"So I tried to think of what were the most unlikely targets and I would tell them these were the three. If I remember correctly, they were Gia Lam airport, Phuc Yen airfield [a major MiG base a few miles north of Hanoi], and one new air base they had just started."

Gia Lam was protected by mutual agreement; it was the base of the International Control Commission, it was a civilian field, so-called, but it was the site of the North's air defense command. ". . . And I was enough of a cynic to believe the Air Force would never let [the Navy] hit a MiG base because if we hit a MiG base, the Air Force [pilots] couldn't shoot down MiGs and become aces. How the hell can you shoot down MiGs if there aren't any?

"All this got them off my back for the morning. Then in the afternoon they started this play for the mad bomber of Hanoi routine, which was to be the theme for the next whole two weeks. And, basically, for the next two weeks, it took this framework:

mornings were devoted to talking about military matters, afternoons and evenings were devoted to political indoctrination for me and trying to build up to . . . the bombing of Hanoi.

"On Saturday night, the last interrogator was some old fart they called the camp commander. They'd always run one of these guys up, a military type, not a political interrogator. He said I must obey the rules of the camp, this, that, and the other thing, and we'll give you a good deal."

He was taken, under arms, from this interrogation room and locked up in a nearby maximum-security cell in a section of Hoa Lo known as Heartbreak Hotel. He was given an old, nib-style wooden-handle pen, an inkwell, and writing paper. He was ordered to write down everything he had told all of his interrogators that day, and to write truthfully. If he failed, he would be severely punished. He knew he had not outfoxed them: he knew one of his interrogators, a buck-toothed, jug-eared man with a good command of English, had taken notes on everything he had said, to any interrogator, at all three sessions that day. The fact he could not hold the pen seemed not to make the slightest difference. His transcript was to be ready the next morning.

Despondent, he stared at the door, a great, heavy wooden door bound with iron straps and pierced with a peephole. He shivered with pain and cold. The temperature he estimated at about forty degrees. He already knew his arms were infected.

For a long while he sat on the cement bunk that was to be his bed; a rat scuttling out of the large drainhole in the corner of the cell startled him, but he did not move.

What in the name of God had he done?

"Picture yourself in your skivvie shorts at forty degrees, about the temperature of your icebox. And then picture the terror of every time you hear keys jangling out in the hallway and the squeak of the outer door, not knowing whether it's to [be] you . . . or one of five other people hauled off to a night interrogation. Picture a pint of water a day. Picture your arm the size of a thigh . . . throbbing with pain and suppurating from about five different points. Picture yourself unable to move your arms above the level of your shoulders, or to retract your hands. Picture the overwhelming smell of urine and offal. Picture a cold rice meal with one little piece of pigskin with the hair still on it. Picture cold brussels sprouts hard as pebbles. Picture no sleep. Picture the desire to die, to commit suicide.

"Yes! Had I had the means then, even though I do not believe in it, I perhaps would have done it. After they broke me, I felt I had betrayed my country and my fellow men and my officer corps."

He huddled in the corner on the bunk and stared across the cell at the pen and the white sheets of paper, upon which he was to write everything he had said during the interrogations.

This was the final humiliation. He stared at the papers and somewhere inside him the black Irish rage flashed. Slowly, painfully, he crawled off the bunk and stood with shaking knees.

With his stiffened fingers, he undid the drawstring of the filthy britches and let them drop. He grasped his penis and with his last reserve of liquid urinated on the papers. He gathered up his britches and made his way back to the bunk.

A guard discovered his defiance.

He returned with others. They produced a length of rope saturated with urine. Stratton was tossed onto the floor and held. His right arm was yanked out straight and the rope passed around it at the elbow, where the wound was from the torture straps. They sawed the filthy rope back and forth and back and forth, cutting deeper and deeper into his arm. He struggled and screamed. He was held fast. When they had finished, they left him in a heap sobbing on the floor.

He awoke at dawn to see a large swarm of mosquitoes swoop through the cell's high and solitary window. The rat stayed out of sight in the drain.

The temperature never went much higher than forty; his pain did not stop; his arms kept swelling.

The mosquitoes left at dusk.

CHAPTER 11

Late in the afternoon of January 5, 1967, Lieutenant Commander Richard Dean Mullen, USN, a squadron operations and targeting officer for Air Group 19, finished the paper work on a mission he would fly the next day over South Vietnam. No sooner had he entered the wardroom than he learned Richard Stratton had been lost. Mullen's square, handsome face collapsed in grief.

"It was a sad occasion for me because we had been good friends and Dick had always had that very fine, humorous personality that was always a strength to everyone. It was very sad."

Mullen checked the battle reports. There was a good chance, he decided, Stratton was still alive.

In the wardroom, Stratton's fellow fliers offered prayers for his well-being. Mullen joined them.

"The lights were dimmed down . . . and the priest . . . (each of the carriers has a priest and a minister aboard) gave a prayer for Dick and of course we, to ourselves, all added our own prayers for his safety and his welfare and that he'd make it okay."

The following evening, the fliers gathered again in the wardroom. This time it was the ship's minister who led the services. Richard Mullen did not attend. The prayers were for him.

* * *

Richard Mullen was a gentleman so courtly and refined, his shipmate Richard Stratton once remarked, that "he wouldn't say 'shit' if he had a mouthful." It was ironic that the wardroom had nicknamed Mullen "Moon" after cartoonist Frank Willard's skirt-chasing, roughneck hustler; the only thing the two Moons had in common was a birth in Chicago.

The soft-spoken, silver-haired Mullen was flight commander of a F-4D Skyraider section at FAGU, the Fleet Air Gunnery Unit, at El Centro when he first met Richard Stratton. Stratton was training with a light attack section. It was 1957. A bond had been struck between the two and it continued through the years. The friendship was revitalized aboard the *Ticonderoga* in October when they found themselves assigned to squadrons attached to Air Group 19. Their separate responsibilities as an operations and a maintenance officer prohibited "buddying around," to use Mullen's phrase, "but in the wardroom, why, frequently I'd see Dick and find a place to sit down next to him. We'd chat about the 'good old days' at the gunnery unit and some of the good times we'd had in the past." It was a comfortable and comforting relationship between two old friends suffering the loneliness of separation from wives and children.

Richard Dean Mullen was born on February 12, 1931, in Chicago, one of two sons in what he describes as a middle-to-lower-income family. Like young Richard Stratton fifteen hundred miles away in Quincy, Mullen worked a variety of jobs to keep pin money in his pockets and to help ease his family's financial burden.

Mullen graduated from high school in Evanston Township. His college life was brief: two years at Wright Junior in Chicago.

He joined the regular Navy in 1951, after a brief stint as a "weekend warrior." He was twenty years old. It was natural selection: his father had been a submariner in World War I; his brother was a naval aviator. His brother administered the oath when Mullen was accepted as a Naval Aviation cadet in 1953.

Also like Stratton, Mullen was a deeply religious man and devoted to his family. He had married Jeanne Louise Riggins and they had two daughters, Sandra and Karen, now five and three.

* * *

Mullen awoke January 6 to find his mission to South Vietnam scrubbed. Instead, he and his wingman, Ensign Denny Shoup, were to pilot their F-8 fighter-bombers to a coastal area near Cape

Falaise, about fifty miles south of Thanh Hoa, North Vietnam. There, they were told, they would find a series of caves in a great cliff that stood out of the Gulf of Tonkin. The caves were being used as an ammunition dump by the enemy.

Aircraft from the *Ticonderoga* and other carriers had given the area a pasting by the time Mullen and Shoup swooped into the sector late in the afternoon. Mullen's plane carried high-velocity rockets and bombs; Shoup's, only rockets. The two planes ran in close for a look, banked away from the landfall, and once again over the Gulf lined up on the target and cranked the engines up to attack speed.

"On our first pass [we fired] the rockets into the caves. It looked like we got some good secondary explosions. My wingman didn't have any bombs so I left him out over the water (while I made one more run). I was just going to drop my bombs into the top of the cliff where the magazine area was.

"I was just pulling out, starting to bank back out over the water, when I got hit; probably it was 37 mm ack-ack fire. I lost my hydraulics [which control the aircraft's ailerons, elevators, rudder, and trim tabs, among other things] and the aircraft became uncontrollable. I knew I was in real trouble."

The F-8 rolled wildly, and at a frightening speed; its instrument panel was a flashing pinwheel of fire warning lights.

He ejected.

The plane hurtled away from his soaring seat and exploded. His parachute dropped him rudely in a rice paddy. The reception committee was heavily armed and inhospitable.

Mullen's flight suit and fatigues were ripped from his body. So were his flying boots and socks; he was wrestled into peasant clothes so violently they ripped. He was prodded at gunpoint away from the paddy, up a long hill through a canebrake to a poorly paved macadam road. The militiamen started running him up and down the road until his bare feet were nicked raw and bleeding. Satisfied he would not lope off into the countryside, his captors marched him toward a coastal hamlet; they did not interfere with a horde of angry peasants who beat the flier with sticks or battered him with clods and stones as he stumbled along, his arms bound just above the elbows. Once at the hamlet, he was put into the back of a truck and driven to a second village farther up the coast. He was held there a day and interrogated by an official of the village whose techniques were as poor as his English. Mullen gave only his name, rank, serial number, and date of birth. He was assured in fractured but certain terms he would speak more freely soon enough.

He was put into another truck for the journey to Hanoi, a trip made longer by numerous stops where he was taken from the vehicle and given over to angry citizens. He arrived well thumped and frightened at Hoa Lo prison early Sunday morning, January 8. He was taken immediately to Room 18 and they were waiting for him, had given up their Sunday liberty for him. There were the usual interrogators, the cloth-draped table and chairs, the table lamp, papers, and ashtrays.

It started without fanfare: what was his name, his rank, his serial number, his birth date? He rattled off the answers in prescribed fashion.

"Now, Mullen, what is your squadron?"

"I'm sorry. I can't tell you that."

An interrogator took an ashtray and shattered it over Mullen's head.

What is your squadron, Mullen? Your ship? Who are your squadron mates? What kind of airplane do you fly? What is its air speed? Its operational ceiling? What is the thrust of its engine? What is the radius of its turn? What kind of weapons system does it carry? What are your next targets?

Nothing.

Mullen was introduced to Straps and Bars.

Interrogation and torture continued off and on all that day and long into the night. They broke him.

"Finally I just got to a point where I said to myself there's only two things I am not going to tell them. That's the targets and that I am married. Why I stuck with those two things, I don't know."

So he told them, told them in bits and pieces about weapons systems, about turn radii and engine thrust, about operational ceilings and air speeds, all of it true or most of it true but not for his own plane, not the F-8 fighter-bomber; instead, true about aircraft he had flown long ago, obsolete birds no longer in the fleet. He did not tell them that. They wrote down all his information carefully, nodding over their papers, exchanging knowing looks over this windfall.

Now, Mullen. The targets. He shook his head. He didn't know anything about targets.

Straps and Bars slipped a noose about his neck. His wrists, severely damaged from earlier tortures, were forced back into manacles; his wrists inverted behind him, his arms were drawn up high and a taut lanyard run from the manacles to the noose. As his arms dropped, the noose cut into his throat. He began to strangle, gagging, gasping for air. His peripheral vision went first; the light faded slowly to gray and he fainted.

He came to at dawn. He lay like a heap of dirty laundry in the middle of the floor. The ropes and the manacles were gone. He was very cold and afraid. He knew he was badly hurt.

He crawled across the floor and up onto the cement slab that served as a bunk and buried his head under his arms in the corner.

"I looked into that corner and someone had taken a nail or something and scratched in very small, little letters, in the corner, 'God, country and family.' . . . That started to give me nourishment, spiritual nourishment. And the more I thought about Him, the more I felt His presence, and the more I felt that someone—even though I was hurting so badly—that someone really did love me and was really there watching over me.

"And of course I started thinking about my wife. We've always been a very close family, and I started getting back on the spiritual part of it. . . ."

* * *

At that same moment in the Heartbreak Hotel section of Hoa Lo, perhaps not sixty feet from where Richard Mullen huddled in a corner of his cell, Richard Stratton's morning interrogation began. That final terror Saturday night had put his life in peril; he was feverish and in great pain. He was at bay.

Two of his interrogators wore the uniform of the North Vietnamese Air Corps; the third interrogator he had seen before—a "political type."

What were the aerial defense tactics used by the U. S. Navy against the Vietnamese MiGs?

He did not know. Carefully Stratton explained he had never seen a MiG; further, an A-4 light-attack ship, which carried a fixed bombsight and less than fifty rounds of ammunition for its solitary 20 mm cannon, would not engage a MiG in combat. Not normally, anyhow. More questions. The "political type" left the cell. The three fliers were alone.

"Another man from your ship is in the other room."

They stared at each other silently. One of the North Vietnamese reached into the pocket of his tunic and took out a pad of paper and a pencil. He wrote the name slowly as his companion watched. He tore the sheet from the pad and handed it to Stratton. Stratton's crippled hands could barely grasp it.

"Moon Mullen."

He looked up into their faces. They were not enjoying this; he could sense it. He shivered. Jesus. They were sincere. It *was* true. Oh, my God, they've nailed Moon. Painfully he handed the piece of paper back. One of the North Vietnamese took out a pack of cigarettes, withdrew one, placed it between Stratton's lips, and lighted it.

"Now, they didn't ease up on their questions but it was an [example] of one aviator respecting another: 'You poor bastard. Your best friend's been shot down. Have a cigarette.' Neither did they indulge in any physical brutality. They knew they were not going to get anything out of me but they were trying to use my answers about my ship against Moon. But . . . they did not indulge in any physical brutality. No North Vietnamese Air Force interrogator ever used physical brutality on me to get an answer. They would threaten and bluff and play games but never once did they raise a hand or call a turnkey to come in and beat me up.

"I think it's analogous to the situation in Germany during World War II, where, in fact, the Luftwaffe kept control of American airmen shot down and tried to keep the Gestapo away from them. I think there is that bond between airmen."

Stratton knew he was in trouble. Alone, perhaps, he could bluff them, play with them, and Mullen could do the same thing. But with two men from the same ship captured within hours of one another, locked up only (he presumed) feet apart but unable to communicate, the interrogators could play one set of answers off against the other.

". . . I thought I was being very clever and giving them nothing that was valuable or of use to them and then they'd beat me down. 'Mullen says this. You say that. Now, which is it?' And gradually they closed in on [a reasonable knowledge of our tactics].

"I didn't feel bad about that because . . . what we used on our ship was no different than what everybody else used. In other words, you had a series of compatible dive angles with your ship and what you used depended upon the flak at the time. And I did not *have* anything to give them and they couldn't have gotten it out of me had they wanted to except, as I say, the tactics sections. But we were using the same damn tactics during the whole war and between their radar, their rangefinders, their naked eyes, and the torturing of any number of us here" the North Vietnamese knew about all there was to know.

Within three days his captors no longer sought that kind of specific information.

The routine of Stratton's interrogation established that first Monday continued day after day, a morning-afternoon-evening medley of questions, lectures, indoctrination, and bullying. It was beyond him what they were doing. He had nothing really concrete to give them and what was concrete had been extracted. He was in terrible pain, fearful of blood poisoning and gangrene. He still wore the filthy peasant clothes he had arrived in. He still was in a cold and solitary cell.

What it was all about was the making of the mad bomber of Hanoi. He would even write his own "confession."

Who made the decision to cast Richard Stratton as a leader of terror bombing raids against Hanoi in December of 1966 is unknown. But such a decision was made. Richard Stratton "confessed" to such crimes.

The Vietnamese were pragmatic: he would take medical treatment (and thereby concede defeat and start writing his daily conversations) or they would have to amputate the severely infected arm to save his life. (If he died, without the operation, they were not responsible. He had killed himself by refusing their offer of

107

medical treatment.) He had no choices left. So it began. At the end of each day, as best he could with crippled hands, he scratched out his recollections of the discussions with his interrogators. Only he knows what terrible torment and turmoil he faced in that decision.

"I think they made their final determination that I was going to be it on the seventh to the tenth day, when they gave me medical treatment. They were obviously upset that I was injured and they were greatly worried about whether or not I was going to lose my arm. They were not worried enough to give me expert medical treatment but they did clean up the wounds, put in sulfa powder, and pump me full of penicillin, [which] at the time I thought was probably truth serum or dope. (The reason [my "confession"] was delayed until March was my health wasn't, simply, restored.) I was on a downhill path and really going out.

"One arm had blown up to the size of my leg, the red streaks coming up the middle and nodules hanging out of the armpit. Every indication of blood poisoning and everything else. [Stratton had also lost nearly 30 pounds by this time, down from 185 pounds when he was captured.] The thing that actually saved me turned out to be the nails that had been bent back and the so-called cigarette burns because they provided drainage. . . . I found that if I could put my thumbs in warm water I could get a drainage going and drain out some of this stuff, could suck some of it out. . . ."

And as far as his continuing interrogations went:

". . . I never understood what they were after until March, and that was to piece together in my own words battle-type information they could put together into a story. The Rabbit [the jug-eared interrogator, later identified as aide-de-camp to the North Vietnamese commandant of prisons] actually wrote the 'confession' out of all the stuff he got."

It is difficult a decade after it happened to reconstruct the North Vietnamese hysteria and the international impact caused by the four raids of December 1966 in which Hanoi itself sustained bomb damage, difficult to piece together what actually happened, hard to put it in perspective.

According to a summary of those raids in *The Pentagon Papers,* "the major result of the raids close to Hanoi December 2, 4, 13,

14—all inside a previously established 30-mile sanctuary around the capital—'was to undercut what appeared to be a peace feeler from Hanoi.' " Allegedly, some beginning arrangements for talks between Washington and Hanoi had been begun by the Poles. Poland was a member of the International Control Commission in Vietnam; initial talks were to be opened in Warsaw in December. *The Pentagon Papers* continue:

" 'When the attacks were launched inadvertently against Hanoi in December . . . the attempt to start talks ran into difficulty. A belated attempt to mollify North Vietnam's bruised ego failed and formal talks did not materialize.' This is an allusion," the *Papers* explain, "to President Johnson's decision to restore part of the bomb-free sanctuary around Hanoi. The analyst does not explain why he considered the raids inadvertent. Recapitulating the public furor over the bombing, the study comments that 1966 'drew to a close on a sour note for the President.'

" 'He had just two months before resisted pressure from the military for a major escalation of the war in the North and adopted the restrained approach of the Secretary of Defense,' the study continues, 'only to have a few inadvertent raids within the Hanoi periphery mushroom into a significant loss of world opinion support.' "[2]

Public anger in the United States over the bombing was exacerbated by Salisbury's dispatches from Hanoi. Salisbury himself believed that some raids were accidental.[3] The Vietnamese, while in an understandable fury, were nonetheless shrewd in realizing the raids could be a major issue in the anti-war public relations campaign.

Stratton believes his selection as arch-fiend in the subsequent melodrama was simply luck of the draw.

"Ho Chi Minh says we're perfidious and therefore the peace talks are off and Lyndon Johnson is a liar. So now they're looking for somebody lately shot down. Of course, we go into our Christmas bombing moratorium (to give them a chance to stock up their supplies again), so there is no action over Vietnam where they can capture a pilot. We're the first ones back on the line, it's our second day of operations, and I'm the first pilot down. So now they have a chance of saying *I* led an attack on Hanoi and [proving] Lyndon Johnson is a liar.

109

"Moon is shot down the next day. There is no way you could make that gray-haired gentleman out to be a mad bomber of anything. And here *I* am: I've got the big nose, sloping forehead, the crew cut, the pot belly; I'm everything their cartoonists use to portray the typical American aggressor on the land, sea, or air; and I've got the loud mouth; I was the arch-type of what the mad bomber was going to be. Moon just didn't fit it. Besides, Moon flew an F-8 tactical fighter and I flew a bomber, so the choice, naturally, fell on me. But they waffled; they really didn't start pressing the Hanoi bit until after Moon was down, in camp, and interrogated.

"The second thing . . . perhaps equally as probable was that Dr. John Takman was due in town [heading an investigative team] for the first Bertrand Russell war tribunal for investigation of American war crimes. [The Vietnamese] had to have some good evidence . . . that we were indeed hitting popular targets. They had to have some material . . . red-hot off the press that showed we were using antipersonnel weapons, intentionally striking civilian targets. They had to produce, and produce fast."

On January 24 Stratton was bound and blindfolded and taken to Cu Loc prison in southwestern Hanoi, where he was put in solitary confinement. Cu Loc, called the Zoo by its American inmates, was a former motion picture studio.

* * *

Moon Mullen was still huddled in the corner of his cell when the interrogators entered. They started in pretty much where they had begun the night before.

". . . I kept telling them things that I had told them before, some of which was true, like the names of some of the people in the squadron, but things I did not think were going to hurt anyone else. That went on for two or three days and there were many threats and they would put me back in the manacles for a while; I held to my stories and it just sort of went back and forth like that. I can't even remember for how long. They moved me out of my cell and into another all the way around back and I was there for a couple of days. Then they moved me back into the interrogation room, the Meathook Room, for a couple of more days and there were more threats, the manacles, and everything else. But it was nothing compared to those first two days."

The regular interrogators were joined by two men dressed in the uniform of the North Vietnamese Air Corps. They wanted to hear again about weapons systems. He went into his litany. The reaction was cold. That is not what the other pilot said. Mullen was at once frightened for fear of more torture and buoyed instinctively that the other pilot might be Stratton. They challenged other answers. Caution got the upper hand. He was being cross-checked, mousetrapped. They kept trying to trip him up.

Things eased a bit after that. Finally one of the interrogators said another pilot, shot down before Mullen, was being held and interrogated also.

Mullen said, "I would like to see him. I would like to see him very much. Is his name Stratton?"

The response was predictable.

"They didn't say yes, they just sort of gave a 'yessing' nod. But they didn't say, 'Yes. It is Stratton.' "

Mullen's physical condition had deteriorated alarmingly. His wrists were dangerously infected and his general health alarming enough to warrant concern. Finally, on the fourteenth day after his capture, his wounds were cleaned and packed with sulfa powder and bandaged. His hands were numb and he could not use them.

"When you get those manacles on, I guess animal instinct sort of takes over. It reminds me of a wild animal caught in a trap. If he can, he will chew a paw off to release himself from that trap. You are really in the same sort of situation. The pain [from the manacles] is so excruciating you are constantly working your wrists so that, hopefully, you can even make your hands shrink to try to slip out of those darn things. You are always working them. Well, what you are doing is just cutting your wrists to shreds. And all of us there were just so susceptible to infection. I got a severe infection in both wrists. The scars are still there where the manacles dug in and, you know, all that. . . ."

The North Vietnamese had finished with Mullen at Hoa Lo. In the afternoon the guards came and bound and blindfolded him, hustled him down to the main courtyard, and put him in the back of the truck. He was taken to Cu Loc, the Zoo. He was put in solitary confinement in a building called "the gatehouse" and there he would remain for more than one hundred days. His medical treatment was continued. It consisted of occasional fresh powderings with sulfa and clean bandages.

Some days after he had been there, an interrogator he had seen at Hoa Lo entered his cell.

"Mullen, wouldn't you like to have a roommate?"

"Yes, I would. Very much. I am led to believe Stratton is here. I would like to get together with Stratton."

The North Vietnamese walked out of the cell without a word. The door was closed and bolted.

* * *

It was a long time after the roommate incident. He was permitted now to visit the bathing area. It wasn't much: a muddy enclosure with a dirty little tub covered with what looked like an old-fashioned, small-paned storm window. The window panes were gray with grime.

As he bent down to slide the window off the tub, he noticed written in the grime on one of the panes the words "HUD'N HUD'N."

He stifled a cry of joy, blinked back tears. Only one person could have written that, he knew. Dick Stratton.

"Hud'n hud'n" was a piece of wardroom silliness that had grown out of the boredom that accompanies war. It was pronounced gutturally and was supposed to imitate the engine sounds of that most masculine of machines, the motorcycle. "Hud'n hud'n." Lots of laughter, the brotherhood of the piston. The 194th Squadron of Air Group 19 had adopted it as its own personal password.

The silly words buoyed Mullen nearly to giddiness. He was ecstatic. Dick Stratton was alive, alive and nearby.

He waited more easily, hoping that a reunion was perhaps in the offing.

He prayed for it.

CHAPTER 12

Mr. Lang watched from the shadows as the antique bird bucked and rumbled toward the darkened terminal, and finally stopped at the apron. The engines shut off. A dull yellow light illuminated the flight deck. The Boeing 307 Stratoliner carried a special passenger tonight from Pnompenh and the elfin Mr. Lang, a functionary in the Foreign Ministry's press department, had been dispatched to Gia Lam to meet him, ease his way through customs and immigration, and fetch him back to Hanoi in the official, black Moskvich sedan. Mr. Lang had worn his blue suit; he had signed for the machine.

Ahh. Mr. Lang hurried forward. He looked up through his practical, steel-rimmed eyeglasses and smiled.

"Mr. Lee Lockwood? Welcome to our country." Into the baggage-laden arms of the slightly startled American Mr. Lang thrust the bouquet of blossoms he had carried from the city.

Guided by Mr. Lang toward the immigration desk, Lee Lockwood was fatigued by his long journey, begun hours and hours before in New York; but weariness could not diminish his elation.

His arrival in Hanoi signaled a journalistic coup as dramatic as any in this crazy, controversial, confusing war. He had a right to feel elated. Lockwood was a photographer with the Black Star organization; at this moment he was on special assignment behind enemy lines for *Life* magazine, the most prestigious photojournal

113

in North America. And in this capacity he was the first American photographer invited into North Vietnam since 1954.

It had all begun on a shooting assignment in Havana about a year before. It had gone well, and he had produced a book on Fidel Castro and Castro's Cuba. On a hunch, a whim, he had stopped by the North Vietnamese Embassy in Havana, Hanoi's lone outpost in the Americas, "just to see how the fellows were getting along." Apparently, just fine: he had applied for a visa and received it about twelve months later. Now he tumbled off the ICC's vintage airliner. After stops in Mexico City, Havana to pick up his precious visa, back to Mexico, and onward to San Francisco, Seattle, Anchorage, Tokyo, Hong Kong, and Pnompenh, he had received, finally, the floral welcome of Mr. Lang.

Lockwood was a man of many parts. Outwardly he was a medium-complexioned person gentle and controlled in manner and speech. Part of that was illusion. Inwardly he was passionate and dedicated. Through all photographers, from Niépce and Daguerre on, runs a thread of crazy. In Lockwood this bit of professional heredity showed itself in an assertive intensity and doggedness that surfaced upon command. Nor was he a man unaware of history or his place in it as its recorder and chronicler. Imagine his frustration when the lowly customs clerk told him he would be prohibited from photographing the Fatherland in color. Mr. Lang was nonplused; Lockwood was vexed.

He had made it a point in Havana, from the beginning, to state he wanted—and intended—to use color film in his cameras. To be prohibited now from doing so would, in the end, greatly diminish the impact of his story.

Customs was firm: it was sorry, but color photography was not permitted. Regulations. And what regulations were those? The regulations that said all films exposed in the Democratic Republic of Vietnam were to be developed in the Democratic Republic of Vietnam, and that meant black and white film because the Democratic Republic of Vietnam did not have facilities to process color film. Not that Mr. Lockwood was distrusted, nothing like that, but the government wished to ensure that nothing of, ah, strategic value had been photographed inadvertently by an outsider. Those regulations.

But color photographs were of the greatest importance.

Well, in that case, the matter would have to be taken up with the proper authorities, with the correct ministry, and special permission would have to be granted. But as a gesture of friendship, Mr. Lockwood would be permitted to keep his color film with him instead of having it impounded at the airport, the normal procedure, if he gave his word he would not use it until the matter had been resolved. He promised.

Settled into the cushions of the black Moskvich, Lockwood and Mr. Lang chatted softly as the sedan rolled across the Doumer Bridge toward the capital, and Lockwood's prearranged lodgings at the Metropole.

What was it Mr. Lockwood wanted to do?

"I said, 'Well, there are several things I want to do here, but certainly at the top of the list if it can be arranged, I would like to see some American prisoners of war, interview them, photograph them, be with them awhile.' Surely from their point of view this would be 'excellent propaganda.'

"'If you want to show that your treatment of American prisoners is humane by comparison to the way prisoners in South Vietnam are being treated as you have been saying publicly all along, if you really believe your treatment of American prisoners is humane and you want some response from the American public, this is the best way to get it. Just let me prove this thesis by talking to some Americans personally.'"

For most Americans, Lockwood explained, the war was a kind of abstraction, matters of tonnage and bombs dropped. There was no human component in the way Americans perceived the war in North Vietnam. A way to gain that component was to let Americans see their own kind in a favorable prison setting.

"I must say I do not believe any prison camps are humane. I don't think it is possible to have a prison and have it be humane under any circumstances. It is a contradiction in terms, whether it's a civilian prison or a military prison. But I gave them the benefit of the doubt. I had no idea what their prisons were like.

"Well, the [North Vietnamese] said, 'This will be very difficult but we will work on it.' About every two or three days, we'd have a meeting and they would ask me for a revised list of places I wanted to photograph and I'd bring this up again. I would always bring it up. I'd say, 'This is *really* important.'"

* * *

Once, a long time ago, Hanoi was gay. This dowdy city with its Frenchified architecture and glittering lakes, its ubiquitous sou trees in leafy parade, had been neither the most elegant nor the most exciting outpost of the colonial service. But it had been comfortable, and those days, for France at least, were happier. As in other civilized enclaves in Indochina, there was a timelessness to life in Hanoi. French intellectuals, bemedaled officers well barbered and tailored, colonials with soft-skinned ladies, and wealthy Vietnamese mingled along the peacock alley and around the zinc bar of the Metropole. There was easy laughter, talk of crops and home on mild evenings when that privileged gentry wandered the small garden at the rear of the hotel or settled in canopied, rattan drinking chairs beneath bright Asian stars or a moon that seemed always in reminiscence the color of ripe camembert.

All gone.

"Hanoi at war," Lockwood wrote in *Life,* "is a city of contrasts. During the daily three-hour lunch and siesta break—decreed by President Ho Chi Minh as necessary for the welfare of body and mind—people nap, read, stroll around the lakes. . . . But beneath this surface serenity, daily life is geared to Hanoi's conviction that United States bombers could come in at any hour. Along almost every downtown street, at six-foot intervals, are one-man concrete bomb shelters. Every effort is made to avoid large concentrations of people in a city whose 1965 population was 500,000.

"Tens of thousands of children have reportedly been sent away to rural areas to live. The main department store is open only two hours a day, from 5:30 to 7:30 A.M. The central market has been vacated, replaced by small markets that move around the city from day to day. Even such things as weddings have been affected."

"One Sunday," Lockwood wrote, "two friends of a Vietnamese acquaintance of mine got married. Only close friends attended the ceremony, and afterward they held a celebration in their home. But because no more than twelve people were permitted in a home at any one time, each guest was allotted two hours at the festivities. The party lasted all day long."[4]

He came and went as he pleased in Hanoi, but could take pictures only when accompanied by a ministry official. His visa covered a period of only two weeks, and he became edgy after several days because he was unable to shoot many of the priorities on his list. He had asked for a session with President Ho; the President was ill. He had asked to go to the Demilitarized Zone at the seventeenth parallel; it was not permitted. He was allowed to photograph vessels unloading at the quayside in Haiphong; photographing ships at anchor in the roads was prohibited. Periodically he submitted to the appropriate officials his exposed black and white film. It would be developed and the strips of negatives and proof sheets returned to him. Occasionally a frame on one of the proof sheets would be marked, though never anything big. But Lockwood was the first to acknowledge he was not shooting anything big. He purposely avoided photographing anything even resembling military installations and he could never photograph, anyway, without his guide from the Foreign Ministry.

One thing that did please him was the presence of Bobby Salas. Salas was a Cuban and, like Lockwood, a photographer. They had met years earlier in Cuba and had become friends. Salas, too, was quartered at the Metropole.

On the twelfth day of his visit, the day before a scheduled interview with Premier Pham Van Dong, and on the eve of his departure, the word came down: he would be allowed to use his precious color film.

"Big, big announcement to me in the hotel. So I began shooting color, and of course they thought I was going to leave right after the interview with Pham Van Dong. That was the way things were organized: you had your interview, and then you were told—after the interview—that you were leaving the next day."

So to the Presidential Palace he went, had his interview, capping it with a magnificent color portrait of the smiling Premier cradling a nosegay of brilliant orange and red dahlias from the palace gardens.

"In the heart of every Vietnamese," Pham Van Dong told him, "the flowers of spring symbolize reunification."

In Lockwood's heart was a touch of winter. His journalistic coup was something less than he had hoped for or, indeed, expected. He would write:

". . . As it turned out about two [weeks] were wasted to

bureacracy and ceremony—delays in planning my itinerary and in providing interpreters, interminable formal briefings and greetings, and always that three-hour recess for lunch. I was not unique in this torment; the same thing happens to all foreign journalists, Communists included."

But he did not depart on schedule. The International Control Commission plane did not arrive on the day of his departure, nor did it come again, as it turned out, for another two weeks. Hanoi was stuck with him, him and his innumerable rolls of color film and his incessant demands to travel, to photograph, and to see interned Americans:

"Now they had to find things for me to do. They had my list of requests and they couldn't very well go back on their word. It would be a matter of losing face. Now that I had the time, I began to travel, and since they had given me permission to shoot color, I just kept on shooting it and that's how that story really got put together."

He traveled nearly a thousand miles, visiting remote areas never seen by Western journalists. He talked with village leaders, ate and drank with truck drivers and militiamen. He photographed quiet street scenes and bombs exploding in an American raid, peasants with rifles strapped across their backs planting rice, battered children and destroyed buildings. Still he pushed for interviews with captured Americans, even, finally, enlisting the aid of the Cuban ambassador to North Vietnam.

In the meantime, Lockwood had become desperate enough to compromise: to his Foreign Ministry contact he suggested eliminating any interviews with captured Americans if he could but photograph them. The answer was still no.

"But what we can do," his ministry contact offered, "is have one of our own photographers take pictures with your camera. You put the film into your camera and you give me your camera. I will take it to one of our photographers. He will go to a place where there are American prisoners of war. He will take pictures. You tell me what pictures you want, and I will bring the camera back to you and the film will still be in the camera; it will not have been taken out." Lockwood had told his ministry contact he would be unable to convince his editors, let alone the American public, that some kind of "propaganda deal" was not being worked unless he himself actually saw the prisoners. Now a Leica camera with a 50 mm Summicron lens and a roll of color film were to bear witness. There could be no other way. Much as the Foreign Ministry supported his requests, he was assured, it was impossible to arrange. The prisoners, the prisons, were under the jurisdiction of the Ministry of War, the Army; and the Foreign Ministry exercised no influence over another bureaucracy.

"I knew I had reached the end of the line. I loaded the Leica with some color film and I wrote down the guide number—the speed rating of the film—and said I wanted informal pictures of these people in their rooms, outdoors, at recreational activities, whatever they were doing. . . ."

The camera came back the next day, its film exposed and untampered with.

(Of those photos taken by an anonymous Vietnamese photographer, *Life* would publish seven, four of them head-and-shoulders shots of tense, unsmiling Air Force men posed before a buff-colored curtain; the other three, full-body shots of Air Force officers, including a sullen and unhealthy-looking Lieutenant Colonel Robinson Risner, a Korean War ace, reported missing September 17, 1965.)

But to the almost certain chagrin of the Vietnamese, Lockwood pressed anew for personal interviews.

* * *

Within reasonable walking distance of Lockwood's room at the Metropole, Richard Stratton sat in solitary confinement at the Zoo. He was confused. He was convinced his captors knew he had not participated in any raids on Hanoi. One area raid he had been scheduled to fly, the December 13 attack on the truck repair facility at Van Dien, had not come to pass. The nose gear on his A-4 would not retract. He had had to dump his ordnance at sea and return to the *Ticonderoga*. He was sure they knew this, because Moon knew it. Moon had flown the raid.

Still his interrogators kept pressing, making impossible statements, demanding insane things and seeking his confirmation, "thumping" on him to keep his responses coming along. At one point he was told he had carried on his lone aircraft Shrike missiles, CBU antipersonnel canisters,[5] napalm, other antipersonnel weapons, and phosphorus bombs. It was nonsense.

Then that idea was abandoned (presumably) after Air Force intelligence informed Army intelligence who informed the prison cadre that no one aircraft could carry and drop that variety of ordnance in one raid at one time.

The routine of interrogation and conversation continued. It kept him from being physically tortured, at least, kept him in a new issue of clothing, gave his still-painful injuries a chance to continue healing.

On March 1, the officer with the large ears and buck teeth, the Rabbit, as he was called, presented Stratton—with all the pride of authorship—the "confession." Then Stratton knew what all the questions, all the writing, were all about. He could not believe what he read; he could not believe the Vietnamese were actually going to release this.

What the Rabbit (and presumably other co-authors) had done was to take the December 13 raid against Van Dien, southwest of the capital, and move it into the northeast section of Hanoi, where, indeed, some American bombs had fallen. The single raid had been expanded into several, and Stratton found himself leading strikes to terror-bomb the civilian population.

"[The Rabbit] ended up with one airplane carrying napalm, one airplane carry CBU's, one airplane had this, one airplane had that, all in the same Alpha strike in my section. I led a section of aircraft that had an airplane full of each of these delights, which is asinine, because they are incompatible in an attack mode and everything else. Each one is delivered in a different way.

"That didn't bother them. They, in their minds, simply had to get the [bombs] from the ordnance locker on the *Ticonderoga* to any site they were going to take [the Russell war crimes investigators to] and provide the delivery mode . . . no matter how illogical it was. And I was elected to be it. I was the chosen vehicle.

"They knew better: they knew the compatibility of weapons on our aircraft; they had shot enough down; they had tortured enough pilots to get that information. They knew, basically, what we carried, but they were intent, once again, on molding world public opinion against the Americans for using these types of weapons.

"I didn't even know about the new CBU, had only heard they were working on it; and at that time there was a stricture against the use of napalm north of the seventeenth parallel; phosphorus bombs and rockets were being used as markers for forward air controllers down south because the smoke would come up out of the trees. [Phosphorus] was not used as an antipersonnel weapon. Eventually [it was] used against ammunition bunkers and fuel farms up north to torch them off, but we were not using it on our ship; I do not think we had any [aboard]. But that didn't make any difference to them because they weren't interested in truth; they were interested in fabricating a story that would be believed. . . ."

Stratton was frantic. He had talked himself into a box. In the presence of the camp commander, he bravely allowed that the "confession" was "a bunch of bullshit" and suggested the commandant try to prevent it from even seeing the light of day. He risked beating by further telling the man that his government stood to make a fool out of itself by presenting such nonsense.

"And he said, 'I know that. It doesn't make any difference. Some American pilot did it and you might as well take the credit for it because you are an American pilot.'"

Stratton then refused to have anything to do with the "confession." He would not read it. Yes, he was told, he would read it. He would be stood up before a political rally at the stadium filled with the citizenry, and he would tell what he had done; and then he would repeat it before a group of intellectuals. He refused. They badgered him all morning, apparently wanting him willing; he still refused. Finally, as President Ho's prescribed siesta hour approached, they compromised. He could tape-record it.

No way.

Yes, there was a way, the frustrated Rabbit stormed. Stratton's cell door was opened and through it stepped an old acquaintance. Vegetable Vic stood before them dramatically, silently, wearing his silly hat. In his hands were lengths of cargo strap and sets of manacle cuffs. Now you *have* a choice, Stratton was told. He chose to believe them, that he had a choice to do it.

121

"I reasoned I would rather make the tape under my own free will and try to screw up the tape than get tortured and do a good job of it. . . . Well, once again, there was another mistake. I should have gone ahead and taken it, and I didn't.

"I was in deep shit in the prison system . . . with a majority of my peers . . . for a number of years with regard to my credibility because of that whole routine."

He knew with sinking heart and disgust he had been seriously outfoxed again. In a last defiant gesture, out of fear and anger, he told his captors they could make him tape, but they could not make him say any "confession" in public, nor could they make him appear in public. He was fluent, he blustered, in French and Spanish and English. He would tell whatever audience they put him in front of exactly what had been done to him. They could kill him afterward, they could kill him on the spot where he spoke, but he would tell of his torture and that the "confession" was false.

The taping date was scheduled for March 4.

* * *

"Here are three military types that I never saw before (or since) sitting there with a tape recorder with earplugs on so they can hear at the head what you're saying on the tape, and then they start taping it. I realize we've got *real* English speakers here now, not the clowns I've been used to working with. So what's my choice? My choice was to go back to Toastmasters' lesson which focused on monotone, a lesson called vocal variety. I decided to take every negative aspect of that lesson and apply it to the recording. And that was, to a certain measure, a success because those who heard it, those of my friends who heard it back here in the country, my own family, were convinced that that was not my voice, that that was not me. And I tried to make it absolutely without any inflection whatsoever.

". . . And at that point was the germ of [the idea that] I will appear to have been doped or under the influence of something. That was the germ right there, sitting there right then taping, realizing these guys were listening to it, that they spoke perfect English, because they would correct me, every mistake that I made, and erase and tape and start over.

"It took all afternoon to tape it. And we went into the evening, also, for a final review of it.

"The night we finished taping, they said, okay, you are going to see a group of intellectuals downtown, and in the Orient it is the custom that you will bow. In the prison system the definition of a salute was a ninety-degree bow to the ducks, to the chickens, the VC, and everybody else.

"So, they said, now we will practice bowing. They said, 'Bow!' And I bowed at ninety degrees.

"'Oh, no! You do a fifteen-degree bow. Now, bow prettily, bow prettily,' and this went on for about a half hour. And this is where the germ of this thing starts growing, sitting there talking in a monotone, and the bowing practice."

* * *

On March 6 Lee Lockwood had taken breakfast and was walking through the lobby of his hotel when "in through the door came the foreign press aide and I greeted him and he stepped back, taken aback because he lost a bit of face . . . not expecting to see me. Then he recovered.

"'Oh, Mr. Lockwood,' he said, 'I have some wonderful news for you!' I said I was certainly ready for some wonderful news because until then I hadn't had much. And he said, 'Today you are going to be able to interview American prisoners of war as you have requested. I can't give you any further details right now, but you must stay in your hotel . . . where we can reach you.'

"That's the way he put it. 'Today you are going to be able to interview American *prisoners* of war—plural—as you have requested.'"

Lockwood passed the time in his room. Bobby Salas, the Cuban photographer, knocked and entered.

"Hey, did you hear about the press conference?" Salas asked.

"What press conference?"

"They're going to have a press conference this afternoon. You'd better come. Rumor is they're going to have an American POW there."

Lockwood found that confusing. Why would they have a press conference like that the same day he was to do his interviewing? Perhaps, somehow, they were connected.

He mulled over this awhile. Then came the word, by telephone, that he was to get ready; a car would be sent for him. He loaded his cameras with film and cleaned and checked the lenses. He put a new cassette in his tape recorder, and he waited.

* * *

At the Zoo, Stratton's morning had been routine, not that there was much variation in solitary confinement. But at lunchtime a trio of turnkeys entered his cell carrying a basin of water and a razor.

"Now you shave."

"I said, 'I'm not going to shave.' And they said, well, you must shave and all this routine. They slapped me around a little bit, and said, shave! And finally two guys held me by the hair and one of the gooks started to shave me.

"Well, first of all, it's an old razor and the blade must have been invented in 1890 and in use ever since, you know? But the guy did a beautiful job and left me with a complete razor burn all over my face, which added to my physical appearance. They suited me up; said I looked thin, so they got me a double set of sweaters, which was beautiful, put the set of pajamas over me, got me a set of socks from somewhere and put them on me (and I never saw *them* again after that day) and put a pair of go-aheads [sandals] on my feet.

"About 4:30, they put me in the back of a truck and drove me off—blindfolded—somewhere downtown."

* * *

Lockwood was taken to a large room: "It was like a long dining room, or a hall and rectangular, maybe seventy-five feet by twenty-five. Along one side were french doors opening onto an interior garden. In this room were many tables, small tables with chairs around them, and the tables had been set. . . . There were cigarettes and matches on them, ashtrays, and glasses. I think they brought in soft drinks. Something was about to happen here. There were people coming in. It was clear this was a press conference.

"Up front was a big loudspeaker . . . standing in the middle of

124

the floor, and its wire running somewhere. On the right-hand side was a curtained entryway. The curtain was drawn. You couldn't see behind it. There was a blackboard or a big map in the middle and there was a portable rostrum and a table, as I remember.

"Already my heart had dropped a bit, you know, because I was really excited. I'd been working on this for a long time and I knew how important it would be back home if I could bring it off. So the room starts filling up. The press presence in Hanoi was not that large, so there was much more than press there; embassy officials, press attachés from all the different embassies were milling around, and there was a Japanese television crew. As far as I know, I was the only American there.

"I think I was the only American, and I think it was set up for me.

"I think a decision had been made to have it before I left, because they knew I was leaving [within a day or two]. I think a policy decision had been made to show off this prisoner of war in the context of a big American magazine and that I was to be the instrument. That's the way I look back on it now, although I can't prove it. Anyway, I'm astounded at all the people who have come into this room. We are told to sit down. So I'm sitting down at a front table with Bobby Salas and some of the other photographers."

"And they bring me in through the side door of this meeting hall, take the blindfold off, and sit me down in the midst of the wreckage of Bullpups [air-to-ground missiles], a CBU canister, a napalm canister, junk and fragments. So they've got some cat speaking in Vietnamese [in the main room where Lockwood was] and they've got all this rubbish here and obviously I'm part of a dog and pony show and the pieces are starting to fit together now."

"The whole thing was really in three parts. The first part was before [Stratton's] tape recording was played, and that was a long lecture where they showed ordnance and they used the map. They handed out a press release on it; I believe it had to do with a bombing raid into another area which the Americans had said they would not bomb. It didn't seem terribly important to me and I wasn't paying enough attention to really know what was going on."

"Now somebody gets up and starts speaking in English about CBU's, bombing of places, and all of a sudden it fits. It's part of a press conference, although I can't see out there, somebody's having a press conference and they are going to use [my "confession"] as fact: here's one of the guys who has done the things we claim, [bomb] the hospitals, the leprosariums, and all of the rest of the stuff that they run out."

" 'And now,' said the short, bald North Vietnamese officer, 'we are going to listen to the confession of an American pilot shot down while infringing on the territorial air space of the Democratic Republic of Vietnam.' And at this point all of [us] photographers rushed forward because we knew there was going to be an American prisoner—I thought prisoners—of war and when he said 'listen to the confession' everybody assumed [a prisoner] was going to come in at any second and read or speak his confession.

"So there is a surge forward, and the officer is shouting, 'No, no, no, no! Return to your tables! Return to your tables! First we are going to *listen* to the confession of the American prisoner of war, and *then* we will *see* the American prisoner of war.' "

"Then they start playing my confession. I realize I am going to have to go out and bow. In some way I have to discredit it."

"Then this loudspeaker I have described shrieked with a lot of feedback and leveled down, and this voice came through it, saying:

" 'I am Richard Allen Stratton, a lieutenant commander in the United States Navy attached to VA-192, CAW 19, U.S.S. *Ticonderoga*. The following are statements concerning my crimes committed on the Democratic Republic of Vietnam during November and December, 1966. . . .'[6]

"He read it in a very flat, robot-like voice, automatic, almost dreamlike. Flat, a voice that was obviously American [and to me, then] calm and patently sincere. As he spoke, mimeographed [transcripts] in different languages were being passed out to the audience. Except for one or two points where the tape seemed obviously patched (and that's why I assumed it was a tape and not somebody reading over a mike) he read the entire [five-page] document without stopping. There was complete silence in the room during the broadcast. The voice changed very little in inflection. When it was over, the photographers leaped up and formed an expectant semicircle around the curtained entrance."

"I listened to my own words in the light of the new day and it doesn't sound as stupid as I thought it sounded when I made it. Now I've got to find some additional way to discredit that thing. They have said, you will not speak, you will just simply bow. You will bow and you will leave. They have got a guard behind the curtain with his AK 47 and they've got Dum Dum with his pistol and they've got another guard with his pistol."

"One of the officers spoke a command into the microphone and a noncom appeared through the curtain, did a right face, halted before the officer, right-faced again, and saluted smartly. He had a stern face. Stern and grim, the officer spread out his left arm and pointed. He said nothing. The noncom saluted again and reversed his entrance.

"I think the officer was Major Bui. [Major Bui was North Vietnam's commandant of military prisons.] He was never identified, so I am just assuming. But he was a very ugly, nerd-looking officer. He looked like the prototypical brutal, no-nonsense prison commander or subcommander interchangeable with prison types anywhere."

"The tape stops and they mutter something in Vietnamese and push me out into this room, which has 150 to 200 people in it sitting at tables drinking their beer—the obvious press conference routine. As I walk out, there's a whole mess of photographers running up the aisle toward me."

"A moment later the curtain was yanked back and flanked by two Vietnamese soldiers; in came the pilot. Movie lights went on

127

and he stood still, more or less at attention. He was a big guy, perhaps six-three. He was dressed in striped prisoner pajamas, alternating purple and cream stripes, socks, and sandals."

"Now, the beauty of this situation is I'm still ill. All my bandages are covered, but every day at three o'clock I hit a high fever. I also have a boil in each nostril—just glorious. So my nose is red and about yea-big anyway; I've got this red [razor] burn over me, plus I'm in my late afternoon fever."

"He was not emaciated or infirm-looking. The only thing physically wrong with him (that I could see) was his nose, which was swollen and was colored extremely red, almost as purple as the stripes of his pajamas, as though he'd been hit with a blueberry pie. But his eyes and his entire face were completely devoid of expression. He seemed unaware of anything. He seemed not to be there at all."

"Some obviously were Caucasians, but my assessment was there were no friends here at all; and so, okay, Manchurian candidate. I will pretend I'm drugged, and how does one do that? One stares at the back of the ceiling with a fixed, glassy-eyed stare, acts mechanical in all his motions. I'll do the ninety-degree bow. I'll box the compass."

"His eyes remained blank, his face without expression as the photographers snapped away on all sides. His arms hung limply at his sides. After perhaps sixty seconds of this, during which the prisoner did not move, one of the officers, Bui perhaps, gave a command in Vietnamese. Immediately the prisoner, still without the slightest change of expression or any indication he was awake, bowed deeply from the waist to the audience. He straightened up, did a quarter turn to the left, and bowed again deeply and slowly, his head almost reaching the level of his thighs. Then he . . . repeated the process."

"I bow to the cameramen rushing toward me, bow to the head table over here, I bow to the door I just came through, I bow to the wall over there, and I stand up straight again."

128

"After four bows he stopped. The photographers kept taking pictures. Again the officer barked a command in Vietnamese and again, suddenly, the pilot began bowing as before."

"And then Dum Dum makes the mistake of yelling out at the top of his voice, 'Bow!' So I box the compass again the exact same way."

"Again the officer barked a command and again, suddenly, the pilot began bowing as before. The process was repeated three times. Finally, perhaps after four or five minutes had passed total, the officer gave a fourth command and the pilot did an about face and abruptly disappeared through the curtain."

"Major Bui, who was sitting at the head table, realized what I had done and, whoosh, get him out of here, get him out of here. And that was it!"

"I was stunned by his appearance. I was practically unable to take pictures, to function. I tried to catch his eye while he was doing all this bowing and to show somehow that . . . I thought if he could see me, he would see that I was . . . an American. I was clean-shaven, my hair was regular length, but, I don't know. I thought my clothes, whatever. I didn't say anything to him. I didn't and I probably should have. I didn't know what to do. I was at a loss. I was trying to make a decision. I was thinking about it and decided better not, because I might screw things up for him.

"And maybe, well, I thought I was going to do some interviews, and this was just a prelude to the important thing that was going to happen later. This was all part of my decision-making. And when he was finishing the bowing, standing there again, I got between him and the curtains so he would have to go right by me in order to leave. I could look right into his face, you know? [It would] give him a chance to see I was an American, to get some kind of response from him, because he was giving nothing. And so he walked right by me, even brushed my arm. There was nothing in his face.

129

"I was so shocked. The event was like some sort of oriental pageant. The prisoner had acted like a robot. It was impossible for me to connect the man who had walked out, bowed, and then disappeared with the firm, intelligent . . . voice supposedly recorded just two days earlier. As the shock wore off, I started getting mad.

"What had they done to him? Why had they done it? And why, above all, had they chosen *this* man to show the world an example of how they treat their prisoners? Everybody I had talked to before [that day] who had any light to throw on the status of prisoners had said the same thing to me: that prisoners were well treated, considering their status. That they were given double the normal Vietnamese portions of rations of food, medical care, reading matter and recreation. In sum, that they were given considerably better treatment than Vietcong prisoners are accorded by the South Vietnamese and Americans.

"[The French delegate general's attaché] was there and he was appalled, really taken aback. The Canadians were cynical about the whole war, cynical about both sides, and I never really could trust what they had to say. They didn't have much to say about this when I talked with them. The Cubans were divided. They all thought it was a terrible scene but some of them were trying to find explanations which would, you know, square it somehow. And others, particularly my friend Bobby Salas, couldn't find any way to explain it. It stunk, and they knew it."

"Well, Dum Dum says to me as he pushes me off the [truck] and back into my cell, you did not bow prettily as I asked you to. And I figured, well, I'm going to have a session on that one so I'd better figure out what happened. I think it over and, sure enough, they call me in about 19:30 [7:30 P.M.] and sit me down and say, uhh, why did you bow the way you bowed? The camp commander, Major Bui, wants to know.

"The best thing I could come up with, which they bought, was I'm afraid of cameras. 'You told me it was going to be a group of intellectuals—a small group of intellectuals. It obviously was a press conference. I don't like the press. There were cameras there rushing up the aisle, and in my fright I must have reverted back to my ancient Catholic custom of bowing ninety degrees.' They all

130

knew about Catholics and they allowed as how, indeed, they had told me it was going to be a small group. (Many of them don't like cameras, I discovered later, because they make them look like idiots.)

"So, they bought it. They said, okay, the guy was just scared."

* * *

Stratton's day was not over. Someone who had attended the press conference that afternoon requested a copy of his "confession" in the pilot's own handwriting. (The transcripts passed out by the Vietnamese were typewritten.) Stratton refused to write it all out.

". . . They brought in two armed guards and they 'thumped' me, beat on me to write the 'confession' down in my own handwriting.

"[The Rabbit was] very careful. There were a couple of grammatical and technical errors they had made and they were very careful to make sure those mistakes were exactly duplicated in my handwriting. I was copying from the typed handout. . . . That [copying] took all night, what with all the delaying tactics, thumpings, fooling around to screw it up somehow, and the recopying. So it was about six o'clock the next morning before there was a copy available to anyone in Hanoi that was, in fact, in my own handwriting."

That he could write at all was a wonder. His wrists were not strong enough to carry anything and still hurt severely. Writing itself was hard, but he made a last attempt to discredit the "confession" by changing the shape of certain letters on the theory that anyone comparing the writing in the "confession" with his normal handwriting would notice something amiss.

131

CHAPTER 13

The humiliation of Richard Allen Stratton was a quintessential blunder. The American's performance convulsed the diplomatic and press communities in Hanoi. Certainly it was the major topic of conversation that evening at the Metropole, and correspondents wasted no time in filing dispatches:

"MOSCOW—Tass news agency quoted an American pilot yesterday as saying that raids on the Hanoi area were not aimed at military targets but were meant to intimidate the population.

"Tass, in a Hanoi dispatch, identified the pilot as Richard Stratton and said he was shot down over North Vietnam January 3 [*sic*]. It said Stratton spoke to a news conference in Hanoi. His home town was not given.

"The Soviet news agency said Stratton took part in raids on the Hanoi area December 2 and December 14.

"Tass said Stratton reported 'the raids of American aircraft were not directed against military targets. Their task was to intimidate the population of the Vietnamese capital and show them that they will not succeed in avoiding the horrors of war [*sic*].'

"In Washington, the Pentagon declined comment on the story. A Navy pilot, Lieutenant Commander Richard A. Stratton, is listed as captured January 5."[7]

Photographer Lee Lockwood was stunned. Nothing had prepared him for what he had witnessed. He had spent, as was his wont, much time interviewing and conversing with resident Westerners in Hanoi. Torture, drugging of prisoners, and "brainwashing" never were matters of serious conversation. A few of Lockwood's contacts were perceptive and pragmatic; certainly that applied to François Simon de Quirielle, the French delegate-general, by Lockwood's description the most seasoned and the most intelligent of the lot, a man presumably with a good intelligence network of his own. Even Simon de Quirielle, like representatives of the International Control Commission or the Cubans, even the cynical Canadians, was convinced absolutely that Hanoi's treatment of American prisoners was, if not ideal, humane by any normal standards. In the very beginning it had been, and such was the image Hanoi carefully husbanded, particularly after reckless and wholesale abuse became routine. But few persons or organizations in early 1967 seemed aware that North Vietnam was brutalizing its American captives. If such was suspected, it was a suspicion kept silent. American Naval Intelligence knew. In April 1966 a Japanese television reporter interviewed then-Commander Jeremiah A. Denton, Jr. Even as Major Bui, the Rabbit, and others monitored his performance, Denton's eyes continually blinked T–O–R–T–U–R–E in Morse code. The videotape left Hanoi virtually unedited, was purchased by American network news, and was broadcast nationally. Some intelligence officer picked up the message. Washington did not go public with the information.[8] That was the policy then; mum was the word.

Simon de Quirielle, since retired from the foreign service and residing now in the South of France, said:

"My memories of the facts are vague (they happened nearly ten years ago) and for security reasons I did not keep personal archives during my stay in Hanoi. . . . I can just say that as far as I knew the American prisoners were given not unfair treatment during their captivity. There were, of course, exceptions like the Stratton [press conference]. Prime Minister Pham Van Dong assured me, several times, that [the POWs] were given better and more copious food than the local population.

"The matter of the American prisoners of war was not discussed among the diplomatic corps for the mere reason that all my colleagues were representatives of socialist countries, and dared not criticize the Vietnamese government."

The enormity of their error was not made clear to the Vietnamese until the following day. The bearer of the ill tidings was the man for whom, just possibly, the event had been staged: Lee Lockwood.

Lockwood had suggested earlier to his hosts, in a gesture of good will, that he would be willing to discuss with some Vietnamese journalists the workings of the American press and how American public opinion interacted with it. His rationale was simple: he perceived vast gaps between Vietnamese and American cultures and languages that prohibited any real communication and understanding between the two sides. He believed if there was to be "any meaningful communication" between the two sides there had to be some narrowing of this gap. Perhaps he could help. The Vietnamese agreed, and the meeting was scheduled for March 7.

"The following morning we gathered in a room in the hotel that they had set aside, about ten or a dozen people plus myself. We were all having tea and Vietnamese cigarettes and soft drinks. They asked me a lot of questions and we talked for quite a while and when I saw that they had just about finished (these were all people who were able to speak English) I said to them, 'If you don't have any more questions I have a question I'd like to ask you. I'd like to know what you thought of the press conference yesterday. Did you think it was effective? You are all members of the press and . . . you are interested in molding public opinion. From your point of view, how effective was that press conference?'

"There was some shifting around in chairs and a sort of grumbling silence and then somebody raised his hand. He said, 'I thought it was very effective.'

" 'Well, then I wish you'd explain that to me. What was the effect?'

" 'Well,' he said, 'this was a man, an American soldier who had been flying over our country dropping bombs on our people and our cities. Then he was shot down and confronted with the evidence of his crimes, and he repented. He saw that he had committed'—and I'm paraphrasing now, I can't remember his exact words but it's pretty close—'a crime against humanity and he wanted to apologize very much to the Vietnamese people for these terrible crimes he had committed against them.'

"So I said, 'Apologize? What do you mean, apologize?' Somebody else said, 'Well, in our culture when somebody has wronged another person, the way he expiates that transgression is that he stands before the offended person and bows.'

"I said, 'Okay. Now I would like to explain something to you. In your culture that may be so. In my culture it doesn't happen. We bow to nobody! It has not even the remotest connection with anything Americans can relate to. It is an act which to you is positive, but it can only, by its appearance, have a negative effect in my country.'

"People shifted around a little more. I said, 'This is an example of the problems that arise from the differences between our two cultures. I have photographed this man and seen him bowing. I am a journalist, and I have to publish the pictures I've taken. I would like you to imagine a story in *Life* magazine based on my trip here. Let's assume there are' (and I was guessing) 'a cover and fourteen or fifteen uninterrupted pages of pictures of the war in North Vietnam and the face of North Vietnam—pictures that show everything that you would like to have shown: on the one hand the terrible damage the American planes have been doing, and on the other hand the tranquillity and even the heroism of the Vietnamese people carrying on in spite of all this. All this, and at the end you come to a picture of this American bowing to the Vietnamese people. What effect do you think that is going to have?'

"There was a lot of mumbling and then one of the younger people said, 'Well, obviously it's going to counteract the entire effect of the rest of the story.'

" 'Well, that certainly is a possibility. We'll have to wait and see. But,' I said, 'here's your problem. Really think about it, and for God's sake I hope you don't ever stage anything like that again, because it was the most horrible thing I've ever been part of and I don't understand it. I don't know why he was bowing. I am not convinced he was bowing to apologize to the Vietnamese people, because Americans don't do that. Either there was some other reason or else he was coerced into doing it, as far as I'm concerned.

" 'And I invite you to find a way to convince me otherwise because I am terribly agitated about this. The *best* thing you could do would be to let me talk to him right now to reassure me that he was not drugged or coerced. That is the only hope you have of counteracting the effect this is going to have.'

"Now they were really shifting around. And finally the senior man there said, 'Well, Mr. Lockwood, I think I really understand what you are saying, and it is clear there is a big difference between the effect that was intended and the effect that was produced and we are happy to be enlightened about that fact. But, unfortunately, we really have no control. . . . This was not an event that took place under our jurisdiction [the press section of the Ministry of Foreign Affairs] or under our control. Prisoners of war are the responsibility of the Ministry of Defense. They are responsible and I apologize to you and I can promise you it will never happen again' (or something like that).

" 'Okay,' I said, 'but what you should really try to arrange is for me to talk to that man as fast as you can.' He said he would try, but he couldn't be optimistic because it was a different ministry. . . .

"I never did talk to Stratton."

* * *

The full impact of Stratton's performance hit with the publication of Lockwood's photographs and article in the April 7, 1967, edition of *Life*. Lockwood's chilling description of the incident and a full-page, graphic black and white photograph of the bowing, seemingly mesmerized flier created an international furor. The photographer's predictions to the Vietnamese came true.

"North Vietnam Under Siege" ran sixteen uninterrupted pages, including seven snapshots of somber prisoners of war selected from the roll of film shot by the Vietnamese with Lockwood's camera, a fact willingly acknowledged by the magazine. *Life* also included an emotional reaction to the Stratton incident from then-Ambassador-at-Large Averell Harriman:

"From the photographs, videotapes and descriptions by eyewitnesses that I have seen of the so-called 'news' conference at which Commander Stratton was exhibited, it would appear that the North Vietnamese authorities are using mental or physical pressure on American prisoners of war. We all remember the ugly record of 'brainwashing' during the Korean War. It would be a mat-

136

ter of grave concern if North Vietnam were using similar means against the prisoners.

"Hanoi has said its policy is to treat prisoners humanely. However, it has refused to allow the International Committee of the Red Cross or any neutral intermediary to visit the prisoners, a right required by the Geneva Convention to which Hanoi has adhered. Without such independent verification, North Vietnam's professions of 'humane treatment' cannot be accepted."

* * *

Stratton had accomplished his goal, even though in March 1967 he was not immediately aware of it; in hindsight he conceded he probably saved his own life. When the war was over, Hanoi had to produce him no matter how battered he was, no matter how many scars he bore. Lockwood's bowing picture was constantly in use thereafter, the caption beneath it usually referring to Stratton as Vietnam's "most controversial" prisoner. As Hanoi had made Stratton a symbol of its charges of genocide and terror bombing, it had equally made him a symbol of Vietnamese cruelty, intemperance, and duplicity.

Hanoi had blundered. Its embarrassment was acute and its only course now was to repair the damage to its reputation as quickly as possible. There were many persons in the United States and abroad only too willing to assist in this chore, whether by design or in innocence. But Stratton, the "black criminal" who had created the trouble in the first place, even if not deliberately (for that was Hanoi's view), was going to help it most of all.

PART IV

DOG DAYS

"Tell me brave deeds of war."

Then they recounted tales,—
"There were stern stands
"And bitter runs for glory."

Ah, I think there were braver deeds.
—Stephen Crane

CHAPTER 14

Richard Stratton slouched, exhausted and emotionally drained, on the cement bunk in his cell at the Zoo. He heard the crackle of the camp's loudspeakers as an unknown and unsteady hand adjusted the squelch. Ah, shit. It must be time for the Hanoi hit parade, the Voice of Vietnam's evening broadcast. He tried to shut out the jabber of Vietnamese that had begun. Sound kept intruding; in dismay, he heard the nasal Massachusetts *a*'s of his own voice:

". . . what was happening in Vietnam. The United States policy appeared to be a succession of errors inherited by and added to by succeeding administrations. The general ignorance concerning the country of Vietnam was appalling and mine was no exception. . . ."

Bastards! Those bastards. They wouldn't let it alone. Oh, no: keep jabbing it to you, rubbing your nose in it. Bad enough in front of the Commies, but now for his fellows? Those pricks. Why hadn't he taken more torture? God, why couldn't he?

No! He had taken all he could, given it his best shot, and it should be obvious the "confession" was a phony. Just listen to that crap. He had done what he thought best under the circumstances, for himself and for the Navy. He had done the best he could to screw it up, to make himself look terrible physically, and if anybody didn't like that, well, they could go screw themselves!

". . . ask that the people of the Democratic Republic of Vietnam forgive the crimes which I have committed against them. I

141

ask that they spare my life and continue their humane treatment of me."

He felt like puking. Crimes? Humane treatment? Your ass.

More jabber, jabber.

Silence.

From the wall against which his head rested came a soft, insistent thumping. Four quick thunks, a pause, and three more—in the prisoners' tap code, that was an S. Two more thunks, a pause, and three more after that: an H. With the completion of the first word, there was apprehension; at the end of the second, a smile.

"S–H–I–T–H–O–T–J–O–B," the wall said.

He felt buoyed despite his situation and his pain and his fever and his humiliation. Shit hot job, the wall said: well done, Dick boy. Outstanding!

The message came from the two men in the adjacent cell, men he did not know, had never seen, might never see. They had been tapping to him regularly, trying to keep his spirits up, and he did his best to return the kindness, though he was preoccupied with his own state, which was more acute than theirs. They had identified themselves as two ratings off the Jolly Greens, rescue helicopters that tried to pluck downed pilots out of enemy hands or from the cold gulf. The choppers were sitting ducks for any V. with a rifle.

Stratton tapped back his thanks; they had gotten his spirits up, would keep at it. There was not much else they could do. They didn't know what was going on any more than anyone else did. They really couldn't help Stratton with his wounds or with his guilt or with much of anything else. They had gotten him to smile and there was not a damn thing to smile about. The communications net between the prisoners at the Zoo was all screwed up; the Vietnamese for some reason had flushed the camp out days ago. The men in Stratton's cell block were isolated from the others, much as they were isolated from one another. Without communication, without any leadership from senior officers, the situation for the Americans was very serious indeed. The senior officer at the Zoo, the man who set prisoner policy (what there was of it), the man who made the decisions (what there were of them), was an Air Force major named Larry Guarino. The talking walls could not find him. Trying to re-establish the comm. net was slow, dangerous work. A man caught communicating would be punished, beaten or tortured, perhaps forced to reveal information about the communications system, or who were the current senior officers (who in turn would be isolated further, and tortured), perhaps forced to write a confession about something. With the Vietnamese, you just didn't know: those lunatics were firmly in control of the asylum for the moment.[1]

* * *

Stratton's tenuous feeling of relief that perhaps the worst was behind him was further shored by changes in his daily routine. No longer was he badgered for military information; the nightly write-up sessions were done with, too. The days began to hurry by. Apparently the V. had retired him from public life.

So he was surprised when he was told it had been arranged for him to be interviewed. Nearly three weeks had gone by since his brazen bowing. Now he was to be displayed again. Now what the hell was this all about? Old memories of persuasion made his arms ache.

What it was all about was Dr. John Takman, a principal investigator for the Lord Bertrand Russell war crimes tribunal. Takman had put the War Ministry in something of a pickle. He wanted to interview Stratton firsthand, this first American to publicly acknowledge war crimes, a ranking officer who had admitted his government's policy was terror bombing, who had signed a confession, and who had made that curious, robotlike bowing performance. Yes, Takman wanted to look at that fellow, talk to him about that confession; something in it didn't quite wash. The Vietnamese were wary; Stratton was an evil man, and a dangerous one. He had threatened to cry torture (in three languages) once before, and for him to do it in front of Takman would be dangerous. Still, they could not deny Takman. Anyone but Takman; one could not withhold evidence of a crime from its investigator.

The interview was scheduled for March 26. Stratton was issued strict instructions about his conduct: no matter what was asked, he would reply only with answers contained in the confession. Nothing else, or he would be severely punished.

The beginning of that interview went smoothly enough for Stratton as he recalled it; he had only to listen:

143

"Takman was a motor-mouth and he went on and on about how some girl riding on a water buffalo got killed by CBU's, and wasting his allotted time. Then he came to his point: here was the raid you were on, and here is where you rolled in, and here's the bomb damage. What *were* your targets? It was one of those idiot-type conversations."

"What were your targets?"

"The 'confession' says 'targets of opportunity.'"

"What is a 'target of opportunity'?"

"A target of opportunity is a target of opportunity."

The interview continued along these lines: Takman, with his time now rushing by, seeking information and Stratton, still weak and facing additional torture if he deviated from the "confession," playing the artful dodger. The Vietnamese monitoring the dialogue were sullen and uncomfortable. Stratton was almost surly, answering in mechanical fashion; they had no control over Takman.

Takman demanded a map, the better to show Stratton why he was confused over the claims in the "confession." No map was available, said the Vietnamese. Takman hinted he was suspicious of the types and amounts of ordnance carried on each of the alleged raids. Stratton referred him back to the "confession." Stratton was aware that Takman had, at least, discovered the incongruity of at least one of the raids, which, if carried out as described, would have left bomb damage on the south side of Hanoi and not the north, as was the case.

Takman got nowhere, got nothing.

Stratton returned to solitary. The Vietnamese were displeased with his sullenness and his manner of speaking, but he had not disobeyed and they could not punish him without loss of face. He was given a lecture on how not to act like a robot.

Within a week of the Takman interview, *Life* magazine produced its special on North Vietnam.

There was a great flurry of activity and Stratton, perplexed and not a little fearful, was swept up in it. He, of course, was unaware of the *Life* presentation, unaware that an American had viewed and photographed his performance. All he knew was that he was suddenly hot property.

"They decided to run me up before a whole series of people and

144

I do not remember the exact order. I guess the [first] one was the Russian and his girl friend, no, the Cuban; the interview procedure had been altered [since the go-round] with Takman:

" 'Here are the five questions to be asked. Here are the answers to the questions. Memorize them. That is all you give, or you shall be severely punished.'

"The questions basically were: Who are you? Where are you from? Did you participate in the raids? Were you brainwashed? And, How is your treatment now?"

The reporter's name was López, resident correspondent for the Cuban news agency, *Prensa Latina* (*Latin Press*). López spoke English and he opened the discussion on a touch of brotherhood:

"I am a friend of yours," he said, "from the Western Hemisphere. I have come to exchange a few ideas and see how you are doing here."

Stratton did not respond to the pleasantry. The Cuban sat down and placed a tape recorder in the center of the table, switched on the record button, and asked the first question. Stratton replied as woodenly as possible in the words he had memorized.

López told Stratton that Washington was alleging ill-treatment. Was that so? Stratton concealed his surprise and responded with the prescribed answer:

"Get enough to eat. I don't show any signs of undernourishment. [Stratton was now about thirty pounds underweight.] In the camp I can listen to the radio Voice of Vietnam, and receive the visits of a Catholic priest. I go to confession and communion. For the Tet holiday [the Vietnamese New Year observed for three days beginning at the first new moon after January 20] we had the traditional holiday meal on a table decorated with flowers. The camp commander even came to present his holiday wishes. For Easter there was turkey on the menu. We get the medical care we need."

López asked Stratton if he considered Washington's allegations "pure invention."

"As far as I am concerned, yes."

López put down his sheet of questions, and asked another not on the list:

"*Were* you drugged, physically abused, or coerced in any way to make that confession?"

"Get enough to eat," Stratton answered. "I don't show any signs of undernourishment. In the camp . . ." It was the answer, word for word, tone for tone, that he had given to a previous question. But López either missed it or ignored it or Stratton miscalculated his effectiveness in delivering the line. The Cuban closed his notebook and turned off the recorder. He stood up and looked at Stratton.

"You have a wife and children," he said, and faced away from the flier. In a wink, he turned around. Gone was the soft, modulated voice.

"How could you, the father of children, bomb these innocent children, who have done nothing to you, in a faraway land?"

Stratton was on his feet, shouting back, before the startled guards could get to him.

"Some of us would do anything to stop you and your kind of philosophy—"

The guards were on him before he could continue. He was pushed out of the room at gunpoint. He was taken back to the Zoo, and solitary. He had insulted a guest and embarrassed the Vietnamese.

López left the interview room, edited the tape, and played it for some of his colleagues in the press corps. In a dispatch from Agence France-Presse, whose correspondent apparently did not hear the tape, Stratton "was said to have given the impression of a man speaking in a relaxed and easy manner."

The next major interview occurred about two and a half weeks later with the Russian. The questions were basically the same, with one change: Were you brainwashed? Brainwashed. Now, that was a hell of a question.

Had he gotten through? Had he fouled up their little party? First Takman asking questions, then the Cuban, now the Russian. Maybe, oh, God, maybe.

Correspondent Yevgeni Kobelev arrived for the interview accompanied by an interpreter and a voluptuous brunette who reminded Stratton (when he thought about it later) of the film actress Elizabeth Taylor. The questions and the answers went by the book. The interview was held in a cozy little room somewhere in Hanoi to which the American had been taken blindfolded in a truck along a circuitous route. Across from Stratton sat the Russians and the interpreter. Beside him was a small table artfully decorated with bananas, candies, cookies, and a bottle of the local beer. The Russian asked the final question about Stratton's present treatment, and Stratton responded with the "Get enough to eat" litany. As he stood to leave, the Vietnamese official who had accompanied him from the Zoo indicated Stratton should help himself to some of the goodies on the table. Without hesitation, the flier lifted the front of his striped prison pajamas, forming a pouch, knelt down, emptied the entire table into the pouch, stood again, and marched stonily from the room.

The incident was not mentioned in Kobelev's dispatch.

"MOSCOW—A captured United States pilot who allegedly confessed to 'war crimes' in Vietnam told a Tass correspondent that he was not brainwashed, the official Soviet news agency reported yesterday from Hanoi.

"The case of the officer, Lieutenant Commander Richard A. Stratton, aroused fears in the U.S. that the Vietnamese Communists were using techniques that were widespread in the Korean War. A photograph in *Life* magazine showed him bowing in Oriental style.

"Tass said Stratton told its correspondent, Yevgeni Kobelev, that he made his remarks voluntarily.

"It quoted Stratton as saying:

" 'On March 4, I spoke at a press conference in Hanoi exposing the criminal nature of the U.S. air war against the Democratic Republic of [North] Vietnam. I did this of my own free will, feeling compelled to do so by my conscience.

" 'I acted not because of some pressure or physical force on the part of the Vietnamese authorities.' "[2]

Upon his return to the Zoo, he was informed that he was an animal, and that he had embarrassed the Vietnamese with his table-tipping nonsense. There were a few cuffs and a slap, but no torture. (At subsequent interviews he was not allowed again to touch the snack-bearing tables; instead, he was given a doggie-bag of goodies after he left the interview room "as my reward for performing like a good Pavlov animal.")

* * *

Communications within the Zoo improved daily. The prisoners "talked" in a variety of codes: thumping on walls, coughs, scratching, anything they could tap or scrape, and hand signals.

147

Stratton was regaining his confidence; and his wounds, despite lack of care, were slowly healing. He knew he would be badly scarred. Through the communications network he learned that others had been tortured, too, some less than he, others worse and for longer periods. Perhaps if he had held out a little longer—no, damn it. He had done the best thing at the time. They had busted his ass, made him shit in his pants, and broken him. A couple of men, he heard, had been tortured to the point where they stumbled around like vegetables. He saw no sense in that. It might look good in a movie, but this was no movie. He was not the goddamn Lone Ranger. If he was going to be effective, he had to keep his wits and his health, or as much as he could hold on to. He did his best to screw up the confession, to tell the world—and his fellow prisoners—that he had not done it willingly. And apparently he had succeeded, or at least scored some measure of success.

He wasn't starring in all the goddamn gook dog and pony shows, getting lectures on how not to act like a robot, all that shit because they liked the way he looked. And that's where it stands, fellas; I did my best, and if you don't like it, screw you, and I am really getting pissed off at being put in a position of a V.

On May 24, he was taken out of solitary and told by the commandant, Major Bui, the Cat, that he was being "rewarded" for having "done for the camp." He accepted this stonily, and not until after he had been placed in a cell with Major Jack Bomar and Lieutenant Colonel Donald Ray Burns did he let go his emotions.

"I was not 'rewarded' by roommates. Every time they put you into a cell, they had a purpose for it. And what they hoped to do with me (because I *had* given the 'confession' and only 'accidentally' screwed it up) was . . . convince Burns and Bomar to, ah, weaken. In other words, they always put in a guy they considered 'on their side' with a guy who was 'against' them. They figured the tough hard-liner couldn't bring the softie up, but the softie would always dilute . . . the strength of the hardliner. We saw that continually, time and time again.

"Donald Ray Burns was, in their minds, the hard-liner; Bomar [who himself had performed badly before a visiting delegation of Westerners, had been—and would be—savagely beaten] was in

148

the middle, and I, was a result of my recent performance, was considered to be a soft guy."

Six days later, Burns was gone.[3]

* * *

Richard Mullen listened to the wall talking. It is his anniversary, his one hundredth day of solitary confinement.

It had begun in a small cell in a building at the Zoo called the gatehouse, so named because the southern side of it abutted an entrance to the camp. Later he was moved to another building and into another cell practically indistinguishable from the first—cement and stucco, badly holed, infested with gekko lizards (and their food supplies, which buzzed or swarmed or crawled until snatched by sticky lizard tongues and converted to sugars or acids or whatever chemicals lizards use to sustain life) and rats frightening in their audacity, lords of Mullen's little gray world, which smelled like other worlds here, with gamy hints of human waste and musty odors like those inside old bass drums stored in unventilated attics.

Thump-thump-thump. The communications network was back in operation. Talking walls, hand signals, coughs, scrapes, lifelines that allowed a man to survive one hundred days watching his wounds heal and counting his toes, news networks communicating instructions, policies, and the trivia that passed for major events in endless, boring, dead days.

Endless running thoughts of food, of home and wife and children, small pleasures remembered, light on her hair, phrases and snatches of conversation rummaged from a hundred or a thousand so, once thought ordinary, or not thought of at all.

Mullen survived because of communication, and so had they all, those who survived. Revelations passed to him revealed he was not the only one who caved in, or was tortured, or was willing, after the hands turned black from the torture cuffs, to spill his guts. Nor was he first with thoughts of suicide or mortification over weakness, self-discovered and believed present only in others.

Thump-thump-thump.

A high point in his one hundred days was the first message from

149

Dick Stratton, thumped, flashed, scraped on the bottom of honey buckets, transmitted slowly and dangerously from wherever Stratton was doing solitary to Mullen.

He was aware of Stratton's confession and, from the same sources, that his shipmate had been badly treated. He was disturbed by other rumors, bits and pieces of remarks he picked up, that a few prisoners claimed Stratton was not resisting—or not resisting enough. Nonsense. He knew Stratton too well.

He learned with some dismay that Stratton had been removed from solitary and lodged with Bomar and Burns, not dismay the event had come about, but that he was not chosen. The Vietnamese had hinted, that one time back, he might get a roommate. Nothing since.

He was confused when the wall told him Burns was gone, packed off somewhere for something.

Mullen's one hundredth day was over.

Thump-thump-thump.

* * *

It was his anniversary. Mullen sat on his cement bunk. It was the 101st day of solitary.

The door of his cell opened. Fear slung up into his throat.

The guards motioned him to pack his gear, hurried him along and out the door, down the side of the building, moving him fast, not giving him a chance to catch his bearings, no good looks at the few prisoners in the yard, down the back of the building on the eastern side of the compound, the one called the Pigsty, down the back to the end to the last cell. Wait! The cell door was pulled open.

Inside, two faces swung sharply toward the light, four eyes instantly wide with apprehension.

Mullen stepped in, and the door closed behind him.

Tears.

Together, Mullen, Bomar, and Stratton hugged in reunion.

They did not stop talking for hours. In the manner of men who knew calamity was only seconds away, they did not waste their time. They exchanged news, and views, whatever they had. There was some time for reminiscence. They decided among themselves to stiffen their "resistance posture," which for them meant, primarily, no more meetings with visiting firemen or traveling delegations, no more co-operation. They all had been badly hurt, and had recovered enough strength to fight back.

No mention was ever made in that room, among those three men, of the rumors of Stratton's alleged weak resistance. But the issue was there. He was in some quarters already the outcast.

A part of the time, a good part of it, was spent watching, watching through holes no larger than the shank of a ten-penny nail, through cracks, under doors, through french slats that boarded glassless windows pulled slightly askew with whatever piece of solid metal had been found, or stolen from careless keepers.

On June 6 they came, an interrogator and a covey of guards, to get Stratton. It had been decided by the camp commander that Stratton would see a new delegation.

No, he would not.

He was seized and taken away. Later, in the afternoon, a guard returned, packed up his gear, and left. Mullen recalled:

". . . They hit [on] Dick first, and told him they wanted him to see a delegation. We had already set up our resistance posture at that time, and he refused. And then they pulled him out.

"Then shortly thereafter, they took Jack [Bomar]. Jack had a kidney problem . . . and he needed quite a bit of liquid throughout the day, and they wanted him to see a delegation. He refused. They put him in one of the hothouses for hours and hours and hours. Finally, he was just completely dehydrated and he consented to see a delegation. And just a few days after that, they wanted me to see a delegation and I refused. They pulled me out and put me back in the gatehouse. I stayed there [in solitary] until September—September 18, I think it was September 18—and then they pulled me out of solitary and sent me back to the Pigsty and I was back with Bomar.

"You know, some [hard-liners] thought that Dick Stratton wasn't really resisting . . . [but] every man has a completely different physical and mental make-up. Granted, we have a Code of Conduct, and granted, we are military representatives of the American people, and it is by the Code of Conduct . . . that each and every one of us would like to perform—to perfection, to be able to withstand an unlimited amount of pain. But some people

151

cannot handle that amount of pain. (I'm not saying that this was Dick's case.)

"The scar on his arm is far more severe than any scar I received. I would say he suffered far greater pain at that time than many, many others. . . . I don't know of a case where an individual didn't give something. It may or may not have been the absolute truth, but I'd be almost willing to bet that everyone gave at least something through torture, and only through torture.

"[Even so,] it eats away at you and you are mortified. The feeling you betrayed your country, I think, was a common feeling amongst every one of the POWs. And Dick Stratton was a very proud and a very intelligent man . . . and it ate at him. But even though you suffer extreme pain and through the torture you give something (as little as you possibly can), you recover mentally and physically and start your resistance posture all over again."

CHAPTER 15

On the first weekend in April, Alice Stratton drove with her sons from Hanford to Palo Alto, continuing her search for a new home. The difficult journey of two hundred miles was not made easier by three small children or by a new anxiety that further strained her patience. Only days ago, she had heard on the radio a broadcast purporting to be her husband confessing to war crimes of a most heinous nature. She had called the Navy; they were unaware of the broadcast then, but confirmed it later. Now, the Navy advised her, a *Life* correspondent recently returned from Hanoi had seen her husband and photographed him. The news was not good.

In Palo Alto, Tom Foy worked diligently selecting prospective properties for the Strattons, but he was no magician. None of the houses so far met her specific needs, whatever those were. What in hell, she thought, did a woman alone know about buying a house anyway? Buying a house was a major investment. Buying a house was a joint venture, a husband-wife venture, except there was no husband. No husband, no divorce, no widowhood. Did she buy to suit him, herself, or them? Just buy? There was not a little resentment mingling with her grief. She was not happy and it was not to get any better for her, not that weekend anyway, not in cruel April.

"We were just about to go home [to Hanford] on Sunday when

Mike, who was then three years old, broke his leg. A ping-pong table fell over on him, clipped his femur, and cracked it up high.

"Tom Foy took Mike and me to the hospital and we were told Michael would have to stay there a minimum of two weeks—two weeks in traction—and then into a body cast. Well, there was no way I could leave that little guy, so once more the Foys moved over and took us in.

"That night, Pat Foy and I went out to the drugstore to pick up the *Life* magazine. . . . I remember picking up that magazine, and it fell open in my hands to Dick's picture. Reaction? I would say chilling horror.

"I remember one of us, I don't know who, said, 'Oh, my God!'

"I felt that insulating protection of a shock reaction; it stayed with me until we got back to the Foys. That night, I remember, we all sat around in stunned silence reading the text over and over, trying to figure out what had happened. I felt stunned, and disbelieving. I didn't know what to think but I just knew something awful had happened. I felt sick to my stomach with worry. I could not eat [for a long time afterward] and probably went down [in weight] to the thinnest I've been in years.

"The next day at the hospital, I met the orthopedist who had set Mike's leg. When I asked him about Michael, I burst into tears. That doctor thought I was overracting a little to a broken leg, but then I told him about Dick. By coincidence he had been [present] at the release of prisoners of war from Korea and he described their condition as 'shocking.' He also described the carrot-and-stick approach used on the POWs. 'That is what they must have done to your husband,' he said, to the effect of 'poor bastard.' And for the first time, I think, the awful impact of what Dick was—or had been—going through really hit me.

"I came back from the hospital, walked into the Foys', and announced, 'Today is our anniversary [April 4],' and then broke into tears. I exposed, once again, the Foys to my discomfort, my painful hurting, and they gave me the soothing balm of their support and friendship, without which I wonder if I ever would have really made it."

Lockwood's photograph haunted Alice Stratton. Other images, implanted accidentally by the well-meaning physician, compounded her agony.[4]

The American press seized upon the *Life* article and Lockwood's photograph of Richard Stratton and his accompanying commentary. The New York *Times* quoted long passages from Stratton's "confession" and carried a lengthy telephone interview with the photographer. A spokesman for the U. S. Department of State told the *Times* his agency was "concerned at recent indications that North Vietnam may be using mental or physical pressure on American prisoners of war to obtain confessions or statements critical of United States policy in Vietnam." Further comments echoed those of Ambassador Harriman quoted in *Life*.

In the end, the government maintained its low public profile regarding prisoner matters.

* * *

The holiday in Barbados had failed to loosen the sadness in Ellen Cooper. Seated next to her husband on the airliner rushing them home, she wondered if she would ever be free of it.

The sister of Richard Stratton, who as a teen-ager carried home the news of her brother's renunciation of the priestly life, was in April 1967 a grown woman, a wife, and the mother of a year-old daughter. She was a person of strong will and ideals. An independent girl had grown into an independent woman who had broken away from the traditional roles of young Irish girls of Boston. Much of the strength and independence she jealously defended was worn thin now, and in danger of collapse.

Ellen had married Dr. Richard Cooper, a physician, in 1959, just six weeks, in fact, before she and her new husband attended the wedding of her brother Dick and Alice Marie Robertson. The Coopers settled in Buffalo, where Richard completed his internship and residency requirements, a process that took two and a half years. There followed, then, a year in Sweden for medical research and another year for study in Cleveland. They returned to Buffalo in 1963, when Richard Cooper set up a practice and continued his research into treatments of breast cancers.

In 1964, out of strong convictions unrecognized by other members of her family, Ellen decided the growing involvement of the United States in Southeast Asia was a commitment without honor or moral foundation.

She did not hold with any of the then popular conspiracy

theories that maintained America had deliberately engaged in an ignoble (and racist) war to secure economic advantage: namely, procurement of Vietnam's potential oil reserves in the South China Sea. But, she maintained, the whole venture "was totally ill-advised. There wasn't any reason to be there. We couldn't help everybody in the world. It was too bad the Vietnamese, both North and South, did not have the rights and freedoms that we [Americans] had, but the Southern government didn't seem any better to me than the Northern government. The government [Saigon] we were trying to shore up was not the same as [Hanoi]; . . . on the other hand it was no better, either. So what was the point of more bloodshed to preserve a government like that?"

It was a decision debated, occasionally with fervor, with her Navy flier brother, who held rather opposing views. Ellen's decision did not necessarily surprise him; she was, after all, the family maverick. For her, Dick was still the older brother-mentor and, despite her free spirit, able to intimidate her. She didn't like that. He didn't set out to do it, but do it he could, she admitted, and she cursed her weakness.

As the war accelerated and the killing intensified, so, too, did the maverick's opposition.

Then in January 1967 her mother telephoned from Quincy to break the news. Ellen was shattered.

"I can remember that quite vividly: the absolute total shock; [being] unable to take it all in for a while; being stunned; what it really meant, and then later thinking, I should have known that would happen.

"I should have known that would happen to Dick. It seemed to me at that time that that was a sort of pattern in my life; that if anybody's brother was going to be shot down and missing, it would be mine.

"And then I thought it was so bad I could hardly talk about it with anybody. It was just so overwhelming that I wasn't able to voluntarily discuss it with anybody, and feeling sad about this all the time, getting up in the morning and . . . you know how you wake up and you know something's wrong and you can't remember what it is, and then you remember? This went on for about four weeks. I said to a friend, 'I'm so tired of feeling sad,'

156

never realizing there would be six years of those mornings, of those mornings waking up and knowing that something was terribly wrong."

Richard Cooper was a compassionate and generous man. He did not agree with his wife's views on Vietnam but he did not try to dissuade her from holding or expressing them; he shared her sadness over the loss of her brother and sensed how deeply shaken and wounded she was. There was a portent in those first weeks and months of a terrible, searing, and eventually debilitating conflict of conscience and loyalty, between personal belief and family love, that would trap his wife. He was there, he made it a point, when she needed to talk or be comforted and, following her lead, kept silent when she chose to contain the sadness within the privacy of her heart. There was some measure of relief when the Navy reported and confirmed Richard Stratton alive and a prisoner; not much, but some. After that the husband put on his doctor hat and ordered a change of scenery. It did not take much convincing to get Ellen onto a sun-baked beach in the West Indies.

The Coopers were linked to the real world only by a nightly five-minute news report in English that crackled and faded on the wireless. One night there was something about an American pilot. They couldn't catch it, and there was no follow-up the next evening.

The airliner touched down in the kerosene haze of LaGuardia International and they deplaned up the ramp into the terminal; there would be a short wait for the connecting flight to Buffalo. Richard Cooper loped off to find a washroom and Ellen wandered toward a news kiosk.

"North Vietnam Under Siege," shouted *Life* in pink and white capitals. She fished thirty-five cents out of her handbag and bought a copy.

"I walked down to the gates, opened up the magazine, and saw Dick. You can't imagine what a horrifying feeling that was. I got up and walked around. The attendent at the gate said, 'Is there anything wrong?' I showed him the picture and said, 'That's my brother.' He didn't know what to say.

"Then Richard came back. It was also in the New York *Times* . . . and he had purchased a copy. I remember flying back to Buffalo and trying to take this all in. Once again it was so much to absorb and it was so bad. What had they done to him? What was going on? Could this be real? I had the same reaction that I did when I learned he was missing: I did not discuss it. Friends came over, and I discussed my vacation. . . . Looking back, I had no control. It was my mind that, not even allowing me to deal with it. . . . The whole thing was so painful for me that for two years I rarely discussed it and if someone had the courage to ask me about it, I answered them in brief fashion so as not to encourage them to ask again."

During the next couple of months stories came from various sources as Hanoi hustled to set things straight: Stratton had not been "brainwashed" and Lockwood's impressions were erroneous. Was there an inkling in all this for Ellen that perhaps her brother had been involved in some elaborate charade?

"I never thought of a show. I felt he could really have been terribly coerced, and I wouldn't expect anybody under those circumstances to continue to be a hero. To me it seemed . . . to be a repeat of the Korean prisoner of war experience. It did not occur to me that this was some sort of a plan or a performance."

Ellen Cooper gave up her anti-war activities.

* * *

Alice Stratton settled finally for a one-story, three-bedroom gray bungalow Tom Foy had found on Nathan Way. The street was quiet, and the lawns green and manicured. Moffett Field was ten minutes distant and the Foy household half that. There was a church a brief drive away and a school close enough for the boys to walk to as each came of school age. It was hardly a distinguished house: California tract design with exposed room beams and ceilings lending themselves to those chain-hung swag lamps mail order catalogues fondly feature. But it suited her present need and she redecorated with warm, soft colors and fabrics. The small front yard was enclosed by a high hedge. An ancient and shaggy pine watched over the larger rear yard, which backed up to, and was fenced off from, a slough. Patrick began badgering her for a tree house.

Alice claimed the master bedroom for herself and installed within it the conjugal bed. It was an act of consummate courage and faith; each time she slid onto the emptiness of its double mattress she could feel the missing.

Stratton's clothes were hung neatly in a proper closet next to hers and there they would remain until he returned. In the dining area, between the kitchen and the family room, she arranged the chairs about the large oak table in the familiar way. His was painfully vacant at each meal. Each meal was begun in grace with special prayer for Dad, a simple, even stark, statement of love and remembrance, nothing more. She was not a woman given to maudlin sentiment, nor would she permit it in her house in front of her children. *Her* children. Lord, it slipped in now, every once in a while.

More than four months had passed since Dick had been lost, and her adjustment to and acceptance of that fact, that he was gone and she alone was mother-father-guardian-referee-comfort-security for the boys, increased. It was by no means an easy passage, this route from partner to sole manager. The picture in *Life* had really undone her, an indication of just how much of an emotionally perilous journey she still was on, and there was that story from Tass, too. Even after the grieving had pretty much passed, there was always an underlying anxiety. Was he alive, or dead? Had he survived another day?

Would she?

Sometimes she wondered what would become of them all without Dick. And what had become of the trained, professional social worker able to cope with life at its basest. Part of her problem, of course, was that she had no one, really, to talk to, to bitch to, to just one day sit down and simply dump all the damn load lodged there inside her chest, and breathe deep again. Not that she didn't have friends in Palo Alto. Thank God for the Foys, and there were now the Marrs, who lived near her on Nathan Way, and there were the Foys' friends who had begun to take her into their circle. No, that was not it. No, the problem was that even with these people, even with the Foys, she was guarded when it came to *him*.

Dick's circumstances were not subjects for open conversation or idle chatting. This was something Washington was really firm on and the bureaucratic reasoning, at the time anyway, sounded logical. Or so she reasoned.

The official line (somewhat refined a decade later) went like this:

159

"Our officials knew that not all Americans who had been captured by the other side had been identified as prisoners; that those whose capture had been acknowledged were not characterized as 'prisoners of war' but as 'war criminals'; that most had been denied any communication with their families; and that none was receiving the humanitarian treatment prescribed by the Geneva Convention. Our nation's leaders believed that if these conditions were to be corrected, they could be achieved only through quiet diplomacy. . . .

"Families were, of course, provided with information that their husbands or sons had been captured or were reported missing, and except for officially classified data, they were also advised as to the circumstances surrounding the men's capture or disappearance. At the time, however, they were told this information was extremely confidential and not to be discussed with others."[5]

Unfortunately, the period of "quiet diplomacy" whispered along through more than five years, virtually obscuring the needs of the families of the men held prisoner or listed among the missing.

* * *

On April 6, a few days after the *Life* article about the POWs appeared, the number of men held captive or reported missing in Southeast Asia was increased by one when a seaman named Douglas Hegdahl was reported missing and presumed lost at sea in the Gulf of Tonkin.

Hegdahl was a member of the deck crew aboard the missile cruiser U.S.S. *Canberra;* his absence was discovered when he failed to arrive for his watch. The *Canberra* turned about and crisscrossed the waters where Hegdahl presumably went overboard. No body was found.

Four days later, the ship's company held a memorial service at sea for the young victim. Photographs of the last rites were sent by the Navy to the parents, Mr. and Mrs. Abe Hegdahl of Clark, South Dakota. Douglas Hegdahl had been in the Navy for less than six months.

Edith Hegdahl insisted her son was alive. She hoped he had not lost his glasses.

CHAPTER 16

Clark, South Dakota, where Abe Hegdahl moved his family in 1953 after he bought the local hotel, sits midway on a seventy-two-mile stretch of U.S. 212 between Watertown to the east and Redfield to the west. It is a fast piece of road, for once inside South Dakota the prairie quickens.

Long hills flow deliberately and ever more sharply westward, dashing against the Black Hills and on, toward the Continental Divide and the hard peaks of the Rockies. This is old land, Sioux, Crow, Nez Percé, Cheyenne land, graveyard land. Twenty miles north by east of where U.S. 212 parallels the Belle Fourche River and nips into Wyoming three hundred miles west of Clark, a government plaque sites the geographical center of the United States of America.

Abe Hegdahl had acquired with the Clark Hotel a smaller motel, and soon purchased a second motel on the outskirts of town. He and his wife and his sons did all the work themselves: no maids for Abe. Douglas, his middle son, often served as desk clerk at the hotel and in the warm midwestern summers worked, too, on the local farms, moving irrigation pumps, hauling hay, and the like. By the time he was a senior in high school and ready to graduate with his class of thirty-eight other teen-agers, in June 1966, the boy stood a little over six feet in height and carried an inflated bulk of 225 pounds. He had a big, open Norwegian face and an easy grin that was only a breath away from a cackling, atonal laugh. The eyes behind the thick glasses were at once guileless and shrewd, intelligent but without apparent intellect. He had what his mother's generation called a peaches and cream complexion, topped by a good head of curly yellow hair, bushy on the top and close-trimmed on the sides where his eyeglass bows slipped behind squarish ears.

If his schoolboy confessions are taken at face value, he was a town badass. Prodded (and blushing), he admits to being a "gang" leader of twenty or so other badasses who harassed teachers out of town and locked class weenies out on school fire escapes in twenty-below weather. These activities were hardly on a par with mid-1960s Berkeley or Bedford-Stuyvesant, but given the midlands temperament, one may assume there was a collective sigh of relief (at least from the school board) when Abe and Edith Hegdahl drove Douglas to Watertown and packed him aboard a bus for Fargo, a night at the Bison Hotel, and a four-year hitch in the United States Navy.

"I wanted to see the world, be on a boat. I was gung-ho! Didn't want to see the war end before I got into it. Well, not really, but I would have enlisted even if there hadn't been a war. I was pretty much . . . pro [Vietnam war]. I felt it was something we had to do. Funny, my mother is very conservative but when it came to one of her kids she was a little reluctant. I remember her saying, 'I don't know why we have to go over there and fight their war for them.'"

Hegdahl was shipped off to San Diego for boot camp and from his description of it, rendered a decade later, it was the old Gang from Clark all over again.

"Did some crazy things in boot camp. Got a picture of me with my head sticking out of a laundry hamper. Hippity-hop, company stop! Pitter patter, detail scatter! We were the worst company [but] I did do pretty good in swimming."

He took boot leave at Christmas of 1966, an early furlough because of the holiday, and headed back to Clark squeezed into dress blues. He returned, reluctantly he says, to the "prison" of San Diego and, because he had already had leave, shipped out directly overseas on the U.S.S. *Canberra*. His entry into postal clerks' school was delayed six months. The Navy needed crews to

162

man ships of the line in 1967 more than it needed clerks. He was assigned to Division 3, a deck crew, and sweated in the ammunition gang manhandling heavy shells for the ship's cannon.

Viewed close-up, the war didn't seem quite as great or glamorous as when he daydreamed about it in Clark. The *Canberra* took a hit from a North Vietnamese coastal battery and a couple of Hegdahl's shipmates were torn up. He wanted a positive memory of the cruise and that, he determined, was to see a night engagement, which was spectacular, according to those of his shipmates who had witnessed it (in violation of standing orders prohibiting men on deck during combat).

The *Canberra* was due to stand down from the line in two days' time.

"Gosh! I didn't want to miss out, you know? So this night before I went on watch, I went up to see the shelling. The ship was shooting from the port side. I was on the starboard side. What I wasn't aware of was that the ship was in the process of making a turn and I walked under one of the five-inch gun mounts. It went off and apparently the concussion knocked me senseless. I went over the side, and as soon as I hit the water, I smacked it so hard it brought me fully to. And the ship was swerving so I was very fortunate I wasn't pulled into the blades [propellers]. . . . I thought we'd got hit by shore bombardment."

He lost his glasses in the water; without them, he saw life in a blur.

He swam for nearly five hours in the black, choppy sea. He worried about sharks. Dawn revealed a heavily overcast sky. A crust of bread floated by his nose. Finally he spotted "a thing" floating ahead of him, and he removed his T shirt and waved it slowly over his head. He was close to exhaustion.

"Turned out to be a Vietnamese fishing boat. It looked like a Viking ship coming through the swells. Those people treated me real well. They hadn't got the party line yet. They fed me and they didn't beat me up or abuse me."

The tired sailor was stripped of his wet clothing and re-dressed in rude burlap. He was seated in one corner of the boat and motioned to stay there. The fishermen shared food with him and offered him some raw clams or mussels. When no one was look-

163

ing, he dumped them over the side. The smell of them made him sick to his stomach. One of the fishermen asked, *"May-bay-my* [U.S. aircraft?]?" Hegdahl's reply was a grin.

Toward evening, the Vietnamese brought the boat about, reset the sails, and headed westward toward their village just north of Thanh Hoa. The boy was hustled ashore and into the arms of the local militia. A member of the political cadre delivered a hysterical speech on the beach that stirred up the villagers, and Hegdahl was hustled away to a central building. In Clark, South Dakota, he would have called it the courthouse. He was seated in a chair beneath an outsize portrait of President Ho Chi Minh. The villagers crowded in and the handful of militiamen was nearly helpless before their collective anger. An elderly person, a woman, he thought, clubbed him savagely in the face, bloodying his nose and splitting his lip.

The crowd was brought under control and the guards eased it out of the building. Hegdahl was fed and locked in a small, cell-like room beneath a small stage in the building's central room. Later that night he was spirited away, marched and jogged on foot, finally put into a truck, and driven to an interrogation center inland.

He volunteered his name, rank, serial number, and date of birth. That much he did remember about the Code of Conduct that he'd read on a bulletin board in boot camp. He did not answer the next question, because the code said he did not have to; he remembered that, too. He was asked another question and he did not answer.

A rifle butt slammed into the back of his head, nearly knocking him senseless.

The interrogator told him he could expect to die unless he corrected his attitude and told the truth.

They took away his shoes and jogged his feet raw.

Two days later, confused and fearful, he was put into a truck and driven to Hanoi and locked in a cell in the Heartbreak Hotel section of Hoa Lo.

When Hegdahl's absence was discovered, the *Canberra* put about to search for him. Four days later, the memorial services were held, his gear was collected and put away, the ship stood down off the line for a breather; the family was duly notified, the picture of the services sent, and sympathy cards began arriving at the family home in Clark.

But the Hegdahls did not buy it. Edith Hegdahl told *Life* reporter Margery Byers, "I was positive he was alive. We always thought the phone would ring and it would be good news. We're Lutherans and we believed God was taking care of him."[6]

Except for interrogation, he was kept in solitary and remained in solitary until early May, when the Vietnamese transferred him to the Zoo and into the cell of a startled and incredulous carrier pilot named Charles D. Stackhouse. Stackhouse was a lieutenant commander who had flown A-4 attack planes off the U.S.S. *Bon Homme Richard*.

"Sir," explained Hegdahl, "you're not going to believe this. . . ."

Probably not. It had taken the Vietnamese more than a month to believe him, to become convinced he was not a spy, to become convinced that this was, without a doubt, the most faceless, ignorant peasant criminal they had ever seen. It was a long month for Hegdahl.

"I was never tortured. But at the time I thought it was bad. I was put into a lot of stress positions, standing for hours, fully clothed, with my hands over my head, things like that, not because I was a John Wayne or kept my mouth shut but because they didn't believe me.

"They took me to a point where they were going to torture me. One of the interrogators looked at me and said, 'Heddle, I will have you tied very tightly and thrown in a dark place.' And I was almost at a point where I said to myself, 'Well, shit, I'm going to have to make up some kind of cock and bull story,' and that's when they let off. And thank God they didn't do it. But at the time I was at my wit's end. They had me standing with my arms in the air or kneeling with my arms out or handcuffed with my hands behind my back, but nothing like . . . the straps and ropes, nothing that severe."

It dawned on him that his natural ignorance of military matters was a plus, and the more stupid the Vietnamese came to believe he was, the more dim-witted he acted.

"I realized I had something going for me. And then the [Vietnamese] started teaching me like I was a child. My biggest coup was I never had to write a confession and that was not because I was able to withstand torture, but because . . . they thought I was ridiculous. They asked me to write anything, by God, they had to work hard for it; not because I refused to do it but because I asked them to spell every word.

"They had put themselves in a position as my teachers and they couldn't be dumber than me. I would ask them how to spell a word, they'd have to go look it up in their Vietnamese dictionaries. Back and forth, back and forth.

"Then one day, they wrenched the pen out of my stained little hand and away from my blue tongue (because I sucked on the point) and they almost never asked me to do jackshit in writing again!"

Hegdahl was with Stackhouse exactly fourteen days, and then separated and lodged for eight days with Air Force Lieutenant Joseph Crecca, Jr., and then put back into solitary confinement again for "corrupting" the flier.

His cell was called the corncrib, a small, stifling brick cubicle with a tin roof. He alternately baked and shivered there for the rest of May and the first five days of June, when he was blindfolded and put on a truck and transferred to a prison camp called Plantation Gardens. From under his blindfold he could see the handcuffed hands of another prisoner being transferred with him; the thumbnails were all black and twisted and the areas above the wrists looked as if they had been severely infected.

* * *

Stratton felt his throat tighten. He had a glimpse of their faces before the guards slammed the door shut behind him, Bomar's angry and tight, Mullen's pale and anxious.

They marched him across the yard and put him in a small tin-roofed hut, a sweat box that performed perfectly under the June sun. He remained there all afternoon.

They came at dusk and got him, snapping his wrists into manacles and trying, unsuccessfully, to blindfold him; but his beak was too much to wrap and he could see beneath it by tilting his head when he sensed no one was looking. He had been allowed to shed his standard prison pajama outfit and was dressed, "for your comfort, Stratton," in his T shirt. He didn't believe that for a minute.

166

A truck waited and he could sense there was a second man in it, a fact he was able to confirm later quite easily. The second man was forward, up against the cab and shrouded in a heavy, army-issue tarpaulin. He himself was covered with a similar tarp. Two guards climbed in back. The truck's engine turned over, coughed, and started. The gears shifted, and the vehicle moved away.

"And by a circuitous route through Hanoi, we came to what obviously had been a downtown soccer stadium. We were being followed by a two-and-a-half-ton truck full of soldiers—which I could see from under the beak. We drove into the center of the stadium.

"The two-and-a-half-ton truck pulled up behind us, turned on its bright lights. They pulled the tarp off me. Then they turned on the [stadium] lights. And all hell broke loose for about twelve or fifteen minutes, and everybody had free whacks on me.

"It sounded like the whole town turned out: and folks, here's a real live one for you! Fortunately, the tailgate and sideboard of the weapons carrier (for that was what the vehicle was) covered my kidneys and I was high enough so they couldn't really reach my head, so I was just getting poked, really.

"But it was enough to impress you that, yeah!, they were ready to play another Hanoi March routine, you know, and they really didn't have very good control over their people. Two of the guards ended up actually having to slug and beat away people to put the tarpaulin down. They turned off the lights and we drove out, and we were transferred to the Plantation.

"The other man in the truck was Douglas Hegdahl and Doug and I were among the first two in that place, which they were just actually opening up as a camp."

The Plantation, or Plantation Gardens, or the Country Club, was none of those, but the former residence of the colonial mayor of Hanoi. In short time it became a show camp and the mayoral mansion was transformed into administrative offices and interview rooms where visiting delegations could chat in comfort and at leisure with selected prisoners. The mansion and outbuildings that housed the cells resembled a quaint European farm like those that speckle France and the Scandinavian nations. It was surrounded, and studded within the central grounds, by tall, old trees; upon closer inspection many of the buildings were seedy and in disrepair. When Stratton arrived in 1967, "it was still in pretty rotten condition.

"Apparently Russians had lived there prior to us because there were Russian magazines and papers laying around . . . [and pictures of] pin-up girls in the big house, Russian pin-up girls, you know, in overcoats? They put me back in solitary confinement again . . . and they kept saying you *will* see an American [delegation], you *will* see an American! There was constant harassment, though not [actual torture].

"They would get you all wet by making you go out there and clean up the place. They'd roll you around in the dirt and punch you. The guard would withhold water from you. They sent me barefoot into a bomb shelter in my skivvie shorts with a stick to chase out the rats, clean out the spiders of various varieties, and all the stuff they didn't want to do themselves. It was a period of constant physical harassment twenty-four hours a day.

"Once again, if you have to make mistake points in logic—I said, finally, fine [I'll do it]. Any *American* I can get in front of I can pretty well let know what happened or, anyway, negate the value of what has happened. Why beat myself down into giving a memorized pitch again?

"Without the *physical* presence of Vegetable Vic or Straps and Bars, the option was you will see him or you will be severely punished. But this time (once again, I say it was a mistake) I didn't even make them produce the torturer. And I should have realized that by this time they probably would not have tortured.

"Basically, I talked myself into it: I would go ahead and play it out. It was obviously going to go on and on until it was exhausted."

* * *

"Heddle, how would you like to meet an American?" Major Bui asked slyly.

"Boy, I would just *love* to meet an American."

The major blinked, then slowly smiled.

"Good, Heddle," he nodded, smiling at the Vietnamese woman interrogator standing beside him, "good. If you do strictly correctly, no punishment for your breaking of the camp regulations."

On his first day in the Plantation, Hegdahl had been caught tapping to a prisoner named Julius Jayroe and had spent the afternoon standing with his hands in the air. By nightfall he was exhausted, and when he was ordered out of his cell for the meeting with Major Bui, he feared that severe punishment finally was to be his.

"[Major Bui] acted so surprised that I wanted to meet another American. It never dawned on me he was talking about some antiwar group. I thought he meant another American prisoner; maybe I was gullible. He gave me his name, Dave Dellinger, and it didn't mean shit to me, you know? Oh, I thought, another prisoner—Dave Dellinger.

"Then he asked me, 'What would you say to him?' and I thought that's weird.

"Oh, I didn't know. We'd talk about home and family. (I didn't want to wreck it, meeting another prisoner.) Then he started telling me, 'You mustn't talk about conditions of the camp; you mustn't talk about where you are at.' It was cockeyed."

Later, Major Bui suggested Hegdahl write a letter home. He resisted, saying his father had a heart condition and the sudden shock of receiving a letter from Vietnam might be too much. The major insisted. Hegdahl consented. He was ordered to include in the letter a warning to his brother not to get drafted, and a request that his parents join the Spring Mobilization to End the War in Vietnam, a current peace movement in the United States.

Hegdahl sabotaged the letter by extending his draft warning not only to his brother, Dennis, but to a ninety-year-old resident of Clark and a cartoon character.

The interview was scheduled for June 8 in a new conference room in the mansion at the Plantation.

* * *

Major Bui was deeply troubled: as the commandant of the Ministry's Camps of Detention of U. S. Pilots Captured in the Democratic Republic of Vietnam, he was responsible for prisoner affairs. Because of his apparent ineptness in handling the black criminal Stratton, the Fatherland had lost face. This was a terribly, terribly serious affair.

The seriousness had been compounded by the subsequent interviews, which, while proper, seemingly had failed to correct the initial bad situation. The anti-war movement in the United States was gaining strength; some groups within it were empathetic or sympathetic to Hanoi's position and all opposed the bombing. There was dissension over the conduct of the war within the Johnson administration and that certainly had been proven in February when Johnson's message, through Moscow, stating negotiation terms was undercut by the State Department's more conciliatory message sent through private channels. Before the President could reply to either message, the bombing resumed, stirring another welcome controversy over the Americans' unwillingness to talk peace. The Russell tribunal had convicted the Americans of war crimes; Hanoi certainly had an upper hand. The Stratton business threatened to diminish Hanoi's increased measure of good will if the West believed American prisoners were being brainwashed or drugged. Stratton had not been brainwashed, and Major Bui and Stratton were going to make that clear, once and for all, to an *American* delegation.

Then they could get rid of Stratton, once and for all, send him home, get rid of the troublemaker and repair their reputation as a lenient and humane government. That made sense. And, for good measure, not only would Stratton be released but perhaps some others, too; perhaps the poor defective peasant Heddle.

* * *

On June 8, 1967, in the afternoon, Richard Stratton was taken from his cell and escorted to the mansion. Waiting for him were Major Bui, cool and immaculate despite the murderous summer heat, a second Vietnamese he did not recognize, and two Americans, one portly and smiling, the other young and looking ill at ease.

The older man stepped forward. "Hi, I'm Dave Dellinger." Stratton retreated behind his customary glower and studied his countrymen.

David Dellinger was fifty-two years old, with a large, square head that was being slowly abandoned by its hair. He was soft-spoken and that, with the gentle eyes, the balding pate, the puffy body, belied an intense passion for his cause. Dellinger was the kind of American who scared hell out of those congressional committees whose job it was to keep America pure; he was the kind of

American who kept J. Edgar Hoover assured a steady flow of investigative pin money.

As Dellinger sat down with Stratton now on a hot summer afternoon in Hanoi, he was the determined chairman of the National Mobilization to End the War in Vietnam, a loose coalition of about 150 American anti-war groups as diverse as pebbles on a beach but collectively dedicated to getting the American military out of Indochina. A month before, he had been one of three American delegates to Lord Russell's war crimes tribunal in Stockholm, which had convicted the United States (and three of its allies) of "crimes" against peace and humanity. The G-men said Dellinger ran with the Reds; actually, he ran pretty much alone. He just didn't care much about a man's politics, as long as they were pacifist. For that was Dellinger's cause, pacifism, and he had martyred himself for that ideal.

He was the son of a Wakefield, Massachusetts, attorney, and graduated from Yale with the class of 1936; he continued his education at New College, Oxford, and it was in Europe, when he found himself in the middle of the Spanish Civil War, that he identified and firmed his pacifist beliefs. He refused to register for the draft in 1939 and pulled a year in a federal penitentiary. In 1943, with the world war at full fury, he refused to submit to a pre-induction physical and was sentenced to two more years in prison. He was beaten in Newark, New Jersey, where he was working as a printer, after speaking at a rally opposing the Korean War. A year after that, on a peace mission bicycle tour of Europe, he wound up in the Soviet Zone of Austria, passing out leaflets to Russian soldiers urging them not to kill or hate. He opposed nuclear testing, and when Vietnam exploded, he was back on the picket line and back in the slammer—thirty days for a civil disobedience demonstration outside the White House in 1965.

He had made his first trip to North Vietnam in 1966 and had his passport revoked in 1967. He was now a journalist and edited and published *Liberation* magazine, which supported the anti-war, anti-establishment line. Like all advocate journalists who emphasize advocacy over journalism, he had critical blind spots.

The second man, the younger one, was Nicholas Egelson, a former president of the Students for a Democratic Society (SDS). He was one of the lesser pantheon of anti-war activists, without the national profile of Thomas Hayden, an SDS founder, or the moralistic, dramatic flair of Rennie Davis. His expenses were being paid by the Peace Committee of North Vietnam, and it was his first trip to Indochina. He had a somewhat heart-shaped face atop a long neck that emphasized his Adam's apple, a curly romp of dark hair, and soft, dark eyes behind dark horn-rimmed glasses: altogether, a rather pleasant and innocent face.

Dellinger has said he requested the Stratton interview specifically because of the Lockwood bowing photograph.

"[It] upset me very much because the reason I was anti-war was because I wanted to be pro-human, and no matter what terrible things [the Americans] might have done, I didn't think this was the way even people who commit war crimes should be treated. And I asked to see some prisoners [Dellinger arrived in Vietnam May 26, and departed June 9, 1967] and I asked specifically to see Stratton since he, apparently, was the number one exhibit of somebody who was being mistreated."[7]

Stratton has said, "I granted the interview as a result of continuous harassment that I had simply had enough of. I was getting far too weak in my isolated state, both physically and mentally. I figured I could get the [Vietnamese] off my back and basically buy some time for myself. I made this quite clear to the government when I came home: this was, in fact, a technique of survival, to buy time."

Whatever other notions he might have entertained about "getting his message" out were dispelled almost at once.

"Then I saw Dellinger [Stratton pronounces the name Dillinger] and Dellinger started motoring off. I realized . . . that you weren't going to say anything to Dellinger that would even get back."

"[Stratton] seemed cautious and suspicious at first, but I felt he was at a terrible disadvantage and I wanted to establish human contact with him. And so I talked about having put in three years in prison . . . myself, but it took a long time to break down his defenses. He was very upset to think that anyone could think he was brainwashed. It sort of hurt his ego, his pride. He kept telling me over and over again about all the education he had had, and

172

how intelligent he was, and he guessed he would know if he was being brainwashed."

"[Dellinger] brought up the brainwashing. In fact it was from him that I first learned about the *Life* magazine article, see? I never knew there was a friendly or a Western caucasian in the crowd. . . . So this was the first I'd heard, and rather than say no, I hadn't heard about it, and have the Vietnamese shut him up, I just nodded to him. . . . I was learning the resistance game. You see, I was not trying to show that I was brainwashed. I was trying to show that I was doped."

"[Stratton] had a perfectly logical explanation: he had bowed from the waist and he said to me, 'Well, I always knew when in Rome do as the Romans do, and here they bow. In the American Army we salute, but in here we bow.' And he said, 'So I have decided that I would bow, too. I was a Catholic altar boy and I reverted to my Catholic upbringing!' I am not even familiar with it, but that was the way he said it."

"Sure, [Dellinger] asked me what the story was on [the bowing] and I gave him that . . . Jeez . . . especially after he told me his wife was a Catholic. What ritual except that of a priest at a solemn high mass, at one point in the mass, goes through a formal bow routine? Even in the liturgy of the Church it is something reserved to the clergy at the old, Latin, solemn high mass. It is never done by the congregation. There is no bowing for the congregation anywhere, it's a genuflection. And I figured to repeat that story for a guy who had a wife who was Catholic would just reinforce [its negativeness], not realizing the guy was so stupid."

"Having been in an American prison, I knew that when we were living among the most abominable conditions that visitors came, distinguished visitors, and toured the prison, and they went out saying how liberal and humane the institution was and I knew that prison was virtually a hellhole and a disgrace. That's why I didn't come out [later] and say, 'Well, Commander Stratton says they're being treated very well.' "

"[Dellinger] had that [guy] from Swarthmore with him. . . . He was a thing of rare beauty. I asked him (I got a chance to say a few words), 'Hey, who are you?' He said he was the leader of the anti-draft movement at Swarthmore. . . . I said, 'What are you going to do when *your* number comes up, lead them off to Canada or to jail?' 'Oh, no,' he said, 'there's no chance of that. I'm 4-F.' I thought that was an interesting insight into a rabble rouser prepared to lead them to the fore. . . . Well, that convinced me that there was no one who came over from our side that was going to be all that sympathetic or willing to deduce what we were saying or read behind the lines. They were prepared to accept whatever the V. said as gospel. . . ."

Stratton's interview lasted about ninety minutes, and he was taken back to his cell. Hegdahl was brought in to see Dellinger, clutching a handful of letters.

"Hi, I'm Dave Dellinger."

"Here is my letter, and here are five they just gave me to give to you."

There was a marked contrast between Stratton and Hegdahl, Dellinger recalled, "because [of] Hegdahl's elation at seeing a fellow American; it was all very obvious on his face."

"I did look elated, sure. I was terribly super-hyper when I met him. I had just been through this business of being caught communicating, and then had just been handed these letters from other prisoners . . . before I went in there. (I stood outside and memorized the names: Joe Crecca, Ed Hubbard, and three others. And when I went in, I told him I had just gotten them because the letters implied these were my comrades and we were together.) Also, there were a lot of lights in there and it was only shortly before [the interview] I realized he was not another prisoner.

"My interview was kind of short, about twenty minutes. Major Bui kept looking at his watch, and I was not required to do anything that I thought was propaganda. (Later on, I realized just being there was propaganda.) I remember at one point [Dellinger] asked me what I did all day long and I said, 'Oh, I stare at the ceiling,' and Major Bui went, 'Harumph!' and we looked over at him. 'Uh, I've got a radio, too,' I said, and Major Bui nodded approvingly.

"Dellinger said, 'You've got a radio?'

"'Well, a speaker.'

"'Oh. One of *those*.' Dellinger seemed truly sorry for me, or at least that's the impression I got, but, Jeez, I never said those things they said I said."

Upon their return to the United States, Dellinger and Egelson called a press conference to 'refute" what the *Daily Worker* reported as "tales spread in the U.S. press recently that U.S. pilots shot down over Vietnam are being 'brainwashed.'" An extended report in the New York *Times* said:

"According to Mr. Dellinger, Major Bui and Commander Stratton explained that it was the custom for North Vietnamese Army men to salute the prisoners and for the prisoners to bow in return because, clothed as they were in pajamas, saluting was inappropriate. . . .

"Mr. Dellinger said Commander Stratton had described the long conversations he had 'from time to time' with Major Bui as being of great help in passing the time and keeping alive his mental faculties and then had added:

"'I have never felt any pressure from him, and I respect him as a fellow human being even though it is obvious that I disagree with him in some areas.' Mr. Dellinger, who had separate talks with Major Bui, said the officer explained that, in his conversations with the prisoners, 'we simply explore as fellow human beings the kind of world it is and the kind of world we would like it to be.'

"Mr. Dellinger said that during the prison-camp interview, Commander Stratton indicated views on the Vietnam war that did not coincide with those of either the United States or North Vietnamese Governments. He reported that the pilot had voiced great pride in his Navy career but then had compared the military services to a policeman who failed if he had to use his gun. The Vietnam situation, Commander Stratton said, according to Mr. Dellinger, marks just such a failure."[8]

Dellinger quoted Hegdahl as saying he wished there had been a peace movement in his home town in South Dakota so that he might have "avoided the situation he was in." Egelson quoted

Hegdahl as saying the young sailor "has hopes that he will be released by the Vietnamese because he believes that unlike the pilots he has not done anything to hurt the Vietnamese. His final words to us as we left were, 'Tell my mother and father I am in good health and am not being brainwashed or anything like that.'"[9]

(A decade later, Hegdahl for the first time saw copies of Dellinger's and Egelson's remarks and his face turned red. "That is a bunch of bullshit, I'll tell you. Bullshit! Good grief, I don't remember saying anything that could even remotely be construed as that. Nothing like that was ever said.")

Later that day, well into the night, in fact, Dellinger was shown a cell at the Plantation, supposedly Stratton's; Stratton's roommate was absent, taking a shower, he was told. He was given a description of camp life, and this he reported so:

"Stratton and Hegdahl said they were given ample servings of food consisting of rice, meat dishes and bread. They said they felt guilty because they were given more than they could eat. [Despite the structuring of this sentence, Stratton and Hegdahl were never interviewed together and were living apart in separate solitary cells.] Each room housing three prisoners is twenty-feet by thirty-feet with a sleeping mat for each and two blankets, a table and chairs. The men take showers. They are allowed to receive and send mail and are given a limited amount of reading material."[10]

"At that time," said Richard Stratton, "it appeared logical to me (although it is slightly illogical now) that by appearing not to be brainwashed to Dellinger, then the only conclusion should be [the Vietnamese] used some kind of dope against me."

Stratton was wrong. The conclusion finally presented in the United States was that prisoners were well treated. That was that. Neither Dellinger nor Egelson ever asked the hard question.

The Dellinger interview and Stratton's performance at it were given high marks by Major Bui and his staff. Maybe things were under control, perhaps the black criminal could be trusted, had learned who was the master here. Another test, perhaps, and then the solution to the Stratton problem could be put into effect.

At the end of June, the Vietnamese welcomed Walter

Heynowski and his colleague Gerhard Scheumann and their staff at Gia Lam airport. Heynowski and Scheumann were East Germans, a documentary film team on assignment in Vietnam to do a report on the American prisoners and the conditions of their captivity. The two men, and their staff, worked for DELAG, a multifaceted communications industry managed by the government of the German Democratic Republic. The bulk of the filming was done at the Zoo and the Plantation, where more than half the prisoners there were placed in the crowd scenes. Stratton and Hegdahl and a few others had supporting roles; ten prisoners starred in lengthy interviews before the cameras. The interviews went well, but once outside the interview room, things were more difficult for the Germans.

None of the prisoners smiled. They were given chores for the cameras, and did them sluggishly or kept turning their backs to the camera. Once the bristle part of a broom broke off; the prisoner never missed a beat, sweeping steadily with the pole alone. There were guards behind every third tree and around every corner and they were difficult to keep out of the shots. Stratton and Hegdahl got their first close look at one another as they were photographed taking a shower together (but discreetly, with a woven bamboo screen between their bodies and the camera).

"Sir," Hegdahl whispered out of the side of his mouth, "what do you think of this, sir?"

"Personally," Stratton rumbled, making no attempt to conceal his talking, "I think anybody who takes pictures of people taking showers has gotta be a little queer."

Stratton was filmed and photographed in a cell, a huge tank of a room perhaps thirty feet by forty feet. There were tables and chairs neatly arranged when Stratton was marched in. Before the photographers arrived, he moved everything, except the bunk, into an unsightly pile in a far corner. The photographers arrived and captured the (sullen) American with a wide-angle lens: a perfect composition, with the man sitting alone on a wooden bunk in a corner, with perhaps as much as ten to twenty feet of empty wall on either side of him.

The Germans entitled the film, and a book containing a description of their assignment and the ten separate interviews, *Pilots in*

Pajamas.[11] *Life* purchased rights to many photographs and a commentary by the two reporters. The pictures and text were scheduled for publication in the fall.

* * *

Hegdahl was on his cement bunk staring at the ceiling when they came for him. He was suffering terribly from heat rash.

It was July 11.

He walked across the compound and from the mansion house he could hear voices, for it was summer in Hanoi and all of the doors and windows of the building were open. He could hear the soft, high-pitched voice of Major Bui and a deeper, booming voice of an American.

"I walked in, and he was sitting there. He looked like he needed a shave, which was kind of normal for Stratton. He got up and we shook hands. Major Bui said, 'He is from the air and you are from the sea, and now you live together.

"'Remember, Stratton, everyone must do for the camp.'"

Their new home was a large cell that had been used as a show cell for the East German filmmakers: perhaps twenty by thirty feet, it had colonial, high-posted ceilings with rectangular ventilation openings up in the walls. The windows and the doors were barred and shuttered with french slats. Painted on the wall, over Stratton's bunk, in black paint were the words "Clean & Neat." Overhead, one of the smallest light bulbs in the history of electric power glowed day and night in a metal shade suspended from a black wire strung wall to wall.

Stratton assumed the title of "Mr. Clean"; Hegdahl was "Mr. Neat." Furnishings were sparse: two ill-constructed bunks with mosquito netting, a small table, stools, and two foul waste buckets for toilets.

Hegdahl literally still bubbles with the memories of that day:

"We jabbered all night long, and smoked. We had both stashed cigarettes because we thought the other might want one, and I produced mine, 'Tah-dahhh!' When I had gone through the [mansion], I'd stolen all the cigarettes I could find; stuffed 'em up my sleeve. Apparently, he'd done the same thing. Neither one of us smoked, but we smoked that night. We sat over on my bunk and we talked and talked. And that was the happiest, happiest time of my captivity, the time spent with old Beak."

CHAPTER 17

The days slid along one after another bright with summer heat, like white keys on a grand piano, monotonous, nearly identical, separated briefly by black slabs of night. The first hours of euphoria for Stratton and Hegdahl, hoarse talking into the dawn, were replaced by a pragmatic routine of endurance against the most terrible odds.

"The gong would go off about 5 or 5:30 A.M. Six o'clock you'd get the Voice of Vietnam—Hanoi Hannah—for a half-hour broadcast. Okay? You would take out your toilet bucket, well, sometime in the morning. You would get issued three cigarettes a day. You would eat your first meal about ten in the morning, your second about four-thirty in the afternoon. You would listen to the Voice of Vietnam again at night. That was it! The rest of the time was 'free time,' just sitting in your cell."

This is Douglas Hegdahl describing a "typical" day in the late summer of 1967 when he and Richard Stratton were cellmates at the Plantation. He continues:

"In some camps you were not even supposed to get off your bed, but that rule was not enforced stringently. We did a lot of pacing, watching the shadows; there was a twenty-watt bulb in the room that burned night and day. There was very little variation.

"If they didn't have a water shortage [and a prisoner was not in solitary] you were allowed to go wash once a day except Sunday. Sometimes there was a water shortage or sometimes it was just too cold to go out. In wintertime, it got too cold. . . ."

It is true that men were tortured and otherwise brutalized in the North Vietnamese prison camps. Unendurable pain and the constant threat of it drove some prisoners insane. At least one man was tortured to death, more than one died of infection from untreated wounds sustained bailing out of crippled aircraft, sometimes in the torture rooms broken limbs were further savaged. One Vietnamese interrogator masturbated, so it was told, while watching his bloody, sweating victims writhe in pain; another bludgeoned day after day an American flier so taken leave of his senses he reacted not at all to the blows and was incapable of attending to his own bodily functions or recognizing his fellow prisoners as Americans, too. This is the stuff of drama guaranteed to titillate a rubber-hose mentality.

But it is also true that these dramatic accounts distract from an equal, perhaps ultimately more terrifying brutality: isolation and boredom. Here is Hegdahl again:

"We were in a barren cell and there was very little to do. The worst thing was the boredom, unbelievable boredom, forced inactivity day in and day out. . . . Many times you lived in a daydream world; sometimes it was your *whole* world. If you tried to maintain your mental alertness (as it is now) you'd probably go crazy in there. I can tell you, it was pretty grim being in captivity and you had to gear yourself down to it, gear yourself down so the smallest little thing became the biggest event. Dick had coined the term 'Events.' Everything was an Event. Eating was an Event. Smoking your three cigarettes a day [was] three Events."

Boredom and frustration occasionally jacked tensions to dangerous levels.

"Well, yeah. You can imagine how you get on if you're married? A lot of people who are married have fights. But imagine living in the same room twenty-four hours a day, always together, except when one was taken out for interrogation or something. But we worked it out, and we talked.

"We talked. Talked about everything. Food! Food was a big subject and we always had names for the food, like Pale Green Death Soup. And one thing that I thought that was funny: Dick would take the bread and it was so old that summer (later, it got better) and he'd pound it on the table and he'd say, 'Awright! Everybody out! EV-erybody out!' and the weevils would tumble out. He had a sense of humor even when things were kind of grim.

"We always judged the meals. Dick had a crazy way of judging the meals: how many T's for taste? and B's for bulk? and P's for palatability? and then we would add them all up. Well, that would take about half an hour and it would kill some time. The highest award we could ever give was the Finger Lickin' Good award. That only happened one time. The camp commander had given us a piece of fudge out of the clear blue for no apparent reason. That was Finger Lickin' Good.

"That summer the food was pretty much pumpkin soup and bread, that old bread. Twice a day. Hardly any variation. Always about the same. Or else you'd get Deep Green Soup. We called it Jungle Soup. Some countries burn their jungles, some of them hack them away, and the Vietnamese, they eat theirs or at least they gave it to us. And in your soup sometimes you got pork— pork fat, pig fat. A lot of times it still had the bristles in it. (But if it had bristles, at least the Vietnamese wouldn't eat it.) The guards [tried] not to let us see [what they ate]. The bulk of our food was more, I would say, but the quality not as good, and in wintertime it got kind of scarce.

"I always thought of chocolate milk, thought that it would be great to have chocolate milk. Dick used to talk about clams and having clambakes. All the time.

"Before we roomed together, the Vietnamese filmed us eating one time. It took them all day to get the stuff ready. We walked into a room and there was fresh bread, pineapples, bananas, fruit, and all kinds of soup. And a problem . . . cropped up. We couldn't carry all that food out. They were filming propaganda so they had to go out and make some trays to put the food on. When I walked out of there with my food the tray was still wet with paint. I got paint on my pajamas and my arms.

"We talked about other things, things out of the routine that might have happened during the day. We had a pleasant night once when he told me what his family used to do for Christmas. We talked about sex, of course, but not like you did when you were, say, in college or high school or something like that. Actually, when you are hungry and you're hot or you're cold, sex goes down the list. Your sex drive probably isn't as great in most cases as when you're a free man. You are physically down.

"And we talked about our lives and our families, but the subject almost always eventually got around to food.

"They called Dick and me out together one time and they said, 'You know, other prisoners have been complaining about the food. Of course, they will receive resolute and serious punishment. What do *you* think of the food?' Dick said, 'Well, in that case, I think it's pretty good.'"

* * *

Stratton had been in captivity more than seven months by the time he and Hegdahl became cellmates, and he had, by the young sailor's account, received only one letter, presented to him on the Fourth of July, "and that was the biggest event of his life. Oh, that was neat. I think he read that letter until he wore it out.

"He was very much an officer and a commander. He had a very commanding personality, a booming voice, and he was most considerate of me. We got along on a first-name basis. He called me Doug and I called him Beak.

"I do not know what it would have been like if I'd lived with Dick [for the rest of my captivity]. When it ended, us living together, we were still on the honeymoon. But I can tell you quite frankly some of the happiest moments in my life took place in there, in the prisoner of war camp, because everything is relative. Going from solitary to getting a roommate . . . like Dick Stratton was a bigger event than almost anything I can think of. Really.

"He would be very depressed sometimes and I would try to cheer him up. He would never discuss, very much, what he had been through, the torture and that. He wasn't the kind of guy who would tell you. He would be very warm and friendly about pleasant things, but he didn't get into a lot of details [about the other]. I was always reminded of it when his sleeve would come up and I'd see the scars. . . .

"Usually after we ate, one or the other would invite the other over to his 'stateroom'; most of the time I think we went over to mine because it was closer to the light bulb. We'd have a cigarette and then we'd talk. I had a feeling he really didn't want to talk about too many things because the room might be bugged. So we'd always talk on pretty light subjects or things that didn't have to do with the camp.

"But, as a prisoner, you get into a position that for your own good you don't unburden everything you know. I sometimes wonder if the Vietnamese moved me in with him because they had kind of figured Stratton out a bit. He had a 'troop' now, he had someone to be responsible for. You know, it was one thing to go it alone and be responsible for what's going to happen to you. It's quite another to have a troop under you (and unlike almost every other officer in the military, Navy or Air Force, that I knew, he had a real sense of command). I am speculating, but I think the Vietnamese got awfully burned by Dick's performance and you make a man desperate and he's going to be pretty dangerous, not very reliable. So I think they wanted to give him something to lose . . . some kind of dog biscuit they could hold over him in case something happened, and that was bad treatment for somebody else.

"I remember one time Dick said to me, 'Look, Doug, I'm not telling you everything about everything because it's for your own good.' I always respected that. I think Dick felt very guilty many times about having done anything, and I felt terribly bad about how he had been treated, because I hadn't been treated nearly as bad as he had. I never was tortured. Never was. But [I was] scared shitless half the time, and after a while I just got numbed out of it."

It is hard to generalize about the lives of the American prisoners of war in that summer of 1967, and the year before and the year after. From all accounts there seem to have been no standards of administration of the camps, which were, with the exception of Hoa Lo, which was designed as a prison, makeshift jails. In some camps, men were repeatedly tortured in 1967; Stratton and Hegdahl, at the Plantation, were not, nor were many of the others there.

The terrible boredom and solitary confinement were sometimes broken by camp chores assigned to various prisoners: Stratton and Hegdahl were occasionally shipped to the coal bins to make fuel balls, hand-made baseball-sized pellets constructed of coal dust and water. Lugging water for prison consumption was another task, and there were the infrequent and never-looked-forward-to question sessions and indoctrination lessons. Some of the questions seem most bizarre. Stratton was asked one time the proper way to have a clambake. On another occasion he was asked by an interrogator, called the Sugar Plum Fairy, if he could help translate Mark Twain's *A Connecticut Yankee in King Arthur's Court,* a copy of which Alice had sent her husband (along with his rosary) as presents for his thirty-sixth birthday.

Other bracings were designed to keep a man off balance.

Stratton was called out one day to face a group of Vietnamese interrogators. Apparently, in their minds, he was being uncooperative and there were threats of what would happen to him if he failed to mend his ways.

"Stratton, if you die, wife will be very sad," a Vietnamese said with a knowing look.

"Oh no," said Stratton, looking very surprised.

"What?"

"She wouldn't be sad. You see, I have life insurance. I bet this company: if I die I win. If I don't die I lose. So don't worry about that, don't worry about my wife, because if I die I win and she gets all that money."

There were looks between the Vietnamese and hurried talk among themselves, quick looks at Stratton, whose face conveyed only childish innocence and concern for his captors' worry. Stratton cleared his throat, politely, and the Vietnamese looked up.

"In fact," he began, "if you wanted to do wife a real favor you keep me two years—and then shoot me!"

"What, Stratton?" There was genuine confusion now.

"Yuh. Wife would still be young enough to remarry and she would have all the benefits of the life insurance plus the salary for that time."

"They tried to get under his skin in ways like that but he wouldn't let it get to him," Hegdahl said. "It was just funny, fantastic, the way he could come up with those little things."

But it was not so funny, let alone fantastic at the time; it was a desperate gamble to resist in any way possible, to be stalwart against an enemy in the presence of one's peers, to make fun of these little idiots with their dictionaries and goon squads, a half-assed game with half a deck. One misstep, a wrong look, a slip in an established pattern of behavior, would bring disaster.

Stratton said that for the first time in his life he "experienced the other end of racial prejudice. Much of that was done, I feel personally, as a backlash against the humiliation they must have felt at the hands of the French for a hundred years, and now it was their turn to be in the saddle; hence the insistence on the ninety-degree bow to everybody, to see the white man cry, to see the white man bow, to see the white man dirty, to see him urinating in his pants."

While captivity did make Stratton and Hegdahl equals, there were still an age gap and military propriety in their relationship, lines over which neither would cross. Hegdahl had respect for Stratton's rank, age, and education and he was the acknowledged leader. Stratton recognized Hegdahl's courage, native wit, and incredible retentive powers, an ability to memorize with a quick study and recite it literally backward and forward; while Hegdahl was the junior member of the team, Stratton did not treat him as either a batman or a sibling.

"I genuinely liked Doug Hegdahl. He just appeared to me to be a senior in high school that you could exchange ideas with. Doug made a remark once, to this Major Bui we both hated, something like rooming with Stratton is sort of like living with your father. I do not think, though, that he was [my] substitute son. I've done a lot of thinking about that, and I don't think it was a transference.

"I like young people, would like to teach when I get through with my military career, and I have an affinity for them. For some reason I am able to establish rapport with them, probably because I genuinely like them, and I genuinely liked him. As I said, he seemed to me to be just like a senior in high school. I respected him as a person. Of course, I try to respect my own children as individuals, as people. My own philosophy of bringing up children is that they are people and you treat them like people, and as long as they respond in that manner you do not go into this authoritarian regimen. I don't think Doug was a son substitute. I think he was a friend, a young friend, but a friend.

"Doug went to them one time when they were pumping him up and asked, Are you going to send Stratton home, too? And they said, Well, maybe we are going to send him home, but do not tell him. They always told Doug, Don't tell Stratton anything.

" 'Don't tell him *anything*. . . . Stratton's an officer and you're an enlisted man, and if you were back on board ship or back in the United States, Stratton wouldn't even talk to you.'

"Doug came back and he said, 'You know, they told me again not to tell you what we were talking about in there.' And I said,

'Yes.' And he said, 'Well, what we said was . . .' [Later on] he said, 'They told me that you'd never talk to me.' He looked kind of plaintive and looked at me and said, 'You'd talk to me, wouldn't you, if we were back home?' It was really touching in a way. These people were making their point. These people were very subtle, planting their little seeds of doubt."

But the Vietnamese were shrewder than Stratton or Hegdahl gave them credit for being. There was the plan to rid themselves finally of Stratton and, for good publicity, the peasant Hegdahl. Treatment of the two Americans unexpectedly improved: more food and of better quality, served three times a day; kinder looks; little sightseeing trips into Hanoi. [And then, when he was fat, well traveled, and feeling benevolent to his hosts, he could be shipped home, an example of the humane and lenient policies of the Democratic Republic of Vietnam.]

"It appeared to me," insists Richard Stratton, "that as early as 1966, but definitely in 1967, the North Vietnamese were considering sending home American prisoners for various reasons. Now this is all WAG [wild-ass guessing] . . . [but] the Vietnamese wanted to reward the peace movement and strengthen it to prove to a cross section of the American public that the peace movement was indeed [influential]. . . . And I think they were trying to establish that they had a 'lenient and humane' treatment, and if they could find some healthy prisoners who were not antagonistic toward North Vietnam . . . they probably would be able to make inroads in their effort to influence the prisoners. This was a carrot-and-stick approach. The stick was torture, release was the carrot, and now, if you are 'good men,' then you will have a chance to go home. I think they thought, hopefully, they would get a stampede going and we would walk over each other's backs trying to do things for them.

"I think in August 1967 Doug Hegdahl was being prepared to be sent home in September with an [American] reporter and his wife, and there were some others, too. My guess is I was one of them. There were three Air Force officers whom we observed— we did not have contact with them—who were going through the same preparation ritual. They figured they may have to give up three, so they would prepare five or six so they would always have

186

an alternate in case something went wrong at the last minute. But Doug, definitely; and sending me home would counteract this brainwashing publicity they'd received."

Hegdahl was taken alone to the mansion. Major Bui waited for him. It was a brief and relaxed conversation, at least for the commandant. Hegdahl was suspicious. Finally Bui put on his avuncular face, cocked his head, and smiled.

"Heddle, how would you like to go home?"

Just like that, right out of the blue, another piece of fudge. Hegdahl stammered, not sure what the proper response should be. Bui let him off the hook.

"Now, you think about it, Heddle. You go back to your room and think about it, but, Heddle"—and the voice grew stern—"you must not tell Stratton, for he is a very evil man."

Hegdahl was taken back to his cell.

". . . and the Cat says they want to send me home."

Stratton whistled softly, and Hegdahl added, "I asked him if they were going to send you home, too, and the Cat said maybe they would send you home, too, but not to tell you. Well, I am not going. I have an obligation to stay here with you guys."

The argument, in whispered tones, went on for some time and, finally, Stratton turned to face the young sailor directly.

"All right!" He hardened the words for emphasis, and his face darkened with pique, the same way it had when Hegdahl, who had the duty chore that day, had, in haste, not set out their eating utensils so the sun would dry them properly.

"All right! You are a *seaman* and I am a lieutenant commander. I am giving you a direct order. You *will* go home and you *will* take this information out of here if you get the opportunity to go home with honor. And if anyone on the outside gives you any guff about why you've come out, you tell them, and I will stand by it when I come out. If I am wrong in ordering you out of here, then I will accept the responsibility for what I have done and they can have my butt, not yours.

"Do you understand?"

"But Beak, sir, what if they want me to do all kinds of propaganda?"

"Well, they might want you to write a letter of amnesty. I believe the word 'amnesty' implies guilt. Don't use that word unless you can't get out any other way, but if you must use the word 'amnesty,' use it. Doug, that's an order! Accept that release."

"Well, Beak, what about you?"

"Not me, Doug. I think somehow I've hurt them; I get the feeling they would like to get rid of me, and I am not going to let those bastards off the hook."

They agreed that if they were forced to go, either or both, they would go on their own terms, and they would look as poorly as possible. The first victim of their resolve was the special food. Into the honey buckets that night went fresh *pommes frites*. Hegdahl watched numbly as the sweet-smelling, light golden strips of potato were overwhelmed and sank out of sight in his own feces.

Stratton's resolve was firm.

"It seemed to me our release was definitely what they were after and I wanted to make sure I did not go home, because it was important to me; I was just getting the picture of how much damage had been done to them [by my bowing] and it would all be countered if I went home early. That was one point. Another point was . . . an early go-home was a special favor we were not permitted to take under the Code of Conduct. . . . The third thing was you in fact, would be breaking faith. . . . And there's a basic principle in the Navy that you always take care of the enlisted men first. If anyone should go home from Vietnam, it would first be the sick and wounded and second the enlisted men. And Doug was about as enlisted as you could get. Also, he had a very retentive memory (he could recite the Gettysburg Address forwards *and* backwards) and he had acquired and could bring out a lot of information. So if anyone was to go home, and an honest release was possible, he should be the one to go."

Hegdahl felt Stratton's directive was truly heroic, though he shied from using the word because he knew Stratton would disapprove.

"I do not think he would want to be regarded as a, uh, hero. But, back in those days, what he did was a pretty revolutionary thing: that was putting himself on the line, so to speak, giving an order like that. It might be regarded as not being 'correct.' But he was that kind of man; he would not shrink from responsibility, and he felt this was his responsibility.

"I guess what I am saying is that he made a decision that was a very controversial decision, to tell me to accept release which ended up implying that I might have to write a letter using the word 'amnesty.' He felt the information I had about the camps would outweigh the propaganda value of releasing a seaman . . . and he felt, he always felt, since I was not a professional soldier . . . that I hadn't really known what I had gotten into; he had been trained, went through [survival] schools, was an officer, and was trained to take these chances."

The Vietnamese were confused. Something had gone terribly wrong. The Air Force men selected for release appeared to be doing reasonably well; not so Stratton and Hegdahl. For one thing, the special food was making no change in their looks or weight. Guards assigned to check their condition reported this. Secondly, Stratton appeared even less co-operative than before. Was it possible Hegdahl was really so stupid he had *not* told Stratton about the release plans? Anger replaced confusion. Stratton really was a criminal. He would have to be tested. As it turned out, it was a ready-made example of supply and demand.

Stratton says, "I wanted to get off the bandwagon, this Hansel and Gretel routine. [And finally] I think they gave me a little obedience test. At nine o'clock on a Saturday night, they came in and gave me a whole mess of propaganda purportedly written by other Americans [a camp-produced magazine titled *New Runway*] and they wanted me to copy it all, including the drawings. . . . That's the only night they had liberty, Saturday night, so you knew there was something fishy going on when they came in and did that.

"And there was nothing in it that was critical as far as time went, and of course I told them I wouldn't do it."

"Dick's exact words were 'I respectfully refuse,'" said Hegdahl. "He wasn't going to point-blank refuse and this way he got off the [release] bandwagon, and the Vietnamese looked at me like 'he really didn't tell him, did he.' His unco-operativeness really baffled them."

Stratton knew he had flunked his test.

"At that time, any time you refused something usually meant you'd get another beating of some kind and I was concerned about it. I said to Doug, 'Boy, I hope I can do this without getting my tit in the wringer again because I really don't want to get beaten again.' I'd really had enough of that. . . .

"Doug was the eternal optimist. Saturday night went and nothing happened. 'You've got it beat,' he says. Sunday night came and nothing happened. 'You've got it beat,' he says, 'got it beat.' 'Aw, c'mon,' I said. 'That's just because they don't work on Sunday around here. They're too lazy. You wait!'

"Monday, we are out carrying stones or something and he kept saying, 'You got it beat, Beak' (he was a great morale booster), and right then, about ten in the morning, they whistled me over and dressed me up in full pajamas and took me over to the Cat. There's Major Bui sitting there; he says, 'You are going to write that.'

" 'No. I am not going to write it.'

" 'That is unfortunate. I stood to ease your way out of here, Stratton. Now I ask you one more time. Will you obey my order and write that?'

"Actually, I was quite polite to this guy because he was a senior officer and at that time I was trying to maintain a certain measure of American dignity—at least with the seniors—because they were calling us criminals and animals. I wanted to show that they couldn't beat us down. So with a measure of military respect (he was equal in rank to me), I said, 'Thanks very much for coming down and trying to help me out' (I knew he was trying to crucify me), 'but my decision is made. I cannot do that kind of thing because it is against my Code of Conduct, and I accept full responsibility for the consequences of my actions' (which used to be a favorite saying of theirs)."

Major Bui was furious. It was now a matter of face. Stratton, a prisoner, could not be allowed to defy an order.

Stratton was marched under guard to a room in the back of a long building called the Warehouse. As he passed through the baffled entry constructed like that of a photographer's darkroom, a guard was on a stool unscrewing the light bulb from its socket. The guard climbed down, the others left, and the door was closed and bolted. There were no windows. Pinheads of light seeped through random holes in the ceiling and walls, but essentially the room was black: no walls, no floor or ceiling, no sound, no night, no day, just a black bubble suspended in time.

* * *

There is a survival training center at Fort Belvoir, Virginia, for young Army lieutenants who may, in the event of another war, become prisoners. The camp incorporates experiences learned in Vietnam. For example, outright defiance of captors is discouraged in favor of more subtle forms of resistance. Those who choose to be hard eggs, answering belligerently or defiantly, are put into the Belvoir version of a dark room: a two-and-one-half-by-six-foot locker buried in the ground.

The maximum confinement is ten minutes.[12]

In Vietnam in August of 1967, it took Richard Stratton about ten minutes to regain control of his emotions. The day went by, and another, maybe, and another, maybe, and another. He lost track of time.

More days.

He chatted with God; thought about Alice; thought about the boys; thought about clams; thought. Talked to hear his own voice. Felt the dimensions of his black bubble.

More days.

More.

What made the dark all the more terrifying was that he could not defend himself against attack from cockroaches and rats, who literally battled him for his bread ration. Finally, when he heard the rats coming, he would break off a piece of crust and throw it away from his body. The rats left him alone. The cockroaches were not fooled. They scrambled for the bread, crawled over his face as he tried to get the food into his mouth. He never knew how many of those dreadful insects he ate.

The heat and the dankness of the place soon eroded his skin, and a terrible itch seized his genitals and moved slowly over his body and up to his chest. He could not shave, nor was his hair trimmed.

Three weeks, maybe, give or take a century. He was losing. He knew they were going to beat him, break him again. There were blanks of time in his mind; he was hallucinating. He lost his grip on sanity. He thrashed, striking out, and suddenly the black somewhere struck back. Noise! He heard thumps; and when his mind stabilized, he heard the tap code, the sweet sounds of the tap code, the sheer symphony of a hand thumping against a wall. There was somebody in the next cell. A trick?

No; the thumps said it was Major Jack Van Loan of the Air Force; Van Loan quickly realized Stratton was in trouble. Communications were soon set up, and Van Loan soothed Stratton, brought him back into a time frame, gave him news, and, more important, time hacks. Stratton was saved.

"The communication is what saved me. Realization that others had gone through it and were able to recoup and that other people have their problems, too, and that I wasn't the Lone Ranger spitting silver bullets.

"Picture twenty-five days [in this room] when you start to lose your marbles and you realize you have gone through half of the day and you don't know what time it is or where you are or what you are doing.

"Jack Van Loan had marks for the sun out in the yard which they could look at through their holes [like a rudimentary sun dial]. This guy gave me a time hack thereafter, every hour. Even when the guards were in his room shaking down his cell, he would, with his hands up against the wall in the classic frisking pose, bang his head against the wall and give me the time tick so I could maintain my sanity and survive."

He searched the blackness and found a nail he had missed in his first days, and with it he drilled some holes in the boards covering what had once been a window or ventilation port. He worked and worked on the holes, enlarging them, adding more to make a pattern, and when the light was right he would stand and walk toward them in the manner of an aircraft following runway lights at night. He regained his balance, and slowly exercised flaccid muscles.

"And everything started working out. I could continue indefinitely."

He continued for forty-eight days.

* * *

The October 20 edition of *Life* magazine carried still pictures taken by the Germans Heynowski and Scheumann. The report, "U. S. Prisoners in Vietnam," said *Life,* provided "the only glimpse so far available of prison life in North Vietnam."

The cover featured a photograph of Navy Lieutenant Paul Galanti (who had been bagged June 17, 1966) sitting in the large Stratton/Hegdahl cell under the words "Clean & Neat."

Lamented *Life:* "Suddenly the fate of these [captured] U.S. servicemen is in the hands of God and the enemy. . . . Just as

Vietnam is no ordinary war neither are the Americans who fall captive treated in the orderly way prescribed by the Geneva Prisoner of War Convention of 1949. As justification for its way of doing things, the Hanoi government, which signed the Geneva agreement in 1957, cites the fact that this is an undeclared war—though the Convention covers not only declared war, but also any other armed conflict.

"Thus, North Vietnam treats its prisoners almost as nonbeings. It refuses to let the Red Cross make inspections, refuses regular exchange of mail and relief packages, refuses even to reveal the number of prisoners or location of camps where they are held. Occasionally, prisoners are subjected to public harassment, paraded through the streets and reviled as 'air pirates' and 'war criminals.'

"Early this year, one captured U.S. flier, Lieutenant Commander Richard Stratton, was put on display at a Hanoi press conference and 'confessed' his 'crimes.' But the intended propaganda effect of this zombie-like performance backfired and Hanoi was charged in many quarters with brainwashing. To counteract this, Hanoi has allowed certain visitors inside what appears to be a model prison housing thirty to forty Americans. . . .

"The U.S. government believes the camp is a deception and that many pictures have been staged. Ambassador-at-large Averell Harriman denounces them as a 'travesty.' Other U.S. experts see disturbing parallels to harsh treatment meted out to American prisoners half a generation ago in North Korea. . . ."

There were photographs of the "capture" of an "air pirate," photos of camp-written magazines like *New Runway*, of the massive luncheon complete with new trays, bananas, pineapples, and soups, of an Easter mass, and of Hegdahl and Stratton solemnly sweeping in the yard and taking a shower, and the terrifying picture of Stratton alone in a huge and barren cell. There was another remarkable picture that somehow escaped those persons in charge of such things: an American prisoner, his back defiantly turned toward the photographer, with the middle finger of each hand stiff and extended. *Life* sidebarred the main photo piece with a clever series of interviews with and candid snapshots of some of the kin of known captives.

"He looks so good, you want to have him home right now,"

Alice Stratton told *Life* correspondent Margery Byers. Looking at the East German photographs, she continued, "I know he is all right in these pictures."

Byers asked about Alice's reaction to Lee Lockwood's bowing picture, and the response was cautious and laconic.

"Well, that was a bad day. It was horrible." And, "Whatever was wrong then, he's better now."

In understated prose, Byers wrote of the interview:

". . . sitting at ease in the sunlit living room of her comfortable West Coast home, Mrs. Stratton displays an outward calm. She looks at the pictures taken by the East Germans, noting her husband's familiar cropped haircut. She smiles, 'I'm encouraged,' she says.

"Brushing aside her own worries, she speaks with compassion of those whose men are listed as missing. 'That takes real courage,' she says, 'going day to day and not even knowing that there's a warm body over there.'

"Mrs. Stratton recently moved to a new house to be near some of her and her husband's old friends. Neighbors pop in and out, the phone rings often. Coping with her three young sons helps fill her days. 'I don't have time to think,' she says, obviously grateful to have it that way. 'It really isn't a problem with me.' Her youngest son, who is almost two, doesn't remember his father, but his brothers, four and six, often talk about Daddy. Patrick, the six-year-old, frequently asks when the war will be over so that his father can come home.

"She has been told that prisoners in North Vietnam may receive one letter a month, weighing not more than twenty grams [a little more than half an ounce]—'letter, envelope and stamp,' she says ruefully. The three she has received from Stratton are full of family talk, and to her, the tone and handwriting ring true. 'Consider this a long cruise,' he wrote in the first letter. . . ."

Alice Stratton chose not to be photographed; instead, she gave Byers a ten-year-old picture of her husband, her "favorite picture," a left three-quarter profile taken when he was a lieutenant (j.g.) in 1957, a small, black and white that de-emphasized the nose and showed a sensitive, strong mouth and firm jawline. It must have been something of a shock for *Life* readers to see it and compare it with the scowling countenance of the same man on the preceding page.

Byers also interviewed Abe and Edith Hegdahl in Clark, South Dakota.

"The Hegdahls worry," Byers wrote, "about simple things— whether he has enough books to read, whether the prisoners can visit each other, how his teeth are (they spent the usual fortune straightening them), whether he salvaged his glasses. 'I hope he remains the same boy he's been,' Mrs. Hegdahl says softly. 'He's full of heck, a practical joker, always smiling and everybody liked him. He didn't talk religion or talk pious, but he never missed church.'"

* * *

Late on the afternoon of August 20, the guards returned to the cell to gather up Stratton's gear; Hegdahl was gathered up as well and taken to the mansion for a brief talk with Major Bui.

"He gave me a look like, You dumb shit! You really didn't tell Stratton, did you? I think they were working to get to Stratton through me, to give him a taste of the good life, to get him to accept release. I think they were really surprised. My God, they could not imagine anyone jeopardizing his own release, but how could they punish me for doing what they had told me to do?

"For a couple of more days, I think they toyed with the idea of [my] release and they were still giving me fattening-up food. I was back in solitary and still throwing the food in the shitcan (and during that winter I thought, my God, what had I done, throwing all that food away? That was a real grim winter). Anyway, I was still throwing all that rich food in the shitcan and then they dropped it. One day it just ended. On September 9 I was moved back in with Joe Crecca, and we were together until November 30. During the time I was with him, I met those two delegations: Tom Hayden's and the Women's Strike for Peace."

Hegdahl's meeting with the Women's Strike for Peace occurred two days after he was reunited with Crecca. The delegation consisted of Mary Clarke, Ruth Krause, and Dagmar Wilson, all active in a variety of committees and councils opposed to the war; they were visiting Hanoi as guests of the North Vietnamese

195

Women's Union in Hanoi. Hegdahl was "informed" he would meet the group one day before the actual meeting. He was warned, as he had been before the Dellinger interview, not to discuss the organization of the camp or its conditions.

According to Hegdahl, the interview was held in a room at the Plantation's mansion. The women were seated at a table with some of their Vietnamese hosts; Hegdahl sat alone at another table. Hegdahl was told by one member of the group they were in Hanoi "to reveal the devastation in Vietnam . . . and take back the true facts to the American people." Hegdahl asked if they were Communists. No, was the reply, and then as an afterthought: "What's wrong with the Communists?"

Hegdahl did not answer. After the interview, the women were allowed to view Hegdahl's cell. When Hegdahl had been in solitary, after Stratton left, his small cell had contained a bed and a toilet bucket. Now he and Crecca both had beds, there were a table and stools, and the place had been scrubbed clean by the two men the day before on orders of Major Bui. Hegdahl recalled that the women commented that the cell, while "bare," was no worse than conditions for the average Vietnamese.

Several days later, the camp's loudspeakers broadcast a tape in which the women deplored the war and its injustices. "I am sure you all want the war to end so you can go home," and, "It was too bad you had to be caught up in this unjust war."

In the October issue of *MEMO,* the house organ of the Women's Strike for Peace, a photograph of the meeting was published showing the three American women on the left, the young American prisoner on the right. The photograph had been cropped, making it appear the four sat at the same small table.

The meeting with Hayden and his anti-war delegation of six occurred a month later. Hegdahl sat on a low footstool; the other Americans sat on chairs in a semicircle around him. One of the group was Rennie Davis; the others were four young women and a man dressed in the garb of an Anglican or Episcopal priest. The priest chattered to no one in particular about his anti-war record, which gave Hegdahl a chance to look over the others; it was obvious, he says, that Hayden was the leader, though precisely *who* he was and who Davis was he did not know. As the minister talked on, Hegdahl caught Hayden's eye and, as the anti-war leader

196

stared in surprise, Hegdahl balled his fist and stiffly hoisted his middle finger. Hayden smiled and returned the gesture.

Hegdahl remained noncommittal to the few questions he was asked and steered the conversation to the Beatles rock group; that discussion, he recalled, took up just about all the remaining time. This was an outright defiance of orders, for he had been instructed to say he believed the American forces should be withdrawn from Vietnam.

Why were they there? Says Hegdahl, "It seemed to me they just came over because they wanted to see the conditions in Vietnam, and they asked to see prisoners and they were allowed to come and see me."

On November 11, 1967, the Vietcong released into the care of Thomas Hayden two captured U. S. Army sergeants, Daniel Pitzer and James Jackson; a third sergeant, Edward R. Johnson, was pronounced seriously ill and released privately. The releases were made in Pnompenh in a ceremony conducted by a diplomatic representative of the National Liberation Front, the parent organization of the Vietcong. Hayden told reporters that "the idea for releasing some American prisoners was first broached in September at a conference in Czechoslovakia of forty American intellectuals and Vietnamese Communists."

There were about two dozen American correspondents in Pnompenh, admitted to Cambodia to cover a one-week visit of Mrs. Jacqueline Kennedy. They remained after Mrs. Kennedy's departure to cover the preannounced release. Only two were permitted at the actual ceremony. By contrast, a Soviet television crew and thirty other communist and "carefully selected" correspondents were admitted.

* * *

Hegdahl was returned to solitary at the end of November after he and Crecca were caught communicating with two fliers in an adjoining cell. He was closely questioned and severely chastised but was not otherwise abused. In another turnabout, he was given a new roommate on December 10, an Air Force junior officer named Tom Smith. Hegdahl for once would have preferred solitary.

"Nothing bugs me more than to hear . . . somebody say the

197

officers behaved themselves so good [in captivity] because they *were* officers, and gentlemen. Well, this guy was an [Air Force] Academy graduate, for crying out loud . . . and he would complain, 'I'm just cannon fodder,' and he would cry and carry on and moan. [He was] a totally self-centered guy, requesting special food all the time from the Vietnamese, *and getting it!*

"I was so pissed off at him one time for getting special food that I broke off some of my bread and put it on the dish for [the American POW] dishwashers. I said to him, 'I don't know if you understand this, but there's only so much bread they bring into this camp, and if you get special food, that means somebody else's rations are cut back.'

"He said, 'Oh, bullshit, oh, bullshit.' Finally, he took a little piece and threw it [on the plate]. . . . 'But ah'm soo hongry.' He was a real baby. He was one of the guys released in the first group."

* * *

On one of his infrequent trips outside his black room, Stratton had gotten the impression that he might end his solitary by seeing a delegation due in Hanoi in September. He did not acknowledge the hint. With Van Loan's wall taps, he would stay in their fucking hole till hell froze over or the war ended, whichever came first.

On his next trip (while his cell was being searched for any contraband he might have acquired) he was blinded by sunlight, slipped, and fell into a sewage ditch that ran along the side of the building. His face smashed into the stucco wall, "and every wound that I ever got in Vietnam turned into livid red, then purple, and stayed that way for about six months; I was a thing of rare beauty"—and hardly presentable to a visiting peace group.

"So because the [delegation] thing falls through, there's no need to keep me in there, and I wasn't going to break, and I think they realized it."

Finally an interrogator paid a social call.

"Stratton, if you apologize to the camp commander, we will let you out of the blacked-out room."

"What do you mean, apologize?"

"Oh, I don't know why you put yourself in a position to be severely punished. All you have to say to the camp commander is 'I apologize,' and you are free. But if you do not say that"—and the words took an edge here—"if you do not say that, we will *severely* punish you!"

They were literally giving him the code words out, an acceptable answer. Stratton capitulated.

"So I said, 'Oh, my goodness. I did not realize I had offended the poor camp commander. I would be delighted to say "I apologize" to the camp commander.'

"'Oh, you will?'

"So they run in the camp commander, who's obviously been standing around the corner; they go out and get mushmouth and he runs in and says, 'I understand you have something to say to me.' And I said, 'I understand my behavior offended you and [sarcastically] I wish to apologize.'

"'Oh, you are a good man.'

"And they bring me out of that room and into another room that's blacked out; five minutes later, a guard comes in with a smile on his face and a light bulb in his hand and screws it in. You are a good man! So it's all over.

"Now, they had bigger fish to fry and, I think, they had decided it was the end of the road for the bowing incident, that they had protested too much and it was getting them into deeper kimchee and they had gotten all of the mileage they could get out of me. I think that was the break: When they told me, gave me the answer to tell mushmouth, I apologize, it was a whole new ball game.

"It was not clear-cut; it was a transition; I still did not know whether the [torture] ropes were right around the corner or not. I did end up [getting beaten badly again] . . . considerably later, supposedly after the brutality had stopped in the spring of 1970."

PART V

DIGRESSIONS
1967–1969

CHAPTER 18

When questioned, should I become a prisoner of war, I am bound to give only name, rank, service number and date of birth. I will evade answering further questions to the utmost of my ability. I will make no oral or written statements disloyal to my country and its allies or harmful to their cause.

—Paragraph 5,
The Code of Conduct

The professional military environment is all but alien and incomprehensible to workaday civilians. Further, in a republic that until recently utilized periodic citizen armies, raised desperately in crisis and disbanded quickly in peace, there is great distrust of professional military men who do not go into mothballs with the excess tanks and destroyers.

The Founding Fathers saw grave danger in maintaining a standing army. Hamilton, writing as "Publius" in the Federalist essays of 1787–88, warned: "The violent destruction of life and property incident to war, the continual effort and alarm attendant on a state of continual danger, will compel nations the most attached to liberty to resort for repose and security to [standing armies] which have a tendency to destroy their civil and political rights. To be more safe, they at length become willing to run the risk of being less free."[1]

Understandably, the professional military officer thinks of himself not as a debaucher of liberty but as the defender of it; he views with distrust the citizen, or at least that citizen who casts aspersions or unwarranted criticism upon the service, or hamstrings its mobility by shutting off or reducing funds necessary for its maintenance. This is alien and incomprehensible to the professional.

For, quite simply, careerists see themselves as extensions of the state. Richard Stratton uses a medical analogy: "The air arm of the Navy is a scalpel; it does the cutting. But somebody upstairs at the White House or the State Department determines the operation is necessary. . . . The Commander in Chief of the Pacific is the master surgeon and he does the cutting. I am the cutting edge."

And Richard Mullen's stark assessment is: "We are military representatives of the American people."

And writer Ward Just, whose understanding of the military environment is as thorough as any, adds a contemporary note: "Identifying the [military services] with the society can, with brisk logic, become the vice versa. In a nuclear age a military man naturally confuses one with the other; in an atmosphere of more or less permanent menace, military strength is the one thing that makes all the other things possible. For a society to succeed, it must first be secure. To be secure, it must be strong. From the perspective of the professional soldier then, the very life of the society depends on the quality of its military force, both men and machines, but mostly men."[2]

There is no stronger fealty than that of a professional military man to his nation, his commander in chief, his service, and his fellow officers—not necessarily in that order. The professional military begins at the service academies, at West Point and Annapolis and Colorado Springs. The Corps of Cadets furnish MacArthurs, Pattons, Marshalls, Halseys, and Zumwalts, thirty-eight-year-old colonels and forty-two-year-old admirals. Teen-age plebes are early weaned from civilian life and civilian laxness: the military with its rules and codes and orders and disciplines becomes parent, habitat, environment.

And then there is the peereval: from the moment the young man (and, now, young woman) steps onto the sacred soil, he is subject to the peer evaluation system. Its impact at that moment, and through the remainder of the professional's military career, cannot be overemphasized. Peer pressure and peer evaluation can make or break a tyro, can wash him out of flight school, can drum him out of the corps or force him into the ranks. For the evaluations are done not only by officers and instructors but by the other cadets: the boys you room with, sleep with, play football with, suffer hazing with, eat with. Constantly your closest friend, your most distant enemy, are looking over your shoulder evaluating your performance, your attitude, your attention to orders, your responses, your appearance, in class, out of class, at work or at leisure, in the clattery din of Commons, in the quiet of your room. The academy codes of honor allow no extenuating circumstances. If you foul up, even your closest friend must write you up. The intensity of structured military peerevals is matched perhaps only by the group cruelty of children, whose need for homogeny can in a wink exile the obese girl, the defective boy, the terrified crybaby, the colored alien.

There is a rationale for this in the military: before a man can be a good general, he must be a flawless private performing assigned tasks without hesitation, without quibbling, without lying. If in combat a professional tells you his rockets have eliminated the impeding snipers' nest and you can now move your troops into the area, you can move your troops into the area because the snipers are indeed smeared over the landscape. You need have no fear for your platoon. You can have faith in the professional's word and judgment; his peers still watch.

The professional military environment with its standards of discipline, its codes of honor, its view of the world in hazard potential, is a society nearly unbreachable by those whose lives are lived in mufti. A price of failure in a civilian job is, at worst, eyestrain from scanning the want ads, perhaps a shattered ego or marriage; for the military officer, it is life, perhaps his own, certainly his troops, conceivably his nation's.

In "Soldiers" Ward Just quotes Marcus Aurelius quoting Plato quoting Socrates:

" 'The truth of the matter is this, gentlemen. Where a man has once taken his stand, either because it seems best to him or in obedience to his orders, there I believe he is bound to remain and face the danger, taking no account of death or anything else before dishonor.'

"That is the Roman standard, and the romantic conception of the hero in America as well: a man disciplined and obedient, brave and fatalistic, Gary Cooper on a street without joy. The Prussians call it *Stramm,* military qualities, more precisely, military bearing, without which no soldier could succeed."[3]

Within the military environment the training and competition, the tradition and standards of academy men, set them apart from all others who wear the uniform. They are princes of the realm, the blood royal, not earls or dukes or lords who, no less noble in bearing, have nonetheless entered an exclusive society by common means.

The ideals set by the military academies filter down through the military society. (One can imagine the shock of a somewhat worldly twenty-five-year-old Richard Stratton in Officer Candidate School being evaluated on his attitudes by gung-ho youths four and five years his junior. Once the initial shock passed, the impression stuck.) And while a Richard Stratton could politely (but not literally) thumb his nose at the military establishment, it was unthinkable for him now to do so at his peers. Whatever his claims to being something of a physically inept, lumbering dolt, a rebel, they must be viewed either as exaggeration or his own peculiar brand of self-deprecating humor. Were it otherwise, the peerevals would have, to use one of his own favorite expressions, nailed him right between the running lights. He would have washed out of OCS, out of flight school, out of tactical training, maybe right out of the Navy.

Contrarily, there was no way at his "advanced" age that even the military could completely suppress his natural independent nature, that shard of fine Irish madness that had always set him apart from other boys, other men. And when, finally, in a prison camp in North Vietnam, he stood against the traditions of the military establishment, he found himself a survivor—thanks to his personality—but a survivor in deep, deep trouble with his peers.

It was something of an irony.

Facing the enemy, any enemy, on the battlefield or in a prison camp, the professional accommodates himself to fate. In extremity, as Just puts it, he acts alone, on "inner motion."[4]

Herein, precisely, lay Richard Stratton's dilemma.

* * *

"Someone eventually is going to sit down and figure out which is the best way to resist the enemy under certain circumstances; there's [one] school of thought that is hard-line straight-on meet the enemy every time. I maintain a person like myself cannot do that for ten years and survive and come home with honor. God did not give me a very strong physique, I am not a strong man physically, nor a well-co-ordinated man, and I am not an athlete by nature or by temperament. But God did give me a brain, and I have a certain practical Irish sense that I picked up from my parents. Everybody had their own forte and mine was to get into their knickers in a different way, and my fellows would not give me that credit.

"Once I found out that I was unable, physically, to battle the enemy, it was a very crushing blow. . . . This idea of endless pain, I couldn't hack it; I couldn't take what they had to hand out. (They were not going to kill me, that was obvious. Because I would cheerfully die, that doesn't bother me one bit. I am prepared to meet my maker, I hope, knock on wood, at any time. . . . Supposedly you live in this world to go to eternity anyway. What is the difference if it is today or tomorrow?) I had to try to develop another method of [resistance] whereby I could exist for [a decade]. My way was an even pull for a long haul: if you are going to succeed and not come out of there a mental vegetable . . . you damn well better not shoot your wad on the first go. So I was thinking . . . of other ways to resist them, the bowing session, for example; the picture of me sitting alone on the bunk in the big cell scowling, my natural visage; giving a subtle finger and ruining a picture."

The Vietnamese are essentially a prudish people, and very conscious of their image. It must have come as a terrible shock to their morality and a blow to their "face" when some Western visitor explained to them that an erect American middle finger (such as appeared in a photograph of a POW in *Life* magazine) was an obscene and impudent gesture.

206

"Stratton! Stratton, you criminal, you even give the vagabond sign!"

"Huh? Vagabond sign? What do you mean, vagabond sign?"

"You know what I mean. The vagabond sign. *This!* To the pigs, to the women, to everybody you give the vagabond sign. You even do it in church! You . . . you are an animal!"

"The Vietnamese had me pegged as a troublemaker because they kept throwing me back in solitary every once in a while for four or five months. They just couldn't stand me and they were watching me like a hawk. They don't do that with their friends. So I had no trouble convincing the V. I was resisting.

"Because my approach was different, the hardest time I had was with my fellow prisoners, and their lack of understanding. We worked together very well. It's just I knew they had these doubts about me. I knew some of them didn't like me and everybody wants to be liked, especially in a hellhole like that, and it was just the damnedest, toughest time trying to establish with somebody, I'm resisting. I'm resisting in my own way."

But Stratton had stood against tradition and had brought down upon his head the wrath of the so-called hard-liners, and of the "super-heroes" within the society of the prisoners, which numbered more than one Naval Academy graduate among its ranks.

"The hard-liners," said Stratton, "fought the V. right down the line. They used to think every time you saw a gook, you kicked him in the nuts. . . . They had been broken and they could never forgive themselves; part of the way they healed themselves was to exhort all sorts of people to do what they wished they could have done."

There was an added complication here: for a civilian in a foreign jail, there is no implication that his behavior while a prisoner affects his future career. Every military man knows his actions in prison, to the contrary, have everything to do with his future. No matter what the conditions, he is always subject to military tradition and military law; upon repatriation, he may face reprimand or, worse, court-martial and disgrace if he has behaved poorly, dishonorably, or illegally, or was thought to have done so. This knowledge can have profound effects on a man in prison, and later on in his readjustment to freedom.

Stratton's resistance methods angered the hard-liners to a considerable degree and his reputation among those at the main prison, Hoa Lo, and at another camp, Alcatraz, reserved exclusively for the hardest of the hard, was, to put it mildly, unsavory. This was not the case at Stratton's own camp, the Plantation.

When Stratton had been released from the black room, the Vietnamese apparently were content to let him stew in the trouble of his own making. It is all but inconceivable to believe the Vietnamese were unaware that Stratton was as unpopular with many of his comrades as he was with his captors. Major Bui, the commandant of prisons, was not an ignorant man, and he spoke and understood English well, if not the fly-boy idiom.

Stratton had humiliated Bui and his aides, had jeopardized their careers, had caused them and the Fatherland to lose face. Now it would be Stratton's turn: there was no more talk about going home; there would be no more public appearances, for he could not be trusted; there were other ways, other humiliations. A picture of Stratton smiling, looking at pictures of wife and children (and Bui had such a picture), would humiliate Stratton. If Stratton were in trouble with his colleagues, that knowledge could be used to keep him in line. Stratton would do for the camp; Bui probably remembered that once Stratton had read the camp news over the loudspeakers; he had been "rewarded," given a lid for his teacup. The man had nearly wept out of fury, and humiliation.

Stratton was neutered.

If this was the major's thinking, he was wrong.

* * *

"[The other prisoners] needed me; they couldn't make me an outcast. Had I been in the Hoa Lo system altogether, I'd have been an outcast. But because I was moved to the Plantation, I was one of their main strengths. I had a wealth of information others didn't have about the prison system and what the V. were doing.

"When I hooked up with Jack Van Loan, I found out about the whole bowing incident and Harriman's statements and the Department of State's statements and . . . I had everything in perspective, and that's one of the ways I was able to determine [the Vietnamese] had gotten all the mileage they could out of me. . . . It was safe to go on another track. Senior officers had come and gone and were always kept in isolation. [With Van Loan, my reputation] was pretty good. Van Loan knew me as a result of the dark room and he had developed confidence in me. I was able to give the rules and regulations. No matter what I may have done, I was always preaching and acting in that situation on the hard line, *but within reason.* I wasn't saying [give only] name, rank, serial number, date of birth. I was preaching . . . that the war here [in the prison camps] was not for military information, it was for propaganda.

"They were taking people directly from the shoot-downs without torturing them and bringing them directly to the Plantation, and they were having a field day with them until we could get a hold of the new prisoners and let them know what the hell was going on, that they were being used, and what the V. were really after: propaganda.

"The best thing we could do was minimize the V.'s net gains. And: you're no good if you got yourself tortured like I did, ended up like a mess of putty without your wits about you. So push them as far as you can at any one time and make sure that they're not bluffing, and once you realize they're not bluffing, then you go into a mode of minimizing their net gain.

"Most of the people I was dealing with knew that I had been through it, were convinced that, indeed, I had been tortured and not making up the story. Some guys did make up a story, claimed things that weren't true to explain why they did something, were less than honest, and the lie always came out.

"So they knew I was true. They all saw the marks, and the marks really helped. The [Vietnamese] really screwed up. After they got through with me, they used to torture guys with shirts on because it left fewer marks, smaller marks. Marks were obviously a passport: yuh, we saw the marks. He obviously has been abused. That established credibility.

"I think largely because of our efforts, Van Loan's efforts, Charlie [Navy Lieutenant Commander Joseph Charles] Plumb's efforts, my efforts, Doug Hegdahl's efforts, we were able to do this, and what was supposed to be a patsy camp ended up falling flat on its face, ended up being just like the other prisons. It had its hard-liners and its soft-liners and an over-all mix of personalities."

By late 1969, after the death of President Ho Chi Minh and the organization of the National League of Families in the United States—made up of POW and missing-in-action families—things in the prison camp appeared slightly less bleak. Torture of prisoners virtually disappeared, food improved, and discipline, in some of the camps, anyway, was less severe.

Major Bui would vanish (presumably disgraced), never to be seen again by any American.

But conditions were not entirely rosy. Some men were still beaten. That much had not changed, at least for those unlucky few who felt the truncheons or rubber whips of the guards.

There was nearly always a price tag on a beating. It was not simply a matter of refusing a request by camp officials, receiving punishment, and that was the end of it. After the punishment came penance: a written apology, a signed statement of continuing lenient and humane treatment and thanks for it to the Vietnamese people, meeting a delegation, taping something, "doing for the camp." In Stratton's case, more often than not, it was taping the "news" for the camp radio.

"The camp commander would say, 'I order you to tape the news over the camp intercom system.' And I would say, 'I will not do it.'

"'You will do it, and you will order the others to do it and we will beat you if you don't do it, and we will beat you again and you will do it again.'

"'Okay. Beat me.'

"They did.

"So okay. I'll tape your damn [news] until I get my strength back, and then I'll challenge you again.

"I was moved at this point [June 1, 1970] back to Hoa Lo, the main prison, and into an area where they are holding the guys from Alcatraz—the real hard-liners. So I walk in there, taping, and they're pissed off to a fare-thee-well. Captain Thaddeus B. Hoyt[5] sends a message through saying it is my order, as acting senior ranking officer, that you not tape. Give only name, rank, serial number, and date of birth.

"Well, I send a message back saying you may think torture and beating are over, but I have just been beaten and I am rolling now (that was our expression), and when I get back my strength, I'll challenge them again; but it's going to be a long war, Charlie, and I am going to do it at my own pace.

"Well, this was unacceptable to him; first, he did not believe I had been beaten, and second of all, there was [my] 'confession.'

"[Hoyt expressed doubts about Stratton's credibility with regard to his initial torture session (which, he said, was too fast and accelerated to be wholly believed) and the attempted removal of his thumbnails (Stratton did that himself, flailing about the rough tile floor).] Well, this was hilarious after [hearing] Hoyt's story; he'd been through the same wringer I had. If anyone should have been sympathetic with me, it was him. He had 'confessed' to 'war crimes' and he had been before delegations and he had made all these statements. [Now] he was telling me the V. were through with physical brutality: 'They won't lay a hand on you.' And I said, 'I am sorry. I do not believe you . . . because I have just been through it.'

"So there he's down on me until, finally, as more people move in, my [Plantation Camp] reputation catches up with me, and he is basically silenced. And, indeed, I did stop taping, and, indeed, I got gradually back on the communications network. One of the things I was able to do was establish communications and liaisons, and able to relay policies that made sense . . . getting people to work together, and stuff like that. That eventually wore him down."

Down, perhaps, but not out.

When the prisoners of war were repatriated, each man filed peerevals, fitness reports on the men they had worked with or been in contact with. In the last years of imprisonment, the POWs set themselves up as a military organization, with a chain of command right on down to recommendations for awards and decorations.

Thaddeus Hoyt had his revenge.

"He really did. He gave me a bad one. I sure was disappointed. It came through Commander James B. Stockdale [one of the senior POWs, and a hard-liner who, Stratton says, gradually accepted Stratton's method of resistance and was himself, in turn, assailed for weakness by some of his fellow officers in the prison system] and Stockdale passed it along, but nonetheless softened anything

211

[Hoyt] had to say. Of course, [Hoyt] stands out; he is the only one who had anything bad to say about me. But [Hoyt's] a little bit demented, to my mind, anyway."

"Many who have engaged in intensive interviews with returned prisoners of war," writes psychologist William Miller, "are convinced that for some prisoners, the complete and candid revelation of all their thoughts, fears, and actions in prison are necessary for good, psychological catharsis and rehabilitation. A number of men have a strong desire to 'tell it like it was.' At the same time, the career military men are aware of what they must project in order to earn a reputation of having maintained a posture of maximum resistance and strength in the prison situation. It will take an exceptional career man to divulge behavior at variance with this model.

"The result of this dilemma is that men are considerably less than candid, deny certain behaviors, omit others, and, generally, paint their experiences in the best possible light. Whether they can live comfortably with this deception for the rest of their lives is an individual matter."[6]

CHAPTER 19

> . . . The missing is always underneath. One day
> when I went shopping at the PX . . . I saw a
> young officer from behind. He was putting on his
> hat, and the tears came streaming down.
>
> —Alice Stratton, 1969

Alice Stratton inhabited a world that most of us, fortunately, can only speculate upon. As with living with a dreadful illness, one must be stricken to understand: to hurt in a white, sterile bed in a room of institutional green, or cling desperately to the rim of the world in a sanatorium; how else to comprehend the despair of helplessness, nightmares and periodic insomnia, and flashes of rage that descended upon that woman as sudden and uncontrollable as a summer line storm; how else to reason with unexplained guilt or self-loathing, sudden erosion of self-confidence, unexpected frenzies of joy over otherwise insignificant suggestions of hope; how else to accept the fragility of human courage?

It is overstating the case to compare Richard Stratton's predicament in Hanoi with his wife's in Palo Alto; but certainly both were victims, trapped by circumstance. If Stratton accommodated himself to fate, acted alone on "inner motion," so, too, did Alice. There is but a slim body of study on military families pitched into this quandary. One of the most recent dealt specifically with Vietnam casualties and the inherent difficulties of women like Alice Stratton:

213

". . . Among other tasks, mothers assumed greater responsibility for making decisions, disciplining the children and handling family finances. The children inherited father-related responsibilities including a heightened awareness of a responsiveness to the mothers' demands and needs. Those family members assuming such responsibility were called upon to lengthen their commitment in recognition of the fact that their father might not return. Many wives reported in the interviews that their relationship with the children was perhaps a closer one than it would have been had the father been present at home. The statistic indicating 'time for dual mother-father role' as being a lesser problem is deceptive; while it may be true that the *time* required to perform the roles may be of little consequence, the responsibilities were perplexing as well as difficult to cope with.

"Even under normal conditions it is difficult for the average mother to raise a family single-handedly. The PW/MIA wife had total responsibility for the family and planning for its future. She often experienced feelings of frustration and guilt, realizing that she was to be held accountable by her husband for whatever the outcome of her efforts upon his release."[7]

Even the most mature and stable among us can experience emotional problems under stress. Alice Stratton's public image was not only that of a mature and stable woman, but of one unflappable and cool under fire, so to speak, all that mythic stuff assigned the ideal military wife and handed down (no doubt by military men) through unnumbered millennia since patient Penelope endured two decades of chaste loneliness (and assaults on her wine cellar) waiting for her wandering Ulysses. This is not to sneer at Alice Stratton's image, which was outwardly calm, or her chastity, which was inviolate, or to diminish her courage, which was hardly mythic. Rather, it is to explain that underneath that stylish façade, which she shed occasionally in the privacy of her home, lived a very real and troubled woman, as vulnerable as any of us.

Several years earlier, when Alice Stratton was a student and a potential instructor at the university camp for troubled children, she was required to undergo—as were all the staff—a psychological examination. The results of that test, her professor confided, showed she was a person too careful about revealing her true feelings; it showed, too, there was some anger. One day, she was warned, it might cause problems. And surely it did.

"[That anger] caused me trouble when I was alone with the boys. Having to deal with the problem of those young children over and over, and constant aloneness, I would get furious at times, and experience feelings of rage. I would get it with Patrick because he was difficult. It was difficult to raise those boys alone. Even though you had a lot of support from family and friends, there were times when you were all alone in your house. You are [already] uptight about a lot of things, the children are being children, doing kinds of things kids do, and you fly off. . . .

"I would be just dead tired and they would be . . . running around, wanting to do this or that, or fighting or up to some [mischief]. I'd scream, 'Shut up! Everybody shut up, and go to your rooms!' And I hate those words, 'shut up.' At times they deserved it, but at times I found it difficult to be the disciplinarian, the listener, the giver giving each of them what he needed. I found it . . . an almost impossible, monumental job. I think it is almost impossible to give three kids that close together all they need—alone."

Patrick was the eldest child, high-spirited, imaginative, loving, and devilish; set against a mother in delicate balance, conflicts were inevitable.

"One time, I had friends over," Alice Stratton recalled in mock horror. "In fact, it was an MIA wife and her kids, and Pat was misbehaving—running around, getting too wild—and I was trying to calm him down. But he wouldn't settle down and at that point I got him into his room and talked to him sternly. He probably lipped off at me; I have no memory of it. I just remember cracking him.

"His nose started bleeding and he screamed. And I felt what a terrible mother I was. And my friend is hearing this, and it made it a little worse when the whole world knew you'd lost control of yourself and smacked your kid and the blood was running." And, humorously, "I mean he could have been quiet about it, right?

"Oh, he was a feisty kid and difficult for me to manage. But he and I were close, too, because he remembered Dick and we had some of the nicest, warmest times at night when finally the pressure was off and the other two were settled down; Patrick and I would sit down and talk about Dick for hours sometimes. He remembered his dad and wanted to hear the family stories again and again and about what happened and the shoot-down. I never told the gory details, but I did really tell him—them—what happened, in general; so we talked about that, and we dreamed together what it was going to be like when Dad came home. So Patrick and I had a nice closeness, and then, ha-ha-ha, he'd put it to me that next day in the daily living situation. But we got closer [sharing our grief] than maybe we would have if Dick had been home all those years. He grieved more than Michael and Charlie simply because they didn't know Dick. Charlie knew him not at all and Mike had only spotty memories. So Patrick and I had in common our missing that man and that brought us close. The others were not excluded, of course, oh no. We would talk about the family and stories about the family. I would tell them over and over the things Dick had done with them. I told them so much, just to keep it alive. I never knew, afterwards, how much they really knew, whether they had real memories or just what I had told them."

She was, indeed, what she had come from, and that was a pious Canadian farm girl/mother, not easily cowed by adversity. Like her husband clinging for survival to his Celtic passion, Alice Stratton fell back and dug into the bedrock of her roots.

"[Over the years] as I was alone with those kids, I got in touch with myself and accepted the fact that I had rage, accepted the fact that I had problems and was not Miss Wonderful in control of everything. I *had* to accept it. There it was: the screaming, loony mother coming apart at the seams.

"It was a big step for me to come to grips with that, and I think it helped me be a more compassionate person with others. If you can see your own faults and accept them, it is so much easier to accept them in others. I suppose I would have come to it in other ways, but this accelerated it, having to do it all alone. It was probably a good . . . growth experience. But I would just as soon not had it quite so intensified."

She decided shortly after she settled in at the new house (and after her initial period of grieving passed) that, in the interest of her sanity and her relationship with her sons, she had to be something more than keeper of the flame. Over the objections of a few family elders, she returned to work. It was a decision she knew Dick would support.

Alice joined the staff of the Catholic Social Services clinic in Mountain View, a community adjacent to Palo Alto. It was a part-time job with a flexible schedule. Depending upon her case load, she could work three hours or twenty-three, as she chose. She fitted in easily and she thrived on the work. Her decision had been a sound one. In contrast to her previous jobs, she no longer dealt exclusively with children.

"It was a piece of cake. I had grown up. I had kids of my own and I had put some stuff together. . . . I found it easier to work with parents. I knew how parents felt now, and I had been in their shoes. I was tired of struggling with my own kids and I didn't care, sometimes, if I never saw another one. Seriously, it was good, and I was lucky to have that kind of work, to like it, to have a good experience with it, to be able to get out of the house and listen to somebody else's troubles, and maybe help them a little. Jeez, everybody's got a lot of burdens, and I discovered I was not alone. Helping others helped me, but also hearing others' problems just made me much more aware, when I went home [at the end of the workday], that mine were not so big."

It was obvious that Alice's work had no adverse effect on the three Stratton boys and had a positive one on Alice. Whatever cultural objections to her employment remained were no longer voiced. There never was, of course, any withdrawal by the family of support for her and the boys. Her parents visited every Christmas; Charles Stratton, Dick's brother, living in Los Angeles, was a frequent visitor. She regularly exchanged letters, phone calls, and news with the senior Strattons in Quincy; Ellen and her husband, Dr. Richard Cooper, kept constant contact and would come West and pack Alice and the boys off on vacations. In turn, at some emotional cost to herself, she and the boys annually traveled East and visited the Coopers, her parents, and the senior Strattons in Quincy, and stayed at the summer camp operated by the University of Michigan for its alumni. It was important, Alice said, to get the boys back East to visit their roots.

In Palo Alto, the Foys were the bulwark; her circle of friends increased gradually. In addition to her work, she was active in Our Lady of the Rosary Church, and another facet of community

217

involvement was added to her life when Patrick entered first grade. She was actually beginning to enjoy herself.

"Every once in a while, I'd feel bad about that. Oh, not so bad I'd stop having fun for a very long time. But it happens and I've written that in my [articles]. I'd realize—all of a sudden—that I would be happy, and I'd say, Jeez, how can I be happy? How can I when that poor man is rotting away in a prison camp and I am actually enjoying myself?"

One must not assume infinite hedonism replaced perpetual anxiety. There were still times or instances when she would find herself terribly sad and depressed; a feeling of hopelessness would sneak upon her, quite unexpectedly, and tears would come. Those were hard years; she would say that later, "hard years and I was just hanging on, just surviving, but it got better as the children got older."

Two things were inescapable: the war, and Dick's absence. She was reminded of the latter every night when she went to bed and every morning when she arose, every time an appliance broke down, and every time Charlie got stuck up in Patrick's tree house in the back-yard pine. There was no one to share troubles with, or the joys.

"He was fun living with, Dick was, and that is what I miss," she told a friend. "And that's the big, awful thing, when you are told he's gone, such a big part of you is taken away: your husband, best friend, lover, just taken away, just . . . gone. That is the worst thing, that awful feeling of loss. We really had a lot of fun. Oh, we had fights, too, but we had a good time fighting." And later, in a blue funk, she despaired. "There were periods when I couldn't get him into my mind. I would sit and I would look at his picture and I'd say, 'Where are you?' I couldn't get that image of him laughing and there would be periods of time when it would be awful. I would have nightmares of him in the cell and that would be awful. I don't know why it came and went, this inability to recall him, his face, his characteristics, not to be able to feel that special quality of his.

"The image of your husband freezes, because there is nothing to change it. The letters were sterile, and yet his strength came across in those letters. He had faith. He had picked up his cross over

218

there, and I would do the same. He had made the best of an unalterable situation. So would I."

The tension eased away from her face and she smiled; she said, to herself, really, "Yuh, all you can do is live one day at a time and maybe the next one will be better. You've got a fifty-fifty chance. I try to pass that on to the boys."

It was not difficult keeping alive the image of their father for the boys; she was working harder to keep from turning him into a mystique, and at that she was not always successful.

"They brag about him to their friends," she said. "They tell them, 'He's the bravest man over there.' [But] I want the boys to know of the dad who is human; nobody can help you do that."[8]

For Ellen Cooper, the years after her brother was imprisoned were a different kind of hell.

"It was terrible. That conflict was awful and it was constant. It seemed like every decision I made involved that very conflict and I felt caught in between the Left and the Right. I felt that the Right (and this is probably an unfair generalization) . . . felt that everything was right about the United States, nothing was right about North Vietnam, and they cared very much about the prisoners. The people at the other end of the spectrum felt nothing was right with the United States, everything was right with Hanoi, and they couldn't bring the prisoners into their scope, or the prisoners were bad.

"There I was with a brother who was a prisoner and very concerned about his treatment and eventual release, and yet I had these feelings against the war. Frankly (in my view) sometimes the United States seemed right. Sometimes it seemed wrong. Sometimes I could see Hanoi's point of view. Sometimes I had the feeling wasn't anybody looking for the truth? Was everybody else just boxed into a predetermined position and only trying to support it? I felt so terribly alone.

"Once the Left here in Buffalo realized that I was anti-war (and after I had begun speaking out against the war again) they sort of began to exploit me, just as I felt the government exploited other prisoners' relatives. And here I am, basically a trusting, open person . . . who likes to be liked . . . faced with all this controversy, having to think of this conflict every single time somebody asked me to do something or say something, having to think of its effect on Dick, yet bringing into it my feelings on the war."

Ellen's views on the war sparked vehement disagreement between her and her father, who held to a my-country-right-or-wrong point of view (and alone endured who knows what conflicts as he grieved terribly for the loss of his son); her mother, on the other hand, felt sorry that she had strong feelings and was concerned by the obvious emotional conflict it was causing. That noble lady fell back upon her religion, confident that one day God would show her why her son Richard had fallen into the hands of an enemy, and with that view accepted the terrible situation that she, alone, could not change. Brother Charles, the ebullient chum of her childhood, held likewise to a contrary view of the war: a little high explosive detonated where it would do the most good far exceeded the value of diplomatic words or nondecisive battles in the Vietnamese jungles.

It was inevitable, with the passage of time and shock and an increasing awareness of how deeply, through one man, they both had been affected by Vietnam, that Ellen Cooper and Alice Stratton would clash on the war.

"Fortunately," said Ellen Cooper, "we have a very good relationship. I like Alice very much and I admire her enormously, so that really helped in terms of disagreeing about an issue that was so emotional for both of us. Without that basis of mutual fondness, it would have been awful; [with it] we could afford to argue vehemently without damage to the relationship itself. We visited approximately once and sometimes twice a year, both here and there, and spent long hours talking to each other about these questions.

"I would get very upset, sometimes, and then later I would feel guilty: Why did I have to do that to her? Why did I have to ask some of those questions and state my views so forcefully? Didn't she have enough [to worry about] without me?"

"[Ellen] raised conflicts in me because she asked piercing questions," says Alice Stratton. "They were good questions and they made me think. Once she said (and I do not remember what the issue was), Well, the President could have tried! Well, I remember going back and reading the magazines again (I was reading everything, boy, *U.S. News, Time,* and *Newsweek* every week, anything on the war in the newspapers just to help me understand what I did believe about this whole thing) and I thought, Jeez, she's right. He sure *could* have tried. Why didn't he? And always underneath it was, I want my husband home. But also, I have got to understand what is going on with this whole war business. So Ellen did a good thing for me. She did it in a friendly way. . . . [In] the colleges [later, when she was on speaking tours] they were saying, What do you think about your husband dropping bombs on innocent people? Why should we be there anyway? She felt the same way they did, but she was saying it kindlier."

"It was a nice dialogue," said Ellen Cooper. "Alice is a very intelligent, relatively open-minded person, so she would truly listen to me, she just wasn't waiting for silences to fill up with her own thoughts. Sometimes she would come close to agreeing with me, but then she would go back to her own thoughts and come to another conclusion.

"But she was in such a totally different situation than I was. She was the wife of a military man. I did not have that sort of stricture on me. And I was married to a man . . . in a position where it didn't really matter . . . how controversial I was. It wasn't going to affect him. It wasn't like being married to someone in the military or in a large corporation and the next-higher-up was going to dislike what Richard's [her husband] wife did. So I had complete freedom in that sense. But Alice was in a totally different situation, the wife of a military man—not that she would have necessarily thought differently in a different situation. She very possibly would have, but it would be highly unlikely. She just didn't have the same orientation that I did."

"I remember," said Alice with a wry little smile, "going to the first [POW/MIA] wives' group and I remember somebody talking about Ho Chi Minh. I am ashamed to say I didn't even know who the hell that was! I really didn't. Your know, you've been busy with your life, with the babies. Well, it didn't mean that much to me. (I knew there was a war on, but even that didn't mean that much to me until Dick got shot down. And boom, did that change.) I went home and thought, I'd better get a hold of myself here and get to know what's going on. All of a sudden, I began to read and read; Jeez, what did I think about this? There was Ellen on one side and [on the other] what I thought Dick

221

thought; well, I didn't know for sure what Dick thought about the philosophy of what he was doing. I mean, we had talked about it some, but not really about the philosophy. I had to come up with it for myself, what *I* thought. I talked about it with the other wives, with Ellen.

"Then I felt that was my whole life. I talked about it all the time and finally began to come to grips with what I thought and felt about it.

"I think I came to the same conclusions that Dick had. I felt very similar, almost exactly as Dick had felt, but I felt proud that I hadn't come to it because that was the way my husband felt, swallowed his philosophy hook, line, and sinker. I . . . came to my [conclusions] after much conflict over what was right and wrong in war, and what was good and bad, and reading and listening, and finally, my decision was it had to be done.

"At any moment, I would have loved my husband to be out of it; I could have had him out of there any time. And I didn't feel very patriotic about it."

When Alice Stratton first moved to Palo Alto, she had not seen herself involved in POW activities. She had not thought much beyond her own circumstances, to begin with. And in mid-1967 government policy discouraged inter-POW-family relationships and concealed the identity of those lost in Indochina. A wife who wished to pursue the matter needed energy, patience, and the talent of a gumshoe. Alice Stratton discovered she had those qualities, as did a handful of other wives.

"We were sort of told to lay low, right? The government just didn't . . . want any publicity. But I did eventually get in touch with other POW and MIA wives, and we [organized] our own group, and we made contact eventually with another small group nearer San Francisco. First of all we were together socially, just for support, and then when Sybil Stockdale started [the National League of Families] we formed up the league's northern California chapter."

The government's policy of keeping mum over the prisoner issue—and warning the families of prisoners and men listed as missing to do likewise—collapsed in May of 1969. The given reason was concern for the imprisoned men, those it knew about and those many more it did not. But government is made of politicians, and however well-meaning or sincere the words of concern, the fact remained that hundreds of hushed-up families rebelled, and Washington did what it did best: reacted smoothly to save its reputation and what good will it had left.

Rebellion began (quite politely, one should note, for that is what the military expects from its officers' ladies) in earnest in 1966 with one woman, Sybil Stockdale.

She was the wife of Commander James B. Stockdale, the commander of Carrier Air Group 16, shot down, listed as missing in action first and later as captured, in September 1965. He was the senior Navy officer held in Hanoi and remained so until war's end. Now, Stockdale had one of those careers upon which the Pentagon smiled with pride: 1947 Annapolis graduate, flawless record, crackerjack flier, craggy good looks, a small man, flinty and tough. He was a native of Abingdon, Illinois, a hamlet south of Galesburg and about thirty miles east of the Mississippi where it passes Burlington, Iowa, on its way south to St. Louis. His wardroom nickname was "Cag," as in CAG, an acronym denoting either a carrier air group or the man who bossed it. "Cag" and Sybil Stockdale were the epitome of Navy establishment; he was well on his way to flag rank and major commands.

Was, until he got smashed up, captured, and viciously tortured. It was a great leveler, that prison in Hanoi. For Sybil Stockdale, military social status in no way soothed the shock, pain, and terrible loneliness. But she was a tough woman, with a sense of humor and a lot of luck. In time, Stockdale was one of a handful of prisoners (who included Hegdahl and Stratton) allowed to write home occasionally. The Stockdales also lived in San Diego, by any description a military community. Quietly, in keeping with the government's policy, she began exploring—after the first letter or two from her husband—"the various government avenues of communication."[9] And living in San Diego as she did, she met late in 1966 the wife of another man taken prisoner. They proceeded to track down thirty-three other POW or MIA families in the area and started informal gatherings to share news, sorrow, and support.

It was slow, hard work but eventually other small groups were formed, such as the one in northern California to which Alice Stratton belonged. Even by mid-1968, a majority of families who

223

had relatives listed as either prisoners or missing knew of no other families in similar straits; and where there were more than one thousand men so listed, only about one hundred families—total—received any kind of mail from Vietnam.

At least it was some information: code words and other secret phrases identified some men whose fate had been unknown, or indicated conditions of imprisonment that were less than what Hanoi claimed. This information was collected whenever possible and, in October 1968, in defiance of Washington, released to the press with predictable results: the isolation of POW and MIA families ended literally overnight. Riding the crest, the Stockdale group and others organized a campaign to deluge the North Vietnamese delegation to the Paris peace talks, expressing concern about the prisoners and demanding an accounting of the missing. It was the first organized undertaking in which a large number of families participated.

In May 1969 Washington gave up. The Secretary of Defense announced that the government would place the prisoner issue before the court of world opinion and demand action to reverse the "shocking conditions" of the prisoner camps and Hanoi's snubbing of the Geneva agreements.

Mrs. Stockdale called an ad hoc meeting of the various POW/MIA groups in May of 1970, and on the twenty-eighth of that month the National League of Families of American Prisoners and Missing in Southeast Asia was incorporated. Sybil Stockdale was named chairman.

The northern California chapter of the league, organized by Alice Stratton's friend Mae Rose Evans, an MIA wife from Alameda, went to battle stations with something approaching a vengeance.

"The first thing I remember," Alice Stratton said, "was Sybil having us sign up for times to send telegrams to Xuan Thuy [head of North Vietnam's Paris delegation] to protest the violation of the Geneva Convention and urge for better treatment [of the prisoners]. She also suggested writing to newspaper editors all over the United States urging better treatment, so at that point I went up to . . . San Francisco and spent the weekend [with a fellow POW wife] and wrote . . . editors. The Foys had the kids . . . and I was free to just really bang away at the typewriter.

224

[Later in the year] I sent a list of those editors with my Christmas cards asking my friends to write, too. As a result of those letters, I had my first voluntary publicity, an interview in the Palo Alto *Times* on July 17, 1969. The reporter came to the door because the phone was still unlisted.

"Next we wrote to senators and legislators, and by this time it was late summer or fall. Our campaign had really swung into full force, and the league was now a national league."

Urged on by Barbara MacKenzie, a POW family co-ordinator in Palo Alto, and by friends in her church parish, Alice was persuaded to go on the stump. With wobbling knees, she made her first speech in October of 1969 to a friendly group at her own church, and followed it up with a second talk (with increased confidence) to an officers' wives' group at Stanford organized by another of Alice's friends, Bonnie Duck, wife of the school's professor of Naval Science. (Mrs. Duck's group remained active until the war ended.)

The talks, those two and those later, were delivered in near-monotone because she refused to let her emotions come through, or perhaps was afraid to. But the effect was electrifying. At one point, the wives' group asked some members of Toastmasters International to advise them on more effective public speaking. Alice and her monotone received no hints, just encouragement. One of the Toastmasters took her aside.

"I don't understand it," he said, smiling gently, shaking his head. "I don't understand it, but that monotone is still effective."

"That's all I can be on this one," Alice Stratton replied. "If I stand there and start letting the emotion come through, then I am going to cry through the whole thing, and that's stupid."

Shortly before Christmas 1969, she was interviewed by Peter Stack, a reporter for the San Francisco *Chronicle*. It was a typical *Chronicle* venture, which is no reflection on Stack himself, a talented writer. Something had come over the wire machines, probably in connection with the Paris talks or the league's letter campaign. Richard Stratton's name was listed as a prisoner, and his home town as Palo Alto. It was a slow Sunday; Stack was available. Let's get a piece on the wife and kiddies, Christmas and all.

He went to Palo Alto, located the house, knocked on the door, and got his interview. It was fairly mild stuff.

225

"She has managed," Stack wrote, "to take on 'an exterior of resignation.' 'As long as I know he's alive, it's at least one thing to cling to,' she said. 'But the missing is always underneath. One day when I went shopping at the PX [at nearby Moffett Field] I was in the parking lot, and I saw a young officer from behind. He was putting on his hat, and the tears came streaming down.'

"Mrs. Stratton," Stack concluded, "along with a number of other POWs' wives, have [sic] formed the National League of Families of POWs in Southeast Asia. They write letters to every conceivable influential source, and they talk, and then write more letters hoping the campaign will bring their men back.

" 'There's every sort of feeling about the war among them,' said Mrs. Stratton, who thinks of the POW situation as a separate issue. She is divided on her feelings toward the war in general.

" 'It's easier if you take the position that he won't be released until the war is over,' she said.

"She looked affectionately at Patrick, who had brought out a framed photograph of his father in his Navy uniform.

" 'He's having his first communion in the spring,' she said, mussing his blond hair. 'That'll be a big moment. Maybe he'll come home then.' "[10]

It ranked as a minor interview for the *Chronicle*. Still, Alice impressed the young reporter, who was sent to Palo Alto with little or no background on the Strattons or the POW issue. "That Alice Stratton was a nice lady, real attractive. She had kept it pretty well together, as I recall. The kids were there and it made the interview awfully difficult. She seemed to be holding back a lot and I think she was trying to spare the kids."

His observations were correct. She was holding back a lot, more than Stack could guess, and she was sparing the boys. What she knew now, what she held back that cool December day, would traumatize them. Good God in heaven, it had traumatized her.

Alice Stratton knew: she knew about Hoa Lo, about Room 18, about the "confession," the isolation, the torture, the beatings, the humiliations. What Stack believed was resignation was a sorely maintained shell to contain her fears—and her fury.

Alice Stratton had talked to Hegdahl.

CHAPTER 20

I hope he doesn't spend half his life there. It's
all right for a little while. It's an experience for
him, but . . . he's kinda bored, I betcha.
                              —Abe Hegdahl to reporter, 1967[11]

It was February and it was cold and he felt foolish and humiliated, sitting alone there in his cell with his head shaved. Douglas
Hegdahl wondered what the penalty was for disobeying the order
of a superior officer.

He was in trouble, he thought.

He had screwed up his own release.

Against his wishes, his memory kept tormenting him, scurrying
back to August and dragging out those last few seconds with the
Beak:

"Remember what I told you, Doug, I won't see you again. Tell
Alice what has happened to me, to us. If it means more torture, at
least I will know I am being tortured for something. Good-by,
Doug. God bless. Tell Alice I love her." And Beak vanished—
into a black room, he learned later. Next day, the Rabbit came,
suggested he write a letter to Ho Chi Minh requesting amnesty
and release. Stratton had warned him it was coming. He fell to his
Uncle Tom role, struggling mightily with the pen, spilling ink,
misspelling words, asking definitions, fumbling over the individual
letters. The Rabbit became agitated, began dictating. Hegdahl

227

rewrote the draft and included a promise never to return to Vietnam if he was released.

A passable copy was finally obtained, and Rabbit took it to his boss, Major Bui.

Then came the succession of roommates and finally Tom Smith, the visiting delegations, and Christmas, and New Year. About January 17 he and Smith were joined by a new roommate, Navy Ensign David Methany, a blond six-footer suffering the effects of 104 days in solitary and an untended infection. Methany, Hegdahl suspected, was the third member of the release group. They were herded out of their cell and across the compound to an interrogation room in the big house, and there was Stratton sitting on a low stool. No conversation was allowed, but Hegdahl and Beak grinned at each other. Now, Hegdahl thought unhappily, we can all go home and report Stratton alive, smiling, and unbrainwashed.

Bullshit. He did not want to do this, go home like a coward tugging on his forelock. Methany was ill, and Smith, well, Smith would have to live with himself. Hegdahl was well, or well enough; he was vital to the camp communication network. His place was here. He wished Stratton had not ordered him to go. He saw no compromise; he had to go and prayed Stratton had told other POWs he was not leaving voluntarily.

Two days later, the trio was visited by an aide to Major Bui known as the Soft Soap Fairy, a sobriquet testifying to his cloying approach to the prisoners, his obvious effeminacy, and his suspected homosexuality. When the major figured there was more to be gained from his charges with honey than vinegar, Soft Soap Fairy got the nod.

"What is your greatest aspiration?" he asked. What did these three desire most? Smith was the senior prisoner; he answered first and according to Hegdahl showed no signs of coyness. He wanted to go home. Methany suggested medical treatment for his infection. Hegdahl wanted eyeglasses. He was supposed to say "go home," too, but could not bring the words forth.

Three days later, the Fairy returned carrying writing tools and paper. They should write a letter to President Ho Chi Minh requesting release. The others set to work; Hegdahl did not.

"Heddle?"

"Naw, I wrote last fall, sir."

It was not an act of defiance. It was just that, sometimes, enough bullshit was enough. It was a dumb thing for Hegdahl to do.

The Soft Soap Fairy (sadly) told Methany later that week that Heddle would not be going home. Methany told Hegdahl, and Hegdahl panicked. Was it a trick to pressure him into writing another letter, or was it for real? He could not take a chance. He had his orders and his 260 names. He prevailed upon his two fellow prisoners to memorize as many names as possible. Smith said he was no good at memory work. Methany volunteered to have a go at it, and learned 70 names before Hegdahl was taken out of the cell and put back into solitary. An Air Force major, Norris Overly, was substituted for Hegdahl and on February 16, 1968, Overly, Smith, and Methany were released by the Vietnamese into the custody of two American pacifists, Howard Zinn and the Reverend Daniel Berrigan, S.J. Before leaving, the POWs taped messages expressing gratitude for release and hoping the war would be shortened. One at least expressed the hope he would not have to return to bomb again.

The following day, Hegdahl was given his glasses. Then he was taken to the cell vacated by the departed and was made to clean it. Then his head was shaved, signifying disgrace. He was not fit to release.

The departure of Smith, Methany, and Overly devastated morale at the Plantation. When tapes of their departure messages were played over the Voice of Vietnam, morale crumbled in the other camps as well. The departure sparked an angry debate over release, which reached near-hysterical proportions. The general opinion was that Overly, Smith, and Methany had disobeyed orders of senior camp officers, broken faith with their fellow prisoners, and given some comfort and a large measure of aid to the North Vietnamese. The early-release tactic was dubbed the "Fink Release Program" and its participants past and future called "slipperies" or "slimies" and worse. Debate continued for months about release. With all this swirling about him, it was with a measure of relief that Hegdahl received a message from Richard Stratton, smuggled into a toilet area in the bottom of a waste bucket, rescinding his previous order that Hegdahl go home. Stratton had been overruled by the Plantation's POW senior ranking officer, Air Force Lieutenant Colonel Hervey Stockman. Stratton was convinced Hegdahl's information was vital and must be gotten out. Stockman believed Hegdahl's release and its potential threat to already deteriorated morale was too high a price to pay, however valuable the Hegdahl data.

On February 25 Hegdahl was taken from solitary and moved in with James Low, an Air Force major and a Korean War ace, a fact he concealed from the Vietnamese. Low was perfectly candid, according to Hegdahl. He did not like the Vietnamese, he did not relish captivity, and he would speedily quit Hanoi if he could.

Hegdahl put it all together—Low's attitude, which was honest, if nothing else; the impact of the previous release—and figured he was being softened up for release again. Except this time he could not go. He had orders.

He roomed with Low for five months and ten days, a humdrum period highlighted by the announcement on March 31 that President Lyndon B. Johnson had canceled the air war against North Vietnam and would not run for re-election. Johnson's announcements were broadcast to the prisoners, who assumed, briefly and incorrectly, that some sort of truce had been reached and perhaps the war was all but over. Johnson had made concessions to get the prisoners home. It was an assumption that created a lot of woe. Hegdahl recalled:

"Most of us felt we were there for a purpose. Then, when the bombing stopped, we felt maybe the war was over. Well, we were still there. The Vietnamese said, Your government has forgotten you. It got very depressing. They would say, you are at our mercy; you are in our hands and we can do what we please with you.

"When you boil it down—and it might not do much for your ego—basically you are a hostage. It was not like Korea, you know, where they had programs to re-educate you, make you a communist. The V. realized that was a bad word with Americans; they didn't even try to any great extent. They were socialists, or nationalists. But you were a hostage. That was the main thing, a hostage held for future negotiations."

On August 2, 1968, Low, along with Major Fred Thompson and Captain Joseph Carpenter, was released to an American antiwar group.

Hegdahl's head was reshaved.

"Heddle," chastised the Soft Soap Fairy, "it is not the extent of your crimes, it is the degree to which you repent."

Hegdahl was put into solitary. Why? "I guess they figured they'd just teach me a lesson. . . ."

* * *

He had been in solitary perhaps two weeks when a guard came and fetched him to the big house and into one of the interrogation rooms. In the room was an aide to Major Bui and a table holding a pair of American dungarees and a striped French sailor's underblouse.

"Heddle, this is what you wear in Navy?" asked the interrogator.

"Yes, we wear those." The dungarees that were being held up before him had the name "Carter" on the back and a service number, which Hegdahl immediately memorized.

"This, Heddle?" The shirt. He nearly said no and then just as quickly grinned and said yes. He almost knew what was coming.

"You dress up."

He did.

He was blindfolded and placed in the back of a truck. From the chatter, he estimated there were three guards. In the cab, a driver and probably an officer.

They were rolling East at a reasonable clip when his blindfold was removed. Everybody was grinning like a Cheshire. From a box under a bench one guard took four bottles of Vietnamese beer, gave one to Hegdahl, and handed the others around. After the second round, things got frisky. There was an officer in the cab next to the driver, as Hegdahl had guessed. Unfortunately he had a stiff neck, which required of him some effort in turning around to check on his troops. He telegraphed the move every time, and Hegdahl's blindfold would be slipped back over his eyes.

The third round.

The guards serenaded Hegdahl with what he assumed were anti-war or soldiers' songs. Lots of laughter and knee slapping.

Fourth round.

"Old McDonald had a farm, E-I, E-I, yoooh," warbled Hegdahl.

The guards, fairly plastered, applauded.

The officer in front turned slowly around.

231

Back on with the blindfold. A lot of giggling, but that ended the song fest.

They traveled eastward a better part of a day and then swung north near the coast to a little village north of Haiphong, probably on Ha Long Bay. The guards dismounted and helped Hegdahl out. They shared mess, and then the young American was stashed in the village pagoda as evening came. An armed guard was posted outside the door.

It was a cool night, and he could smell the sea. He was not sleepy despite the long ride and the beer. Perhaps it revved up his juices. He never knew what came over him:

"[It] was when the guard fell asleep. I was scared to death, but the guy was sleeping. It was the closest I ever made to any kind of escape.

"Ever try to open a door and do it quietly? Each sound is exaggerated in your mind. I'd get the door open, and then I would run back and sit down, then a little more open, then run back.

"My feet were like lead. That was my womb, that pagoda, and those were hostiles out there.

"There was a canal outside. I was thinking of getting into the canal and taking off, just torn with it, you know? Well, the decision was taken out of my hands. The guard awoke and caught me out in the courtyard of the pagoda. He was sure nervous. Pulled me back inside.

"I thought, oh, shit. I'm really in for it. And the guard looked at me, and went, 'Shhh! Shh!'

"I never got any flak about it; I assume *he* didn't tell anybody about it because he had fallen asleep on watch."

The next morning, after a light breakfast, Hegdahl was taken to the beach; set up and ready to work was a Vietnamese film crew. Standing around the shooting area was a pride of small, excited brown-eyed children, mothers, and elderly persons. In halting English, the film director explained to Hegdahl that he was to wade out into the war, struggle with a guard, be overpowered, and then, humble, be led in to shore and "captured" by a group of other guards who would remain on the beach.

On the first take, Hegdahl dressed in his French sailor shirt and American dungarees stormed the beach like MacArthur in the Philippines, grinning and waving.

He was reinstructed. He did it again.

The director called a break. Hegdahl played with the children and allowed a crone to stroke his beardless face.

Third take. Hegdahl began struggling with the guard, dumped him in the water, and held him under. The guard thrashed, surfaced, and screamed in terror, and Hegdahl kept dunking and holding.

Cut. The director was hysterical. The crowd enjoyed all this excitement.

Another take. Another flub.

They ran out of film. Hegdahl was run back to the Plantation.

The film was never released.

Major Bui was unhappy with his performance. Hegdahl was back in solitary. There would be no roommate.

For his twenty-second birthday, September 3, 1968, Myron Lee Donald, an Air Force pilot, slid a cigarette under his door. But other than that bright moment, solitary was beginning to lean on his nerves. When a prisoner in an adjacent cell became violently ill, Hegdahl was belligerent.

"Bao cao! Bao cao [guard!]," he screamed, "that man over there is sick. Help him. Help him." His anger and noise concerned the guards more than the needs of the ailing prisoner.

"I guess they got pissed off at me, and I think they laid a trap for me; they knew we were echoing our voices through the [cellblock corridor] and talking. They caught me, and they read the riot act to me. They called me a *criminal.* I told them I did not care what they thought, I was a *prisoner of war,* and the V. really went apeshit."

He was marched at bayonet point to the corncrib, the isolated brick and tin solitary-confinement cell he had visited once back in 1967. It was one of the few times he really blew; perhaps it was the tension of the moment that prevented the guards from realizing Hegdahl, in a dangerous lapse, had blown his cover as a dumb, bovine imbecile.

He was pitched into the cell, and his mat and cup tossed in after him. He was still quite agitated, trying to control the build-up of rage his cover would not let him vent.

"I could not openly defy them alone, the way Dick and I had done together. But I was pissed. They had used me for propaganda, and if they were going to use me [again] for propaganda, then I was going to look shitty.

"So I went on a hunger strike. That is when I lost most of my weight; in the end I couldn't have weighed more than 120 pounds. [The figure represents a total weight loss of 105 pounds from the time Hegdahl enlisted until he quit his fast. Pictures of him taken in early 1969 show him indeed looking as he had wanted.] I was not dumping the food but cutting the regular ration down. It became an obsession. The Vietnamese really did not know what was the matter. The weight loss was so gradual, they really did not notice.

"Then they were going to have a Japanese film crew take pictures of me. I didn't protest or anything: sure, I'd be happy to. Well, I'm weighing about 120 and I figured the best defense was a good offense. So I went in there and those were the pictures that came out of me. I was so weak, at times I'd pass out when I stood up real fast. I stayed on that hunger strike until February 25, 1969."

"But sometimes I wonder, looking back on it. When you lose your physical health, you kind of lose your mental health, too, and other guys saw it. Dick [Stratton] was very concerned when I would see him (when I was allowed out of the cell occasionally) and he would look at me [and make eating motions] and I think they were wondering what was happening."

The long months in solitary changed Hegdahl. If he had never thought much about what he believed, or who and what he was, he had the opportunity now, if only to keep his mind active and divert its attention from his shriveled stomach. Occasionally he was given pamphlets or magazines by the Vietnamese in their efforts to improve his mind. The magazines, usually from communist countries, were heavily censored, which offended him. And he couldn't make much sense out of political tracts with titles like *The International Conference for Solidarity with the Vietnamese People Against the U. S. Imperialist Aggression and for the Defense of Peace.*

"Most of them were so poorly written . . . you really couldn't get through them. I was lectured about Americans committing the most awful outrages, and they gave me a book called *American Imperialists* [which said] we cut off the ears of Vietcong and pickled them. . . . Things like that. And they told [me] about the anti-war movement, of course.

"When I was in prison, I probably met the whole Chicago Seven somewhere along the line. They came through the camps to look at you, you know. At first [I] was very angry. Why did [America] allow these people to come over here? It was hard on the morale of the prisoners: you were not only facing the enemy, but you had your own fellow Americans coming in to tell you it was an illegal, immoral, and unjust war, as the Vietnamese used to put it. You had these anti-war groups coming in and parroting that!

"They would quote a [United States] senator or congressman [making a statement opposing the war] and then say, now, these people are not traitors, are they? They say this, why shouldn't you?

"They gave us Albanian magazines or Korean magazines . . . but they were censored. You would open them up and find the pages pasted together (I would still open them up and then paste them back together) and to an Oriental or a communist who doesn't know freedom, it didn't bother them. But to an American it is a repulsive thing.

"They gave me [anti-war] articles out of *Time* magazine, or *Life,* especially *Newsweek,* but it got to a point where I would look . . . at a picture of a group of demonstrators and the police trying to hold them back, and I thought, why, you dirty bastards can't do that! That's what America is all about. That's what freedom is. If you crack down on these peace groups and forbid them [to demonstrate] you will be no better than the North Vietnamese and their Stalinistic little society where censorship is not even repulsive.

"I am not saying this feeling came immediately. At first I was very bitter against [the anti-war movement]. But it dawned on me books [opposing the war] were printed in the United States and allowed to leave the country, peace groups were allowed to leave the country, and all I could think was, what a contradiction. We don't know what suppression is in the United States. We are a free people. In fact, we take it for granted. I don't think anybody really realizes the extent of it until you are in captivity in a place like a communist country.

"So, after that, any time they showed me an anti-war statement, or something like that, instead of it being hard on my morale, it was good for my morale. All I could say was, 'Only in America! That's a pretty damn good country we have there.' That's what we treasure, that's what we zealously treasure . . . that freedom. Even if it appears sometimes to be counterproductive, you cannot suppress it or defeat America's whole purpose.

"Dick Stratton said, 'Doug, these people represent everything I hate. Though they may seem kind on the outside sometimes, they represent everything I hate. I hate repression. I hate their attitude toward religion, their way of life, and I recognize it as something I would never want to live under.'

"In the United States, you appreciate just being able to say what you want, even to a senator, some representative, some politician; you just tell them what you think and you don't worry about the police coming to get you.

"America is crazy, but it's the best thing going. That's the kind of attitude . . . most of us had."

The photographs taken by the Japanese were released. They appeared in a Defense Department exhibit in Washington and were circulated at the peace talks in Paris. Shortly after that, guards presented Hegdahl with a stalk of eighteen bananas; he was ordered to eat them all; he was given a pep talk on going home; his face, covered with ringworm, was treated with iodine; he was allowed out of his cell for sunbaths. He asked for a roommate; it was refused; he stayed on the hunger strike.

On February 25, he was taken to the big house. He was told a meeting with "an Italian lady" (Italian journalist Oriana Fallaci) and a Japanese delegation had been arranged.

"Heddle. These are the questions to be asked, and these are the answers."

"Sir, if they ask embarrassing questions, I am going to give embarrassing answers."

"Heddle," said the Rabbit, "if you give the answers to these questions, you will get a roommate. I am trying hard to get you a roommate. You will get Stafford for a roommate."

"All right. I will see the delegation, but I will not tell them I received excellent treatment."

The Rabbit was very angry. "All right," he said, mimicking the American, "you will not get a roommate."

The Vietnamese unexpectedly capitulated. He did not see any delegations, and that night he joined his new roommate, Hugh Allan Stafford.

* * *

It was on again in March. A triumphant message was sent through the communications net:

"Fox says if forced you go [home] with our blessings. Wizard."

Fox was the code name for Colonel Theodore Guy, USAF, who had replaced Hervey Stockman as the Plantation's senior ranking officer. "Wizard" had replaced "Beak" as Stratton's code name. Guy had followed his predecessor's hard-nosed attitude regarding early releases ("The rule is, NOBODY goes home early and doesn't that kid understand it?"), but Stratton, using his reserve supply of Irish wit, cajoling, and arm-twisting, had pressed his case; he wanted Hegdahl out, he wanted Hegdahl's names and information out, and that was that. Guy finally relented. And Hegdahl, again under direct orders and still recovering from his self-imposed fast, was less adamant about opposing release. He himself was convinced now that he had a mission, and believed he could do as much good outside Vietnam as he could do inside the Plantation. Now Hegdahl had to convince the Vietnamese to let him go. He did his public best, Uncle Tomming and being carefully polite to the Vietnamese (while privately helping develop a new communications setup in his cellblock):

"On the tenth of May, 1969, the shit hit the fan."

What smeared Hegdahl's fan was the escape from the Zoo of two Air Force Captains, John Dramesi and Edward Atterbury; it was an escape that had been more than a year in the planning, and was ill-fated. The two fliers were quickly recaptured and brutally punished. Dramesi survived; Atterbury was never seen again. The escape provoked wide controversy because it set off a period of retribution, the most savage wave of tortures and punishments of the war. Every camp was shaken down, every cell inspected, almost every prisoner beaten or questioned. Carefully built communications systems were destroyed; personal effects garnisheed.

Hegdahl and Stafford had drilled a series of message and notepassing holes in the wall between their cell and the next, which held a prisoner named Ron Webb. (Webb could have passed for Stratton's double, had the same attitude and respect for the Viet-

237

namese; in fact, they were roommates for a period.) As guards swept through the camp, the holes were discovered. Stafford was savagely beaten; so was Webb, whose wrist was broken in the process.

Hegdahl was not beaten, but he was dragged roughly from his cell and tossed into solitary. All of his personal possessions were taken. So were his extra clothes and his blankets. Gradually, during a two-week period, his possessions were returned. On the sixteenth day he was taken to an interrogation room in the big house. His interrogator was a hard-looking officer he had never seen before.

He was seated at a table. On the table were paper, pen, and ink. The guards remained in the room; the officer's voice was cold and angry. He would have trouble Uncle Tomming this one, he thought.

"Write what I tell you," the officer said. "To the Camp Commander from Dog Heddle, a disclosure about prisoner activities . . ."

"No, I cannot write this."

"Write Fox is senior officer."

"Write what?"

The interrogator's face darkened. He motioned to the guards with a short, jerky sweep of his arm. Hegdahl was grabbed and pulled from the table. His arms were bound. He was knocked to the floor and wrapped tightly, round and round, in a bamboo mat, a piece of Dakota melon in a slice of Vietnamese prosciutto. The hors d'oeuvre was left stifling and claustrophobic on the floor for an hour. That was enough for Hegdahl.

He Uncled. The Vietnamese was soft-spoken.

"Write! Fox is SRO. Beak is Stratton. . . ."

And he wrote. It was nonsense: old code names no longer in use; scribblings on a diagram of the prison compound of no earthly consequence. Nothing vital, as it turned out. He signed it.

He was returned to his cell.

* * *

The tea party, appropriately enough, was held on the Fourth of July. Major Bui poured. Hegdahl, who was one of the guests, guardedly studied the Cat. The years of strain running the camps (or mismanaging them, as the case might be) showed on the major's face. He had developed a tic under one eye. His old smoothness was gone, though his manners and appearance were still immaculate.

The other guests were Navy Lieutenant (jg) Robert F. Frishman and Air Force Captain Wesley L. Rumble. The prisoners were served bananas and advice with their tea. If they showed correct and proper attitudes, said the major, they would be considered for release.

As the gathering broke up, Major Bui took Hegdahl aside; Frishman and Rumble were taken out of the room. Bui's mouth smiled, but his eyes did not; the tic was flicking double-time.

"It is true, Heddle, this time you go home. But if you say anything bad about the camp authorities or about the Vietnamese people when you return, I will see these documents fall into the hands of your government. According to your Code of Conduct, you will go to prison for revealing secrets of your comrades."[12] His hand softly patted the papers Hegdahl had written and signed the month before.

* * *

Hegdahl, Frishman, and Rumble were moved together July 9, and Hegdahl, entering the cell, felt compelled to remind his two comrades of POW policy: officers were not supposed to accept release.

"I did it the first thing when we were moved together. This was my third group of officers and I reminded them of the policy and that's all I did. I wasn't going to get preachy or jeopardize my position this third time. I just told them what the policy was. They did not respond to it at all." (Hegdahl said Frishman later told him he had been ordered home by Hervey Stockman, former SRO at the Plantation; both Frishman and Rumble were ill and had suffered from wounds, Hegdahl added.)

Feeding of the prospective releasees increased to three meals daily, and they were taken outside in the sun several hours each day. The Vietnamese arranged tours: a visit to the bomb-leveled town of Phu Ly, south of Hanoi; a trip to Hanoi's parks and the city's art museum.

On August 3, 1969, an American peace delegation headed by

239

Rennie Davis arrived to take the prisoners home. The delegation and the prisoners met first in the main interrogation room at the Plantation's mansion. Later, all of the Americans, without official Vietnamese supervision, dined at the Metropole. The prisoners were instructed not to mention the names of any other prisoners while still in Vietnam.

"Let me remind you, Heddle, that we have ways of getting even; we have your statements, and we have friends . . . even in the United States."

On August 4 the Ministry of the Army officially turned the prisoners over to the Vietnamese Committee for Solidarity with the American People, who in turn gave custody of the trio to Davis's group, the American Committee for Solidarity with the Vietnamese People. It was a major do: lots of people and toasts to peace. The prisoners were offered their choice of presents in a room full of them, and they politely declined. Speeches had been prepared for the prisoners, and Hegdahl managed to foul his badly; no one realized it in all the excitement, and when the error was discovered, he was made to do it again and he fouled it up again.

The American peace delegation expressed its thanks, and as the Vietnamese applauded and smiled, Hegdahl edged over to the camp commander's desk and stole his cigarette holder.

"He was real proud of that cigarette holder, so I took it, right then. Couldn't hardly have done it before; they would have searched the camp."

The Vietnamese refused to let Hegdahl keep his skivvie shorts. He was wearing them when he had been captured, and after he was imprisoned they were returned to him with his prison number stenciled on the front in red.

* * *

The former POWs landed at Kennedy in New York at 4:15 P.M., August 7. Frishman's and Hegdahl's families were there to meet them and a forty-five-minute reunion was held inside the plane. The peace group that had escorted them out went its separate, jubilant way and held a press conference. Rumble was ill. He was taken immediately from the plane and transferred by police station wagon to an Air Force medical evacuation plane.

240

Hegdahl and Frishman were transferred to Bethesda Naval Hospital for treatment and debriefing.

It was decided that Rumble's list of names was the more accurate, and it was his that was used as the "official" list. Hegdahl's phenomenal memory was used as the cross-check and further picked over for an incredible array of information.

"Sir, the Plantation Camp, also known as the Country Club, is located at the intersection of Le Van Binh and Le Van Linh."

The innocent one was home.

Now he had to talk with Alice Stratton; he was under orders.

PART VI

CRUSADES
1969–1973

The students started to let go their feelings on the war, and how did we feel about it, being the wives of—nobody actually said being "the wives of killers," but they skirted around it [enough] so you got the picture."

—Alice Stratton

CHAPTER 21

When Hanoi announced on July 3 it would release three prisoners of war to acknowledge Vietnamese humanity and American Independence Day, Alice Stratton surrendered cautiously to the desire that her husband would come out. She was not alone in this hope; Hanoi was devious and did not name the prospective releasees. More than a month passed, finally, before release occurred. Richard Stratton remained a prisoner. By that time, Alice and the boys were in Buffalo with Ellen and Richard Cooper near the end of the annual summer trek East, and preparing for return to California.

She telephoned Washington to see if the Navy had learned anything about her husband; yes, she was told, there was some news. One of the men just released, Douglas Hegdahl, had roomed for a while with the commander; would she like to see Hegdahl?

She left the next morning for Washington, leaving the boys in Ellen's care. She took a taxicab and motored the ten miles or so between National Airport and Bethesda Naval Hospital, which is situated in Maryland just beyond the District of Columbia line.

Hegdahl's room was on an upper floor and off limits to all except authorized personnel. Frishman was squirreled away up there, too; with an escort, Alice passed easily around the ribbon barrier signifying sanctuary. Hegdahl was sitting in a chair, his bones wrapped in a Navy-issue bathrobe, preparing for a debriefing session with an operative from Naval Intelligence, when Alice arrived.

The spook was piqued by the interruption.

And Hegdahl, getting to his feet to greet Alice Stratton, Hegdahl lived now in bits and pieces in a body physically and emotionally spent. He recalled, for example, only parts of his trip back to the United States; he remembered the reunion with his mother and father, who had come on from South Dakota, their tearful embraces and Edith Hegdahl's concern over his teeth; he did not recall how he had arrived at the hospital, beyond a helicopter trip to Washington, or how he had come to find himself in this room.

"I was," he conceded, "in pretty much of a drifty, being-led-around mood. I was exhausted. Everything was so incredible and my folks were there and I had to see them by appointment, practically. And when they said [Alice] was there (as if—'Do you want to see her?'—as if there were any question) it was kind of surprising.

"Of course I want to see her!"

Continuous interruptions had already upset the debriefing officer; he was anxious and sullen—and determined. He remained in Hegdahl's room throughout Alice Stratton's visit. "He was so apprehensive about the whole thing," said Hegdahl, "he made me feel kind of weird."

Hegdahl was equally determined and his obligations to Fox, Wizard, and Alice Stratton were, at the least, equal to those he owed the intelligence people.

Of course he wanted to see her. How absurd.

"And I remember Alice came in and . . . it was kind of sad, the way she looked. She was after any information at all, you know? I asked her if she wanted anything to eat. No, she was interested in just getting some news."

Alice sat down. Hegdahl began slowly: Dick was in adequate mental and physical health; he wanted Alice to know he loved her and that love sustained him; wherever she wanted to live after this war was done was her decision to make; never again did he wish to be in a position where he was separated from his family; his family, Hegdahl said, was more important than his career.

He began then, as gently as possible, but directly, the accounting Stratton had directed him to give: the capture, the interrogations, tortures, humiliations, starvation, solitary, forced propaganda; a full explanation of the bowing incident, "the whole nine yards," as Stratton said. The debriefer scribbled and occasionally winced; no one had briefed Hegdahl on what was classified material and what was not.

Alice sat ashen and still in the chair. No flicker of emotion corrupted her face, and Hegdahl was too woolly to pay attention to her eyes.

He relived the long days, the endless hours of captivity and black rooms; he touched on moments of happiness and relief from the monotony.

"I said . . . I said, 'Dick is very pleased with the way you've raised the kids. He's just tickled you are handling it so well.' That was the only time she kind of smiled.

"I felt so bad because she acted so grateful and I guess I was in sort of an exalted position, being a returned POW. It was if I was really doing her a big favor by talking to her. . . . And I felt, I felt I just wanted to reassure her. I remember mentioning that I thought he was doing very well, and I think the things I related let her know he was certainly all right: the fact he knew little things about the kids and stuff like that (from the few letters of hers that had gotten through). Later, things she said about the meeting, well, that surprised me a little bit, that perhaps she was as naïve as she had been. She just didn't let on when I was talking with her. She didn't talk very much, she just listened mostly.

"Oh, I don't know. I always felt Alice was grasping, just grasping for anything. I just wanted, really, to reassure her. . . ."

Alice Stratton's life forever altered in those merciless, brief moments. The devastation would have been no less had she been raped.

* * *

"Now I knew.

"I remember walking out of that room and into an elevator in a total state of shock.

"It was such a shock. That really was a shock. I had no conception of what had happened, that he had been mistreated to that extent. I had never even allowed myself to even think that . . . that . . . that anything so bad had happened.

"It was easier when I didn't know during those years . . . because you can pretend: you can pretend he's been given a shot in the arm and drugged, or something. Even when Methany came home, I asked him what really happened to Dick, the bowing and all? He said, 'I think you'd better wait and let Dick tell you about it.' He was not going to tell me. He was telling *other* people and I remember a story getting back to me, but I still didn't. . . ."

* * *

One look at her sister-in-law and Ellen Cooper's stomach turned sour.

"I can remember [Alice] coming back . . . upset . . . under control. I knew she had some terrible things to say. I kept sort of putting her off: 'Well, I'll just finish the dishes and *then* we'll go in the living room and talk,' as if I just didn't want to hear it.

"Then we did go in the living room. She told me. . . .

"These things, one after another . . . just so horrible, were beyond anything I'd ever experienced. It seemed to take me days to take it in. She told me that [Dick] had a chance to come home, and turned it down. That, too, was extremely difficult for me to comprehend. I was incredulous . . . a father of three sons giving up a chance to come home? I could not understand it. In the military context [perhaps it was] a good, brave thing: Dick and Alice had a belief in this conflict—and the purpose of it—which I did not share. Perhaps it was easier for them to understand than it was for me.

"After Alice left [for California] it was three or four days before I told Richard, my husband. I could not say the words. The words would not come out, they were so bad. . . .

"That was the beginning of the acceptance of the reality of torture and it was so difficult for me to accept that any human being could do that to another human being. And while others' reactions seemed to be more personal—you know, how could that happen to *Dick?*—I never fully recovered from the knowledge of what bad things we do to each other.

"I felt so strongly about it that it changed me totally. Whether I was incredibly naïve, I do not know. [Before,] I lived in a world where, I thought, people were basically good; I had to accept some of the badness of human beings, and it so disillusioned me, it changed me from an idealist to a would-be cynic. (I wouldn't have quite made the grade as a cynic; I'm not really a cynic.) But [that incident] took away a lot of illusions I had lived with because, I guess, in . . . growing up during World War II, war was bands playing and savings bonds and heroes coming home.

"So here I was in my early thirties discovering the reality of war: it was horrible. Intellectually I knew it was, but had never truly felt it so inside."

* * *

Alice remembered little of those days; she operated by instinct, one imagines. When she arrived back in Buffalo, she opened up enough to tell Ellen almost all Hegdahl had related. She continued the next day with packing and got herself and the boys back to Palo Alto. She did not tell them much of what she had learned, nor did she tell her parents or the senior Strattons. She did tell her brother-in-law, Charles.

A week went by, perhaps longer, and only gradually did anger displace shock.

"One of the wives asked me what had happened to Dick. I lied. I just couldn't talk about it. I just couldn't believe it. It was too much. I really was shocked. I *really* was shocked.

"Probably wasn't too wise [going to see Hegdahl]. Total shock. Now, the [Navy] didn't know that, don't think they could have realized what it did to me. I could not get hysterical, so I just closed up.

" 'Nothing more is coming into me.'

"I didn't know how to deal with it.

"I don't think Dick realized how naïve I was about the way they were being treated. I guess he assumed I knew more about war, how horrible it is, and about prison camps; he had the background from the military. I just didn't have any conception of it, of man's inhumanity to man. And to have it happen to your own. . . .

"How could they do that to my husband?"

Her reading intensified—anything about prisoners, other wars, other prison camps, other survivors. She realized that "this had been happening since the beginning of time. Where had I been? Was it just the Asians who treated people like that? No, of course not. The *English* treated people like that!"

From Washington, in the midst of all this, Hegdahl (and later

Frishman) telephoned her. The government wanted to go public with the Stratton story: a full-scale press conference to relate what was going on in the Hanoi camps. Would Alice give them permission to tell what had happened to Dick?

"I thought about it, and worried about it, and finally said yes," said Alice Stratton. "It didn't occur to me it might save his life, because I worried the other way. Perhaps I'm too much the worry wart, that they might take it out on him. You just didn't know which way it would go. None of us knew the [North Vietnamese] that well. There were guesses . . . that it might help him.

"But I felt uncomfortable because I was speaking for the family. I felt I should have asked Ellen and Richard Cooper, all of them, but I . . . I didn't. I just . . . I mean, what can you do? They would have all said yes, no, maybe . . . and the Navy wanted a decision. I talked to the casualty department: what's your recommendation? They said, there is a risk, but it is a better idea to go ahead and get some publicity now. I had to trust them."

"I imagine," said Hegdahl, "Alice was going through the same thing I was. I couldn't sleep knowing we were going to go public. I was worried they were going to zap him or something. We really couldn't tell for sure."

" 'Okay, do it,' " Alice told Hegdahl. " 'Do it.' I was very nervous they would thump on him again. [And after the press conference] Dick decided not to write for fourteen months, which reinforced that nervousness terrifically. Wow! It was the one time I was not sure he was alive. I didn't lose hope, really, but I [thought], maybe he is not there. I don't think you can really, fully consider it. You can peek at it, but not allow yourself to emotionally think of that."

* * *

The government's major press conference September 2, 1969, at Bethesda Naval Hospital, opened with a government spokesman charging the North Vietnamese government with violating basic standards of human decency. The spokesman, reading from a strongly worded statement by Defense Secretary Melvin Laird, said:

"There is clear evidence that North Vietnam has violated even the most fundamental standards of human decency. It consistently has claimed, through propaganda statements, that our men have been humanely treated. Information the Department of Defense has received clearly refutes those contentions."[1]

Behind him on a dais, Frishman and Hegdahl sat awaiting their turns to speak. They were pale and thin, but self-possessed. They were dressed in starched summer uniforms, white as fresh-split marble. On his sleeve, Hegdahl wore his new rating: the single inverted chevron of a third-class petty officer.

"It may be," the government spokesman continued, "that top officials in Hanoi are unaware of the shocking conditions within North Vietnamese prison camps. Nevertheless, North Vietnam is accountable to every human being for these flagrant violations of human decency. North Vietnam is also accountable for its failure to release sick and injured prisoners and for its failure to permit the men to correspond freely with their families. Hanoi knows about these violations.

"Some of our men have been in Communist prison camps for more than five years. Over 200 have been there longer than three and a half years. We are concerned that the passage of so many months of captivity could have long-term, adverse effects on the well-being of our men. . . ."[2]

The two returned prisoners were introduced. Frishman, the senior man, spoke first and upstaged Hegdahl; inexplicably, because Frishman had never spoken to Richard Stratton. The young South Dakotan, a slight flush on his pale, thin cheeks, sat tight-lipped as Frishman described the ordeals of himself and Stratton, the tortures, Stratton's press conference, and its aftermath in the black room. "I feel," said Frishman, "like I am Stratton's chance to blow the whistle and get the facts out. Actually, I've seen Stratton and he's in fair shape despite the torture. He's a real example for me to follow. Stratton knows I've been released. He told me not to worry about telling the truth about him. He said that if he gets tortured some more at least he will know why he's getting it and he will feel that it will be worth the sacrifice."[3]

He concluded with a plea for Hanoi to live up to its claims of lenient and humane treatment, and for the American public to make itself aware of the abuse of American prisoners in North Vietnam.

Frishman dwelled briefly on his own difficulties in North Vietnam: medical treatment for his shattered elbow was denied unless he agreed to give information. Despite his wound, he was roped to a stool, finally lapsing into a coma after two days. When his elbow bones were finally removed, the shrapnel was left in the arm, and the wound took six months to heal. Most of Frishman's twenty-seven-odd months in captivity were spent isolated in solitary confinement.

(What he did not know then was that Navy surgeons would be unable to mend his tattered arm well enough for him to resume his Navy flying career, and he would go on limited service; neither did he know that the strains of captivity would finally end his already shaky marriage.)

Hegdahl delivered an unembellished précis of 353 words. He described the state of his health, which, he said, was excellent, his tumble from the deck of the U.S.S. *Canberra* and his rescue by North Vietnamese fishermen, his imprisonment and stretches in solitary confinement, and the paucity of mail received by POWs; and he gave an assurance to reporters that Washington was diligently working to get the remaining prisoners out of North Vietnam.

(Frishman held center stage again during the question-and-answer period that followed the formal statements, and continued to hold it in the weeks that followed as the major subject of a lengthy article in the Washington *Evening Star,* as the author of a briefer piece in *Reader's Digest,* and as a star witness—preceding Hegdahl again—before the House Committee on Internal Security investigating the Students for a Democratic Society (SDS) for its members' travels to communist nations, its alleged active support of Hanoi's war effort at home and in North Vietnam, and its involvement with POW repatriation. Other pro-Hanoi American groups were also under study.)

The tales of Frishman and Hegdahl made real the worst fears of the National League of Families, and that organization—now fully vindicated—increased its efforts and its pressures on both the American and North Vietnamese governments and upon the American public.

The revelations of torture provided as well a bond where responsible citizens divided over the war itself joined together. The plight of the POWs became to great degree a separate issue over which there was little dissension, although hard-line anti-war activists insisted the stories were fabrications by the Administration designed to undermine the peace movement.

* * *

On September 4 in Hanoi, Ho Chi Minh died of heart failure. He was seventy-nine. The nation went into mourning.

Whatever evil Ho represented for the Americans, he was beloved by his own, a poet-philosopher-politician who lived simply in a converted stable behind the Presidential Palace. Though Ho eschewed deity, he was not unaware of the myths and legends grown up around him, which he helped perpetuate, or of questions about his past and his name (he was born Nguyen That Thanh in 1890 in Nghe An Province, the son of an impoverished scholar, and took his pseudonym while he was in jail between 1942 and 1943 after his arrest by the Chinese secret police).[4] "Little mysteries," he called them. Pressed once about his past by Bernard B. Fall, the eminent Vietnam scholar, Ho demurred with a sly smile: ". . . I am an old man, a very old man. An old man likes to have an air of mystery about himself. I like to hold on to my little mysteries. I'm sure you will understand."[5]

He was not without wit ("Tell me, is the Statue of Liberty still standing? Sometimes it seems to me it must be standing on its head").[6]

And he understood well the deprivations of imprisonment from his own experience:

. . . Four months leading a life in which there is nothing human
Have aged me more than ten years.
Yes: in a whole four months I have never had a comfortable
    night's sleep,
In four months I have never changed my clothes, and in four
    months
I have never taken a bath.
So: I have lost a tooth, my hair has grown grey,
And, lean and black as a demon gnawed by hunger,
I am covered with scabies.
    Fortunately

253

Being stubborn and patient, never yielding an inch,
Though physically I suffer, my spirit is unshaken.[7]

North Vietnam was a wail of misery. Radio speakers throughout the nation sobbed with dirges. In the streets weeping Vietnamese chanted his name over and over and over again. The prison guards and administrators wore mourning patches on their tunics and were short-tempered and agitated.

A majority of the prisoners in Hanoi's major camps declared a temporary truce in their resistance war, a few out of respect for some honest guard's misery, the majority sensing grave danger in baiting warders made unstable by grief. But for the passing of Ho himself there was only joy for most POWs, who learned of the news before day's end or surmised what had happened.

In his examination of the POWs, John G. Hubbell wrote: "The speed with which Ho's political heirs moved to improve life for the prisoners seemed to indicate some degree of understanding that the old regime's policies had been counterproductive."[8] Ho appeared, Hubbell added, to have dangerously misjudged the feelings of the American public for the captured men.

How much of his attitude was based on judgments of impassioned anti-war activists visiting his country can only be a matter of speculation. The activists' judgments were wrong, too. Frishman and Hegdahl made the United States POW-conscious. Ho's death permitted the government to instigate more lenient POW treatment, although it was hardly full-scale prison reform. There never would be a full accounting of all the men; mail was still impeded; no Red Cross officials inspected the camps; punishments for infractions were still out of keeping with the alleged crimes.

But there was change.

A promoted Soft Soap Fairy made it a point to tell senior men they would not be tortured as long as he was in camp administration. He was true to his word.

Food altered radically, in amount and in quality; soups were aromatic and swimming in vegetables; bread was fresh and abundant.

Major Bui was in disgrace; he had lost a star off his collar, was relieved as commandant of prisons and made a camp commander at Hoa Lo. At one point he alledgedly told an old nemesis, Commander Jeremiah A. Denton, Jr., that for thousands of years the official policy of [Vietnam] had been humane and lenient treatment, but that in the case of the Americans, he and a number of officers and guards had misinterpreted and misapplied this policy. They had all, he added, been made to publicly confess their errors.[9]

The statement, if accurate, is all the more remarkable when one considers Vietnamese "face."

Within a short time, he was gone. This devious, immaculate man with his careful English who held all power over all POWs simply vanished.

Several prisoners were granted roommates and, while communication between compounds and buildings was still forbidden, no apparent attempt was now made to stifle exchanges between prisoners within the compounds or buildings themselves.

Still, food and inter-cell communications did not alter entirely the prison situation. The Vietnamese were determined not to allow the prisoners to organize en masse, and were equally determined to maintain the prisoner propaganda mill of news broadcasts and such. Prisoners were not tortured; still, the threat was always there. For most of the prisoners, resistance remained a primary function and a high-risk endeavor.

(When, for example, in the spring of 1970, just before he was shipped back to Hoa Lo, Richard Stratton claimed leadership of the Plantation prisoners—and demanded Vietnamese adherence to the Geneva Convention, in writing—"it was an affront the Vietnamese could not take." He was wrestled to the floor of an interrogation room and flayed with bamboo rods.)

* * *

The year 1969 was a pivotal one for the war effort, the prisoner issue, the anti-war campaign, and the Vietnamese policy regarding its captives; 1969 was the watershed, the last hurrah of a sometimes loony, often insane, bloody, divisive decade.

It began with a changing of the guard: Johnson gone, Humphrey trounced, Nixon in, in to an unmeasurable degree by virtue of his "secret plan" to end the war in Vietnam. The Democrats' chief negotiator in Paris, Ambassador Averell Harriman, was replaced by the Republicans' Henry Cabot Lodge. The peace talks resumed January 18, expanded now to include representatives of the Thieu government of South Vietnam and the National Liberation Front. The Nixonians were under pressure; support for the war eroded steadily in the face of no discernible peace progress or battlefield victories; more than 30,000 servicemen were dead; 549,000 U.S. troops packed South Vietnam.

On May 8 the National Liberation Front offered a ten-point peace proposal to Ambassador Lodge that contained two key measures: unilateral withdrawal of all American troops from Vietnam, and NLF political participation in South Vietnam. President Nixon countered a week later with an eight-pointer, seeking mutual troop withdrawal from South Vietnam and an internationally supervised cease-fire. The Nixon proposal was as silly as the NLF's: America would not dump out unilaterally, if only for reasons of face; North Vietnam always denied its regular forces fought in the South, so it could not withdraw troops that did not exist.

Summer went no better. South Vietnam's President Thieu suggested in July that the NLF participate in his nation's elections, but the elections must be internationally supervised. The communists denounced this "obvious trickery."

In August, shortly after Henry Kissinger and high-ranking North Vietnamese began secret peace talks, the anti-war forces were delighted with the courts-martial under Article 118 of the Uniform Code of Military Justice of several Special Forces (Green Berets) officers and noncoms for the murder of a South Vietnamese. The charges were dropped when the dead man was identified as a double agent and the Central Intelligence Agency refused to allow its agents to testify.

An otherwise insignificant American Army second lieutenant was ordered September 5 to remain on active duty pending investigation of alleged offenses under Article 118, UCMJ, while serving with C Company, First Battalion, Twentieth Infantry, Eleventh Brigade, in Quang Ngai Province. The officer's name was William L. Calley, Jr.

In November, President Nixon announced his plan to "Vietnamize" the war by withdrawing all American ground troops on a secret timetable. Two weeks later, a quarter of a million anti-war protestors invaded Washington; congressional leaders demanded concrete dates for withdrawal, and Lieutenant Calley was indicted for the murder of 109 civilians at My Lai.

Navy Commanders Charles Conrad, Jr., and Alan L. Bean of Apollo 12 landed on the moon November 18. It was the second American moon landing in five months.

The stories told by Frishman and Hegdahl were retold and reread in Hanoi. Stratton's name figured prominently in these. He was braced one day by a member of the political cadre at the Plantation, a former interrogator and sometime camp administrator named Frenchy:

"Stratton, you know Heddle?"

"Yeah, I know Hegdahl. He was one of my roommates."

"He is a very stupid man!"

"That is one opinion."

"He even say they pull out all of your fingernail."

"No, they didn't do that. . . ."

"See? He is a stupid man, Stratton."

". . . Just two of them, just two."

"You even tell him you were burned with cigarettes and you were tortured."

"That is true."

"Is it true?"

"Yes."

"Stratton, you are the most unlucky of the unlucky."

CHAPTER 22

The grooming of candidate Nixon as peacemaker garnered him votes from lots of folks who normally never would have voted Republican, and for whom the man himself represented the nadir of American politics. But there were many who held to the view—Ellen Cooper, for example, who voted for him—that following Johnson's self-imposed exile from Washington, the bombing halt, and the continuing dialogue in Paris, a new Republican President would have an opportunity to end the war and bring the prisoners home right then and there in January 1969.

They were wrong.

Peace did not come. The troops and the prisoners remained in Indochina. And when, after all the fruitless talk in 1969, the President ordered in April of 1970 a combined American–South Vietnamese invasion of Cambodia (ostensibly to cut and destroy communist supply depots and border sanctuaries), his image of peacemaker tarnished perceptibly. When, by the fall, he had reduced troop strength in South Vietnam to 368,000 men (or by nearly 200,000 troops) critics suggested the boys were coming home because B-52s did a better job bloodying the enemy.

The next year was no better: the American anti-war movement, still sputtering and suspicious after the Cambodian invasion, was cheered when the President signed legislation repealing Johnson's Gulf of Tonkin Resolution, and flung into frenzy less than a month later when Nixon lent American air and artillery support to a messy, ill-advised, and ill-fated forty-four-day South Vietnamese invasion into neutral Laos.

American troop strength dropped to 208,000 men; American bombers dropped record amounts of ordnance as the birds filled the manpower vacuum.

That just about tore it.

At least, it tore it for Ellen Cooper. Her disaffection with the Administration had driven her out of the closet in 1970. She went back on the picket lines and resumed her activities in the anti-war movement, ever cautious, though, that zealous colleagues did not exploit the fact she had a brother in Hanoi. The year 1971, with its endless peace proposals, counter-proposals, talk, Laos, endless air war, POWs still in Hanoi, moved her to an incredible state of frustration and anger. On December 24, 1971, she vented her feelings of rage and betrayal on page 2 of the Buffalo *Evening News:*

"Dear President Nixon:

"Must my brother be a prisoner of war again next Christmas? He will have spent four Christmases in a North Vietnamese prison camp since you were elected in November of 1968. I voted for you in that election because you pledged to end the war quickly. I hope that mistake will not cost my brother his life.

"Time is running out for these men in their quiet rooms in Hell. POWs are freed by ending a war, not continuing it. I beg you to end the war completely before the 1972 election. Do not mislead the American people by telling them that we need a residual force in Vietnam as long as there are prisoners there. On the contrary, as long as there is a residual force in Vietnam, there will be POWs.

"The men who have died in Vietnam cannot be brought back, but it is still not too late to save the prisoners.

"Ellen Cooper/Buffalo, N.Y."

That letter (which Mr. Nixon did not answer) said Ellen Cooper, made her a controversial figure. It was a quarter page and cost her husband $800, but it was money he considered well spent; Dr. Richard Cooper now agreed with his wife on Vietnam.

Ellen decided she "would vote for Nixon on the basis of the fact that he was of another party; it wasn't his party's war and he [rather than the Democratic candidate, Vice President Humphrey] would be in a better position to say those Democrats got us into it, now let's get out of it.

"On the strength of that, I was patient with that man. Waiting. I gave him—I think—until the spring of 1970 [the time of the Cambodian invasion], when I became extremely upset. He gave one of his little talks on television one evening and it was like a light bulb going on over my head. I had been patient. I was wrong. This man was lying. I was furious . . . and I never believed him again. I hated that man enough to understand why some individuals end up killing a head of state. I do *not* mean a total nut, but someone who had a rational basis; I understood that amount of frustration and anger. I am not saying that I positively entertained the fantasy of killing the man but I now knew [what would prompt someone to do it]. A lot of [what I felt] had to do with Dick, and Nixon's exploitation of the whole prisoner [issue]."

The letter gained her a measure of regional attention, though in no way did she ever figure as a prominent, national anti-war activist. But by virtue of her politics and her brother's position she was a rare bird.

Ellen Cooper may not have wanted to be controversial, but she could not have it both ways. The anger, the turmoil inside would finally be resolved only by professional help; it was a perilous state for a woman who genuinely wanted to be liked and preferred anonymity.

"But I knew I would have to live the rest of my life with what I did during those years, and I had to follow my conscience. That was the only way I was going to make it and it wasn't easy because, contrary to what my family thought, I really did not like controversy. It is hard to appreciate . . . how hard this was for me; these things were not easy for me to do."

How deep Ellen Cooper's commitment was is illustrated by two incidents in Washington, where she was attending meetings held by the National League of Families. She was one of only twenty or twenty-five persons present who were Navy relatives. The group was invited to luncheon by the Chief of Naval Operations, Admiral Elmo Zumwalt. That same noon, anti-war groups had organized a demonstration in front of the White House.

"I went to picket the White House because I felt it would be better for Dick. I knew he wouldn't like it and [he probably still thinks] I would be somewhat amused by picketing the White House.

"I hated it!

"I was embarrassed by it. It was lacking in dignity. I would rather have not been in that position, but, feeling the way I did, I had to follow my conscience and do that rather than sitting with some admiral chatting about niceties."

The second incident the following day involved a more difficult choice.

"It was suddenly announced at this meeting that the President of the United States was coming [to greet us]. The doors flew open, and in came the secret servicemen and President Nixon.

"The crowd went wild. People were yelling, screaming, cheering, Women were throwing themselves [at] him. It was a fantastic display of emotion. I was faced with a terrible decision: what was I going to do?

"I made the instantaneous decision that I would stand up for this man because he represented the office of the President of the United States. . . ."

She stood amid that adoring, applauding chorus, tears in her eyes, her hands at her sides clenching the seams of her skirt.

"It was so hard for me. I had so many strong feelings about this and I have tried to put so many of them aside. At one point I even spoke to a psychologist about some of these feelings. I just had to get out all sorts of anger I had about this. And also, I had worked so hard during that time to be independent, to be in control, to be brave, so to speak, that I think I turned away support that could have . . . helped me in dealing with it. Perhaps [had I accepted it] I would not have felt so alone."

Even with support, one suspects she would have been alone: the war was controversial, her brother was controversial, and the subject of Vietnamese treatment of POWs was controversial; spokesmen for the anti-war movement gave little credence to increasing stories of ill treatment of the POWs, and no acknowledgment of poor prisoner treatment or battlefield atrocities by National Liberation Front guerrillas or North Vietnamese regulars.

"Here were these people who probably had the same views about the war that I did . . . quibbling about whether or not [the Vietnamese] actually pulled out Stratton's fingernails. This was very hard on me, to wake up one Sunday morning and read Anthony Lucas [J. Anthony, "Tony," Lucas of the New York *Times*] writing that it was a bunch of baloney about Stratton. Once William Sloan Coffin was here on the television in Buffalo [the Rev. William Sloan Coffin, Jr., the chaplain of Yale University, and an anti-war activist] . . . saying something like, And that *Stratton* story, of course, is *not* true, but . . . some sort of propaganda the Right was using to make the Vietnamese look bad. I once wrote him a letter about that; he conveniently did not recollect, but he was sure he didn't say that. Well, he *did* say that!

"They all believed it, including Ramsey Clark, who . . . came back [from Vietnam] and said they were the best-treated bunch of prisoners in the world, or something like that.

"It was very hard. [As I have said before] I wondered if anybody was looking for the truth, or was everybody just boxed into a predetermined position?

"When the chips are down, how terribly alone you are."

What compounded Ellen Cooper's agony was the disintegration of her faith in the Church (not her faith in Catholicism, but the establishment) and in her government.

"I always felt that people were questioning my patriotism, and I felt I was a patriot, too, despite my views. I criticized my children and I loved them and I wanted them to be better; I felt the same way about my country. But I could not accept . . . this war I did not believe in and this government that was exploiting [my brother] and seemed uncaring, and a Church that I had been brought up in that seemed determined to be irrelevant.

"And I resolved it, finally, by not believing much in authority. Once Dick said to me when we were having a discussion about the Church, 'The trouble with you is you don't believe in anything but yourself.' But the Church made me very angry, and sometimes I suspect Dick felt the Church abandoned him.

"Here was the country being torn apart by this war and I never heard it mentioned [by the Church]. When I approached the Church about help for the prisoners, an humanitarian issue and a natural for somebody who didn't want to get involved in a political conflict, it was mostly nonresponsive. This was in the diocese in Buffalo. I began writing angry letters to the bishop and the monsignor.

"But I also felt the same thing about Quincy: my parents had been good, solid parishioners at Sacred Heart parish for forty years and it did nothing, absolutely *nothing,* when I wrote to the monsignor to inquire whether it would be possible to say a few prayers for Dick, a man who grew up in the parish, on a certain day set aside for the prisoners. There was no response to my letter.

"So when I heard a year after the war was over that the church in Quincy was dedicating a new flag and flagpole to Captain Stratton . . . it really made me angry. I'm not sure how Dick felt about it, but it was too late for me. They were not going to endear themselves to me by these gestures following the war because they suddenly discovered they had a war hero on their hands!"

* * *

Alice Stratton was spared the authority crises and the internal turmoil of her sister-in-law; but, like Ellen, she followed her conscience in efforts to help her husband. The shock of Hegdahl's story passed, replaced by terrible anger.

Though she constantly worried that the international publicity given Frishman's and Hegdahl's stories might mean additional punishment for him, she felt she had no choice but to keep the facts in front of the public. It was all she had to fight with. And with Charlie in kindergarten, she devoted more time to her league activities. Time did not lessen the anger.

"How could they do this to my husband? I was going to tell the world, and this coincided with the government's feeling that the world should be told. I had natural material to move in with. With our local [league] chapter and the one we formed at Moffett, we really got rolling; we were just going to tell the world. I wrote up what [Hegdahl] told me had happened to Dick and I just read it off at meeting after meeting . . . in a monotone, because [once again] I could not let the emotion come through. . . . We spoke to service groups, Kiwanis, Rotary, at schools, to anyone who would listen, frankly. Generally we did not take much flak, but at a few places, at junior colleges and colleges, we did. One particular one, I remember, I think it was De Anza in Cupertino, they really give it to us.

"There were two of us, Sondra Bors [the wife of an MIA] and myself; luckily, there were two of us for support. The students started to let go their feelings on the war, and how did we feel about it, being the wives of—nobody actually said being 'the wives of killers,' but they skirted around it [enough] so you got the picture.

"I was angry at having been treated this way, but it was because I was somewhat unprepared. Again, it forced me to ask, what do I believe, and not to be defensive the next time. And how did I feel about what he did? Again, it was like my mother's faith. You accept it. I had never even thought about it a lot . . . until I began to hear these kinds of things. Up until then, I don't think I'd really come to grips with what I thought about it, which is surprising. Anyway, [that Cupertino incident] was good for us, because if we were going to be out there, we'd better know what we were talking about. We always stressed the humanitarian issue, which was not for or against the war. But you really had to know what you believed in; otherwise, you get awfully defensive and awfully upset. Some people thought I was becoming tough and hard. Sondra thought she saw it happening, but I don't think so. You learned ways to put on an exterior to protect yourself, but wise ways so you could legitimately answer a question and get your point across."

Eventually, at the instigation of Bonnie Duck, the wives were given a room in the office of Moffett's willing chaplain, the Reverend John Berger, with phones and desks and filing cabinets, the hardware of a movement. Standing committees for speakers, publicity, community liaison, and the like were organized; endless petition drives throughout the Bay Area collected signatures in support of the POWs and MIAs. A Big Brother program for the children of fatherless families was organized; there was a "freedom sing" in San Jose; Frishman was trotted out once to make a speech; Hegdahl himself was on the road now, and always willing to speak; Shirley Temple Black visited Red Cross centers on behalf of the wives.

Chaplain Berger and his aunt, Dr. Evelyn Berger Brown, a psychologist, developed and directed a series of retreats for the wives where they could meet alone, away from daily cares and chores, to discuss their situations and together face their anxieties and fears. It was a monumental chore, considering the emotional time bombs that were ticking in those women and their various family situations and philosophical outlooks, but it worked.

Alice Stratton attended three such retreats, one in 1971 and two the following year. The first retreat was conducted by Evelyn Berger Brown. "We all liked her very much," recalled Alice, "and it was at this retreat that I first came to grips with my fear about the possibility that Dick may have changed.

"She was talking about the fact that these men [might] come back different. . . . I broke into tears and I was surprised at my reaction because I was not aware, until then, how really afraid of that I was.

"On the second retreat the leader was an Air Force psychiatrist. We had some girls from Southern California on this retreat, as well as our northern California group, so some of us were strangers to one another. One girl's husband had just recently been shot down [this was the spring of 1972]. In one of our group sessions, she began to sob out her anguish and despair that she could never make it alone, and feeling the loss and the missing of her husband. I remember the same feelings welling back up into me and I tried to choke back the tears. Soon my throat was aching for the effort and the tears flowed anyway, as they did for many of us. We all knew what she was feeling.

"It was a very emotional time for me and it hammered down what I had learned over and over in my work with people.

"When I went as an instructor to the University of Michigan's summer camp for emotionally disturbed boys . . . we received (as I have said) a week of training. I called it 'combat readiness.' Bill Morris, the director, set the tone the last night before the kids arrived with a story of a boy from the slums of Detroit. This was a kid who had never been outside the slums, and when he came to camp he was taken on an overnight hike. He looked up at the stars as they all sat around the campfire and he said, 'Will you look at all those goddamned, motherfucking stars!' It was said with awe and wonder.

"Bill was trying to point out that these were kids, regardless of their language, who could still experience just as much as any other kid. I think that story epitomized my feelings about working with these kids. And I was reminded at the retreats how similar our feelings are underneath [regardless of our language] once the defensive layers are peeled away.

"It has been my experience that always, always, once the spiny retorts and sharpness we carry around as a defense have been cleared away, there is a great goodness to people. This is not to

265

say there is still not weakness and vulnerability, but in no case have I not seen man's goodness.

"I guess that's why I love social work so much. It allows you to see so much beauty in folks."

* * *

Thank God, she thought, the roughest times were behind her; thank God she could go out on the line and do battle for her husband and the other prisoners and the missing. How she grieved for those other women, women who did not know whether their man was in a cell or in pieces. Thank God she had outlets now, friends, the league, the retreats, a place in the community, a kindergarten for Charlie, and the money to pay for it.

(Dick had been promoted to full commander and the increase in pay was welcome; she had had to struggle, sometimes, on the allotment paid to her; it amounted to just over $1,000 a month, not a small sum, but with a mortgage, a car, and three boys, not a large sum, either.)

Yet the emptiness was always there. She lived day by day, and the days segued to weeks to months to years. How many more years?

"If I hadn't had outlets finally," she once told a friend, "I . . . I can understand how parents crack up, beat their kids; I can really empathize with them now, because even with everything going for me as a single parent, it is the hardest thing I have ever done. Then, you always have the worry, are you doing it right?

"For instance, when Patrick didn't learn to read right away, I didn't even dream he might have a learning problem. I thought he had *emotional* problems because he missed his father and I hadn't done things right; if only I hadn't been so hard on him.

". . . When the psychologist said, 'Mrs. Stratton, your son has a learning problem [dyslexia],' I went home and cried, cried with relief that *I* hadn't ruined him. It *wasn't* me! He'd been born with it.

"Whew!"

* * *

Douglas Hegdahl gave up his rating and accepted the Navy's offer of an early honorable discharge. (His enlistment originally ran to October, 1970.) He found imprisonment had marked him.

266

He was a compulsive pack rat and his bachelor apartment in San Diego was filled with tinfoil, tin plates, TV dinner trays. He could not bear to throw it all out.

"It was very scary getting out of the hospital," he would later tell a reporter for the New York *Times*. "You have to gear yourself back up to a fast pace, and they're throwing all these decisions at you. They're not really doing that, but it seems that way, and even the smallest decision is a tremendous thing when all you have had to worry about is when you are going to eat a chunk of bread."[10] He added, as an afterthought, that once he decided to eat, he would nibble away for an hour, just to kill some time.

He found, he said, so many people "zooming around in a mad dash" that he sought solitude by driving out to the desert and camping alone.[11]

He was the first to admit that it had been rather nice, all the attention he was getting, and the publicity. How many boys from Clark, South Dakota, after all, testified before congressional committees in Washington? The key was, however, that he *was* a farm boy from South Dakota, and gradually he stopped believing his own publicity because he found the hubbub annoying, and he "felt like some sort of weirdo."

"After a while you feel used. I don't know how many times a Senator put his arm around me and smiled into the camera, so he could say how much he was doing for the POWs."[12]

Hegdahl made two tours around the country speaking on the prisoner issue for concerned groups like the National League, not as a "hero," but as a man with a tale to tell, a mission for the men he'd left behind. He wearied of the one-night stands and the incessant travel and the absence of solitude, but he kept at it, he said, because it was important work. He had also some insights and he wanted to relay them, things he had learned in Hanoi.

"Most Americans think of everything in terms of black or white," he said; "there can't be any shades in between. Then you look at the Vietnamese: they have sixty shades of right and sixty shades of wrong."

And:

"I never realized how abundant everything is [in America]. When you see the waste that goes on, it really makes you wonder."[13]

On a trip to Texas, he was contacted by a man named Murphy

267

Martin. Martin was secretary to H. Ross Perot, a mildly eccentric Annapolis graduate who had made a bundle in computers. From his Dallas headquarters, Perot carried on an impassioned war of his own against the Vietnamese and for the prisoners and their families. He was rich enough and powerful enough to do it. Tales about him and his colorful exploits were legion. It was believed Perot money paid the way for POW/MIA wives to Paris and Asia to protest Vietnamese treatment and seek information on their men. Rumor had it that Perot employed his own intelligence operatives throughout Southeast Asia, who gathered information on the Vietnamese, prisoners, anti-war groups, anything that could help on the prisoner issue. Perot once contacted Alice Stratton and offered to pay her way to the Orient to bargain for her husband's release, an offer of kindness she appreciated but gently declined on the advice of Naval Intelligence and her own common sense.

Now Perot money helped pay for Hegdahl's travels around the United States, and two more tours in Texas.

"Doug, how would you like to go to Paris?" Martin asked.

To Paris: to harass the Vietnamese, to gain more publicity for the plight of the prisoners and the missing? How would he indeed.

Hegdahl and Martin landed in Paris in December of 1970 and checked in at the Hilton. They spent some time making up lists of demands to present to the North Vietnamese and getting the lay of the land, so to speak.

"Some of the demands were outrageous," Hegdahl recalled with delight. "Things like letting the Red Cross in to inspect the camps; things like letting me go back to Vietnam with a news team and film the camps with the Red Cross. Some were serious, too.

"We didn't have much success, of course, but then it was mainly to harass [the Vietnamese] and keep the prisoner thing in the news. Oh, we'd pin little notes in French [they had an interpreter to assist them] on their door, things like that. They were embarrassed."

Hegdahl suffered an acute attack of paranoia and was uncomfortable at the lush Hilton. He felt people were watching him, and that he was followed. He worried their plans might go awry if anyone discovered him and Martin at the same hotel. Martin understood, and Hegdahl moved to a small, out-of-the-way pension by himself, rooms fit for a poor poet, he imagined. He had some time before taking on his old enemies, and he enjoyed himself. He did the sights, tested the food, walked the boulevards. Once, in a bookstore, he met and chatted for twenty minutes with Erich Segal, author of the best seller *Love Story*. To Segal he was just another friendly American. Hegdahl was relieved.

Hegdahl telephoned the North Vietnamese legation and made an appointment for the following day. They let him in.

"They knew who I was, but I don't think it really dawned on the guy I talked with. And the first time, I was so secretive, I assume they thought, Hey, this guy may be working for *us!*

"Well, I arrived and went in. Martin was not with me; the Vietnamese wouldn't have seen him, and if they had found out I was working for Perot, they really would have been, well, pissed off.

"I guess they thought I would harass them [because I was an American] but I was very polite. I sat under another big picture of Ho Chi Minh. I was *very* polite, and they started giving me their dog and pony show about the POWs.

" 'Don't you understand Nixon's using the prisoners to further his own belligerent war plans?'

"I said, 'Hey, this is a perfect time to prove it. If indeed you are treating the prisoners humanely now, you can prove it. Show Nixon up! Let me go in with the Red Cross and film the camps.'

" 'We couldn't guarantee your safety.'

" 'I'll sign a waiver.'

" 'And our treatment of the prisoners [always] was lenient and humane.'

" 'I don't think you understand. I was a prisoner there.'

" 'Oh.' "

Incredibly, he was allowed a second meeting. He arrived at the legation trailed by newsmen and television cameras. Once inside, he began again presenting his demands. As each in turn was rejected, he came up with another one. The meeting lasted ninety minutes, and that was that. He was not invited back.

He held a press conference on the steps of the legation.

"I am very disappointed," he said, solemnly, "because I thought the Vietnamese would have responded to this very humanitarian plea on behalf of the families of the prisoners."

He never understood why they let him in at all. On the delegates' picture roster in the hall of the legation, he saw the photograph of a Vietnamese officer he recognized. The man was known to Hegdahl only as Smoothie. He had been one of his interrogators in Hanoi.

He left shortly after his meeting with the Vietnamese. He was home for Christmas.

Later he appeared on the Dick Cavett television talk show.

Still later, he was hired by the Navy as a civilian lecturer and instructor for its survival training center. He moved back to San Diego.

He kept in constant contact with Alice Stratton and made occasional visits to Palo Alto.

His war was done.

* * *

In the western half of Hoa Lo prison, a large area in the shape of a crude right triangle standing on its head and dubbed Camp Unity by the POWs, Richard Stratton was feeling better than he had in a long time. It was the Christmas season; New Year was approaching and soon it would be 1972. He had been at Unity more than a year. At first there had been only the Hoa Lo prisoners, but then, as the Vietnamese began closing outlying camps, the population had swelled to more than three hundred men.

It all began, Stratton reckoned, with the Son Tay raid. He recalled how he was heartened when he heard the news: an American commando raid on Son Tay prison camp; the POWs had not been completely forgotten.

That raid, he would later learn, was the personal crusade of Colonel Arthur Simon, a thirty-year veteran of three wars. Simon personally had selected and trained his force of seventy Green Berets, most of them Vietnam combat veterans. The mission read like an Ian Fleming novel: a lightning strike deep inside enemy territory (Son Tay was only twenty miles north of Hanoi), rescue the POWs, and carry them home.

Simon went in by helicopter on November 21, 1970. As many as thirty North Vietnamese soldiers lost their lives defending empty cells. The Son Tay prisoners had been moved to Camp Faith, the next prison down the line and closer to Hanoi, four months before. The raiders were on the ground less than half an hour; there were no fatalities among the Americans and the only casualty was a twisted ankle.

Military intelligence came in for a roasting, but Simon was philosophical; the prisoners could have been moved at any time, he said, even minutes before the would-be liberators landed on the ground. He and his men were decorated for their derring-do. The POWs, when they heard about it, were elated. The Vietnamese, fearing more raids and the possible loss of valuable bargaining material, began closing outlying camps, moving the men into Hanoi and eventually to Hoa Lo. That was when Camp Unity opened. For the majority of the POWs, it was a beginning of compound living with large numbers of their fellows and the end of cellular living, either isolated or with only a very few mates.

Unity was large, the northern and eastern edges of its triangle about 375 feet each, and the third side perhaps 400 feet. Instead of tiny cubicles, there were seven large and three smaller undetached cell buildings, each with an individual or shared front yard, so to speak, delineated by a fence. In the center of the compound was a distinct octagon building that housed showers, and later a kitchen, and two rectangular buildings with rooms for the guards and prisoner interrogations.

The "new" men moving into Unity in early 1971, when outlying camps started closing, brought new information, new prisoner groups, and the camp was a flurry of messages and intelligence. (The Vietnamese did not let compounds mingle in the beginning days of Camp Unity.)

Stratton's wrists often ached at day's end from the hundreds of words he was required to flash by hand signals to other buildings. He was also quite busy with his class on international affairs. There were lessons and lectures to prepare for the prisoners' recently organized "school." If a man had a specialty in any field, he was invited to "teach" it to other prisoners. It helped kill time and bolstered unity and morale.

The POWs had organized themselves now into the Fourth Allied POW Wing. Colonel John Peter Flynn, the highest-ranking captured officer, assumed command. The hapless Hoa Lo authorities had assigned to a single large cell not only Flynn but nine other senior officers; in the past it had kept them isolated from each other and the other prisoners. It was a strategic error. The senior men were now an easy signal away and found it simple, in turn, to set policy and issue orders.

The wing's motto was "Return with Honor," and the senior officers issued blanket amnesty to any prisoner who might have collaborated to any degree for whatever reason. The offer was to remain open until war's end.

Morale improved. So did the excitement of sticking it to the Vietnamese—"getting into their skivvies," Stratton called it.

(The camp authorities, highly sensitive to a POW-conscious public outside Vietnam, urged men to write home. The POWs went on a letter-writing strike. It was voluntary. It was during this period that Stratton did not write Alice for fourteen months.)

It was not easy street, still. Men were punished for the slightest infraction or sometimes on whim, locked in leg irons or put in solitary. Prison sanitation facilities, primitive to begin with, were now overtaxed, and perodic epidemics sickened the inmates. Diseases like conjunctivitis were hardly fatal, but extremely painful and annoying. There was a whole host of these kinds of problems.

Stratton had tooth trouble, for example. A year before, he had suffered an abscessed tooth. He had received treatment for it.

"I received that dental care from the guy who was the doctor, an old man, a good man; the [Communist] Party was forcing him to do things he didn't like. But he was also the veterinarian, the butcher, the supervisor of camp medics, *and* the dentist. He sat me down in a broken-armed captain's chair with a block of wood nailed on the back to hold your head, and he broke the tooth off in my head. A year later the thing became infected again and they brought in what I assume was a real dentist. They did have them; some guys went to real dentists downtown. This guy chiseled out the roots. He had novocaine. The novocaine came from Czechoslovakia. It was two years old when they got it. It didn't work. It was extremely colorful.

"[Real] medical treatment was given to people who were either traitors or about to be given publicity; it was given *in extremis,* for they did not want you to die, most of us anyway. Some, I believe, they did let die; anyone in between did not get medical treatment. There was no such thing as preventive medicine except in rare cases or when they thought, over the years, we might be going home. One time they thought they had a cholera epidemic and we were inoculated; I remember getting [inoculated] that first year when they thought the peace marches in San Francisco and New York were going to win the war for them. They ran around giving people shots. [The stuff in the hypo] was mucky-looking, like something they'd picked out of a mud puddle. The interrogator said it was four shots in one. The [medic] came through and inoculated the whole cellblock. He used the same needle; he never cleaned it.

"If you were a 'good man' like Miller and Wilber [Marine Lieutenant Colonel Edison Wainright Miller and Navy Commander Walter Eugene Wilber],[14] you received medical attention almost continuously whether you needed it or not. . . ."

* * *

Moon Mullen was in Camp Faith when the Son Tay raid occurred. Since 1967 he had bounced through different cells and solitary and the like, winding up at Faith; after Son Tay he moved to Camp Unity and through the communications network learned that his old shipmate Dick Stratton was there, too. As the prison population grew, there was some reshuffling and they found themselves within tapping distance in adjoining cells. It was a short-lived reunion.

Around Christmas, Mullen's cell had a beef with the camp officials. There were fifty-two men in that cell designed or at least comfortable for no more than twenty-five; they were ordered to do camp labor. Being unsure of the object of the work, they refused to do it. The senior officer was pulled out. So was his replacement. That left Mullen in charge. And he quickly got into trouble.

"It was New Year's Eve, and you know this was after the big Christmas thing. During that whole holiday season there was a great deal of spirit and pride in all of the POWs in their heritage and so forth. Well, midnight comes and we are very quietly humming 'Auld Lang Syne' and a bunch of things, and one of the guys said, 'Hey, let's sing "God Bless America"!' I said, just super. Let's do our thing. Well, we just boomed out 'God Bless America' and it was a beautiful thing; I really had tears in my eyes. We all knew what the consequences might be, but we just felt so good and we were just expressing ourselves and the way we felt toward one another and toward what we were, what we really were, and we just boomed it out. Of course, the North Vietnamese didn't particularly care for that, they rattled on the front gate of our cell, and . . . the very next day I was pulled out.

"I was put into Heartbreak . . . for, I don't know, a month or something like that, [with three other] guys living in a two-man cell, two up on the slabs where you normally sleep and then two sleeping athwartships on the floor beneath the slabs. It was pretty cramped. . . . Then we went on out to Skid Row [a maximum-security prison that had been built by the French about ten miles southwest of Hanoi. It lacked lights, good ventilation, and sanitary facilities. Its holding areas were primarily small, heavily barred cells]."

Mullen remained in Skid Row for a year before he was moved back once again to Hoa Lo and Camp Unity.

* * *

For the prisoners who remained at Unity, perhaps the greatest benefit of the new prison regime was a slightly relaxed rule regarding incoming mail and packages. The men received more letters, though certainly not all that were addressed to them; more pictures were left intact. Many prisoners, for the first time, saw new homes in which their wives had been living for years, and pictures of their children, some of whom had not been born when they left for war. In return letters, for the "no-write strike" was over, prisoners demanded minute details of the new homes, mortgages, interest rates, and so on, and when they received them compared notes, redesigned buildings, built new ones in their heads, or enlarged and landscaped the old ones. It killed some time.

Stratton was shocked by new pictures of his sons. The boys were positively *shaggy*. HIS sons!

"The kids' hair kept getting longer and longer. My friends were [urging caution]. 'First of all, I'm going to say, Cut your damn hair!' My friends would say, 'Don't do that. Have faith in Alice.'

"'I think I'll say, then, Do you think there are any barbers left in Palo Alto? Do you think she'll get it?' 'Yeah, Dick, she'll get it all right, and you're in trouble.'

"'Well, maybe I can say, ahhh, Would you check in and find out what time they're shearing sheep in Montana? How about, Did you ever think of getting [the boys] dog licenses, just so there's no confusion with city authorities when you're out in the park?'

"Finally one guy said, 'Dick, remember your father's advice: Keep your mouth shut and your eyes and ears open. Remember, if you really want to lose those kids when you go home, all you have to do is tell them to get a haircut,' and I started to calm down."

Instead of one-liners regarding his hirsute offspring, he wrote:

"21 March 1972

"Best wishes for a happy birthday is offered with an unequaled love. The images of our good memories of April and our wedding, Alice, is an anniversary I cherish. My thanks for a love and a friendship that have never wavered. Thank you for all you have done from a deep love of me and our sons. I hope you will follow the practice of having an annual physical examination. I hope that you understand that I want you to make full use of that last commanding jump in pay whenever it came for yourself and new furniture. Love to Pat, Mike and Charlie."

He really wanted to go home.

It was a good thing five and a half years in prison had taught him patience.

* * *

On May 8 the President announced that North Vietnamese ports, including Haiphong, would be mined and land and sea routes to the North would be "interdicted" to prevent further delivery of material for the war effort. Air strikes, too, would continue, he promised.

Mining began the following day.

In a Paris suburb on a sultry July 19, 1972, Dr. Kissinger met secretly with Le Duc Tho.

Le Duc Tho was a member of the late President Ho's old guard. A tough, hard-line communist and ultranationalist, he was a handsome man crowned by a thatch of shining silver hair. His well-tailored appearance belied a spartan life-style. He was a worthy adversary for the tubby, bespectacled, former Harvard professor. Tho was a member of the North Vietnamese Politburo. He had been chief adviser to the North Vietnamese delegation in Paris. Now he was its chief negotiator.

The word war had finally been joined.

275

CHAPTER 23

Workers hurrying into the city moved quickly through the suggestion of winter in the gray dawn. It was October 11, 1972.

At Gia Lam Airport, air defense personnel shed their padded tunics and settled in front of their machines for another day of waiting war.

In the diplomatic quarter, situated in the eastern part of the city near glittering Lake Haankien and a block away from the National Assembly building, the French mission prepared for a busy day. The secretary to M. Pierre Susini, the French delegate general in Hanoi who had succeeded François Simon de Quirielle, checked the day's agenda again. Mr. Susini expected a visit from the Albanian ambassador, and the fifty-two-year-old French diplomat wanted all in readiness.

At the Army depot edging the west bank of the Red River, about a half mile from Susini's office, a group of militiamen were hard at their morning exercises.

Hanoi is well named: literally, "ha noi"—"inside the river." The city sits with its lakes and its sou trees on the west bank of the Red River at the extreme head of the Red River delta, about sixty miles inland from the port city of Haiphong. In one sense, Hanoi is like Amsterdam or Venice—one cannot travel far in any direction without coming to a water crossing of some sort. Because of this, Hanoi's communications system and transit routes are particularly vulnerable to air attack.

Perhaps a coast watcher was daydreaming or an American destroyer in the gulf jammed an early-warning radar station. Perhaps a wire broke, or a tube loosened. No one ever did know. The planes came without warning, screaming over the city even as the air raid sirens sounded and the bombs fell. It was 11:30 A.M.

At the French mission, the Albanian arrived on time. Susini personally greeted him at the door and urged him quickly inside as an American plane shrieked by at rooftop level. The building erupted with a deafening roar. Screams of the wounded were heard even before shattered masonry stopped falling.

Ocher-colored smoke oozed from the center of the mission complex and billowed slowly upward in thick folds. The Albanian, dazed and bleeding, got to his feet. His colleague, Susini, was buried to the neck in rubble and bleeding heavily from head wounds. He was barely conscious.

Four Vietnamese employees of the mission were dead, a fifth gravely hurt. Frantic staff members and rescue workers extricated M. Susini and rushed him to St. Paul's Hospital.[15]

* * *

Reaction to the incident was swift. Georges Pompidou, the President of France, accused the United States of "a deplorable act." The North Vietnamese delegation to the peace talks denounced the Nixon administration for "these serious and repeated attacks which reflect a bellicose policy."[16] Formal apologies to the French were quick in coming from Washington, but Defense Department spokesmen hinted darkly that it was all a Hanoi hoax: the destruction of the mission was probably caused by a grounding North Vietnamese SAM missile fired at one of the twenty attacking American aircraft. That shibboleth was proved false three weeks later. Defense conceded an "error."

The timing of the raids on Hanoi that morning during a period of intense diplomatic activity recalled incidents in 1966 and 1967 when fledgling talks between the Johnson administration and the North Vietnamese delegation were shattered by heavy American bombing raids around Hanoi. Full-scale talks did not begin finally until May of 1968.

The talks in October of 1972 did not stop. There was evident strain, but the meetings in Paris continued, and continued deep into October. Paris filled with whispers of a breakthrough. From one end of the capital to the other, it was said the Americans and the Vietnamese had reached accord. There appeared to be sound basis for the rumors. Dr. Kissinger had returned to Paris on October 19, eight days after the raid, and had been closeted since in the most intensive sessions with Le Duc Tho and no less a figure than Tran Van Lam, the North Vietnamese Foreign Minister. A sulky President Thieu of South Vietnam was also in Paris and spent long periods of time with the American delegation and Dr. Kissinger.

Kissinger returned to Washington on October 24. Within hours of his arrival, the White House ordered cessation of bombing north of the twentieth parallel (about seventy-five miles south of Hanoi). Two days later, Radio Hanoi announced agreement with the United States on a cease-fire and a peace treaty. Dr. Kissinger presented himself to an excited and overflow press conference in Washington.

Peace is at hand, he told the reporters.

Kissinger outlined a nine-point accord, but disclosed few details. The United States recognized the independence and unity of all Vietnam as set down in the 1954 Geneva accords. The cease-fire would be effective twenty-four hours after the peace documents were signed. All United States and allied troops would quit Vietnam within sixty days after the signing. Bombing and mining North Vietnamese territory and territorial waters would stop. The "political" side of the document was vague: free and democratic elections, but no specified date; provision for a so-called National Council of Reconciliation and Concord to administer demobilization and organize the elections in the South, but not how it was to be chosen.

Finally, the United States and the Democratic Republic of Vietnam would enter a new, equal, and mutually beneficial relationship with an American pledge to aid postwar reconstruction.[17]

This document was unsigned, Kissinger admitted.

The draft accord in no way restricted the United States from maintaining its Thailand air bases; American ships of war still steamed through the Gulf of Tonkin. The hard details of peace were still for the bargaining.

Relations between the United States and South Vietnam were

strained and became more so after the accord was revealed. President Thieu of South Vietnam felt he had been served up to Hanoi so that Washington could extricate itself from the war and recover its men held captive in the North. Saigon began incessant complaints. Hanoi heckled Washington to sign the Paris document immediately. Was the United States deliberately delaying settlement?

Spokesmen for the National Peace Action Coalition refused to take Dr. Kissinger at his word. The organization's demonstration against the war scheduled for November 17 would still be held in major American cities "regardless of Kissinger's announcements and regardless of who is [elected] President [in the forthcoming presidential election November 7]." Other peace groups expressed suspicion, too.

The North Vietnamese set an October 31 deadline for signing the agreement. That day came and went. The document was unsigned. Kissinger in Washington and Le Duc Tho in Hanoi were silent. The North Vietnamese Foreign Ministry, however, denounced the United States for failing to sign the agreement, adding that it had betrayed a promise to do so. In Washington, government spokesmen said the United States had tried to meet the deadline but could not because some "minor" issues were still unresolved. The "minor" issues were not revealed. Peace seemed to be slipping inexorably away.

(So were the fortunes of the Democratic Party: Richard M. Nixon of California was re-elected to his second term in office on November 7, 1972, by one of the largest landslides in American political history. U. S. Senator George McGovern, the Democratic standard bearer, a liberal and a peace candidate, did not carry even his home state of South Dakota.)

Six days after the election a spokesman for the North Vietnamese delegation in Paris told reporters his government would be willing to resume discussions with the United States. There was one thing, though, he added: the agreement announced on October 26 last was complete, unchangeable. The Americans' chief delegate to the Paris talks, under orders from the White House, was attempting through leaky secret channels to resume the talks, not to ratify the October accord, but to modify—if not completely change—it. The differences over the document that had been called "minor" were now labeled "substantial" by the President.

279

The October deadline gone, pressures on Washington increasing, Saigon's Thieu again began to argue his case. Washington had long ago dealt him out of the war; he would not be dealt out of the peace or his shaky political hegemony. He complained that the National Council of Reconciliation would or could turn into a coalition government with the communists; he reiterated his demand for withdrawal of all North Vietnamese troops from South Vietnam; he insisted a border between North and South be established, then sealed off to prevent infiltration of communist troops (and to shore up South Vietnam's claims of sovereignty). These counter-proposals to what Washington and Hanoi had worked out without him represented almost certainly the victory Thieu had never won in the battlefields or villages of his nation.

The United States certainly did not need Thieu on the sidelines coaching it in the pursuit of peace. On the other hand, he could not be altogether ignored without shattering in this crucial time myths it had taken years to weave about the independence of South Vietnam and its officials, and the disinterestedness of the Americans in that nation's internal affairs. On November 20, with the Thieu memoranda in hand and, one assumes, a shopping list from Mr. Nixon as well, Dr. Kissinger rejoined Le Duc Tho in Paris to re-attempt a cease-fire and pave over the stumbling blocks in the road to peace. Discussions continued toward December with Kissinger shuttling between Washington and Paris and Washington. On December 2 he flew back to Paris to begin a whole second round of talks. It was a wasted flight.

It was perfectly clear, as 1973 approached and the war continued, that Kissinger had sparse basis for his October statement that "peace is at hand." After ten days of intense, often acrimonious, deliberation, negotiations deadlocked. Kissinger returned to Washington. Le Duc Tho flew to Hanoi.

Washington, Hanoi complained, had reopened all the major issues of agreement, in effect attempting to call back everything North Vietnam thought it had won in October. Hanoi, countercharged Washington, had reacted to the "modest" questions of the Americans by presenting drastic new demands that destroyed almost everything Washington thought it had won back in October, including its promise to release all American prisoners of war when United States forces quit Vietnam and linking release instead to the release of political prisoners held by Saigon.

* * *

It all began innocently enough: a lengthy press conference called by Dr. Kissinger on Saturday, December 17, to deflate what was left of his October optimism for an early truce and to lay much of the blame for failure on the North Vietnamese. He detailed his hard days in Paris and concluded his remarks with a supplication.

"And, so, what we are saying to Hanoi is: we are prepared to continue in the spirit of the negotiations that were started in October. We are prepared to maintain an agreement that provides for the unconditional release of all American and allied prisoners that imposes no political solution on either side, that brings about an internationally-supervised cease-fire and the withdrawal of all American forces within 60 days.

"It is a settlement that is just to both sides, and that requires only a decision to maintain provisions that had already been accepted and an end to procedures that can only mock the hopes of humanity."[18]

In Saigon, in Thailand, in the ready-room on Guam, on the flagship of the Seventh Fleet steaming in the Gulf of Tonkin, the orders from the commander in chief had been decoded. Ground crews were already loading the bomb bays of the B-52s and packing the belts of cannon and machine gun bullets into the wings of the fighter-bombers; rockets were in their pods, checklists completed, maps up to date. It was December 18, 1972. The target: Hanoi.

They waited for night.

CHAPTER 24

They sat resigned in the dimly lit air defense center at Gia Lam. Yellow-green lines circled interminably the little glass hippodromes of the radars, leaving behind for a few seconds during each revolution fuzzy, blister-like dots: enemy aircraft.

The lines circled.

The dots inched across the faces of the glass screens.

There was little movement elsewhere in the room. Everybody watched the machines.

When the planes were thirty miles distant from the city the first air raid warnings sounded. Night traffic moved off the roads. City residents gathered children, elders, belongings, and half-asleep hurried to the shelters. Defense crews raced for the anti-aircraft cannon and rocket sites situated about the city and along the banks of the river.

At eighteen miles, the second warning sounded.

Radar grids pointed straight up, then. The dots were overhead. Inside the air defense center at the airport, they could hear plainly the kettle drum thumps of bombs exploding. Fire glowed in the sky to the north. Scattered missile batteries fired upward into the blackness.

Miles high, a sudden silent blink, white and orange.

A hit!

Cheers from the ground. Watch for parachutes.

The drumbeats moved closer and closer to Gia Lam and the

room from which they directed the defense. The building shuddered. Flakes of paint and dust gently fell on the men and the machines. A storage building bulged and disintegrated in a blossom of dust and concrete and glass. There was a lot of shouting and confusion. The airport was a sanctuary, safe from attack.

The dots vanished. It was 2 A.M. A mile north of the airport, near the capital's major railroad yards where the highway and the train tracks turned toward the sea and Haiphong, the village of Gia Lam was an inferno. The screams of the wounded could be heard over the roar of the flames.

* * *

"MOSCOW, December 18 (Reuters)—United States planes attacked the suburbs of Hanoi tonight dropping bombs two and three miles from the center of the city, according to a Tass report from the North Vietnamese capital. The Soviet press agency said that the raid lasted 40 minutes and that a big glow could be seen north of Hanoi."[19]

* * *

(Special to the New York *Times*)

"WASHINGTON, December 18—The Nixon Administration announced a resumption of the bombing and mining of North Vietnam today, and the White House warned that such raids 'will continue until such time as a settlement is arrived at.'

"Administration officials said that President Nixon, in ordering actions against military objectives in the Haiphong and Hanoi areas, had directed the Air Force and the Navy to strike targets not bombed before.

"Ronald L. Ziegler, the White House press secretary, voiced the threat of continuing attacks north of the 20th Parallel after a halt of nearly two months, while insisting that their renewal was consistent with the policy enunciated by Mr. Nixon on May 8 in announcing his decision to mine the ports and bomb more extensively.

"He said then that the actions would cease when American prisoners were released and an internationally supervised cease-fire was in force.

"Mr. Ziegler also linked the latest action to the threat of another North Vietnamese offensive. 'The road to peace is wide open,' he said. 'We want a rapid settlement to this conflict.' But, he added, "we are not going to allow the peace talks to be used as a cover for another offensive."

"Some military analysts, puzzled, said they knew of no signs of a major offensive. . . ."[20]

Later, Press Secretary Ziegler in a meeting with the press assured them that the road to peace was still open and expanded somewhat on the subject of the bombing: "Neither side can gain from prolonging the war," he said, "and neither side can gain from prolonging peace talks."[21]

Later still, unidentified "intelligence sources" noted that Hanoi had been expecting attack. These sources added that North Vietnamese officials had directed an evacuation of women and children from Hanoi December 4 (the day the most recent sessions of private talks had begun in Paris).

It is difficult to divine meanings behind these statements. There were still more than 300,000 persons left in the city. The North Vietnamese were expecting something, but Hanoi was surprised by the intensity of the attacks. Schools and universities had been closed, the windows of the buildings boarded up, and the entire education system moved to the countryside. Now all public gathering places, with the exception of the city's churches, were closed. Boating on the city's lakes was prohibited.

The first raid that night was followed by more, and more yet. It wasn't long before residents and defense officials worked out a rough attack pattern (though the Americans refused to follow it to the letter in the beginning and followed it hardly at all at the end, with sorties nearly around the clock).

The general concentration of bombings of Hanoi came at late evening, early morning, and early afternoon. The tactical raids by fighter-bombers began shortly after the noon hour and rarely lasted sixty minutes; the night alert usually began about 8 or 9 P.M. and before midnight the B-52s were overhead—the first time they had been used against the capital—and were gone by 2 A.M.; there were some prolonged bombings, though, which kept city residents in the shelters until past five in the morning, just in time to begin the workday.

It was a grim and deadly business the B-52s were about: unlike tactical fighter-bombers, which work close to the ground and bomb with respectable accuracy in most situations, the B-52s flew at an altitude approaching seven miles. Their bomb patterns covered a land area about half a mile wide and anywhere from a mile to a mile and a half long. Each bomb bay could hold up to one hundred bombs, depending on the type. The B-52 was a fearsome weapon. Its psychological impact was as devastating as its ordnance.

Washington's strategy appeared to be simple: concentrate first on the North's communications system—roads, bridges, railroad lines, railroad depots, railheads, repair yards; telephone and telegraph lines and centers, and the air defense network. Next came the defense structure itself: SAM sites, ordnance depots, antiaircraft batteries, airfields known to harbor North Vietnamese MiG fighters, airfields capable of servicing MiG fighters, airfields in general; finally, secondary military targets: supply depots, power stations. Many military targets lay hard by nonmilitary sites. Bach Mai airfield, for example, was situated near Bach Mai hospital; a major military depot and a heavy concentration of anti-aircraft emplacements were less than a mile from the city's diplomatic quarter, and so on.[22] The implication was obvious: nonmilitary property destruction was heavy and civilians died.

By December 22 Washington had sent official apologies to Warsaw for hitting a Polish ship in Haiphong harbor, and to Cairo for damages done the Egyptian Embassy in Hanoi, and unofficial acknowledgment of damages to London regarding the M.V. *Kim Seng,* a 5,970-ton merchantman of British registry hit while anchored at Haiphong.

There were other complaints: New Delhi protested that its embassy in Hanoi had been bombed; Peking suggested it did not take kindly its new friend's strafing of Chinese vessels at Haiphong; the Hungarians and the East Germans reported their commercial missions in Hanoi had been hit by American aircraft, and Cuba said its embassy in Hanoi had received bomb damage. New Zealand filed a formal protest through its Washington embassy opposing round-the-clock bombing. At the Vatican, Pope Paul VI lamented the "painful delay" in ending the war in his annual message on the State of the Church and the World.[23]

The President, vacationing at Key Biscayne, said he was determined to continue the present policy until North Vietnam decided to resume the Paris talks "in a spirit of goodwill and in a constructive attitude." In Hanoi, Defense Mininster General Vo Nguyen Giap said even if Hanoi and Haiphong were destroyed by the bombing, the "North Vietnamese people will not be forced to yield."

The destruction was awesome, even for war-hardened reporters assigned to cover the story from Hanoi. Dispatches by Tass, MIH (Hungary), and Agence France-Presse reported B-52 "carpet bombing" of large sections of North Vietnam and portions of the capital itself. Washington insisted its aircraft were attacking only military targets. U.S. mission officials in Saigon dismissed the stories as propaganda.

"My first reaction to the bombing was euphoria," recalled Richard Stratton, "and then after that, kind of a letdown; sort of here we go again, and then realizing it was probably the only way we were going to get anywhere.

"The Vietnamese, the guards and the interrogators, weren't so much angry as bewildered. Oh, they were corked off with all our cheering and yelling, but that was understandable. They did not cut back on our food or anything, and on Christmas day we had the 'traditional' Christmas meal. They kept shoveling the food at us.

"I guess they realized, too, like we did, that things were about over; they just couldn't sustain that kind of bombing.

"I felt sorry for the guys in the B-52s. After I saw a couple of them get it with a full load of fuel and bombs, I must admit to feeling I was glad it wasn't me up there. . . . They were sitting ducks for the SAMs."

Stratton recalled that the Vietnamese guards made strenuous efforts to keep the prisoners away from the windows, as much to prevent them from seeing what was going on as to protect them from possible mishap. The POWs were also kept out of the prison yard.

By the end of the first week, the day before Christmas, government officials ordered further evacuation of Hanoi. Buses and trucks assembled at key points throughout the city for those who could not make their own way into the countryside. Trucks were hired by groups of families; others went by foot or bicycle. A majority of the city's shops closed; street traffic dwindled to a fraction. On Christmas Day, Hanoi was 75 to 80 per cent evacuated, according to city officials.

(Not all of the evacuees who fled the city found safety in the country. The B-52s were performing daily missions in adjacent provinces. Casualties were heavy. Many of the wounded were returned to hospitals in Hanoi.)

With some perception of the American character, Vietnamese authorities assumed the capital would not be bombed Christmas Eve; a Christmas mass was scheduled. Evacuation or no, the Hanoi Cathedral filled to overflowing. Late worshipers huddled outside in the cold. The cathedral's great pipe organ was not working; the music was provided by harmonium and *a capella* by a mixed choir. The choir included among its younger members a dark-eyed boy with a remarkable soprano range. Gruber's "Silent Night" and Schubert's "Ave Maria" were among the selections. The service and the sermon were delivered in Vietnamese, and a priest summarized the sermon for foreign visitors in French, English, and German.[24]

The planes did not come.

Christmas Day was brittle-bright. Cold.

The planes did not come.

Aboard the ships of the Seventh Fleet, at Guam, in Thailand, on scattered bases in the South, the weary ground crews worked on the aircraft and dined on a traditional Christmas dinner: turkey, ham, dressing, cranberry sauce, whipped potatoes, yams, buttered onions, squash with butter, rolls with butter, milk, coffee, pies, and sweetmeats.

Some POWs were heartened by, even delighted with, the raids. Some men gave up nights of sleep to watch the fireworks. For many, like Stratton, the raids were an act of faith by a government that sometimes, they believed, had abandoned them.

"If we were ever betrayed as a group," Stratton said, "if we ever felt we were betrayed as a group of prisoners, it was when Johnson ordered the bombing moratorium just prior to the 1968 election. We felt we had been sacrificed for political consideration. . . . This was our viewpoint. Knowing the enemy as we did, [most of us were] firmly convinced we were never going home until [the U.S.] laid the wood to the North Vietnamese and in some form which they understood, which was direct force in their own back yard. There was no real hope [for us] until the bombing started again up North, and it never really came up to us until October [of 1972]; by up to us, I mean where we could see it and hear it.

"In October–November, the North Vietnamese told us about the abortive agreements that had been reached and which the United States was now 'weaseling' on, saying to us if you didn't have such a perfidious President, you all would have been home for Christmas [because] it was ready to go. Your side screwed it up. This was the first we had heard of *secret* negotiations [and] indirectly they were telling us things. Once we found out they were talking secretly we believed Hanoi must be serious. We believed, as Harriman once said, they negotiated in public for propaganda and in private for real. Once [the U.S.] started bombing again where we could see it and hear it, we knew that *we* were serious, and the Vietnamese would respond to it. So we weren't disheartened by the fact things had broken down. It was giving us hope, and then in December when they started bombing Hanoi itself and we were sitting under the B-52s and the F-111s and the A-6s, we knew that our side was indeed hitting them where it hurt, hitting them downtown where the policy makers could feel the effects of the war.

"In fact, the [Vietnamese authorities] used to come into our camp. It was the safest place in town. At noon the duty drone would come over and circle round a satellite receiving tower which had been built next to the camp, and use that as a turn point. We used to stand and wave at it. So we knew we were pinpointed and they were bombing close to us. We knew that the Vietnamese were getting hurt because a lot of high-priced interrogators whom we had seen before would be inside the camp, identifying it as a relatively safe place.

"Then we knew we were going home; we were convinced it was simply a matter of time. The bombing stopped just about Christmas time, just prior to Christmas Day. We had about three days of beauts, day-and-night type stuff, real close by and then it was off and we knew they must be talking again."

* * *

On December 26 the planes returned.

It seemed, if that were possible, more terrible than before. Dur-

288

ing the night the B-52s bombed alongside the Kham Thien road, a major thoroughfare that runs past the central railroad depot in the heart of Hanoi's so-called native district. Eyewitnesses said the section was "carpet-bombed." Dwellings there were shanties by Western standards and disintegrated under the weight of the bombs and the shocks of their concussions. Despite the recent evacuations, 215 persons were reported killed, another 257 injured. The whole cratered area was a scene of the most desperate misery. Many of the survivors wept and loudly lamented the loss of their kin as they stumbled through the debris.

The planes came again on the night of the twenty-seventh, and the twenty-eighth, and the twenty-ninth.

Then they vanished. The sky was empty.

The White House called a halt to bombing above the twentieth parallel on December 30. The announcement also said technical-level negotiations between the United States and North Vietnam would resume in Paris on January 2, 1973. Full-scale diplomatic talks between Dr. Kissinger and Le Duc Tho would resume January 8. Despite the bombing, it appeared the two capitals managed to keep in touch with one another. What was not so clear, and perhaps in the final accounting was irrelevant, was whether the impetus to reopen peace talks had come from Hanoi reeling under continuous assault or from Washington backpedaling under increasing foreign and domestic pressure to suspend the raids. Characteristically, Hanoi insisted it had not been bombed back to the bargaining table. Washington refused comment—period.

On January 2 the experts sat down to work up the technical agreements to put a cease-fire into effect.

On January 8 smiling Henry Kissinger greeted smiling Le Duc Tho as the world's cameras clicked away like a conclave of beetles. It was the third round of talks since October.

* * *

It was about this time that they shipped Moon Mullen and the others back to Hoa Lo, and camp authorities relaxed restrictions on yard time. Mullen recalled that "negotiations were going on, we actually got quite a bit of time out in the courtyard . . . and sometimes they'd let all cells out in the courtyard at one time. We went out in the courtyard and that's where I saw Dick once again.

Golly, it seemed like it had been forever since I had had a chance to talk to him. And, as we always [did], we just sort of razzed one another.

" 'Well, Rich, I see even though the chow's been pretty poor you are still capable of keeping a pretty good, hefty nose on. . . .'

" 'Ahh, bull. You guys from FAGU [the Fleet Air Gunnery Unit at El Centro], you never change; you just press it on.'

" 'Well, Rich, you gotta do your thing, keep the spirit going.'

"And once again," Mullen reminisced, "we became very, very good friends, [and] we were finally in the same room; . . . security had relaxed somewhat and the Vietnamese really didn't bother us too much. We continued the education programs. Dick was more than willing to make a contribution and [his lectures] were magnificent; he did a real super job. We all felt it would be a short time before we'd be back amongst society and we were trying desperately . . . to bring everything back into perspective . . . just to help prepare ourselves.

"Everyone knew (the North Vietnamese included) it was sort of coming to an end. . . ."

CHAPTER 25

On this January morning, twenty-four days into the new year, a wan sun with little chance tried to melt the snow lying inch-deep over the hamlet of Beallsville, a community of 452 persons rooted firmly in the wind-slicked Allegheny foothills of Ohio about sixty miles south and west of Pittsburgh, and half that from Wheeling in the West Virginia panhandle. The land in this hard corner of old America is much like the people who have lived on it: worn, rock-solid, austere.

The wind that morning, sharpened to a fine winter's edge, busied itself through the town's three curbless streets, past the high school (where last night, as the President announced the cease-fire, most of Beallsville watched the local Blue Devils drop a basketball game to rival Bishop Donohue), and up the side of Cemetery Hill. Telephone wires sang. Dry grass, shrouded in the winter-brown of death, rustled nervously where it poked through the snow. The rope on the new flagpole slapped monotonously against the tall, white shaft. At the foot of the pole was a simple plaque:

> In Honor of Those Who Served Our Country.
> "He causeth wars to cease." Psalms 46:9.

The flagpole and the plaque cost the townspeople more than one thousand dollars. They were memorials, footnotes really, to a history of the war in Vietnam: seven of Beallsville's sons died in the conflict.

Now the war was over. Bitterness made the town, seemingly, all but indifferent.

"It's a darn shame it couldn't have ended a few years sooner, at least for us here," Joe Decker told a New York *Times* reporter writing a color story on the townsfolk. The reporter, Andrew Malcom, nodded sympathetically. (The newspaper's research department later estimated that if New York State had lost the same statistical share of men that Beallsville had, the death toll to combat would have been 278,000. As it was, New York lost 3,985 in Indochina.)

As Dr. Kissinger began a televised press conference to detail fine points of his cease-fire triumph, Otis Thornberry, Beallsville's mayor, was busy installing a washing machine in Sam Britton's house. Maegene Pittman stopped her dusting and glanced sadly at her son's basketball trophies glinting dully in a glass display case. Young Jack Pittman was the first Beallsville man to die in Vietnam; a piece of shrapnel in his head did the job quickly. That was in 1966.

Along the back roads and hollows that had been surveyed by George Washington eight generations before, shivering children waited for the yellow school bus. Dead soldiers slept in Cemetery Hill under frozen sod and an inch of corn snow.

The rope on the flagpole slapped monotonously.

It was a peaceable day.

In Washington, Dr. Kissinger's precise, accented English continued detailing the accord he had initialed in Paris the day before. The war was over, really over. A lot of people got fooled back in October when the good doctor told them peace was at hand. A lot more steel and words and blood had been spent in the intervening three months.

There was no jubilation in the capital, no celebration that the war was all but over; no clink of glasses, no congratulatory smiles at the White House or on Capitol Hill or in the offices of the National Security Council.

Perhaps everyone was tired, like Maegene Pittman, or busy, like Mayor Thornberry. Perhaps there was nothing left to say. Perhaps it was the general, gnawing feeling that there was no victory. That possibility was noted by George D. Aiken, the Republican dean of the Senate and the senior senator from Vermont. Aiken recalled he had proposed a peace settlement in 1966 (the year Jack Pittman's brain was blown out). It consisted of the United States declaring it had won the war, packing up, and going home. That, in effect, was pretty much what had transpired in January of 1973, or so he suggested.

It was an unusually clear day in midwinter Washington; television producers for the three major networks were pleased about that. It would make for some dazzling exterior shots during coverage of Lyndon Baines Johnson's funeral cortege. Washington was sending the dead President back to Texas today for burial, this day of peace, a fact quickly exploited by quick-witted reporters assigned to cover the story. It had been "Johnson's war." Now it was Nixon's peace. The latter was the sole, surviving heir to all the Presidents of all the administrations that had tramped through bloody Vietnam.

Truman had died in December.

Eisenhower was dead.

Kennedy was dead.

Johnson was dead.

Lyndon Baines Johnson, thirty-sixth President of the United States of America, whose uncertain hands shifted the war into high gear, who made it a matter of Johnsonian pride and national honor, who in the end was toppled and destroyed by it, his pride ashes in his throat and national honor rent.

Now in January of 1973 the long agony was done. Johnson was dead and all the others, save Nixon, were dead and 50,000 American warriors were dead. Peace was at hand, so long in coming, with so many false starts, so much duplicity, so much blood, so many bodies.

* * *

It was midnight tomorrow in Hanoi. There was total silence, and after years of war many residents found it hard to sleep undisturbed an entire night. They were still burying the dead in Hanoi, still rummaging through the rubble left by the bombings. The raids on Hanoi, its suburbs, and the surrounding countryside left more than 1,200 civilians dead, more than 1,200 wounded. The destruction had been frightful, but they had held tough, fought back. There were no missiles left. The accuracy of their defenses was posted on lists pasted to walls throughout the city, and garbed in striped convict clothes in the cells of Hoa Lo prison. They had gone back to Paris and achieved victory.

News of the cease-fire was broadcast on the loudspeakers throughout the city. There was great rejoicing. The Premier had acclaimed the cease-fire a great victory "of the long, hard, and invincible struggle of the Vietnamese people for independence, liberty, and peace. We are full of enthusiasm," he added, "and very happy."

The Premier had given a short but emotional speech, interrupted frequently by joyous, vigorous applause from members of the Politburo and the government. They had met, these men and women, at the Presidential Palace together with members of the diplomatic corps to bid farewell to the Foreign Minister, who was leaving for Paris to formally sign the accord. It was a moving spectacle. North Vietnamese leaders hugged one another and smiled, shook hands and chatted with animation. The President was there, and the Vice-President, the Secretary of the Worker's Party and the Minister of Defense. Through the windows of the palace they heard the loudspeakers that three weeks ago had wailed air raid warnings broadcasting the full text of the agreement the Foreign Minister would sign in Paris. The text was being broadcast simultaneously by Radio Hanoi, whose director of programming planned to have it repeated day and night for the next forty-eight hours. Excited announcers were under stern instructions to read slowly so that people all over the nation could feel the full impact and importance of the texts, and share in the national joy of victory for the Fatherland.

CHAPTER 26

On Saturday, January 27, 1973, Marine Lieutenant Thomas V. Boykin, of Baton Rouge, Louisiana, let down the landing gear under his A-4 Skyhawk, banked into a turn, and settled into the glide pattern for his descent to the runway at Bien Hoa, South Vietnam.

It was 6:40 P.M.

The tires screeched and smoked as they touched the tarmac. The aircraft, its engine at the idle, slowed to taxiing speed and wheezed to a rocking halt in front of its bunker-hangar. The ground crew greeted the young pilot with wisecracks. Someone playfully doused him with water.

Boykin told his crew chief that during his mission he overflew a firefight near Can Tho in the Mekong Delta. He had taken some small-arms fire from communist troops. The crew chief reported the aircraft had not been hit.

His was the last American warplane returned from the last American bombing mission by the last American air combat group in South Vietnam.

It was 6:45 P.M.

The cease-fire would begin in fifteen minutes.[25]

CHAPTER 27

The Western Union telegram from Washington was dated January 28; it arrived shortly after the telephone call.

Her hand trembled slightly as she read it. She did not bother to wipe away the tears sliding toward her chin.

"I am pleased to inform you that your husband, Commander Richard A. Stratton, USN, was included on the list of captured in Southeast Asia provided our government by the government of North Vietnam. It is expected that the first incremental release will be within the next two weeks. You will be notified of any additional information received concerning the release, health and welfare of your husband. This confirms the information passed to you earlier by your casualty assistance officer.

"Vice Admiral David H. Bagley,

"Chief of Naval Personnel."

PART VII

RENAISSANCE

There are enough returned POWs who speak out about these qualities in the Vietnamese to reinforce what I thought many of us were confident about all along. There is a thousand year history of humane treatment accorded the defeated armies of the Mongols, Chinese, Japanese and French. Or have we not read their remarkable history?

My position on the POW issue has been widely misquoted and taken out of context. What I originally said and have continued to say is that the POWs are lying if they assert it was North Vietnamese policy to torture American prisoners.

—Jane Fonda[1]

But on the other hand, did you see what those POWs and their torture stories did to Tom Hayden? Poor Tom; at the end of his good fight it turns out he's something of a fool.

—Michael Miner[2]

CHAPTER 28

DISPATCH

"HANOI, North Vietnam, Feb. 12 (Agence France-Presse)—Buses still bearing the camouflage paint of war arrived at the civilian airport at Gia Lam this morning carrying American prisoners of war in their last moments of captivity.

"As the hour of release approached, the airport was aswarm with more soldiers of varied rank and nationality than anyone here could remember. The formalities were simple and swift. In a little more than an hour, all 116 men were headed by air for Clark Air Base in the Philippines.

"'They were released as rapidly as they were captured,' one North Vietnamese official remarked with a smile.

"Scores of North Vietnamese officials had left their ministries to cross the Red River to the airport for what all present clearly regarded as a historic moment.

"There were North Vietnamese and American officers and enlisted men; Canadians, Hungarians, Indonesians and Poles from the International Commission of Control and Supervision, and some 120 Vietnamese and foreign journalists—none, however, from the United States.

"Also present was a team from the Four-Party Joint Military Commission, formed by the United States, North Vietnam, the Saigon Government and the Vietcong, but Saigon's representatives were reported missing. [They were absent "without justification," the official North Vietnamese press agency said in a broadcast, according to a Reuters report from Hong Kong.]

"The public, however, was not admitted.

"The atmosphere at the airport, which is still scarred from the bombing of last December, seemed somewhat stiff at first but rapidly became relaxed.

"North Vietnamese soldiers invited the crew of one of the American medical evacuation planes to tea in a building whose windows had been shattered. In turn, a group of North Vietnamese clustered around an American jeep to study the functioning of the radio with which it was equipped.

"It was 12:30 P.M. when Lt. Col. Nguyen Phuong of North Vietnam presented to Col. James R. Bennett of the United States the first 20 American prisoners.

"The men had arrived at the airport riding 20 men to each bus. Each group on stepping to the ground was formed into two lines of 10 men each.

"One by one, the prisoners passed before Colonel Phuong and Colonel Bennett, who were seated at a small table under a canopy of green parachute cloth installed in case of rain. The table was in a grassy enclosure surrounded by a wrought-iron fence.

"As each prisoner's name was called, he would step into the enclosure, give his name and in a move signifying repatriation, walk past the table. An American serviceman would then escort him about 75 yards to one of three C-141 StarLifter transports.

"Some of the released men saluted at the table. Some did not. One displayed a piece of white canvas bearing, in blue, the words, 'God bless Nixon and the American people.'

"Twenty-nine of those released today were wounded or ill. Three were carried aboard their plane on stretchers. Two were using crutches. Six of the wounded were said to have been crew members of B-52's shot down in December.

"A list containing the name, rank, birth-date, place of capture and condition of each of the prisoners was turned over to Colonel Bennett.

"By 1:45 P.M., all prisoners were airborne, 40 in each of the first two planes and the 36 others in the third. One more aircraft followed—the C-130 that had brought a medical team, telecommunications specialists, ground crews and the radio jeep."[3]

ENDIT.

CHAPTER 29

Richard Stratton took a pull on the tin cup and rinsed the canned milk around in his mouth. He was sitting, back against the wall, in the large cell he shared with the others in the Camp Unity compound at Hoa Lo.

A blow job, he thought, just another blow job! The releases of prisoners had stopped; it did not appear any more of them were going home. What the hell had happened? A screw-up, or another little blow job by the Vietnamese? Maybe it was time for a few more bombing runs.

He was in a cynical mood. And he was exhausted. They all were. The cell had been up most of the night trying to memorize the text of a mildewed copy of *To Kill a Mockingbird*. It was one book in a pile of musty material the Vietnamese had handed out. They were trying to memorize as much of the stuff as they could (before the guards came back and took it away), just like the book people in *Fahrenheit 451*. In the years ahead, in 1974 and 1975, the books they had memorized would be told and retold. It would help morale and kill time, and keep their minds active.

Things had seemed so certain back in January, and positive in early February. Now, who knew what was coming? It was nearly March.

On January 27 the prisoners had been mustered in the yard by their senior officers, parade formation, the seniors in front. They knew something was in the wind. The Vietnamese had never done

301

that before. The Vietnamese camp commander read the announcement: an agreement had been signed between the United States and the Democratic Republic of Vietnam. The war was over. They were going home.

There had been not a sound and, from what he saw, no visible emotion on any pale face. They had had their chains jerked before.

"Do you understand what I'm telling you?" The camp commander was flustered by the lack of response.

"Yes, I understand." It was the compound's senior officer.

"What do you have to say for yourself?"

"We would like to go back to our cells."

They were dismissed and dragged back to the cellblocks. The doors closed behind them and "then we all went ape," said Stratton. "But we still thought there was something fishy. That evening, an unknown Vietnamese officer, maybe a lieutenant colonel, came by and stuck his head in the door. He started yanking our chain.

" 'What are you so happy about? You are never going home. You are war criminals.' The announcement was all a bunch of bullshit, that was what he was telling us.

"But [three days later] they started handing out mimeographed sheets, one per man, page by page, of the text of the agreements.

"[A provision in the peace agreement itself provided that each prisoner was to receive a copy of those portions of the accord regarding exchange and repatriation of POWs.] We liked to think they were simply trying to jam it to us right at the last minute, but in fairness it was probably their inability to mimeograph [quickly] or get paper."

At the same time, the Vietnamese opened up a warehouse and trucked to the prison boxes of reading material—everything from Adelle Davis on natural foods to *MAD* comics, and a pile of novels, including *To Kill a Mockingbird*. The material had been culled from packages sent to the prisoners over the years by their families and friends.

They also had been fitted for release clothing: black shoes, blue-gray jackets, blue pants, shirts. Each prisoner's name was written on a piece of paper and that was pinned to his pile. The clothes were stacked in an empty room in Camp Unity.

"The Vietnamese rearranged us," Stratton said, "so that we

would be in cells [with those with whom we would be released]. The agreements said we would be released by date of shoot-down. The first group got ready to go; there was no trouble. They waited [for] the designated day of pickup. They were told, 'Tomorrow you will leave.' The Vietnamese killed a couple of extra ducks, pulled out some eggs and . . . beer for a farewell meal. They brought in a road show, a vaudeville show, and tried to get us all out [in the courtyard to watch it]. None of the guys would go out—and there was a big hassle over that—because we thought [the Vietnamese] would take pictures to show how well we had been treated."

The first group of Americans went out on February 12. Before leaving Hoa Lo, some of the releasees were allowed to say good-by to their comrades remaining behind.

Robinson Risner was there, and Jim Lamar, an Air Force flier from Little Rock. Several of the men in Stratton's compound secretly passed messages to the departing prisoners. Stratton pressed a wadded wrapper from a package of Trung Son cigarettes into Lamar's palm. Lamar understood. No verbal instructions were necessary.

Then another bunch had gone. Twenty men were released out of sequence to honor Dr. Kissinger's visit to Hanoi. They literally were forced onto the bus to take them to the airport and freedom. At first the senior officer had refused repatriation for himself, and the others agreed. The Vietnamese had been stymied.

The camp commander confronted the senior ranking officer. They had to leave!

"We have to see a genuine American from the transfer team. He has to walk into this compound and tell me through my locked door that I am supposed to go home. Otherwise, we are not going! I don't care whether Henry Kissinger has asked for us or anything else! We have the agreements right here and this is the order in which we are going home."

The Vietnamese had no choice. One of the camp officials went out and returned with a U. S. Army major; no American not a prisoner had ever penetrated that deep into the camp.

"What the hell are you guys trying to do, screw up the whole goddamned release? Get your asses outa here! Get into your clothes, and get the hell out of this country!"

The Americans understood that kind of talk. They got their gear, and got their asses out of Hoa Lo. The date was February 18.

That had been the end of it. There were no more releases. The second group, Stratton's group, had been given their farewell supper. They had not gone home the next day. Blow job! The bastards had done it again. He was thankful he had gotten a message out to Alice.

"There was a great deal of letdown and resignation. But we'd had so many ups and downs, we'd been through it all before, what the hell. So we kept going, kept at our daily work chores. We were very busy digesting all the reading material. The Vietnamese were trying to keep us from communicating, so [we had to work at that]. The bastards: we'd be here ten more years. To hell with it."

The tension hurt, physically hurt: his neck muscles sometimes were so taut it hurt to move his head. He could feel it in his throat and across his chest. He was not going home today. Not tomorrow. Neither were any of the others. The faces of the guards were somber; tension was draining a lot of them, too. How much longer?

He felt the lump of letters under his butt. He had hidden them under his pallet automatically after the Vietnamese had presented them. He was not sure they would not be taken away. But prison taught you caution. He pulled them out. Already they showed wear. There were forty letters in all. He had received twenty of them, in a bundle, five days ago, and twenty more the day after: forty letters from Alice, the oldest dated in mid-1967, the most recent, 1971. Forty letters. He had felt the fury gorge his throat; it hadn't shown very much on his face, that was something else prison taught you.

He riffled the envelopes slowly, making sure each was in the order of its mailing date. He set the pile to one side and took the first envelope off the top, removed the letter from the envelope, unfolded it, smoothed it out on his knee, and began to read. He tried to picture Alice's hands and face as she had written it six years before, but the image was blurred. He read slowly, studying the words.

When he had finished reading the letter, he refolded it exactly as Alice had folded it all those years ago, and replaced it in its envelope. He put the envelope to one side and took the next one from the pile. He opened the envelope and removed the letter, unfolding it, smoothing it out on his knee. Letter after letter. When he had finished, he rehid them. The morning was gone. After "lunch," he would read them again. Then he would burn them, burn everything in his waste bucket, letters, pictures, everything. He had gotten as much as he could out of those letters, memorized as much as he could. He was not going to give them the pleasure of taking them back. He was not going home (whenever that would be) with the letters in his pocket, the Vietnamese saying he had had them all along. No way, Charlie!

Stratton, in fact, had no desire to come home with any keepsakes of his prison years. He had enough permanent mementos on his body, he would remark later on. Not everyone felt that way, of course. Hegdahl, back in 1969, had wanted to keep his skivvie shorts, but they were taken from him. He settled for the stolen cigarette holder, a tube of toothpaste, and some stamps and money he had also stolen. Several men wanted to keep their tin prison cups. The Vietnamese relented, but the men had to sign for them. Lieutenant Commander Edward Davis, who left with the first group of POWs, smuggled out a two-month-old puppy named Ma Co (the gift of a guard), who later delighted news photographers at Travis by piddling on the runway.

Moon Mullen had a special keepsake he wanted to get out.

"There were certain little things you treasured. One of the fellows, Jim Hivner [Air Force Captain James Otis Hivner], took this brown wrapping paper we used for toilet paper and made his own glue out of bread dough paste or rice paste, whichever, and he laminated layers of this paper to make cardboard and fashioned all this paper into a cigarette box for me. He had written all over it [in ink made] with brick chalk, and [on the bottom] made by the Delta-Sierra Box Co. It was really neat, and it was a nice thing. I [wanted] to get it out as a remembrance of one of the few good things [that happened in prison]."

Like his cellmate Richard Stratton, Mullen took the release delay philosophically, perhaps more phlegmatically.

"With my personality, anyway, . . . it was one of those things you just take in your stride; you aren't revengeful and you aren't bitter because, really, you've waited so long anyhow. You know [release] is coming, and, after six and a half years, what does one more week matter? Or two weeks? It all worked out. It all worked out just fine."

Four days later, March 1, the word came down through the chain of command and there was another reading of the orders. There was little emotion in the yard. They marched back to their cells, and when the doors closed behind them they went quietly nuts. The communications network throughout the prison tapped itself numb. One of the watchers spied several of the guards lugging out release clothing, 106 sets of clothing, one set for each man to be released.

Kasler was going, Colonel Jim Kasler; and Gordon Larson and Jack Dramesi; they were all senior men. They had all been shot down between 1966 and 1967.

Stratton was on the list, too. He was going. His heart thumped and his throat swelled thick. Some men softly wept, but he was not one of them. He did not trust himself to speak, but he did not weep. He had won. They had broken him and made him do their will. They had made him cry in pain, made him shame himself, made him shit his pants; they had tortured him and beaten him and humiliated him, and he had come back each time. He had won; he had beaten the sons of bitches after all.

Now they wondered, the old-timers like Richard Stratton, what was waiting for them. They knew for certain the world they had left in 1965 or 1967 or 1969 was gone. The fliers shot down and imprisoned during the December 1972 raids had told them that. Old enemies like China were new friends. There was "détente" with the Soviet Union. The American domestic scene had altered radically: there were rising prices, rising taxes, and risen hemlines; breasts had been lowered out of brassieres, hair dropped over shirt collars ("I dunno how to tell ya this, Rich, but the only guys with crew cuts stateside these days are queers!"); there was Watergate and "The Waltons," X-rated movies, Z-grams; anti-war vets threw their medals on the steps of the Capitol; American flags decorated the seats of Levi's; there was black power, yellow power, gray power, gay power; there was communal living and natural foods, consumerism, guru-ism. Oakland baseball players wore *white* shoes, and there were double-knit suits cut in the styles of the 1930s.

What awaited him? Who had lived and who had died? What did Alice and the children look like now? The photographs he had received were old. What did she smell like and feel like, how did her voice sound? What about him? There was some anxiety there, he had to admit it. What did the Navy think of him? Where was his career going now? The North Vietnamese had broken him and he had broken the code. What did his family think? Had he disgraced them with that 1967 confession? It ate him, gnawed at him, and he brooded. Then the euphoria of release hit him again and drowned out the worries. He felt like a yo-yo: up and down, up and down.

The hours passed so very slowly, but they passed. The release date, so they were told, was March 4. Everybody believed it and nobody believed it. Just like the gooks to jack you up and cut you down.

"Just prior to the release they came in with an . . . X-ray machine made in East Germany. They brought in a mess of so-called doctors and we went through a so-called complete physical. There was a physical record for each of us, a medical examination form. It was a real dog and pony show."

On Sunday night, March 3, 1973, they received a second farewell meal.

* * *

Alice Stratton's casualty assistance officer telephoned the news: Dick's name was number 30 on a list of 106 men to be released at Hanoi on March 4! She let out a whoop of joy, startling her sons. They never had heard her cry out like that. The carefully cultivated veneer split for a moment; tears came quickly. The boys watched perplexed.

She gathered her composure and comforted them. Later, she telephoned the family to share the glad tidings.

She knew he was all right, or as right as could be expected. She had received a telephone call from a fellow POW wife in early February, a friend whose husband was released with the first group. He had told his wife and his wife told Alice that Dick was alive, safe, relatively healthy, stable; later she got the crab-handed note on the cigarette pack wrapper smuggled out of Hanoi by Colonel Lamar:

"Dear Alice," she read, "let me tell you how much my love for you has grown over these years of darkness. Without you there can be no sunshine for me. Without you there is no strength for me. You have been the source of my strength and will to resist in spite of all odds. You are my love, my hope and my life.

"My desire is that you wait for my return at home just like at the end of any other cruise. I will defer to your desires but want you to have Charlie, Paul Durup or Father Kerrigan accompany you if you decide to meet me anywhere enroute. I do not want you to travel without a male friend of mine.

"I do not know when I will be released. As far as I can see I am in the status of a political hostage held by an uncivilized, brutal, petty people. Your continued support of President Nixon and the Navy Department is essential for my eventual return. I am in excellent mental and physical health due to your and America's efforts on my behalf. I have received less than a quarter of your letters and will have many questions. Do not take the children out of school. I want only to be with you, our families, our familiar and our closest friends. I want no publicity of any kind from any source. The faithful support of you, our family, and our friends has been a constant source of comfort to me.

"If we decide to have more children, they will be older, adopted ones. But if we are to play Vatican roulette again I hope you have purchased twin beds. Even though there is a little snow on the roof there is still a lot of fire in the furnace.

"I am still the same man you married, maybe a little wiser, but my love for you has matured quite a bit. I love you. Hi Pat, Mike, Charlie, Mom, Dad, Charlie, and Ellen. Love Rich."

The letter was dated at Hanoi, February 7, 1973. It helped, as she read and reread it, carry her through the time when repatriation halted.

Alice Stratton's odyssey had come full circle. In the beginning, after Dick was lost, her days were painful and long. Long days were back, but no pain. Getting through each day to get to the next to get to the next to get to the day when she could see him get off the airplane from Hanoi was giving her knots in her stomach. She drank endless cups of instant coffee and drafted endless lists of things to be done before Dick came home. Some of the load she shared with close friends; they had stuck by her through all the years of ordeal and now they had a right to share joy. The tasks were labors of love. As the days moved toward March the small gray house shined from polishing. Flowers were planted in the back yard at the base of the high redwood fence that blocked the view of the sluiceway, and alongside the house in the small greenway there. Windows were washed, cupboards cleaned, toys reassigned to boxes and shelves. She worked steadily through piles of the children's papers, sorting out those she would save for Dick; she clipped her way through the last of the boys' photographs and assembled them in the albums. During the years he had been away, she took or had friends take hundreds of pictures of the boys for a photographic record of their growing up. There were schedules for meals and baby-sitters that would go into effect once he was home and when she could join him. She shook out and cleaned his clothes, altering the closets from an enforced widowhood to the mixed hangings of marriage. There were everyday things: her work (which finally she temporarily suspended); the care, feeding, and discipline of three boys; church; neighbors; POW/MIA correspondence; and a few private moments stolen here and there for herself. She was exhausted each night, but the routine hurried the hours past and permitted little time for worry.

"Anyone who isn't a *little* apprehensive is either stupid or unrealistic," she said in the umpteenth interview requested of her since the release list was made public. She had turned down very few calls. The swell of publicity, the price of her role and activities in the POW/MIA movement and Dick's controversial image, was tedious, but she felt she owed something to those reporters who had supported her and the league during the years she had been identified with it. She did lose her composure, however, when a United Press International photographer smacked Charlie in the face with a Nikon. The blow was accidental and not serious, but the boy wore a small mouse under his eye for days afterward.

She knew, too, that once the euphoria of reunion was over, a long and perhaps difficult path of readjustment for all of them lay ahead. Dick would need breathing room; they would need to get to know one another again as parents, as friends, and as lovers; and it probably would not succeed without much hard work and plenty of empathy. She was concerned how the boys would react to the return of a father with stricter, sterner ways.

"After the initial joy is over," Alice confided to Bill Cook, an old Stanford acquaintance of her husband's and a reporter for *Newsweek,* "we will have to get down to the nitty-gritty of bringing Dick back into our family. But we're so ready now, we can't get any more ready."

There were domestic crises to deal with: three active boys with banged knees, scrapes, squabbles, school homework. There was trauma: Mickey's guinea pig was killed by a dog. The child was heartbroken. He had wanted so to show it to his father. They wept softly together and pasted a picture of the little animal in Michael's photo album.

She studied her sons, these three individuals she had nursed, fathered, and mothered for six years: Michael, sensitive, vulnerable, in a world of animals and day dreams, who sometimes wore his sneakers (if he could find them) on the wrong feet and never noticed, not all day; Patrick, lean, and blond, and fiery, the athlete who, perhaps more than the others, carried the pain of his father's imprisonment deep inside him; and Charles, moody, bright as a penny, shy, dark as the others were light. She recalled, poignantly, that Charlie's teacher had asked his class to draw a picture of their greatest wish. Charlie's paper showed a row of cell doors drawn in brown crayon, with bars on the windows in black. He had written beneath it three times, "I wish my Daddy were home." When the teacher asked them to draw the wish fulfilled, he had written across the bottom of a paper, "My Daddy is home." The rest of the sheet was blank.

She loved her sons so deeply.

Mail was pouring in, twenty-five, sometimes thirty or even forty letters a day from all over the nation. Letters wishing her well, one or two wishing otherwise. Letters from persons wearing POW bracelets with Dick's name on them, asking when they should be returned. She made a promise that once Dick was home every letter would be acknowledged, answered personally; more than eight hundred were stacked in the living room right now.

She remembered to buy herself a new bottle of perfume—Chanel No. 5.

Yes, it was over. She was very glad it was over.

CHAPTER 30

Stratton awoke before the reveille gong sounded; it was March 4, 1973, the 2,251st day of his captivity. With any luck he would not be here for the 2,252nd.

He felt a thick mixture of joy and apprehension, a combination of emotions that often afflicts children Christmas morning.

Finally the gong sounded. He turned to, pulled on his prison pajamas, and helped get the toilet buckets ready for emptying. There was quiet joking; it did not relieve the tension.

Shaves and showers all around.

Breakfast: milk, bread, some sugar.

They fretted through free time.

The day grew older. They policed the cells. Release-day instructions had been issued two days before: fold the sleeping mats and mosquito nettings just so, stack them just so; cells were to be clean and neat, not left littered.

They were lined up and Stratton tramped with the others to the other side of the prison. The release clothing was stacked in piles, a prisoner's name pinned to each individual bundle. Stratton stripped as he was ordered, everything off. After he was searched, he put on his release clothes. He dressed quickly. Even though it was noon and the sun was out, it was chilly. The black shoes pinched and his clothes did not fit very well. He felt uncomfortable and conspicuous until he realized everyone else felt the same way. Shit, did it matter? He would have left bareass naked if that was the choice.

When Moon Mullen was marched over, his cigarette box was discovered and confiscated. He flew into a rage, but quickly controlled it. He did not want to screw up his release, or anyone else's. Sadly, he left the box behind.

Inside the main entrance to Hoa Lo was a large and carefully groomed garden compound. The prison officials took great pride in it. "Camp Unity" could be falling apart with age and neglect, but the garden grew on forever. It was the first sight that greeted visitors and it had often been photographed and described by persons as disparate as Gerhard Scheumann, the East German journalist, and an elderly California lady pacifist who had toured the Republic in 1970 and taken tea with the Premier. It would be the last view of Hoa Lo for the POWs now being assembled in the garden for release.

Stratton walked in the garden with the others, nodding to acquaintances, chatting softly with intimates. They were lined up and marched through the gates, under the wall, and into the sunshine on the other side. No one was blindfolded. The buses waited, new buses, East German, Stratton reckoned, maybe Czech, still daubed with wartime camouflage. Beyond the buses was a crowd of Vietnamese civilians, a small sea of wide brown eyes, dark clothes, straw hats, and soft chatter.

Stratton was apprehensive at first.

"Since the crowds were absolutely under their control, what were they going to do to us out there? The crowd was all along the street, watching. [But they] were very quiet and curious, which belied this natural hatred they (allegedly) had for the Caucasian air pirates. It's all a play and the Party played them like violins. If they had really hated us that much they would have wanted one last shot at us. . . ."

The buses were loaded, twenty men to a bus, roughly; the doors closed. Engines rumbled to life, gears shifted, and the vehicles, one following another, moved slowly down Hoa Lo Street away from the prison and the onlookers. Nobody was sure, *really* convinced yet, that they were going home. They sat and looked out the windows at a city they would never forget, which promised not to forget them.

312

The route through Hanoi to Gia Lam International Airport where they were to be repatriated was a long and circuitous one. Hanoi at siesta: it had the musty charm of a turn-of-the century Paris suburb. The war came into brief focus as the buses passed through the Kham Thien district, which had been peppered in the December 26 raids. (Stratton would later recall that he himself saw no areas he could call "carpet-bombed.") Hundreds of workers, most of them women, swarmed over the rubble.

From the bus windows the city looked far from desolate. Life streamed by on foot and in oxcarts; there were endless passings of pedicabs, military vehicles, Chinese trucks, and occasional World War II–vintage motorcycles with sidecars. The late President Ho Chi Minh smiled down from a picture on the façade of the National Bank. Across the street was the guest house in which Dr. Kissinger stayed while in Hanoi to negotiate the prisoners' release. Along Dien Bien Phu Street, where the more important Party members lived alongside foreign diplomats, the villas were banked with bougainvillaea and hibiscus plants. A keen eye might have spotted the wreckage of a downed plane protruding above the hedges of one of the houses. On Lake Hoan Kiem in the center of the city, off-duty soldiers rowed in tiny boats; old men sunned on the benches. A sidewalk artist had set up a display of his wares.

The buses slowed as they entered the traffic patterns of the Doumer (Long Bien) Bridge, spanning a mile over the beds and marshes of the Red River. The bridge was again in repair. All five traffic lanes were open, two for pedestrians, two for vehicular traffic, and one, in the middle, for the wheezy little steam locomotives tugging long lines of wooden wagons to and fro. Once they were across the river, on the rutted road to Gia Lam, evidence of the recent bombings was unmistakable. Roadside spinach fields were cratered; rows of jerry-built huts of straw housed refugees; the Gia Lam railhead was a fire-blackened scrapyard.

"My God," Stratton said as he passed the ruins, "they crucified it. Just crucified it, really laid it low."

They turned, heading east, for the airport. There was a good deal of apprehension when the buses finally stopped in front of a corrugated-steel outbuilding. It was some distance to the flight line. What now? Goddamn! They were ordered out of the buses and into the building. It was filled with church pews, rows of

313

them. The prisoners were told to sit down. They sat, quiet, edgy. Suddenly the guards were around them, chattering and smiling. It was a goddamned box lunch social, cases of Hanoi beer, baskets of little cookies that tasted like the shortbreads Lorna Doone used to write her name on. The men drank and ate, killing time. Obviously there was some kind of delay. It was really quite bizarre.

Then that nonsense was over. Back on the buses they went for a short, gear-whining drive to the flight line. The buses stopped. They climbed out the buses and lined up in front of their respective vehicles.

"The word from the seniors was that we would leave with dignity," Stratton said. "We would not act like a bunch of animals sassing them or yanking their chains. We wouldn't act like a bunch of idiots jumping up and down; until we crossed the line, it was to be no smiles, somber, straight business, pure military. We realized the photographers would be there with the happy prisoners departing and we wanted to make it clear when we crossed that line we were happy, when we were on the [Vietnamese] side, no way, Charlie. They were a bunch of bastards!"

Across the field, perhaps one hundred yards distant, three mammoth C-141 StarLifters waited, their silver skins shimmering in the midafternoon sun; tail markings identified them as belonging to the 10th Aeromedical Evacuation Squadron, Travis AFB, California. Between the prisoners and the planes an imaginary border line temporarily separated two nations: on the far side of the line, American medical personnel paced, watched, or waited; on the near side of the line the Vietnamese were assembling, watching a signal corps crew setting up a microphone and speaker. Straddling the boundary line was a small, grassy enclosure in which Colonel James R. Bennett, USAF, and Lieutenant Colonel Nguyen Phuong, ADRV, stood chatting in brief sentences, two professionals, neither friendly nor hostile, in carefully pressed uniforms, doing their jobs.

A North Vietnamese officer with protruding teeth and large ears stepped up to the microphone.

"American military captured personnel, listen to your name called and step out from your line."

The Rabbit was giving orders right to the end.

314

"I am going, and that little shit is staying," thought Stratton; there was some justice in the world.

The Rabbit read off the names of the assembled prisoners. One by one they walked forward to the table where the two senior officers stood, saluted, spoke their names, and crossed the imaginary line into the welcoming arms of their countrymen. The Rabbit droned on; the ranks of waiting prisoners thinned. Stratton fidgeted, waiting to hear his name, watching the others go, watching the Rabbit, feeling hate and disgust churn in his guts.

Finally. His back stiffened and he marched forward, his face angry, his lips pressed thin, whitening with fury. Colonel Bennett returned his brisk salute and reached out to shake his hand.

"Welcome aboard."

"Sir, get a picture and get the name of that cocksucker that is reading those names off on the microphone. That bastard is responsible for torturing over 90 per cent of the prisoners here." Phuong was impassive, but his eyes glittered. Bennett held tightly to Stratton's hand, soothing him, saying softly, "We've got him. We've got him. Now, don't worry about it. Just get on the airplane. We've got him."

He was firmly moved across the line. There were a lot of blanks after that.

He was startled by the cool beauty of a flight nurse standing at the bottom of the plane's boarding ramp, and curious about the C-141 ("I had never been inside one, you know, and I remember just looking around and marveling at it and sitting down").

With all aboard, the aircraft's jet engines whined, fired, and came to life. The plane taxied slowly to the head of the runway for take-off. The other birds would follow at intervals. The engines were run up. The C-141 strained against its brakes.

Inside, the tension was awful. Stratton gripped the arms of his seat. The plane started rolling. Nobody was certain they were going to make it.

"It's just like the cocksuckers to shoot us down on the way up and blame it on an American aircraft."

Rolling . . .

"Some stupid son of a bitch ain't got the word and he'll fire a SAM at us and we'll buy the farm."

Rolling . . .

315

"With our luck, some little old lady will be pissed because we knocked off her husband and she'll fire a lucky round and hit an engine and blow the shit out of us."

The StarLifter was rushing now, rolling faster than their minds could concoct disasters. The engines strained to lift the heavy ship off Gia Lam's short runway.

Talk stopped.

The nose lifted.

The main gear bumped free of the earth. They were pushed forward into their seat belts. The co-pilot hit the levers retracting the landing gear and the rate of climb increased. The ship gained altitude, crabbing onto course for the three-hour flight to Clark in the Philippines. In a manner of minutes they crossed the coastline and were over the Gulf.

The passenger section was in bedlam. Yells, cheers, magazines, pillows, paper flew through the compartment.

They were free.

CHAPTER 31

The American military had achieved a triumph in its own steady, muddling way. Its repatriation program for returning Vietnam POWs was nearly perfect. For years the Pentagon had designed, plotted, changed, studied, reported, restudied, tested, and finally committed to orders a procedure for the returnees. The entire operation was designed to ease their path back to civilization and, at least in the first weeks home, to de-emphasize the shit-shower-shave-shine tempo of military life.

Of course, the program was named "Ozone Prize," then "Operation Egress Recap."

The Secretary of Defense hastily renamed it "Operation Homecoming," before the first men came home.

The name mattered little, except as an anecdote about the military. The program mattered a whole lot.

The operation contained built-in buffers and safeguards, carefully balanced diets, and total security from the press. In contrast to the intimidating battery of intelligence operatives and psychiatrists that had faced the Korean prisoners of war twenty-one years before, each Vietnam POW was greeted by an escort officer, a man of rank, service branch, background, and experience comparable to those of his charge. The escort officer was the buffer between the POW and the fast-paced world, a safeguard even against the military bureaucracy itself. He carried in his official black briefcase up-to-date news for the returnee about his family

—the good with the bad—and other personal matters; he had a file full of more mundane information: current rank, decorations and/or citations, accumulated back pay, and what to expect by way of the scheduled "debriefings" that lay ahead.

Operation Homecoming's foreign outpost was Clark Air Base, a vast installation lodged for decades on the dusty Luzon plain in the Philippines; summer-baked and monsoon-soaked, it was the place where all returning prisoners landed after their release. Operation Homecoming went well in its initial tryout in February and was polished when the second batch of twenty came out. There had been some changes made, with accumulated experience: more cigarettes and coffee were put on board the medical-evacuation planes carrying the prisoners to freedom. Normal high-calorie American meals would be offered the men at Clark now instead of the blander fare prepared for and summarily rejected by the first groups. Special meals were again available, but lobster tails and hot dogs had been crossed off the menus for lack of interest. Gone, too, were soups (unless specially requested). Because a majority of the returning prisoners were reasonably fit and mentally alert, internment time at Clark's medical center had been cut from eight to ten days to four or less in most cases.

* * *

Homecoming wasn't all that easy for Richard Stratton.

"If that is the best you can do, shove it up your ass! I don't need beaver shots, for chrissakes!" The stunned recipient of this attack was an unidentified and well-meaning individual who had given Stratton a copy of *Playboy*. Thumbing through it, he had discovered, naturally, its gatefold triptych illuminated by a soft, lush mound of pubic hair. Startled by his reaction, comrades separated him from the magazine, substituting instead the 1972–73 winter edition of the Sears, Roebuck catalogue. Not every trend led to unclad females. Outstanding, but what about the beaver? Well, Rich, ahh, things look like they've changed. Jesus, he guessed they had.

Stratton's outburst surprised his escort officer, who exchanged glances with a second man, then wandered deliberately away. The second man, a full commander, sat down next to Stratton. Stratton did not know then, would not know for a while, that he had, not one, but two escorts; the officer beside him now had been flown down from Guam just for this chore.

"I don't remember who he was. Navy commander type. He sat down beside me and started making small talk. After the cheering and all that, I was tired. [None of us] had gotten much sleep the night before, wondering about release and doing our all-night reading, communicating, and everything else. Well, I don't know him and I don't have much to say to him. . . . Then he disappears."

Homecoming officials had established a medical-priorities procedure for the returning POWs. Each individual man was interviewed and his medical condition and needs, if any, established. The process began almost as soon as the aircraft cleared the Gia Lam runway. The information was radioed ahead to Clark. If blood were needed, or oxygen, or wheel chairs or ambulances, they would be waiting at the runway when the C-141 landed. There were no serious medical cases on the plane, and the radio traffic was routine, except for the commander from Guam. He had a different interview to conduct and he did not appear comfortable carrying it out. Stratton saw it in his face: something was up.

"The guy came waffling back over and sat down, and he said, 'I have just been talking . . . to Clark. Just got an interesting message and I really don't know what to do about it. In all honesty, my function on this airplane is to check you out before we land because there's a lot of people and a lot of cameras there.

"They want to know, uh, your . . . mental condition. Now, what the hell kind of answer do I give them?' I laughed at him.

"Was I okay?

"I was fine! I said to him, 'What were you going to do if I wasn't okay? What the hell were you going to do, take me out the back door? Lift me off in a gunny sack?' He laughed too, and he said (and he got serious), 'Well, you are in for it. You are in for the publicity bit.'

"I really appreciate what he did. Here was a guy who was not going to be manipulated by the system. He was giving me the courtesy that, until I proved otherwise, I was a human being. He was giving me a chance. And I was fine. I was. I think, in all fairness, I was worried about what the ultraconservative population of the Navy would think of me and what my fellows thought of me and I think I evidenced this concern. . . . Knowing what the enemy had said was not true and wanting very desperately those that I cared for most—my family and close friends—to know it wasn't true; I was very much concerned about what they thought. These were people that I really had a feel for; some others I could give a shit less, and I really didn't give a shit for the Navy Establishment.

"But I was afraid that perhaps, perhaps some one of them had believed those things; basically, I guess, the 'confession' of 1967. Now, it was some comfort back in 1967 to know that others had been broken, too. But when it came to my family, here and now, well, it didn't matter any more what others had done."

* * *

The plane touched down at Clark a little past 6 P.M.

In a roped-off area near the flight line a crowd numbering more than one thousand cheered and applauded. A color guard in silver helmets stood stiffly at attention. A ramp was wheeled into position next to the first C-141 and a thirty-foot carpet of red nylon plush was unrolled. The welcoming committee standing at the foot of the ramp included Ambassador Henry A. Byroade; Admiral Noel A. M. Gaylor, the American commander in the Pacific, and Lieutenant General William G. Moore, Jr., commander of the 13th Air Force, based at Clark.

Stratton was only feet from American soil.

"We all lined up and they had the order [of deplaning] and one guy was supposed to stand just inside the door and announce over a mike who was getting off. I was standing there waiting and the commander from Guam came up and started chatting and he broached the subject of smiling. *My* smiling. Everybody, he said, was, uh, 'concerned' because they had never seen me smile; that all the pictures that had come out of Hanoi, with a couple of exceptions perhaps, came out without a smile. Then he came right out and asked whether I was going to smile a lot now.

"I said, 'Who the shit cares? I don't turn it on and turn it off. Why the hell should I smile? I'm tired, I'm dirty, I stink. The clothes don't fit and I don't feel like smiling.'

"And the commander said, 'Well, just take it from a friend. If you love your family, you'll come off this plane smiling because they're going to be watching.'

320

"Now had that guy not come to me before and told me about that message from Clark, I would have suspected him of trying to manipulate me. Then, I don't know; funny, what flashed through my mind was the time I was sitting in the A-4 when the tail blew off and I was wondering whether I should pull the curtain or not, remembering Alice's last words about not dying and leaving her with those three little kids; now it was the same thought—Alice. The old lady has probably been worrying for years about those pictures of me. If I walk off here feeling like I do, tired and everything else and so sick and tired of all the publicity and cameras and everything else and figuratively shoot them a bird, it will make me feel good but it will probably hurt her.

"It was good advice that commander gave me; it was the motivation I came off that plane with."

Stratton fairly ran down the ramp. His smile was dazzling.

Network commentators who often sounded as euphoric as the returning prisoners looked could not restrain themselves as Stratton flashed his teeth: "Lookit that smile; never seen him smile like that," and other such noteworthy patter. CBS cut to a film strip and commentary showing Stratton bowing and bowing and bowing at the 1967 confession press conference.

Another commentator, filling dead air with his own sounds, wondered aloud whether Stratton's celebrated 1967 "confession" of war crimes and less celebrated (and subsequent) interviews would cause his ostracism from the Navy and his fellow POWs. Alice Stratton heard that remark, and it registered, but it was a while before she reacted to it.

In Palo Alto, California, watching her husband (live and in color) get off the C-141, seeing the walk, the salute, and the smile, Alice let out a cry of joy. The tears came—followed by an incredible feeling of relief. The desperate hours were over: more than six years of waiting, 2,251 days, 54,024 hours, 3,241,440 minutes of waiting, fear, sleepless nights, raising sons without a father, of helping other wives in the same predicament, of loneliness and anger and frustration, of sleeping alone and fighting alone and hoping alone. All gone. Now she would wait for what she knew would quickly come next, his voice, the standard NOK (next of kin) call she had been told would come soon after the men arrived in the Philippines.

The telephone rang once. She cut it off in mid-jingle.

"Hello?" It popped out mechanically. She knew who it was.

"Hi, hon, I love you. How are you?" The Massachusetts baritone with its broadened *A*'s was still the same, still strong, still him.

The murmurs of love came quickly. The extraordinary moment in which they found themselves permitted that breach of the normal restraint both had exercised with each other on the telephone.

(Stratton had always found it difficult to make love to his wife on a telephone, he said. It was so impersonal. In his salad days in Washington, he dated an operator for the Potomac Telephone Co. She told him how she and her colleagues often listened in on other people's calls, even though the company forbade it. This admission of eavesdropping surprised him and, ever since, he had never quite been sure that when he was on the phone, particularly with Alice, everybody on God's green earth wasn't listening in.)

After the personal exchanges, his voice became serious. She again knew what was coming: the question of publicity. He admitted he was nearly irrational on the subject. But he knew, too, that, beside his own private nature, the years of interviews and cameras and profiles and exploitation he had had while a prisoner had brought to him a great anger. He told her about the incident on the plane and about the advice he had received about smiling. He did not tell her (until later) that behind the smile was a sudden panicky fury at all the cameras and fill lights and an irresistible, erratic urge "to kick the living shit out of the first reporter or photographer that came within reach." Was freedom going to be like prison? He fled to the refuge of a gray hospital bus.

* * *

Unlike some POW wives, Alice Stratton refused to be photographed or televised watching her husband get off the plane at Clark. It was a private moment, and she refused to share it with anyone except her family and a few, very few, intimate family friends. When the NOK call ended, she knew he was all right; hearing his voice, sensing the temper, feeling a touch of his wit, she knew he was safe and stable, or as stable as any man coming out of six years of confinement can be.

But in truth, she was perplexed and she fretted; perhaps she should have discussed the matter with him? No, he had enough to worry about at the moment. What bothered her was the ostracism comment she had heard on the television. She knew whatever he had said or done had been as a result of torture or some other deprivation. Hegdahl had told her that. She knew other POWs had made similar statements for similar reasons. She knew the Pentagon had decided no returnee would be punished for any activity performed under duress or threats of torture.

But maybe he didn't know; he was anxious, she could sense it. Finally, she picked up the telephone and placed a person-to-person call to Dr. Roger Shields, the Assistant Secretary of Defense for POW affairs. She explained her doubts. Shields reassured her Dick was not ostracized.

And later, unknown to her and to the consternation of her husband, Shields delegated a brigadier general to assure Stratton that his role as a POW and position as a naval officer were above reproach.

Reassured, Alice Stratton prepared for her husband's homecoming and for turning command of the family over to him when he was ready for it. She had had something of a long cruise herself.

* * *

"We landed at Clark and they fed us right off the bat, thank God. It was after six and suppertime anyway. They really had a good operation going there. The mess hall was really set up. They had a dietician there, too. She was Chinese-American, a captain, and she was dressed in a miniskirt. It was the first miniskirt I was actually conscious of seeing and that captain was some kind of good-looking. But she wasn't there to dress up the place, she was there to save us from ourselves.

"'What would you like?' she asked. They were specializing in New York steaks, filet mignon, all that sort of stuff.

"'I'll have a dozen eggs. Scrambled!'

"'You can't have *that* many,' she says. She's on an anti-cholesterol kick. I don't know about any of that.

"'I'll take whatever you can give me.'

"'I'll give you, uh, half a dozen.'

"'Fine. Outstanding!'

"'Well, come back if you want some more.'

"I ate that load with ketchup on top and salt and pepper, and when I was finished I came right back up and there she was. I said, 'I'd like my other half dozen now, please.'

" 'Well, okay. But you can't have *just* eggs. You have to have some meat, something of substance with them.'

" 'No, no meat. I don't want any meat. Eggs.'

" 'Not even a filet mignon?'

" 'No. Nothing. Just the eggs, please.'

" 'If you want the eggs, you have to take the meat!'

" 'Okay, I give up. I'll take the eggs with the meat.' And I thought, To hell with you, lady!"

He carried the platter back to the table. One half was filled with a steaming mound of creamy yellow eggs, the other sported a filet mignon oozing just the right amount of blood and decorated with a small fillip of parsley.

"I went back to my table. I ate that second load of eggs with ketchup and salt and pepper. When nobody was looking, I threw the steak into the trash can."

With his stomach full, he attended to some paper-work matters with his escort officer (he was now down to one) and went to his room, which he shared with four other men; they referred to it as "the cell." It was not an entirely humorous designation; Homecoming officials intended to keep them isolated, initially, from a horde of well-wishers and the press to maintain a continuity of repatriation and to protect information the men carried in their heads.

There were restrictions, too, on eating—a four-hour cushion, rigidly enforced, between meals.

Nearly four hours had passed since Stratton consumed his dozen eggs. He was talking with his roommates; one of them asked off-handedly, "Hey, Rich, did you see the salad bar in the mess hall? Oh, man!"

He had not seen it, and now his mouth watered. Salad!

"When my time was up, I went right down to the mess hall and got a tray and found the salad bar. I got two great big dinner plates and I put them on the tray side by side. Then I made a great big fresh salad with greens and everything on one and a great big fresh fruit salad on the other and topped that one off with cottage cheese.

324

"I'm walking down the line now on the way to my table, and there's a new dietician, a male dietician, and he's a nice, gentle soul.

"He says, 'Oh, you like salad, huh?'

" 'No shit, Dick Tracy!'

" 'Uh, oh, uh, well, sir . . .' "

He looked up and smiled, blushing, at Stratton.

" 'Well, don't be embarrassed, sir,' he said brightly; 'some nut came through here four hours ago and ate a dozen eggs.' "

He was free. He was well fed. He had talked with Alice. The adrenalin was washing out, and some of the euphoria with it. He felt a little drained. Back in his room, he sat on the edge of his bed. What luxury! He slid under the clean, crisp white sheets and stretched his legs out as far as they could go and closed his eyes and smiled. The bed was cool. The pillows smelled so clean.

And he couldn't sleep. The bed got hot and uncomfortable. It was too goddamn soft, for one thing. He tossed, he turned; he could not get comfortable; his feet began to sweat. After a couple of hours, he gave up; to hell with it. He got out of bed. He put the pillow on the floor beside the bed and he pulled off the blanket. He lay down on the floor, pulled the blanket around him for warmth, and laid his head down on the pillow. He slept.

Four days later he went home to California.

CHAPTER 32

The return of the Vietnam POWs in February and March of 1973 had all the earmarks of a mass media morality play, something joyous salvaged out of the Indochina disaster, something unifying and relatively clean in a nation divided by war and about to be sullied by its greatest political scandal.

The media tended to reflect the returning POWs as a band of heroes, which they were not. Lingering anti-war hard-liners insisted they were criminals, rogues, and liars, which they were not. And this was all understandable; the media took the easy way because the difficult way was beyond them. The Haydens, Fondas, and Clarks were proved foolish, and at best, naïve. Perhaps the most thoughtful—and anguished—comments on those weeks came from an obscure midwest reporter writing in the *Chicago Journalism Review*. The reporter's name was Michael Miner, and he himself was a veteran of Vietnam:

"[The POWs] are too important for us to slough them off so cheaply—and that is what we have done, with stories that were old the second time we wrote them. I want to know just who the hell these prisoners are, because some part of them is part of me and some part isn't, and the same overlap is true of the country. The country must know what to make of them and at the moment it doesn't, just as we [reporters] don't; yet their return mattered. It was more than just another cheap whiff of sentiment; when they came back, an era ended."[4]

Most of the whiffs of sentiment, genuine high drama and low comedy, were played at Travis Air Force Base, a grand, fat military clutter in a green-gold valley between the farming communities of Fairfield and Suisun City about forty-five miles north and east of San Francisco and the Golden Gate.

Travis was home base for the 10th Aeromedical, which carried Richard Stratton out of Hanoi. In earlier years, in the years when the bloodletting in Vietnam was at its peak, the 10th performed less joyous chores. The squadron's silver C-141s started home the refuse of war: the dead and dying, the wounded and the maimed, carted it home and dumped it on the runway at Travis where Stratton's plane was landing this noon. There were times back in the mid-1960s when 100,000 men passed through Travis every month: fresh troops on their feet heading west, the refuse in its coffins or on litters heading east. Now it was over, and the crowds today, March 8, 1973, gathered at the flight line at Travis were in a jubilant mood. And there she was, the first plane.

Even before the engines of Homecoming Flight Q shut down, there were ragged tatters of applause. The door of the C-141 was opened, Travis' Operation Homecoming information officer, Lieutenant Colonel William Reslie, USAF, clambered into the plane. He stood behind the door inside, out of sight.

"We are attempting," he said through the PA system, "to offload these people in this order. . . . First, since he is the senior officer on board, Commander Richard A. Stratton, United States Navy."

It was a little past noon. Stratton, in full uniform, burst from the airplane like a greyhound out of the starting box.

He was grinning.

He acknowledged the applause, shook hands with the welcoming senior officers, and walked to a battery of microphones set up in front of a thin phalanx of reporters, photographers, film and television crews. His smile faded. The sun was directly overhead. The air was crisp. Several persons in the crowd of onlookers were waving large American flags. Stratton watched the banners as the next four men on Q flight lined up raggedly behind him, blinking in the sunlight. Stratton had wanted a show of unity, and he got it. The four represented the POW presence in Vietnam: Marine Sergeant Richard G. Burgess, Army Specialist 5 Jose M. Astorga, Air

Force Lieutenant Colonel Thomas M. Madison, and Clodeon (Speed) Adkins, a civilian construction worker captured in 1968. Stratton, senior officer aboard the plane, was spokesman for its passengers.

"We stand here today," he began, and he was quite somber now, "as we have stood for so long—shoulder to shoulder. We are American fighting men and we have never forgotten it. We stand ready now to give our lives for our nation. We have kept the faith; we have never wavered in our trust in God, our trust in our country, and our trust in our fellow Americans." His eyes were bright and he looked left and right as he spoke. His head was slightly back, his face pale, still somber. The men behind him looked tense; Burgess, eyes glazed, his flesh an unhealthy grayish yellow, swayed on rubbery legs.

"We thank the Office of the President and the State Department for steering a steady course and a firm hand," he continued. "We thank the Congress for keeping our families in comfort while we were away. Now we are going to join with the rest of America and bring the rest of them home. We will stick together and move the country forward.

"I'd like to say something personal." His right hand grabbed the bill of his cap and his arms flew out in a wide V gesture of joy and he grinned, showing the gap in the upper row of teeth.

"After six years, I have something to smile about. I'm free!" He resquared the hat. The smile faded and the face was pleasantly stern. "America, we love you; we salute you," and he saluted the audience. There were cheers.

"We love you too," a woman shouted from the crowd. More applause.

"All right, men," he said out of the side of his mouth, away from the microphones, "about face and follow me." He straightened his back and marched through them toward the administration building about two hundred feet from where they had been standing. The others followed him. Burgess weaved slightly, but shook off a hastily offered arm of assistance. Stratton's old friend Ted Kopfman ran from the building and met him about halfway. They exchanged an affectionate, back-slapping bear hug. The crowd cheered. They linked arms and walked the rest of the way together. Waiting at the building for them was Lieutenant

Commander Everett Alvarez, Jr. He and Stratton reached for each other and the resulting hug was so forceful that they nearly lost their balance. And they all went inside together, and the name-calling and deplaning continued. There were cheers and applause and a lot of waving American flags, and more emotional reunions.

Several minutes passed and the onlookers, civilian and military alike, showed no signs of leaving. Stratton, who several days before had been in a near-frenzy over the press and was always reserved in crowd situations, was overcome by the euphoria of homecoming. He bounded out of the building and he ran toward the crowd, which again cheered him loudly. He skipped a couple of times along the way. He reached the barrier and began shaking proffered hands at random. William McNair, an invalid in a wheelchair, was wearing a POW bracelet with Stratton's name on it. He offered it and Stratton took it from him and slipped it on his right wrist with several others. He took one of McNair's hands in both his own and chatted animatedly with him, his face only inches from McNair's bearded one. He hugged and kissed McNair's wife. More hands. It was a jubilant moment, and a time-consuming one, beginning to disrupt the military's schedule. Finally Commander Joseph Posner, the public information officer of the 12th Naval District, separated Stratton from his public and ushered him to waiting Navy station wagons that would take Stratton (and several others) in caravan to Oak Knoll Naval Hospital in Oakland.

There another crowd, Naval and Marine brass, and more reporters and cameramen waited.

And Alice. And the children.

Richard Stratton was home from his war.

His wife's ended forty-five minutes later, the time it took an anonymous seaman second (with a heavy foot behind a V-8 engine) to drive from Travis to Oakland.

* * *

Alice and the boys were driven to Oakland from Palo Alto by her casualty assistance officer and literally smuggled into the hospital through a rear door to avoid a crowd of well-wishers already gathered at the main entrance. Once inside and ensconced in the

329

room assigned to Stratton on the hospital's sixth floor, they watched the goings-on below from a window, waving occasionally to friends they spotted in the crowd. A family reunion with relatives would come later; Navy plans called for first reuniting the ex-POW with his wife and children. Inside the building, in the reception area, was a box of corsages, one for each of the returning men to present to his wife. The flowers had been sent and paid for by the White House.

The small caravan from Travis pulled up. Stratton uncurled his long legs and got out of the wagon. He was still the senior officer and stood before a small brown lectern bristling with mikes. The crowd cheered. Two young girls dashed from the sidelines, nimbly dodging around a stone-faced Marine guard, handed Stratton their POW bracelets, and bussed him soundly on the cheeks. He bent, with a smile, to receive the smacks. The crowd responded loudly.

He made a short speech, thanking them for being there, concluding in a rousing voice:

"We stuck together as one in facing the enemy. Please join with us and stick together and get the rest of them out.

"I am happy to be home. It's so good to be free. It's so good to have clean air. It's so good to be clean. God bless you all." And then he waved, smiled, tipped his hat, and was gone.

They waited inside the room, with the door open; Alice was terribly excited and elated and tired and let down all at the same time; the boys, anxious, fidgeting. Then she heard his footsteps, a long-forgotten beat, and her heart rushed inside her chest; she was near coming apart. She didn't think she could stand it, waiting for him to get through the door.

"Hi, hon, how are ya?"

Like a ballet in slow motion, they moved into each other's arms and there was a suggestion of tears. The boys moved around them. Alice said:

"He looked thin, but he looked good to me. Of course, he would have had to look pretty bad to look bad. Oh, that moment was a lot of things: kind of like the happiest day of your life, or Christmas is here and you've been waiting a long time for it. But I was thankful, too, the ordeal was over, sort of a tired feeling, sort of a letdown because we got so strung out there at the last, but finally just an overwhelming feeling of relief.

330

"I think the biggest excitement was when he actually got out [of Hanoi] . . . because I knew then eventually I would get my hands on him. Ho-ho!"

For Richard Stratton, it was a moment of understated joy and delicate renewal.

"The important thing was the kids. If either one of us fell to pieces, it might cause problems for the boys that would be hard to identify later on and take years to correct. We had talked about it before, in the first letter I had sent [Alice] from Hanoi and the last one, telling her that, in a sense, this was just another cruise. I had always asked her not to meet the ship; there was a family tradition here.

"So that's about the way we handled it and it wasn't any real strain. Charlie hid behind her skirts; the other two were right out there. I had a present for each of them, a pair of binoculars and some Mickey Mouse thing which immediately kept them busy so I could, well, to put it crudely, pat her on the arse."

His first impression, or certainly one of the first, was the attractiveness of his wife, who had, in fact, physically changed very little during his absence. His mind had misplaced somewhere in Hanoi a sharp and precise picture of Alice: that clean, cool attractiveness, how her jaw squared ever so slightly, and her smile and long, slim legs, the earthy laugh and the faint hint of Chanel. It sorely tested his resolve; enforced chastity was easier to bear than its voluntary brother. But he had made a vow to himself and he passed it on to her: he was going to get to know her again and she him, and he was going to court her; anything else, he delicately phrased it, would be an insult to her and their relationship. And, he would recall later, it worked out quite well.

"But I admit I was horny. She was a good-looking girl and it had been a long time. Oh, she looked great! She had not let herself go to pot. It really hit me. Here was a gal who thought enough to keep herself in shape with everything else she had to go through and she looked just as good as the day I married her. No. Even better. . . ."

* * *

The Stratton clan drove to the hospital together from a rendezvous at San Francisco International, the senior Strattons from

331

Quincy, brother Charlie from Los Angeles, and Ellen from Buffalo. For Ellen Cooper, it was an unforgettable time.

"On the drive from the airport to the hospital, the talk was filled with light banter hiding feelings of incredible tension. We were all tense about this; getting to the hospital and knowing what was about to happen was a very, very important moment in our lives. None of us were ever going to forget it. Often those important moments—and there are few of them—are disappointing, are wrong in some way. . . .

"So [once we arrived at the hospital] we went through all these doors where there were Marine guards—and we had identification and everything—I kept thinking about this. What were we going to find? How was it going to be? How was *he* going to be?

"It was just unbelievable: walking, walking, walking by lots of pictures drawn by little school kids about the return of the POWs; it was all very moving, but . . . everything in and under control and [finally] getting to his door. The tension was so great. Opening the door. And there he was. He really looked so good and he acted so fine. We greeted him in order: first Dad and then Mother, then me, and Charlie. Dad was really overcome . . . and had to sit down. We each have different memories of that moment, what it meant to us. But for me that moment was perfect. It could not have been a better reunion and I will always remember that."

So began Richard Stratton's renaissance. Those first hours of reunion and emotion, dreamlike in some ways, blended into days of reality, and fatigue. He was very tired, like the rest of them, drained by tension and more than six continuous years of anxiety. Hanoi was so far away now, yet always close. Too close. A jingle of keys on an orderly's belt, or soft footsteps by his door in the middle of the night, brought him bolt-upright in bed, terror-stricken and soaked instantly with sweat. There were medical problems: an enlarged prostate gland, a tendency to go overweight rapidly, bone deterioration in his jaws, a glucose problem, unexpected bouts of euphoria and hyperactivity, and an inability to sleep well at night.

He had also suffered loss of his near vision, a result of the normal aging process—he was now forty-one—and the inadequate prison diet. The military had anticipated these kinds of problems.

It was obvious within the first few hours after his arrival at Clark that he would need glasses. His eyes were tested and a prescription for lenses was made up and radioed to the military opthamology lab on Okinawa. Twelve hours later, the new glasses perched on his nose, a chore, noted one of his waggish comrades, for which that particular organ on that particular face had been admirably designed.

Navy dentists went to work on his jaws and teeth, and Navy psychiatrists on his head to help ease the way to a faster, more demanding life. Intelligence rummaged around in his brain for whatever information he had. All these things—medical, dental, and psychiatric evaluation, and intelligence debriefing—had begun on Clark. They continued on a more intense and regular schedule at Oakland. Intelligence was perhaps the most demanding, for it forced him to relive a nightmare: where the first debriefings sought names of men possibly alive but missing and those still in prison, intelligence now wanted from him an hour-by-hour, day-by-day, year-by-year accounting of his imprisonment, from shootdown to "confession" to liberation; there was no form and no checklist other than that with the names of other prisoners he had given them at Clark. And they went through all that again, too: the name of every person he had ever seen in his years of imprisonment; the name of every person he had ever heard from, or thought he had heard from, or thought he had seen. What were the names and locations of the prison camps he had served time in; who were the collaborators, if any?

They rummaged around in his mind with their questions and their tape recorders: What kind of military information had the North Vietnamese sought? How did they phrase their questions? What kind of political questions had they asked and what kind of politicizing had they done? What kind of military information did they have? What was the treatment like? What methods of torture had they used? How had he responded? Who had done the torturing? Who was the camp commander? Who? What? Where? When? How? On and on and on for three hours a day, until by the week after Easter they had purged him of every scrap of information he had and some, indeed, he had forgotten he had.

Despite the joy of his homecoming and the reunion with his family, it was not an easy time for him. His days were full, even though the Navy had allowed plenty of free time. Sometimes, just overwhelmed, he would go to his room and shut the door so he could be alone, away from everybody and everything. It was not easy on the family either.

"In the next few days [after homecoming] a lot of different things happened," Ellen Cooper recalled. ". . . There was so much emotion going on, it was unbelievable. A psychologist should have been there to record every minute of it. There were times when I was so happy and so proud of him and other times when I felt angry.

"I was probably not very understanding about what was happening to Dick, and he must have been feeling all sorts of things himself that I couldn't know about.

"Oh, I remember at one point—everyone apparently kept alluding to what I had been doing—he finally asked me, 'What on earth *have* you been doing?' and I tried to explain my [anti-war] views, which shouldn't have been a surprise because we had discussed them . . . as early as 1964.

"I remember a specific discussion and I believe Dick said to me, 'That man brought [me] home!' I thought I screamed, maybe I didn't, . . . 'I hate that man!' . . .

"I felt Nixon had exploited him. I felt that those of us who were against the war helped to bring Dick home, but he felt the anti-war people prolonged the war, and I understood why he felt that way and accepted it, but I didn't believe it. . . . I would be less than honest if I didn't admit to some hurt that he couldn't see my contribution.

"He was very busy with other things to do . . . but [the Navy] left time for these men to be with their families. At one point when we were there and I was there, he had lunch with a priest he didn't know; another time he spent a long time watching movies of the . . . air war in Vietnam. This made me angry. I felt we were all there to see him after six years and he was sitting there watching those movies.

"He turned to me eventually and said, 'What's going on here? You seem so angry.'

" 'I *am* angry! Why are you watching these movies?'

" 'Well, I wanted to see how the war was going.'

" 'I could have told you how it was going: we lost!' "

334

If her timing was bad, at least she was honest about what she was feeling, or as honest as she could be. Ellen was going through a new, internal struggle, and facing her brother had triggered the final battle. She did not want to lose.

"I was very conscious of wanting to make it clear to him now, this big brother who had been sort of a formidable figure and with whom I hadn't spent much time in the last decade . . . that I was no longer that intimidated little sister. That I was now an independent, functioning adult with my own ideas that were different than his. And that was sort of mixed in, I think, with that display of anger. . . . It was sort of like, Okay, Ellen, if you don't start right away you'll be engulfed again. You must begin asserting yourself with this strong individual."

Whatever their divergent views, and the pressures of the moment, Richard Stratton loved his sister deeply and, perhaps, even recognized the struggle she was going through. He told her that as long as she had done what she believed in on his behalf within the limits of the law, it was fine with him.

"I couldn't ask for more from a sister, Ellen."

* * *

Days moved into weeks and the buzz continued: medical tests, dental drills, blood tests, urine samples, stool tests, intelligence sessions; it never ended. Thank God for Alice. Always, there was Alice, on the telephone or visiting him at the hospital; she carried news, mail, gossip, papers, and love; she had assembled the photograph albums, but he could not bring himself to look at them, not then, not for a long time. It was too painful to have to look at six years of lost fatherhood, to be reminded he had missed the sweetness of watching his sons mature. Alice took the albums home.

Finally he was allowed to go to the home he had never seen in Palo Alto. The doctors gave him an hour, plus travel time. Alice was driving and the children were in back, just a little self-conscious.

There were some attempts at small talk but things got quiet. He turned around and spoke to them. His face was gentle.

"I want to explain something to you if I can," he said. "It is going to be difficult for you, I know, but you must realize that your mother is my girl friend and my wife as well as your mother. I am going to spend as much time with you as I can, but I'm also going to have private time with Mother, too, and you are probably going to feel left out at times.

"I understand that and I appreciate it, and when you feel that way, let's talk about it, and if we keep talking about it, I am sure we can work it out."

Alice squeezed his hand and smiled.

* * *

Whatever uneasiness Stratton felt on that first trip to Palo Alto centered not on his family or what might await him on Nathan Way but on the California highway traffic; it was safer in combat.

"What a bunch of nuts!"

The actual homecoming was anticlimactic: to his eye, the "new" house resembled the one he had left in 1966 in Hanford and "I had the feeling I had just come home from a nine-month cruise and it was nice to be home again, in my own home, away from all the screwy psychiatrists in the hospital and away from all the people who were prying at me."

He prowled through the rooms, quiet, taking it all in.

"[Dick] appeared quiet," Alice recalled, "and I was afraid he didn't like the house; I had carefully kept it with the old things, the same furniture, so he would remember. But it turned out he was pleased with the house, he reacted quite well.

"It was too short a time; I was disappointed he had to go back to the hospital [so soon]."

Had it been a different occasion, or had he had more time, no doubt Stratton might have needled Alice about her housekeeping.

"Some jerk from the [hospital's] allergy clinic, a doctor, decided I was allergic to dust, leaves, weeds, or something. So he did all the pinprick tests on me and decided that this was indeed the case. He called me in for a consultation and gave me a sheet of paper to take home to my wife.

"The sheet of paper was to tell her how to clean house, how to get the moss and weeds out of the bathroom, the shower, and all that sort of stuff. And I remember thinking: you jerk! I've been away for almost seven years, and I'm going to tell this woman how to clean the house?"

As it was, he let the humor pass for the moment.

Luckily the moss and weeds in the bathroom and the shower did not infect him, and he returned to the hospital, at the end of the appointed hour, intact and without a telltale rash.

*　*　*

The hospital provided a crash course for the returnees on all or much of what they had missed during years of imprisonment. It was more than Stratton or any of them could really absorb: photographs, books, magazines, news materials in short and expanded forms, special films from the National Aeronautics and Space Administration (NASA) and the Department of Defense (DOD), and movies every night at the Oak Knoll officers' club.

(Stratton, attending one of those evening movies at the officers' club—a film considered "racy" by the critics—finally heaved up a yawn of boredom, and snapped his jaw into a gaping and unclosable position. There was considerable consternation among the medical staff and "general quarters" at the hospital where he was rushed. It was a "trick" jaw. Stratton, with "ahhhhs," "uh-uh-uhs," and much pointing of fingers and frowns finally convinced concerned residents and corpsmen to fix it his way. The bone snapped quickly back into place.)

Stratton refused to let himself be overwhelmed; when past or present, crowded him, he went to his room and shut the door. The door had a sign on it: "Yea, though I walk through the valley of the shadow of death, I shall fear no evil, for I am the meanest SOB in the valley." It had a certain intimidating effect on younger corpsmen. The sign was a gift from one of the television crews that covered his homecoming.

*　*　*

Alice Stratton, like other ex-POW "female dependents," was, within a few days, given permission to visit her husband at Oak Knoll on a regular basis, eventually take him home for gradually increasing periods of time, and spend full nights with him at the hospital. It was in these early days, mellow hours, that they began picking up the pieces of their life and looking forward. They began picking up the threads of conversations that had ended in 1966. Would he stay in the Navy or would he resign and pursue

337

now the teaching career he eventually desired? If he stayed in the Navy, would he take a command and put to sea again? It would almost certainly be offered if he could pass a flight physical. If he stayed in the Navy but could not fly, would they stay in Palo Alto or ship out; and if that were the case, would it affect the boys, particularly Charlie with his physical therapy and Michael with his school problems? And between the questions they flirted and got to know one another again, swapped gossip and anecdotes, reminisced, laughed, and sometimes just sat quietly studying one another.

"The first few days were like a honeymoon," said Alice, "but only the first few days. The great beauty of being able to start all over and have all these simple things, well, it's like seeing the grass greener, it was really neat. Every single thing that we did, I felt like pinching myself."

His affection and respect for her were limitless; in another man they might have been unnatural. As a physical token he presented her with a large diamond ring one night at a private dinner at the officers' club. She had never owned anything like it and its value and size made her self-conscious the first few times she wore it. But she wore it.

"I had returned to an extremely attractive and beautiful woman," Stratton said. "And I was glad to see that she had not adopted some of the wild styles. It would have repelled me to see my wife running around in a super miniskirt, hotpants. She is far more of an extrovert now than when I left her; perhaps being dominated by the male Naval Aviator with a big mouth, she never had a chance to shine."

With the luck of the Irish, his first full weekend home was St. Patrick's Day weekend (March 17 falling on a Saturday in 1973). It was his introduction to the role of citizen Stratton in the sometimes rarefied life of suburban Palo Alto: small talk, back-yard barbecues, parish politics, school taxes, and crab grass problems. He took it in stride.

"The adjustment," Alice told a friend, "is similar to what we would have at the end of a cruise. He's coming back from what, as he keeps saying, is just a longer-than-usual cruise; and I keep saying, 'Dick, that was a *very* long cruise!'"

The neighborhood was decked with "welcome home" signs; neighbors were invited to a St. Patrick's Day beer bust and gab fest on the Strattons' front lawn. It was a merry time, everyone a little self-conscious at first, then loosening up as the afternoon wore on. It was sunny, but cool. There were pretzels and green beer and lots of children. Stratton, wearing his squadron cap and a lightweight Navy windbreaker with squadron patches on it, looked pale and a little tired but otherwise fit. He chatted and flirted with the children, kissed wives and daughters, shook hands with the men, talked vaguely about his future in the Navy, vividly of his impressions of the Boeing 747, and stayed mum about anything having to do with his years in North Vietnam. The party broke up about five. He went into the house and fell asleep from exhaustion.

The weather turned warm overnight; Sunday was a real smoker. In spite of it, the nave of Our Lady of the Rosary offered only standing room to late-comers for its second mass that morning. The Strattons, honored guests, had front-pew seats; the commander, in dress blues, looked rested, perhaps just a little tense. The boys fidgeted, until their father's sharp whisper put a stop to that nonsense.

To the north of the chancel, a jazz choir rocked through the opening song and services began, led by the Reverend Terrence Loughran. Father Loughran was a "modern" priest. It was he who had instituted jazz choirs and other innovations he considered liberating and attractive to younger Catholics; he was a kind and gentle man who wore a full beard over contemporary vestments and insisted on being called Terry. When he introduced Stratton to the congregation, his voice was thick with emotion.

"I will simply ask you to welcome with great love, which is human and therefore very Christian, Dick Stratton back to his family and to us. And Dick, if you would like to step forward, we would like to greet you."

Stratton stood and walked slowly forward to the foot of the chancel. The applause and cheers went on for a very long time. He embraced Father Loughran, then turned around and faced the congregation. The choir cut through the applause.

Stratton stood there a bit perplexed by the welcome, a half-smile on his face, nodding, trying to follow the unfamiliar lyrics, hands fumbling at his sides. He held his ground. The applause died away, and the song ended.

It was very quiet. Stratton cleared his throat. He began to speak. His voice was husky.

"I want to thank you all, from the bottom of my heart, for this welcome this morning. I want to thank you for caring for my family and for giving them a home when I was absent. And I have some words that I hold close from the Book of Proverbs, Chapter 31."

Some members of the congregation wept, the tears dropping onto their Sunday clothes, their throats giving off strained sounds of snuffing. A quizzical look crossed Alice Stratton's face. Father Loughran bit his lower lip. Stratton fumbled for a moment, taking a white piece of paper out of his pocket, and, holding it away from himself, began reading without his glasses:

"When one finds a worthy wife, her value is far beyond pearls. Her husband, in trusting his heart to her, has an unfailing prize. She brings him good and not evil all the days of her life. She reaches out her hands to the poor and extends her arms to the needy. She is clothed with strength and dignity, and she laughs at the days to come.

"She opens her mouth in wisdom and on her tongue is kindly counsel. She watches the conduct of her household and eats not her food in idleness. Her children rise up and extol her. Her husband, too, extols her saying, 'Many are the women of proven worth, Alice, but you have excelled them all.'

"That from the Book of Proverbs. God love you, my family."

He gave Alice a long, private look and walked slowly back to his seat.

Late that afternoon, he returned to the hospital.

CHAPTER 33

On March 20 Richard Stratton donned dress blues again and submitted himself to his first formal press conference. It was held in a small auditorium on the ground floor of Oak Knoll Naval Hospital. Stratton's name alone prompted full network coverage.

He was loose, smiling: a man obviously tackling this chore with relish. Carefully he explained to assembled reporters that under a POW bond of allegiance, and for current national security reasons, he could answer no questions about his years in Hanoi. He reminded them that Hanoi still held more than two hundred men. When all the prisoners were free, and security lifted, yes, he would be willing to meet with them again and tell them anything they wanted to know; the story would be "very interesting," he promised.

The press conference began; Roy Neal of NBC asked Stratton a question about his captivity.

Stratton politely demurred, briefly repeating what he had first said.

Another reporter got his attention: How had Stratton changed?

"Well, I am a much more patient man than I ever was before. And six years of waiting for an elevator certainly gives you a little bit of patience. The second thing is, I think, that I am a little bit more of a tolerant person than I was before. I think I was very

341

much given to being opinionated. I would search out an answer for a thing and think that now that I had resolved the answer, that was it. Now I think I have learned that there are many different ways to skin a cat."

And how had his vision of America changed, asked Jack Viets, a reporter for the San Francisco *Chronicle*.

"Perhaps the most interesting thing that I have noticed," Stratton replied, "has been a new freedom of spirit that I was not aware of before I was shot down. I think long hair, short skirts, loud-noised music, fancy cars, the whole nine yards, simply resolves itself to a new and free spirit in the United States and I myself think it is good. I think it is an indication that the country is maturing; we are shedding our Linus blankets, we are beginning to think for ourselves. I'm very happy with it."

And how do you find your church changed, Commander?

"Well"—he smiled—"three times I had to ask my wife if we were indeed in a Catholic church. There were bongo drums, a trumpet, a piano, singers, and sort of like a go-go girl choir. It looked like the poor priest was being pushed off the altar by all sorts of civilians. People were singing jazzy songs that I used to hear teen-agers singing, all during the mass."

It was, one field producer said, "boffo stuff," and it made good copy on a slow news day. And when it went on the air that night, Stratton was really upset (and a lot of persons in his parish were upset with him) because he had gone on to say, and local television film editors had dumped it, "That's all said in humor.

"The mark of a successful Catholic mass to me is how many people approach the communion rail and it appeared as if the whole congregation approached the communion rail. And if that's what it takes to get these people to the communion rail, well, that's fine."

And he had gone on to talk more about the new spirit he had observed.

"Perhaps at the end of the mass was the most striking of all. Normally, up in the Northeast, at least, the most dangerous place to be—like the Los Angeles freeway—is in the parking lot of a Catholic church at the end of mass as they run over each other

342

trying to get home. In the new spirit now, we all adjourned to a hall and had coffee and doughnuts."

* * *

Out of the public eye, Richard Stratton's role, or perhaps, better, his position, with regard to this new freedom was difficult to assess, and dangerous to do so with that particular man, who outwardly projected, as one reporter put it, an almost simple, uncomplicated range of values easy to satirize. Underneath that façade was a learned and complex person with superb self-control and an ability to woo the media on its own terms.

Yes, he had mellowed. But yes, too, he always had a mellow side with intimates. He described himself as more compassionate, less opinionated, less antagonistic. But when an acquaintance agreed with him that before his imprisonment he was opinionated, pigheaded, and sometimes antagonistic, he angrily denied it.

Alice Stratton's insight offered a slightly altered picture.

"He is definitely more tolerant of his fellow men and their differences," she said. "I think he had been like that before he left, but it's greater now." Whatever changes he had undergone, the relationship with Alice was unchanged or, if changed, strengthened.

"Some wives had said that their husbands would never understand how difficult it was to be alone, to have to buy a house or buy a car, make these decisions. Well, I feel this is something Dick has understood and has not looked upon my part of this trial as insignificant at any point and has been appreciative of it, as I have been of his trial. And I think it's just a mutual admiration society."

Well, there were no angry denials of that. Somehow, he once got off on the subject of wardrobe and, with tongue in cheek, revealed a little of himself:

"I didn't care about clothing or what I looked like. I do care now, because of Alice. I want Alice to be proud of me. In fact, I used to wear an awful lot of things that Alice didn't like because of my superior attitude, what I now refer to as my James Bond era, where I was the cock of the walk and I would wear what the hell I pleased and the rest of humanity could jam it!

"I was the hot jet ace! I didn't need anybody. Now I've mellowed a bit; I've humanized a little bit. The prison has been an enriching thing. Right now I care what Alice thinks; as a result she will have some say in what I wear. I realize that all my taste is in my mouth; I have no conception whatsoever of color, matching, or style, or anything else, so why not admit it?"

* * *

By the end of March the remaining American prisoners had left Hanoi. Across the nation, in more than a dozen separate press conferences, the earlier returnees related the horror stories of their years in North Vietnam. Only a comparative handful spoke out but they estimated that between, 1965 and 1969, 95 per cent of the Americans captured by the Vietnamese were tortured or abused. With a couple of exceptions there were no denials of that figure by ex-POWs who had not met with the press.

True to his word, Stratton again appeared at Oak Knoll before reporters and television and film cameras. He was accompanied by Lieutenant Commander Rodney Knutson, a former Marine with gimlet eyes and all the emotions of a screwdriver.

Stratton was grim. Reporters sensed an aggressiveness in him that had been absent nine days before at the first press conference. Instead of dress blues, the fliers wore summer tans with short-sleeved blouses; the bands of scars about Stratton's arms were plainly visible.

Stratton began the press conference:

"I was shot down in North Vietnam in 1967, a military officer in the United States Navy under competent orders. As a result, as it states in the Nuremberg trials charter, anyone who abuses a prisoner of war is guilty of war crimes."

Then he recounted briefly, without details, the torture sessions and the abuses, challenging any "doubting Thomas" in the audience to step forward and inspect the marks, "my Hanoi bracelets," as he called the scars.

The reporters pressed for more information. They wanted to know why Stratton had been tortured and to retell the story behind his 1967 confession. He complied, eliminating the more grisly details.

Knutson was not so sparing. At one point, without a flicker of

344

emotion on his face, he recalled: "I also was tortured. I was beaten. I have had teeth broken, my nose broken, my wrists broken. I have suffered internal injuries, and these were all at the hands of the North Vietnamese during torture sessions.

"Lenient and humane treatment? Not on your life.

"I was beaten to a point until my buttocks were just hamburger. There was blood spattering against the wall each time the club fell."

The torturers then rolled him over again and made him sit in his own gore and waste. He was dressed in a flight suit at the time, and his wounds and the fabric of his clothing congealed together. It took something like six hours, he said, to soak the clothing off the wounds so his comrades could attempt to treat them.

Stratton told reporters that "the anti-war effort in the United States aided and abetted the enemy." Knutson agreed and singled out Jane Fonda for criticism. The POWs had found distasteful a picture of the actress sitting in an anti-aircraft emplacement and singing with the Viet gun crew, while wearing a Vietnamese helmet.

Some days after the press conferences, she responded with her "hypocrites and liars" statement, and as to torture, added:

"While some of the men are sincere, we must question the racism that may color their interpretations and the circumstances of their alleged mistreatment. How many cases of brutality were the result of resisting regulations at any cost? How much solitary confinement was caused by POWs carrying out U.S. military orders to conspire against, even escape, their captors? How many need some justification for the strong anti-war statements they made while being detained to avoid the danger of court-martial?"[5]

Miss Fonda's statement elicited only a snort of disgust from Stratton, but early in April he whooped with laughter at a release from the Vietnamese News Agency refuting his claims of war crimes. By God, he had gotten into their knickers. His claims were "brazen lies" and "slander." Quoting the Hanoi daily *Quan Doi Nhan Dan,* VNA reported that Stratton's statements "still kept in the 'archives' of the Hanoi Hilton [*sic*] confessed that he had taken part in no less than twenty air raids against civilian centres in North Vietnam. On several occasions at his own request, Stratton had issued written statements to condemn his government's barbarous bombing policy and thank the Vietnamese government and people for their lenient and humane treatment. . . ."

VNA went on to say that Stratton had repeatedly "denied" being tortured or brainwashed to interviewing reporters in Hanoi, had "admitted" that the incidents of cigarette burns and fingernail bending were "borrowed" from an account he had read of South Vietnamese treatment of prisoners, and that he had "agreed" in a signed statement "with United States Senators Anderson and Hawkins" that Saigon's treatment of POWs was cruel and should be stopped.

"[Stratton's] threadbare slanders can deceive nobody," VNA quoted the newspaper. "Not a few released American pilots have made their 'declaration of conscience' despite intimidation of all kinds by their government. Navy Captain Walter E. Wilber is one of them. He said . . . he was never tortured and never saw or heard of other POWs being mistreated."[6]

"Beautiful," said Stratton, laughing as he read the text, "outstanding. I still can get into their knickers. Oh boy!"

* * *

At one point during his press conference, Stratton had been challenged by a reporter: was Stratton really serious when he had said he had a new philosophy of life? Yes, he said. "There was no room for bitterness because there was too much to be done."

It was not a complete answer. He was bitter, about the treatment he had received and toward the North Vietnam communists who had abused and tortured him.

It was no mellow man who later described his former captors as "an armed group of paranoid children that have a national inferiority complex and are trying to overcome four thousand years of backwardness by working one day a month.

"So it's going to be most difficult for them to become, as they like to say, the second Japan of Asia. Right now, they are very busy destroying what the French built up for them in the last hundred years. The French did a lot for them and they'll never admit it. They once put me in a cell which had by actual count 391 nail holes in it, chipped into the plaster and making the room fall apart. And everywhere we went, there was the same kind of lack of consideration for property. (You know, once property becomes common, no one cares what happens to it. You could see it. A leak would start in the roof and they'd wait until the whole roof collapsed before they'd replace the one tile.)

"They are going to spend the next four thousand years sticking their fingers in the dikes. Fortunately there are 20 million of them and they may have a chance to survive."

On the other hand, he was not really complaining, either, he said. And that had not been the real intent of his press conference in which he had described the rigors of captivity.

"That's history," he explained. "That happened six years ago and that wasn't, really, the point we were trying to make. It's not the point I was trying to make. . . . We were not trying to say, 'Ouch, we hurt,' because there are so many people that hurt so far worse as a result of that war—both in Vietnam, Vietnamese and disabled vets, American Marines on the lower floors of the hospital that are still there and still hurting. People hurt every day, sometimes worse, many times worse, than I was ever hurt.

"The message I was trying to say was, 'Look, America, the North Vietnamese communists were lying to you when they said we were receiving good treatment. That was an outrageous and total lie. They manufactured outward appearances of good treatment to mislead certain segments of the American public and the world.

"The hurt part we brought out of Vietnam was that there were American citizens who chose to believe the enemy in the foreign capital and not believe their President or their own government. The real lesson to be learned from the prison situation was not that the enemy will torture, but that [the prisoners] survived because we stayed united, because we believed in our country, because we believed in our God.

"You know, in unity there is strength and it's about time this country found it out."

*　*　*

He was not always so serious; Stratton's irrepressible sense of the absurd had survived North Vietnam intact. He was making something of an ass of himself about the hospital, harassing his physician, Dr. Al Kisselstein, whose years of training had ill prepared him for Richard Stratton. What Stratton wanted was a

347

flight physical, and Kisselstein kept stalling. Stratton took to wearing an orange flight suit and his blue squadron cap with "The Beak" stitched onto the back in gold. He was still refused. He threatened to add to this costume a flight helmet and a torso harness and a G-suit; they weakened. Finally he told Kisselstein he would knock off the nonsense altogether if he got the physical and would attempt to be the model patient. The doctor assented. Stratton would receive his flight physical. Stratton gave the flight suits away to admiring nurses. He began wearing a Japanese robe.

On another occasion, his escort officer, Lieutenant Commander Gary Morrow—who had stayed with him even though the Navy had determined that Morrow was no longer needed—managed to talk him out of inserting three earthworms into a requested stool sample. The prank had been suggested by Stratton's eldest son. Patrick even supplied the required worms.

Within a few weeks came the turnabout: he was living at home and commuting to the hospital, instead of the other way round. Soon the hospital would be behind him and he would go on convalescent leave. Operation Homecoming was done, homecoming about to begin.

CHAPTER 34

Alice Stratton relaxed at the kitchen table, sharing a pot of coffee with a friend. It was quiet. The children were still at school. Dick was at Oak Knoll having some dental work done. He would be back in time for supper today. In two days he would be home for good.

She looked tired. On the table in front of her was a stack of letters, some of the eighteen hundred they had finally received and were now answering.

The talk turned to the children.

"Now, the children do tend still to come to me, often, first," she said, "but gradually I'm seeing that they turn to Dick; each time we're together, they turn to him in a more natural way.

"You know, the first few days, they would always ask me. First they would ask me directly; then they would ask me in front of Dick, and then the last time we were together, Mickey came up and said, 'Dad, can I have a Popsicle?'

"And I thought, well, there we are.

"We've made it."

* * *

Michael's Popsicle was a symbol of what lay ahead in the months that remained of 1973, a period of adjustment, reflection, and anticipation so crammed with events and emotions it was nearly impossible for them to absorb it all. Sometimes they just

349

stopped and held one another, not in sensuality or out of thanksgiving, but because they were free to do so. They were both free and they knew as they had never known before what freedom meant.

"I know the strings that were cut in 1967 are never all going to be re-attached or all the loose ends tied up," Alice Stratton said, "but it all has become a strengthening experience, a positive experience rather than a negative one. I find I have been able, after all, to integrate it into my life and grow in a positive way. . . .

"Dick has become more tolerant. I believe I have become more independent [and that independence] is inside me now, it is not just a façade. Dick always wanted it to be that way. He is the type of man who wants his wife to have her own life as well as a life with him. He believes it enriches and adds to what they have together. I find it easier to live in a relationship where both persons feel they are really independent. When one of you doesn't feel a step down, it is a lot easier; if you are both on an equal footing, it is a lot healthier.

"We had very happy, positive years before," she continued. "Now we are building on those, and continuing as before with the added dimensions of my strength and his. Maybe it was all there before but we never had to use it. Now we know it is there."

Richard Stratton echoed his wife's sentiments.

"We are better off than we ever were. It was a good thing that happened to us in terms of our rapport. The separation was good for us; we both got stand-off distance to evaluate what we did when we got married and we have determined it wasn't a bad idea after all. That was one of the positive things that came out of the prison experience."

The Stratton children decided their parents should repeat their wedding vows now that the family was reunited. Whether it was their own idea or whether someone put them up to it was not known. They did not care to comment. Their parents acceded to the request. The boys chose the wedding cake—chocolate, covered with traditional nuptial decorations. The Reverend Terrence Loughran performed the ceremony.

"It symbolized," Alice said, "a new beginning to our marriage after having been through a trial, a separation, and having survived it and come back together again. It was a symbolic way of saying again the vows of commitment to each other. We didn't have to say them but it was, I think, a nice way of beginning our years hopefully of being together forever.

"Dick had engraved inside the [new] ring the dates of his captivity and the name of the prison he was in. He is going to wear it once a year to remind him of where he's been." He also asked her, she said, to put that ring on his dresser in plain view should he forget himself and get bogged down, as he put it, "in trivia and unimportant things."

* * *

Of his stability and increasing good health there was no question; idiosyncrasies he had developed were under control and understandable in the context of his life. He controlled his kleptomania, resisting the urge to steal and pocket small sharp objects, and pencils. Both items were invaluable in prison. (On the plane trip home, from Clark to Travis, he had managed to acquire twenty-five small can openers off luncheon trays without any real awareness he had done so; he lost track of the clipped pencils.) He insisted his table setting include a fresh linen napkin folded inside a silver ring. He developed a taste for California wine and would eschew a snort of good booze to savor an unsampled pressing. Some nights passed badly. Some days, too: he was seized by a momentary attack of paranoia, fearful of some kind of retribution by North Vietnamese communist agents; the police chief in Palo Alto persuaded him he had no need for a pistol permit and assured him further that the local constabulary could provide whatever protection he or his family might need. Assuaged, he did not press the issue any further. There were days when he felt out of sorts, sour or just crabby, and the ring would appear on his dresser. That usually cured him.

"Oh, I'm trying awfully hard," he said. "You don't know how hard I'm trying to come on soft, and everybody tells me, For God's sake you're coming on so strong. Six years of imprisonment and isolation [are] coming out all over the place." Still, he could not deny his natural instincts.

"Dick is already talking about seven to eight is going to be study time," said Alice, "for everybody. Including me! And we're all going to study together whether you read a book or learn a poem. We're going to turn off the television set. I think that's great and I would have liked to have done it and I tried to do it, but it didn't get implemented as well as I think it will now, now that there are two of us. If one of us is tired the other can take over."

"[Alice] has tried to protect the boys from my onslaughts," he explained with a wry smile, "trying to get me to go piecemeal in getting the old programs back on the road. She gets a little frustrated at times, I'm afraid. She recently completed this parent effectiveness training course, is now teaching it, and she is very, very good at it. But she is frustrated because, it seems to her, she is not so effective within her own four walls as she is with those people she is working with at Social Services.

"She has come to realize that, indeed, prophets are without honor in their own countries."

* * *

They talked at length about the future. She decided that for the time being she would continue her social work, and he agreed. He would stay with the Navy. The Navy had been good to him, and to his family while he was in prison. He had served more than eighteen years and the fourth gold stripe of a captaincy was not far off. He had several specialties the Navy could use, aviation for one, political military history and international relations for another. Even though there were others more current, he hoped the Navy might select him for advanced training—a doctorate in international relations; then perhaps posting in the diplomatic service. He applied.

The Navy said no.

If the decision upset him he concealed it well; his status as an ex-POW should not give him a leg up, he said.

By perseverance, he requalified in A-4s, the attack ship he had flown in combat, overcoming a more than six-year layoff, poor eyesight, and his age, which was now almost forty-two.

He was selected for aviation command in October.

He turned it down. And that was finis for a one-time "hot shot" flier. It was one of the biggest decisions he would ever make, and he made it, but not without some longing:

"I miss flying tremendously. If I had my 'druthers' independent of family I'd be back at sea now with my own command. I turned it down because to have successfully pursued it would have meant leaving my family and going back to sea. I do not think I could have faced myself in the mirror each morning knowing I was doing it simply for an ego trip for myself. I turned it down and the family was the reason."

That was one aspect of it. Another was that more than six years in prison and rehabilitation had seen him pass from a young, agile flier in his thirties to a graying, nearly middle-aged commander in his forties. He had, in short, lost his edge.

"You know, I can't read a map any more without my glasses. And I found when I went through the flight refresher course in the A-4 . . . that I was exactly even with the airplane. If you are not ahead of the airplane in carrier aviation, you're dead. I think I made a wise decision."

He began a quiet search for a shore-based command, a command that was requisite if he was to continue in the service in jobs that had challenge, that were more than just positions to mark time to retirement. In the meantime, he was assigned as executive officer to Captain W. B. Abbott, chief of the Naval Plant Representative's Office (Strategic Systems Office) at the Lockheed Missile and Space Corporation in Sunnyvale, California, working on the Trident Missile project. It was not a glamorous job, but it was not without its appeals. Besides, Abbott was a good skipper.

* * *

In the fall of 1973 the Strattons moved from the gray bungalow on Nathan Way that Alice had bought and that they had suddenly outgrown to a newer, larger home Tom Foy found for them on Grove Street. It was a rambling structure of contemporary design, sheathed in redwood, with a two-car garage and large back yard with a tool shed and stately old trees. It sat beside a cul-de-sac lined with more trees and well-kept, expensive homes. It was the kind of street you thought of, or would like to have thought of, when you remembered growing up in Massachusetts or Michigan: quiet streets with pastoral names, safe for children, isolated from war and confrontation, crime and smog. Physically, the new house was quite near the old one and the children went to the same school. But it was a world away. He was proud of it, and even though it was expensive, both he and Alice felt it worth the investment. A lot of their emotions and feelings went into that new place. They didn't talk too much about moving away from it.

He was proud, too, that they had acquired it on their own with their own money. It was no handout to a "war hero." He had, in fact, partaken of none of the largesse offered by a number of local and national corporations to POWs when they came home.

"I was asked," he said, "by a South Vietnamese friend of mine who was visiting here if I had gotten a car when I came home, and after seeing some of the come-on in that I was glad to be able to look him straight in the eye and say, 'I didn't take a damn thing when I came home!' I did write Ford [the Ford Motor Company] and told them if they wanted to give away a car to give it to the hospital over at Oak Knoll and equip it for amputees. Ford never answered my letter."[7]

A little more than a year after Richard Stratton's homecoming he was awarded the Silver Star Medal for the gallantry of his bowing performance in Hanoi, and the Legion of Merit, the Bronze Star Medal, and the Navy Commendation Medal to honor his resistance activities while a prisoner of war. He tried without immediate success to solicit similar honors for Douglas Hegdahl, still working as a civilian employee at the Navy survival school at San Diego, and participated in an ill-fated campaign for the bestowal of a presidential citation on Alice in acknowledgment of her activities in the POW/MIA movement and for keeping her family together against great odds. Even requests by the governor of California, two representatives in Congress, and other POW wives could not budge the Pentagon. The answer was no.

That one hurt.

* * *

An incredible physical vitality drove him: in addition to his work (which involved considerable travel), he averaged twelve speaking engagements a month, a majority of them in the Bay Area, a pace that never slackened from August of 1973 until Thanksgiving of 1974. Somehow he managed a little time for his family, though not nearly enough, as he was unhappily to discover. It was a curious endeavor for a man who craved privacy. Sometimes he was "sick of being a damned professional POW";

354

but there was a certain warmth, too, in the limelight. He was an accomplished and witty speaker and audiences responded to him. Under all of it was a sense of obligation.

"We tried to respond to people who helped Alice or supported the Navy or supported the government while I was in trouble. There were 175 different organizations Alice and I could identify as having made some direct contribution. . . . I think we set out knowing how much it would take out of us, Alice and me, and we made a rule that no two of us would go out on a school night. I tried to do as many as I could on my lunch hours so as not to take time away from the family. We estimated there would be about two hundred talks in all. We came out pretty close to our estimate and we fulfilled what we considered an obligation, telling people what happened. I didn't like the attention and the fuss but I thought [the POWs' and the families'] side of the story should have equal time with those of Jane Fonda and Ramsey Clark. I think we accomplished that."

They were both very tired, and as they discharged what they perceived as their obligations they were able again to spend more and more time with each other and with the boys, who desperately needed more of his time.

Soon there would be his own command, chief of recruiting in the New York–Long Island area; and his captaincy; and another home near what used to be Mitchel Field near Garden City, Long Island. It would be a real trauma, uprooting the boys, but they could handle it.

And there was something else.

Alice's father had died in June of 1973, shortly after Dick had returned from Vietnam. Now they learned that Charles Stratton senior was fatally ill, four months, perhaps, six at the most.

They decided not to tell the children right away.

355

CHAPTER 35

So it was done.

Not that simply said or accomplished, but done nonetheless. They had survived.

They had put a year between them and Vietnam, a year and then some; it had been a difficult passage, for the boys particularly.

"I think," mused Alice, "the basic adjustment was made after about a year. It wasn't until Dick was home a year that we began to come to grips with the realities. There was so much fanfare and hoopla going on, it was just a whirl. . . . I think there will always be scars on the kids as a result of Dick's separation that cannot be taken away. It affected each one of them differently."

Richard Stratton, looking at his sons, realized their struggle.

"The kids lived in euphoria for six months—Daddy's home! They were expecting Daddy to be Superman in sports, only to find out he hated sports; that Daddy could fix anything, only to discover all he did was bumble their toys when he tried to repair them; that Daddy had all the answers, and discovered he didn't. . . .

"I think they spent the next six months hoping I'd go away again, off to sea or on deployment, to give them a little relief. And I believe they have spent the last six months . . . dealing with the nitty gritty, finally negotiating a livable contract with their father. I think they have made the adjustment and they are prepared to live with me. I just came home from a week away on business and there was a sign up by the door that said, 'Welcome Home, Dad!' I think it was a sign of acceptance. I made the initial mistake coming back by trying to compensate, and very quickly came to terms with that. You can't make up for past time. You pick up the marbles and work with what you've got."

"The children have realized that Dick is going to stay," Alice agreed, "despite his jokes about them wanting him to go away, and they have made their adjustment to him—and *his* to them. And we all do a lot of talking about where do we go from here, step by step by step. We didn't really start because Dick was trying to compensate. So when we decided let's start from *here,* Dick cut down some of his public speaking, and we had a chance to communicate. You have to be around to communicate.

"But I think we were fortunate Dick did come back from Vietnam and we had a chance to work on the adjustment as a family and to communicate together. It's slow, hard work, just like having a family is anyway. It's a constant, everyday hacking-out of the rules of the family, its disagreements and its system, what went wrong and where you failed. What we have to realize is that what happened we can't make up for; as Dick said, we have to take it from here and live with it as it is.

"I remember saying once the thing I missed most when he was away was the sharing; it is so nice to have him back, to have a friend to share everything with. It's funny, I do not feel any regrets that he is no longer flying. I do for him. I know he would still love to fly and I know he would love to go back to sea and I feel a certain sadness for him because he can't. But me? I don't miss it a bit." She laughed softly. "It's nice to have him around all the time."

* * *

Alice had said repeatedly, after her husband returned from Vietnam, that he had not changed, and she was grateful for it. Within the narrow context of her meaning, he had not: he was still her husband, loving, solicitous, humorous, strong. But in the greater context, he *had* changed. He was, as he said, more patient, and he was more tolerant. He had made rather a big deal out of these virtues at his first press conference in 1973; months later he found himself having to work hard, often, to keep practicing what he had preached.

"I still have to fight intolerance, some of it, some leftovers from the past. I was intolerant, say, of persons who were slower than I was. I would never slow down for people who walked or worked or thought slower than I did. Their job was to keep up with me. Well, I was intolerant of people who could not hold their booze, for example, or intolerant of people who did not think the same way I did about fidelity in marriage. Now I find my feelings are the same as before but I don't go around applying labels: so-and-so is a bad man because he can't hold his booze, or he cheats on his wife. In short, prison accelerated a maturation process.

"But, you know, there is one thing that still bothers me: long hair on men. It's not important, but I just don't understand it. I mean, I tried myself, tried to grow it a little longer. It didn't work. And I tried real hard with Patrick to get him to look like what in my estimation was civilized. "Finally," he sighed, "I am prepared to accept it. I can look at Pat's golden locks without puking. I don't understand it, but I came to realize, I guess, that it was not necessary for me to understand it."

Tolerance was not the only thing Vietnam implanted in him. He had been, well, radicalized, if that is the word for it; no longer did he consider himself cock of the walk or content to minister only to his own needs or pleasures.

"I was brought up by a very close family, one that treasured its privacy. I grew up believing what I did and how I did it was nobody else's business. I had a right, a heritage, if you will, to sit in my own castle doing my own thing and that was my obligation [to me].

"I served in the military and that was my obligation to society. And I probably would have continued to sit back and devote myself to selfish activities had I not been through Vietnam.

"But I think seeing the communist movement eyeball to eyeball, seeing what a very vocal minority, basically, did to this country in terms of tearing it apart, I can no longer sit back quietly. I was part of 'the silent majority' simply doing my duty as I saw it and going about my business. I will not be silent any longer. I do not think it is in the best interests of my family or my children or my country to remain silent if I have something to contribute in terms

358

of an idea, teaching, passing on experience or supporting people or ideas.

"For example, when I found out Ramsey Clark had won the Democratic primary in New York State, I sent fifty dollars to Senator Jacob Javits [whom Clark would run against]. Now, Jacob Javits has never been one of my national heroes, but I felt it was important a man like Ramsey Clark not represent this nation in the Senate of the United States. I would *never* have done that before the prison experience.

"I wouldn't have gone out on a speaking tour before, either. Had someone asked me to speak, I simply would have said no. I would not have sat down with my wife and compiled a list of persons we thought we could either influence or reinforce.

"I think involvement is essential for the preservation of our democracy, and involvement at every level that touches you, not just the one you have selected as your particular 'charity.' I used to give myself to my country the way I used to give a few bucks to the Community Chest. I was, because of the way I was brought up and the years [in which] I was brought up, very parsimonious, otherwise known as a cheap screw. I wouldn't spend money. . . . Things sure have changed.

"A week before we moved into the new house, we 'adopted' a little girl under the Foster Parents Plan; we would never have had a foster child in Colombia if I had not been through this. Maybe the reasons for it are selfish, I don't know.

"When a letter comes from Clara, it's interesting to watch the reaction the boys have to it. Her whole house, with five kids, isn't any bigger than our living room. It puts a few things in perspective for them, that here in this hemisphere someone is eking out a life that is far, far different than theirs.

"And the other thing . . . Vietnam for me this year and in five years Patrick's going to have to go to South America to fight another war because we were too cheap to share what we had? No way! . . . But I wouldn't have done it before. I know."

* * *

There is in the odyssey of Richard and Alice Stratton an arguable irony. Between 1965 and 1973—and a little before and a little after—many Americans renounced, sometimes with violence, such

359

values from previous generations as unswerving faith in government and law, love of God or faith in religion, filial respect, self-reliance, emotional temperance, and an intangible capacity to persevere against adversity. But it was precisely these qualities, coupled with their own basic fibers, that succored the Strattons (and others like them) in their separate prisons and allowed them to survive. During Richard Stratton's imprisonment the outside world changed radically; in a sense, he stood still. Radical change is dangerous to persons of Stratton's persuasion because it permits little chance to compare old values, old ideals, old principles that should not be overlooked or, perhaps, discarded. Neither Stratton nor his wife was shy about voicing this. Someone (he cannot remember who) dubbed him a "philosophical fossil." But his time-tested values, his father's values, that bound a family together would not be cast off idly.

"When I grew up in New England in the 1930s," Stratton said, "the values that were in my home were shared by the church and the school. If the home lapsed momentarily, the school would always fill the gap, or the church would. This is no longer the case. The values that I hold here today in my home . . . are not shared by the school system, nor the community at large, and they are not shared, or willing to be voiced, by the church. . . . That leaves me in an untenable situation because my children are outside of their home more than they are in it. And it brings me to a position where the only thing I have left, frankly, as the oldest boy passes thirteen is my example. I have nothing else."

The Stratton boys are extraordinarily alert, intelligent children. It was impossible for them not to have noticed, since their father's return, an increased contrast between home life and street life. Their father acknowledged it.

"They react to this split well, right now, because love takes care of a lot. The first real test will come when they reach their mid-teens, the second when they leave home and go out on their own. What I hope to achieve right now is that if a son of mine, for example, steals or lies, there will never be any doubt in his mind when he faces his mirror in the morning that he has stolen or lied, whatever else he may choose to call it publicly. In his own heart, he will know it is a wrong thing to do, an unacceptable thing to do, and he will not be able to kid himself.

"There is a real aberration going on right now and I think a lot of people have lost sight of it: everything's right, nothing's wrong. There is no such thing as a wrong thing!"

Not surprisingly, Alice Stratton agreed with her husband.

"I think the old values are all the more important today. But first of all we need to learn to communicate with one another more effectively. We also need to learn what our values are and preach them, not from a parental pulpit, but in a living, daily kind of way so we can get across to our children what it is we stand for. I think that's more important than a 'wishy-washy' do-your-own-thing son.

"Sure, they can go out and do what they want, but at least they will have something to fall back upon. When you do not have some set of basics, you are really lost, I think. You are going to flounder whenever a crisis comes into your life, and it will come whether it's a Vietnam, the breakup of a marriage, or the loss of a child. Then you have to fall back and say, 'What does it all mean to me?' If you never had any meanings in the beginning, I think it's going to be rougher overcoming the tragedy.

"You know, if Vietnam hadn't happened to me, something else would have. But Vietnam, Dick's imprisonment, changed me. It forced me to fall back and discover what my values were and to learn what I wanted to live by. Otherwise, I might have allowed myself to just follow along on Dick's coattails for a long, long time. That's right! The six years gave me confidence, a chance to prove to myself that I was all right in my own right. I *did* hang on to Dick's coattails and put him on a pedestal (which is no bad thing, he belongs up there), but that meant I had to be just like him, as good as I thought he was."

And of course, that was the rub: Vietnam. Nothing ever again in their lives would ever touch them as Vietnam had touched them. The loneliness, the fear, the terrible price it extracted, and the triumph, what they had salvaged, would be there always, and in their sons.

The point was they had salvaged their lives, survived during a time of troubles, and after. They attributed it to faith, humor, discipline, and self-reliance, and Richard Stratton, for one, saw nothing unique in that.

"You see it in any situation where tragedy can pull a family together or pull it apart. Somehow people have to cope, and what enables them to cope? I think about people under stress, whatever induces that stress; the Vietnam prison situation was a dramatic thing, it received a lot of publicity, but our sources of strength, I think, were still the same. I am talking about faith in something: faith in God, faith in your family, faith in your country. Anyone who has strong faith in something has a greater survivability quotient. People who can talk, discuss, or hash things out have greater survivability. People who are taught the discipline of family, even though it may be broken by death or divorce or something, have survivability. A good family structure gives a sense of roots, of belonging, of meaning, of being responsible for your actions, a conviction that you can do something about your circumstances however limited they might be, and create something for yourself.

"But if there is one essence to survival, a common thread, it is simply this: you have to want it."

* * *

"Someone asked Dick," Alice told a friend, "do you feel now like it never happened, or it's all over? And he said, absolutely not. He remembers all too well. But in a way, for me, having him back erased all that, [but] those feelings of fear . . . whenever a loss is threatened are still very much with me and can easily be evoked.

"There was a picture of three women on the front page of the New York *Times* recently. Their husbands were trapped in a mine and they were waiting to hear their fate. Looking at their faces, I knew what they were feeling. I guess now the difference for me is I know I could survive, if I had to, alone. I just hope I never, never have to do it again."

362

PART VIII

A POSTSCRIPT

Indoors when Miss Maudie wanted to say something lengthy she spread her fingers on her knees and settled her bridgework. This she did, and we waited.

"I simply want to tell you that there are some men in this world who were born to do our unpleasant jobs for us. Your father's one of them."

"Oh," said Jem. "Well."

"Don't you oh well me, sir," Miss Maudie replied, recognizing Jem's fatalistic noises, "you are not old enough to appreciate what I said."

—Harper Lee
To Kill a Mockingbird

CHAPTER 36

The house was quiet save for quarterly chime concerts of the grandfather clock that stood in the dining room. The boys were at the playground; Alice was shopping.

It was Saturday, a lazy, winter Saturday without rain, without any particular urgency. Richard Stratton was relaxed, even a little mellow. He sprawled in his own green armchair in the den he and Alice shared as an office. About him was an orderly clutter of books, papers, letters, marine prints, and a shaggy blue rug on the floor. He stretched his legs, settling his feet atop a weary ottoman that was a cousin to the chair. A mug of coffee steamed in his hand. Dressed in vaguely pressed dark slacks and a nondescript flannel shirt with a bola string tie, the kind that was popular in the 1950s, he could have passed for a Barnstable County town selectman.

Across from him, settled into the upholstered rocker, was a friend. The two men reminisced for a while about other friends and small, agreeable matters suited to the mellow mood of the day. Gradually the talk turned to the war, as it sometimes did between them, try as they might to avoid it; while the conversation remained gentle, mellowness left the room.

Stratton said, "No, I don't think the government deceived us about Vietnam. I don't think it was deceit. I think it was stupidity. I don't think someone sat down and said 'I want this end result but the American people will never buy it. Now, how can I manipulate them into a position where it is inevitable?'

"I don't feel that. I don't feel that Diem was trying to manipulate us in, nor do I think Kennedy was trying to manipulate us in."

"You certainly don't believe it just happened?" his friend asked.

"No," Stratton said. "I think it was inevitable, an inevitable course of action once we decided we were going to let the French back in Indochina after World War II. We chose at that point. We were committed, whether we knew it or not, and we didn't have the brains to know what that commitment meant."

"Don't you resent the fact, then," his friend asked, "that you had to go over there and carry out the commitment?"

Stratton shook his head.

"No," he said, "because most wars are the result of people's stupidity and any soldier that reads his history ought to know that. Every society has garbage. Somebody has to pick it up. The garbageman goes down the street and picks up your garbage; we're a wasteful nation and he picks up more than he should. The soldier, many times, is in the same position as that garbageman. But instead of picking up an individual's garbage, he picks up the nation's.

"There is no man," he said, "who has had his ass shot off, or had it shot at in anger, who is going to sit down and tell you that war is intrinsically a nifty, good deal. In fact, when I find military types telling me war is great, the first thing I look for now is whether the son of a bitch is wearing a Purple Heart or any kind of a combat decoration. Chances are the louder he is or the more irrational he is about the 'wonders of war,' the cleaner his chest is. He may have all sorts of administrative awards and scalps hanging from his belt, but—"

He stopped and shook his head in disgust.

"There are war lovers," he continued. "Yes, I certainly admit that. I recognize that, but they are not the normal kind of people.

"Still . . . with all due respect to athletes, we laud the jockstrap mentality: win at any cost. That's what my kids are being taught in Little League right now. It's sure soured me. Now we keep the Little League world championship within our own indigenous borders because Taiwan won it too many times. That's a great lesson in sportsmanship for my kids to learn. Ah, we've known this all along: in high school, college, in professional athletics, it's all built on winning. This is the mentality you get into. And you can carry it over into warfare: that it is some sort of a big game to kill, to destroy. It isn't.

"Warfare is a tool of diplomacy, after all other things have failed. There's a way it should be done—if it has to be done—and there are certain rules to go by. There are certain restraints to be exercised. I'll stand by that. I don't resent going to Vietnam. I did volunteer. And I went into this business knowing what I was getting into. I did not think I was joining a flying club when I joined the Navy. My children ask me what I do. I tell them I am an administrator, I'm a general manager. I tell others I'm a pilot, and this and that. I'm a professional killer." He was being deliberately dramatic, but he was not joking.

"I am a highly trained, highly paid professional killer. That is my business, death and destruction. If I think anything else, I'm an idiot."

"Good God, do you like it. Really like it?"

"I've used the simile before: if a doctor gets a certain vicarious pleasure out of cutting people open, he's sick."

"Then why do you do it, Dick?" The room was still for a long time. Stratton looked, unexpectedly, old and very tired.

"Because I do not think," he said finally, "war should be left to the war lovers."

APPENDIX 1

The "Confession"

This copy of Richard Stratton's "confession" is the one received by Lee Lockwood in Hanoi the day Stratton was exhibited.

The original remains in Lockwood's possession.

Statement of a Captured U.S. Pilot

I am Richard Allen Stratton, a lieutenant commander in the U.S. Navy attached to VA-192, CAW 19, USS Ticonderoga. The following are statements concerning my crimes committed on the D.R.V. during November and December 1966:

The Ticonderoga arrived in the Tonkin Gulf on 14 November 1966. I had been sorry to leave my family, unsure of the direction which the war was taking and certain in my own mind that most of the people back home did not know or care what was happening in Viet Nam. The U.S. policy appeared to be a succession of errors inherited by and added to by succeeding administrations. The general ignorance concerning the country of Viet Nam was appalling and mine was no exception.

The first mission on 14 November, my first in combat, was against a highly populated section of Vinh. The target was briefed by the Wing Air Intelligence officer, LtJg O'Farrel as being of the highest political priority in that the people themselves must be made to feel the pressures and realities of war.

This would be a four plane flight—all A-4's, the first two aircraft would have 2 CBU's and two 500-pound fragmentation bombs; the second two would have 2 napalm tanks and two 500-pound frags. The tactics would be to come in low in two sections, climb to 5,000 ft next to the city, and dive across from east to west. The CBU's and napalm would be used to catch exposed people. A second sweep from west to east with frags would catch the sheltered areas and spread the flames made by napalm.

I led the flight and flew in as briefed. The time of 10.00 A.M. was

369

chosen so that as many people would be exposed as possible. The weather was good and there was no difficulty finding the target, the first pass with CBU's and napalm found people running for cover. On coming back for the second attack people could be seen lying about or running with clothes afire.

About this time we saw the Vinh BDA photographs. There was obviously no military and no discernible industrial significance to anything in view. It was so obviously a residential area that we had the photo and target coordinates checked against each other. There was no doubt that this burnt out area had been our target. We were disgusted.

During this same period we went on another mission of similar type to a small village about 30 miles north of the DMZ.

This would be another four plane flights. 2 aircraft would have 2"75 rockets, and CBU's, the second 2 aircraft would have 2"75 rockets and naplam. Being a rural area, dusk was chosen to get most of the people gathered together in one place. The tactics were left open since there was virtually no AA opposition.

I led the flight and had a little trouble identifying the target due to the failing light. The first section cut across low dropping CBU's the second section firing its guns. We wheeled back. This time the first section used rockets and guns, and the second dropping napalm and firing guns. We circled the area but could distinguish nothing but shadow running against a background of flame.

On the 22 of November we were to strike Nam Dinh. Since we had spent so much time in the south along the coast, O'Farrel explained that it was felt that the war should be brought farther north.

This was a six plane flight, two F8's and four A4's. The F8's would carry two 500 frags, two Sidewinders and 20mm ammunition. The first two A4's would carry 2 CBU's, two 500 frags.

The second two were to carry 2 napalm tanks and two 500 frags. The F8's were to sweep in first delivering their rockets and bombs and climbing to a position north of the city to provide protection from the MIG's with their remaining Sidewinders. The A4's would come out of the sun out of the east since target time was again 10.00 A.M. to have the maximum number of people exposed. The CBU's and napalm would be delivered first and the frags would be used on the return run to spread the fire and cover sheltered places.

In the debrief my Wingman John Parks stated that it was a useless target, a senseless target and so he brought his frags bombs back. The air wing commander set the policy that anyone who brought his bombs back henceforth would be court martialed. Later photographs showed that LTjg Parks was right, it was a useless target, strictly a wide area of houses, shops and shrines.

The 2nd of December was to be an air wing strike on the suburbs of Hanoi. The area ran from the center of town to ten miles south and is distinctly an area of houses, shops, parks and pagodas. The air wing commander CDR Phillips said that this was an extremely important mission necessary to make the people of Hanoi realize that they were not immune from the ravages of war. Also in a larger sense the mission was for the world at large to show it what could be done and test its reaction.

I took part in the 2 December 1966 raid on Hanoi. At the briefing, beside Cdr Phillips was Cdr Hathaway, commanding officer of V.A.-195; Cdr Jellows, air wing operation officer, Cdr Hill, former commanding officer of V.A.-192; Cdr Moore, executive officer of VA-192; LCdr Estocin, operation officer of VA-192 and over thirty other officers. The brief started about two and one half hour prior to take off.

The target was to be the south side of Hanoi an area from the center of the city extending ten miles to the south. Anti-personnel weapons were chosen to inflict maximum damage on the population. The busiest part of the day was chosen for maximum effect on the population.

The strike would involve four F8 aircraft with two 500-pound fragmentation bombs and four 5-inch rockets; four A-4 aircraft with four CBU's each; four A-4 aircraft with two napalm tanks each; four A4 aircraft with eight 500 pound fragmentation bombs each; three A4 aircraft with four Shrike each; three A4 aircraft with two Bullpups each; six F8 aircraft with two Sidewinders each; all aircraft would have 20mm ammunition.

The tactics would be to cross the city from West to East diving from the North so as to cover the entire southern area of the city in right hand dives. F8 aircraft, Shrike aircraft and Bullpup aircraft were cleared to strike their own direction.

The flight met heavy anti-aircraft and missile fire. It was led by Commander Phillips Cdr Hill let the second group of A4 aircraft and I flew lead of the third group of A4 aircraft. Due to heavy opposing fire from the ground, the group did not act as a unit and commenced separate attacks. I was horrified at the density of buildings and population in the target. Bombs were scattered over the entire South side of the city.

During the debrief, Cdr Phillips announced that not enough of the target had been hit and that we would have to return to the same target again before the month was over. This statement was a result of his own observation of the results while in the air.

Privately most of the pilots were appalled at the pacific nature of the target. Ltjg Parks of VA-192 declared that he would not ever go on one of those city raids again. He had come to fight a military war not a war against civilians. This raid was proof of a policy in force to apply pressure directly against the people of Viet Nam. Yet I not only did not have the courage to refuse to go on the mission, but I did not have the courage to speak out against the mission or at the policy. I was inwardly ashamed at being such a coward.

On 14 December 1966 the Air Wing was called upon to make a repeat strike against Hanoi. Cdr Phillips started the brief by remarking that the 2 December raid had received very little world wide notice. The importance of the mission was again stressed in that it had the direct interest and support of Washington's policy of bringing the war home to the Vietnamese people. The hope was still to motivate the people to bring pressure on their government to accept a compromise situation in South Viet Nam. His remarks were essentially the same as on 2 December.

This strike would also involve four F-8 aircraft with two 500 pound fragmentation bombs and four 5-inch rockets; four A-4 aircraft with four CBU's each; four A-4 aircraft with two napalm tanks each; four A-4 aircraft with eight 500 pound fragmentation bombs each; three A-4 aircraft with four Shrike missiles each; three A-4 aircraft with two Bullpup missiles each; six F8 aircraft with two Sidewinder missiles each; all aircraft with 20mm ammunition.

I took part in this raid. Present at the briefing were Commander Phillips, Commander Mc Kellar, Commander Hathaway, Commander Chessman, Commander Fellows, Commander Moore, Lieutenant Commander Scoffield (VA-192), Lieutenant Junior Grade Eddy, Lieutenant Junior Grade Young (both VA-192) and about thirty other pilots. Ltjg Parks stood up and declared that he was not going to participate in a raid which struck women and children. He was dismissed and told to report to his commanding officer.

The tactics this time was to cross from West to East South of the city, turn North and dive from East to West in order to cover the entire South side of the city from its center to ten miles south. The attack headings would therefore be perpendicular to those of 2 December but cover the same area. These were no specified targets; the target was the general area. The F-8, A-4 Shrike and A-4 Bullpup aircraft were to use their own discretion in selecting and firing upon targets.

On our return the raid was declared to be successful and complete. By being complete we understood that we would not be required to make the same raid again. It was over a week before we understood what the Air Wing Commander meant by successful. Numerous newspapers and magazines made it clear that the people of Hanoi had been made to feel the impact of the war and the world had certainly taken notice of what had happened. If this was the purpose of the mission as they told us, then it was successful.

Privately the pilots were disgusted at their participation in the raids but not many were moved to action as was Ltjg Parks, LCdr Estocin (VA-192) said that if he could find an excuse he would quit flying. I myself was still a moral coward. Twice I had seen what we were doing to innocent people and yet I did not have the courage to act or even to speak out.

The pilots were amazed when in various statements the American Government in the person of a State Department spokesman and even in the person of President Johnson himself denied the raids on Hanoi. They said that we hit only military targets not populated areas. They said that all strikes in the Hanoi area were made with the knowledge and approval of the President. Yet we have flown on these missions. We knew that we had hit populated areas and not military targets. We knew that we had struck Hanoi. These statements of the American Government were obviously false.

I was shot down on 5 January 1967 while conducting a coastal search mission North of Hon Me. I was instantly captured and humanely treated by the people of Viet Nam. Since my capture, I have been led to see the full and true nature of my criminal acts against the people of Viet Nam in terms of injury, death and destruction. I have been made to see how my lack of courage in standing up to the illegal, immoral and unjust policy of the American Government has caused much harm to innocent people who have never threatened the American people. I sincerely acknowledge my crimes and repent at having committed them.

I ask that the people of the Democratic Republic of Viet Nam forgive the crimes which I have committed against them. I ask that they spare my life and continue their humane treatment of me.

March 4, 1967
Richard Allen Stratton

APPENDIX 2

The Code of Conduct

The Code of Conduct for members of the American armed forces was adopted as a guide for future prisoners of war after the Korean debacle. Until late 1977 it read as follows:

1. I am an American fighting man. I serve in the forces which guard my country and our way of life. I am prepared to give my life in their defense.
2. I will never surrender of my own free will. If in command I will never surrender my men while they still have the means to resist.
3. If I am captured I will continue to resist by all means available. I will make every effort to escape and aid others to escape. I will accept neither parole nor special favors from the enemy.
4. If I become a prisoner of war, I will keep faith with my fellow prisoners. I will give no information or take part in any action which might be harmful to my comrades. If I am senior, I will take command. If not, I will obey the lawful orders of those appointed over me and will back them up in every way.
5. When questioned, should I become a prisoner of war, I am bound to give only name, rank, service number and date of birth. I will evade answering further questions to the utmost of my ability. I will make no oral or written statements disloyal to my country and its allies or harmful to their cause.
6. I will never forget that I am an American fighting man, responsible for my actions, and dedicated to the principles which made my country free. I will trust in my God and in the United States of America.

After the Vietnam war ended, a special review panel was convened to study the code and recommend any needed changes. The panel concluded that the code was still functional and necessary and only one change resulted: in paragraph 5, the word "required" was substituted for "bound." The change, said the panel, would allow a POW under torture to give more than name, rank, service number and birthdate without loss of honor or thrusting him into moral dilemma. Leaving the remainder of the code unchanged made it clear, though, that a captured serviceman (or woman) was to take all the torture possible before submitting to his captors' demands.

The change was approved by President Jimmy Carter on November 3, 1977.

NOTES

[1] Unlike some of his fellow fliers, Stratton chose not to carry sidearms in combat; the only weapons he wore in the cockpit were knives. "[We] had a choice," Stratton says, "of carrying a .45 or a .38 caliber Smith & Wesson Police Special. The .38 was mainly valuable as a signaling device because it could carry tracer ammunition. (However, the use of tracer ammunition against human beings is considered to be against international law.) The pistol also would have added another pound and a half of weight I didn't need to carry in case I ended up in the water. We were so loaded down with survival equipment that our weight exceeded the recommended weight for the [aircraft's] ejection system. . . .

"That wouldn't have made any difference. I had made a bargain with myself after seeing *The Bridges at Toko-Ri* [a 1954 adventure film starring William Holden and based on a book by James Michener about an American pilot and family during the Korean War] that I was not going to stand off the entire enemy . . . with a .38, six-round revolver. . . . [But] even though I had made this bargain, had I been carrying the gun when I bailed out, being in an emotional and irrational mood and 'brainwashed' by the American movie industry, I probably would have landed firing and the guy with the AK 47 would have let me have it."

[2] Stratton's thoughts about his aircraft were not quite irrational as they might appear; he had "stolen" the plane his rockets destroyed.

"We had trouble getting the A-4E's that were able to handle the Shrike missiles; it was a wiring problem. So over the Christmas [1966] period we were to pull some swaps with the Marine Corps for aircraft that had been wired properly. When we came up, the paper work wasn't available to make the swaps. The plane I had [January 5, 1967] was literally stolen from the Marines. We left a plane behind for them, but there was no paper work so we really didn't own the one we had, and it was probably about the first hop that it was on. It also had 'double nuts' on the nose and the name 'Billy Philips' painted on the side. 'Double nuts' are the numbers 00 and designate a wing commander [as in 006] and Billy Philips was an air wing commander. I had the distinction of creaming a wing commander's stolen aircraft. Sounds like a 'Pappy' Boyington special!"

[3] Salisbury later compiled his dispatches and experiences into a book: *Behind the Lines—Hanoi: December 23, 1966–January 7, 1967* (New York: Harper & Row, 1967).

[4] Harry S. Ashmore and William C. Baggs set down their experiences as peace emissaries in a book whose title was unequivocal: *Mission to Hanoi: A Chronicle of Double-dealing in High Places. A Special Report from the Center for the Study of Democratic Institutions* (New York: G. P. Putnam's Sons, 1968).

[5] The source of the photo cited was the North Vietnamese Women's Union in Hanoi; it was distributed in parts of the United States by chapters of the Women Strike for Peace. The photo cited is in the author's possession.

[6] Hai Thu, *North Vietnam Against U. S. Air Force* (Hanoi: Foreign Languages Publishing House, 1967), pp. 57, 58, 71.

[7] Tet is the Vietnamese New Year, observed for three days beginning at the first new moon following January 20.

[8] These are official North Vietnamese figures.

[9] "A History of the Air War," *Vietnam Courier,* Special Number 88 (Hanoi: December 16, 1966). The *Courier* was an English-language broadsheet circulated primarily among visiting Westerners and the Western press and in the North's prisoner of war camps.

PART II

[1] Neil Sheehan et al., *The Pentagon Papers, as Published by 'The New York Times'* (New York: Bantam Books, 1971), pp. 9–10.

[2] Ibid., p. 14.

[3] Ibid., p. 25.

[4] David Halberstam, *The Best and the Brightest* (Greenwich: Fawcett, 1973), pp. 151–54; Neil Sheehan et al., *The Pentagon Papers,* p. 85.

[5] Neil Sheehan et al., *The Pentagon Papers:* Document ⚡21, "Report by Vice-President Johnson on His Visit to Asian Countries," pp. 127–28.

[6] Neil Sheehan et al., *The Pentagon Papers,* pp. 88–90.

[7] Neil Sheehan et al., *The Pentagon Papers:* Document ⚡26, "Cable from Taylor to Kennedy on Introduction of U.S. Troops," pp. 141–43.

[8] *Look* magazine (April 21, 1964); statement issued at Washington, D.C., May 24, 1964. Both cited by William G. Effros in *Quotations*

Vietnam: 1945–1970 (New York: Random House, 1970), pp. 206 and 207.

9 Statement issued at Washington, D.C., May 4, 1965; statement issued at New York City, August 12, 1964. Both cited by William G. Effros in *Quotations Vietnam,* p. 179.

PART III

1 Stratton's eardrum had been weakened by earlier injuries. He says, "We ought not to blame the Vietnamese [for rupturing it again] because my eardrum was busted in survival school by a box on the ear in 1959, and again in the same manner in survival school in 1966. I think my [survival instructors] ought to be rewarded for their consistency. . . ."

2 Neil Sheehan et al., *The Pentagon Papers,* pp. 523–24.

3 Harrison E. Salisbury, *Behind the Lines,* pp. 63, 70.

4 *Life* magazine (April 7, 1967), p. 41.

5 "CBU" is an abbreviation for "Cluster Bombs Unit," an antipersonnel weapon that basically comprises a so-called mother bomb and inside that a large number of smaller missiles that are released upon impact. In some models the "baseball" type, for example, the smaller missiles themselves contain even smaller missiles, which in turn are released.

6 The full text of Stratton's "confession" is reprinted elsewhere in this book.

7 "Tass Quotes U.S. Pilot's Raid Story," Associated Press, San Francisco *Chronicle* (March 7, 1967), p. 1.

8 This incident is recorded in two sources: Rear Admiral Jeremiah A. Denton, Jr., USN (ret.), with Ed Brandt, *When Hell Was in Session* (New York: Reader's Digest Press, 1976), pp. 91–92; and John G. Hubbell et al., *P.O.W.: A Definitive History of the American Prisoner-of-War Experience in Vietnam, 1964–1973* (New York: Reader's Digest Press, 1976), p. 177.

PART IV

1 Communication was the key to survival for the prisoners. The basic means of communication was the so-called tap code, which was instituted at the Hanoi Hilton (Hoa Lo prison) by an Air Force captain named Smitty Harris; Harris and some friends worked up the code in a coffee break during survival school training and he remembered it after he was captured and imprisoned. In the code, the alphabet was set out in five rows of five letters each, the letter *K* being omitted to

make the pattern possible. Each letter was represented by two distinct tap patterns, the first to denote its row and the second to denote its position in the row. For example, the letter *A* was the first letter in the first row, and required two separate taps; the letter *S* was the third letter in the fourth row and required first four taps, then three. Stratton's first code name, Beak, would have sounded like this:

B   E   A   C

. ..   .

Because *K* had been eliminated, the prisoners substituted the word *C* (first line, third letter) in its stead.

Other methods of communication were also devised. The tap code could be used on buckets or anything that made noise; a system of hacks and coughs and throat clearings was also used, as was a series of hand signals, which denoted in some cases individual letters or phrases.

This information was told to author Stephen A. Rowan by Robert H. Schumaker, a Navy pilot and Vietnam POW; Rowan cites it in his book *They Wouldn't Let Us Die* (Middle Village, N.Y.: Jonathan David Publishers, 1973).

[2] "Brainwashing' Case," Associated Press, San Francisco *Chronicle* (May 3, 1967), p. 1.

[3] Burns was among prisoners of war repatriated February–March, 1973.

[4] The memory of the Korean prisoners of war was still a provocative one in the mid-1960s, particularly those reminiscences of so-called brainwashings and other atrocities committed against United Nations soldiers by the North Koreans and Chinese, and even more so the shocking conduct of American captives. According to Phillip Knightley in his superior work *The First Casualty* (New York: Harvest/Harcourt Brace Jovanovich, 1975) approximately 10,000 men were held captive in North Korea; more than two thirds of these were Americans. It is estimated that fully 70 per cent of the Americans collaborated to some degree and perhaps 40 per cent eventually died in captivity. Despite minimal security there were no escapes. Conditions in most of the POW camps were bestial. Morale among the POWs withered. Men refused to be organized by their superior officers; the weak were left to fend for themselves; the sick, wounded, and dying were preyed upon and often robbed of their rations by some of their healthier comrades.

[5] Hamilton I. McCubbin et al., *Family Separation and Reunion*, Report No. 74–70, (San Diego: Naval Health Research Center, 1975), p. 2.

[6] Margery Byers, "At Home with the Prisoners' Families," *Life* (October 20, 1967), pp. 34–34B.

[7] Photographer Lee Lockwood says it was he who first suggested to David Dellinger that the latter look up Stratton and seek an interview to see if Stratton had been drugged or brainwashed.

[8] Werner Wiskari, "Captive U.S. Flier Denies Being Brainwashed," the New York *Times* (July 14, 1967), p. 4.

[9] Tim Wheeler, "Talk with Captured U.S. Men, Find Hanoi Treats Them Well," *Daily Worker* (June 26, 1967).

[10] Ibid.

[11] Walter Heynowski and Gerhard Scheumann, *Pilots in Pajamas* (*Piloten im Pyjama*) (Berlin, DDR: Verlag du Nation, 1968).

[12] Ted Gup, "Inside a Mock POW Camp," Washington *Post;* "Punch," San Francisco *Chronicle* (July 24, 1977), p. 5.

PART V

[1] "Publius" (Alexander Hamilton), "The Federalist No. 8," written November 20, 1787, in *The Federalist* (New York: Modern Library, 1937), p. 42.

[2] Ward Just, "Soldiers," Part I, *Atlantic Monthly* (October 1970), p. 60.

[3] Ibid.

[4] Ibid.

[5] A pseudonym.

[6] William N. Miller, "Dilemmas and Conflicts Specific to the Military Returned Prisoner of War," in McCubbin et al., *Family Separation and Reunion*, pp. 123–24.

[7] Hamilton I. McCubbin, Edna J. Hunter, Philip J. Metres, Jr., "Adaption of the Family to the PW/MIA Experience: An Overview," in McCubbin et al., *Family Separation and Reunion*, p. 40.

[8] Peter Stack, "Christmas Wait for Prisoner of War," San Francisco *Chronicle* (December 24, 1969).

[9] Iris R. Powers, "The National League of Families and the Development of Family Services," in McCubbin et al., *Family Separation and Reunion*, p. 3.

[10] Peter Stack, "Christmas Wait for Prisoner of War."

[11] Margery Byers, "At Home with the Prisoners' Families," p. 34.

[12] Actually the code says no such thing, nor is it a legally binding document. A majority of prisoners were unaware of this latter fact.

PART VI

[1] Official transcript of the news briefing, U. S. Navy, Bethesda Naval Hospital, Bethesda, Md. (September 2, 1969).

[2] Ibid.

[3] Ibid.

[4] Jack Woddis, Introduction to *Ho Chi Minh: Selected Articles and Speeches, 1920–1967* (New York: International Publishers, 1970).

[5] Harrison E. Salisbury, Introduction to *The Prison Diary of Ho Chi Minh* (New York: Bantam Books, 1971).

[6] Ibid.

[7] Excerpt from Ho Chi Minh, "At the End of Four Months," translated by Aileen Palmer, in *The Prison Diary of Ho Chi Minh* (New York: Bantam Books, 1971), p. 85.

[8] John G. Hubbell, *P.O.W.*, p. 520.

[9] Rear Admiral Jeremiah A. Denton, Jr., USN (ret.), with Ed Brandt, *When Hell Was in Session,* p. 198; also noted in slightly different form by John G. Hubbell, *P.O.W.*, pp. 518–19.

[10] Steven V. Roberts, "Freed P.O.W.'s Carry Psychic Scars of War," New York *Times* (December 17, 1972), p. 1.

[11] Ibid.

[12] Ibid.

[13] Ibid.

[14] A majority of the returned POWs believed Wilber and Miller willingly collaborated with their captors (and attempted to persuade others to do likewise) to the extent that they voluntarily wrote and recorded anti-war statements, willingly visited with anti-war delegations, and accepted special treatment, food and medical treatment. After repatriation, both men were charged with mutiny by Rear Admiral James B. Stockdale, the senior Navy POW in Vietnam. The Secretary of the Navy found merit in Stockdale's accusations, but dropped the charges after investigation because prolonged courts-martial would be injurious to other POWs and their families. Wilber and Miller were officially censured for their conduct and retired from the service.

[15] This day's events were compiled from eye-witness reports and other dispatches published in the New York *Times* and other journals. The attack on the French legation was witnessed by Michael Maclear, a Canadian journalist.

[16] Flora Lewis, "France Makes Protest," New York *Times* (October 12, 1972), p. 18.

[17] Excerpted from transcripts of Dr. Kissinger's remarks, United Press and others (October 26, 1972).

[18] Transcript of remarks, New York *Times* (December 17, 1972), p. 34.

[19] "Attack on Hanoi Reported," Reuters dispatch printed in New York *Times* (December 19, 1972), p. 14.

[20] William Beecher, "White House Says Raiding in the North Will Go On Until There Is an Accord," New York *Times* (December 19, 1972), p. 1.

[21] Ibid.

[22] New York *Times* (December 28, 1972) and other sources.

[23] New York *Times* (December 24, 1972) and other sources.

[24] Telford Taylor, "Hanoi Under the Bombing: Sirens, Shelters, Rubble and Death," New York *Times* (January 7, 1973) and other sources.

[25] Thomas W. Lippman, "Last U.S. Jet on Final Bombing Mission Returns Safely to Base," Los Angeles *Times* (January 28, 1973), p. 1.

PART VII

[1] Jane Fonda, "Who Is Being Brainwashed?," *An Indochina Peace Campaign Report* (Santa Monica: Indochina Peace Campaign, 1973 [otherwise undated]), p. 4.

[2] Michael Miner, "Messiahs, well scourged, reciting a gospel of values past," *Chicago Journalism Review* (May 1973), p. 4.

[3] New York *Times* (February 13, 1973).

[4] Michael Miner, "Messiahs, well scourged," p. 4.

[5] Jane Fonda, "Who Is Being Brainwashed?," p. 4.

[6] "Hanoi Press Scores Former POW Stratton's 'Torture Tales,'" dispatch in English by Vietnam News Agency (dated April 12, 1973).

[7] Ford was among several American corporations that sought (with varied degrees of publicity) to welcome the POWs home and reward them materially for their services.

SELECTED BIBLIOGRAPHY

Books and Films

Ashmore, Harry S., and Baggs, William C., with Burnell, Ellen H. *Mission to Hanoi: A Chronicle of Double-dealing in High Places. A Special Report from the Center for the Study of Democratic Institutions.* New York: G. P. Putnam's Sons, 1968.

Berrigan, Rev. Daniel, S.J. *Night Flight to Hanoi: War Diary with 11 Poems.* New York: Perennial Library/Harper & Row, 1968.

Birmingham, Stephen. *Real Lace: America's Irish Rich.* New York: Harper & Row, 1973.

Blakey, Scott, with Russin, Joseph M., and Stapp, Blair. *2251 Days,* a documentary film. San Francisco: KQED, 1973.

Buss, Claude A. *Southeast Asia and the World Today.* Princeton: D. Van Nostrand Co., 1958.

Des Pres, Terrence. *The Survivor: An Anatomy of Life in the Death Camps.* New York: Oxford University Press, 1976.

Effros, William G. *Quotations Vietnam: 1945–1970.* New York: Random House, 1970.

Ellsberg, Daniel. *Papers on the War.* New York: Simon & Schuster, 1972.

Fall, Bernard B. *Viet-Nam Witness: 1953–1966.* New York: Praeger, 1966.

———, and Raskin, Marcus G. *The Viet-Nam Reader: Articles and Documents on American Foreign Policy and the Viet-Nam Crisis.* New York: Vintage, 1965.

Fifield, Russell H. *The Diplomacy of Southeast Asia, 1945–1958.* New York: Harper & Brothers, 1958.

Fitzgerald, Frances. *Fire in the Lake: The Vietnamese and the Americans in Vietnam.* New York: Vintage, 1973.

Gettleman, Marvin E., ed. *Vietnam.* Greenwich: Fawcett, 1966.

Giap, Gen. Vo Nguyen. *People's War, People's Army.* New York: Praeger, 1962.

Halberstam, David. *The Best and the Brightest.* New York: Random House, 1972.

Heynowski, Walter, and Scheumann, Gerhard. *Piloten im Pyjama.* Berlin, DDR: Verlag du Nation, 1968.

Hickey, Gerland C. *Village in Vietnam.* New Haven: Yale University Press, 1967 ed.

Hubbell, John G., et al. *P.O.W.: A Definitive History of the American Prisoner-of-War Experience in Vietnam, 1964–1973.* New York: Reader's Digest Press, 1976.

Knightley, Phillip. *The First Casualty.* New York: Harvest/Harcourt Brace Jovanovich, 1975.

Long, Ngo Vinh. *Before the Revolution: The Vietnamese Peasant Under the French.* Cambridge, Mass.: MIT Press, 1973.

McCarthy, Mary. *Vietnam.* New York: Harcourt, Brace & World, 1967.

Moore, Capt. John E., RN. *Jane's Pocket Book of Major Warships.* New York: Macmillan, 1973.

Rowan, Stephen A. *They Wouldn't Let Us Die.* Middle Village, N.Y.: Jonathan David Publishers, 1973.

Salisbury, Harrison E. *Behind the Lines—Hanoi: December 23, 1966–January 7, 1967.* New York: Harper & Row, 1967.

Schlesinger, Arthur M. *The Imperial Presidency.* Boston: Houghton Mifflin Co., 1973.

Sheehan, Neil, et al. *The Pentagon Papers as Published by 'The New York Times.'* New York: Bantam Books, 1971.

Thu, Hai. *North Viet Nam Against U. S. Air Force.* Hanoi: Foreign Languages Publishing House, 1967.

Weiss, Peter. *Notes on the Cultural Life of the Democratic Republic of Vietnam.* New York: Dell Publishing Co., 1970.

Woddis, Jack, ed. *Ho Chi Minh: Selected Articles and Speeches, 1920–1967.* New York: International Publishers, 1970.

Documents

Berg, Lt. Cdr. S. William, MC, USNR. *The Vietnam POW: Different But Not Unfamiliar.* San Diego: Center for Prisoner of War Studies, Navy Medical Neuropsychiatric Research Unit; A paper presented at the 27th National Convention of American Ex–Prisoners of War, Las Vegas, July 27, 1974.

"Investigation of Students for a Democratic Society. Part 7-A. (Return of Prisoners of War, and Data Concerning Camera News, Inc., 'Newsreel.'") Hearings before the [House] Committee on Internal Security, Dec. 9–11 and 16, 1969. Washington: U. S. Government Printing Office, 1970.

Kaiser, Edmond, et al. *Vietnamese Children in Fire and Blood,* and other papers. Lausanne: Terre des Hommes, 1966.

McCubbin, Capt. Hamilton I., MC, USA, et al. *Family Separation and Reunion.* San Diego: Naval Health Research Center; Report No. 74–70, 1975.

Spock, Dr. Benjamin, and Pepper, William F. *Special Report: The Children of Vietnam.* San Francisco: *Ramparts* Magazine, Jan. 1967.

U. S. Navy. "News Briefing with Lt. Robert Frishman, USN, and Seaman Douglas Hegdahl." Issued at Bethesda Naval Hospital, Bethesda, Md., Sept. 1969.

Articles

Ball, George W. "Top Secret: The Prophecy the President Rejected." *Atlantic Monthly,* June 1972; p. 36.

Butterfield, Fox. "Village in Vietnam: Peace Is Still at Hand." New York *Times Magazine,* Nov. 11, 1973; p. 37.

Byers, Margery. "At Home with the Prisoners' Families." *Life,* Oct. 20, 1967; p. 34.

Fallaci, Oriana. "Thieu." *The New Republic,* Jan. 20, 1973; p. 16.

Jones, James. "In the Shadow of Peace." New York *Times Magazine,* June 10, 1973; p. 15.

Lockwood, Lee. "Recollections of Four Weeks with the Enemy." *Life,* Apr. 7, 1967; p. 44B.

Marshall, Eliot, et al. "Vietnam: Some Afterthoughts." *The New Republic,* Feb. 10, 1973; p. 17.

(POWs): "Home at Last!" *Newsweek,* Feb. 26, 1973; p. 16.

(POWs): "POW Showdown: Hanoi Gives In." *Newsweek,* Mar. 12, 1973; p. 30.

(POWs): "Jane Fonda and Tom Hayden—Candid Conversation." *Playboy,* Apr. 1974; p. 67.

Roberts, Steven V. "2 Pilots, 2 Wars." New York *Times Magazine,* June 10, 1973; p. 14.

(Stratton): "U. S. Prisoner Said to Deny Pressure by Hanoi." Agence France-Presse dispatch from Hanoi published in New York *Times,* Apr. 17, 1967.

(Stratton): "U. S. Prisoners In North Vietnam." *Life,* Oct. 20, 1967; p. 21.

(Stratton): "North Vietnam Under Siege." *Life,* Apr. 7, 1967; p. 44.

(Stratton): "Controversial Prisoner Freed." New York *Daily News,*
Mar. 5, 1973; p. 1.

Taylor, Telford. "Hanoi Under the Bombing: Sirens, Shelters, Rubble and Death." New York *Times,* Jan. 7, 1973.

———. "Defining War Crimes." New York *Times,* Jan. 11, 1973.

———. "North Vietnam." *Atlantic Monthly,* May 1973; p. 4.

Wiskari, Werner. "Captive U.S. Flier Denies Being Brainwashed." New York *Times,* July 14, 1967; p. 4.

POW Literature

Chesley, Larry. *Seven Years in Hanoi.* Salt Lake City: Book Craft, 1973.

Dramesi, John. *Code of Honor.* New York: Norton, 1975.

Denton, Jeremiah A., Jr., with Brandt, Ed. *When Hell Was in Session.* New York: Reader's Digest Press, 1976.

Gaither, Ralph. *With God in a POW Camp.* Nashville: Broadman, 1973.

Helsop, J. N., and Van Orden, D. H. *From the Shadows of Death.* Salt Lake City: Desert Books, 1973.

Jensen, Jay Roger. *Six Years in Hell.* Salt Lake City: Horizon, 1974.

McDaniel, Eugene B., with Johnson, James L. *Before Honor.* Philadelphia: A. J. Holman Co., 1975.

McGrath, John M. *Prisoner of War.* Annapolis: Naval Institute Press, 1976.

Plumb, Charles. *I'm No Hero.* Independence, Mo.: Independence Press, 1973.

Risner, Robinson. *The Passing of the Night.* New York: Random House, 1973.

Rutledge, Howard and Phyllis, with White, Mel and Lyla. *In the Presence of Mine Enemies.* Old Tappan, N.J.: Fleming H. Revell, 1973.

INDEX

Abbot, W. B., 353
Academies, service, Code of Conduct and, 203–6, 207
Adkins, Clodeon (Speed), 328
A-4 attack planes, 4, 5, 6, 7, 352–53, 377
Agence France-Presse, 146, 286, 299
Aiken, George D., 292–93
Air Group 19, 101, 102; 194th Squadron, 112
Alameda Naval Air Station (Calif.), 58–59, 66
Albania, 276, 277
Alcatraz (NV POW camp), 208, 210
Alvarez, Everett, Jr., 329
American Committee for Solidarity with the Vietnamese People, 240
Annapolis (Md.), United States Naval Academy at, 52, 203, 207
Anti-war groups and movement, 24, 155–58, 170–78, 186, 195–97, 198, 219–26, 235–36, 252, 253, 254, 255, 256, 258ff., 273, 299 (*see also* Demonstrations, anti-war; *specific developments, groups, individuals*); and POW releases and homecoming, 229, 230, 239–40, 298, 326, 345–46
Apollo 12 moon landing, 257
Army Reserve, 55, 57
Ashmore, Harry S., 22, 26
Asia, background to U.S. involvement in Vietnam and, 74–83. *See also* United States; *specific administrations, countries, developments, events, places*
Astorga, Jose M., 327
Atterbury, Edward, 237

Bach Mai airfield, 285
Baggs, William C., 22, 26
Bagley, David H., 296

Bao Dai, 75, 76
Beallsville, Ohio, 291–93
Bean, Alan L., 257
Bennett, James R., 300, 314, 315
Berger, Reverend John, 264
Berrigan, Reverend Daniel, 229
Bethesda Naval Hospital, released POWs press conference at, 250–53
B-52 bombings, 284–85, 286, 287, 288, 289, 300
Birmingham, Stephen, 44
Black, John, 228
Black, Shirley Temple, 264
Bomar, Jack, 148–49, 150, 151, 166
Bon Homme Richard, U.S.S., 3, 165
Bors, Sondra, 263
Boston, Mass., 45–50, 51
Boykin, Thomas V., 295
Brainwashing (charges and issue), 133, 136–37, 146, 170, 173, 175, 187, 193, 346, 380
Brown, Evelyn Berger, 264–65
Buffalo *Evening News*, 259
Bui, Major, 127, 129, 130, 133, 148, 168–70, 174–75, 176, 178, 185, 190, 195, 196, 208, 210, 228, 231, 233, 238–39; in disgrace, relieved of his command as NV military prison commandant, 254–55
Burgess, Richard G., 327, 328
Burns, Donald Ray, 148–49, 150, 380
Byers, Margery, 165, 194–95
Byroade, Henry A., 320

Calley, William L., Jr., 256
Cambodia, 81; invasion of, 258, 259
Camp Faith (POW camp), 270, 273
Camp Unity (POW camp), 270–73, 274, 301, 312
Canberra, U.S.S., 162–63, 164
Carpenter, Joseph, 230
Carter, Jimmy, 375

Castro, Fidel, 114
"Cat, the." *See* Bui, Major
Catholicism, Roman. *See* Roman Catholic Church
Catholic University, 55, 57
CBUs, use of, 120, 121, 126, 144, 379
Central Intelligence Agency (CIA), 26, 28, 256
Chicago Journalism Review, 326
Chicago Seven, 235
China, Communist, 74, 75, 80, 81, 84, 285, 306
Clark, Ramsey, 262, 326, 355, 359
Clark, S. Dak., 161, 162, 164, 165, 267
Clark Air Base (Philippine Islands), 299, 316, 318, 319, 320, 321, 322, 323, 333
Clarke, Mary, 195
Code of Conduct, POWs and, 151–52, 164, 188, 190, 202ff., 229, 307; peer evaluation and, 203–6, 211–12; text of, 374–75
Coffin, Reverend William Sloan, Jr., 262
Collingwood, Charles, 22
Colorado Springs, United States Air Force Academy at, 203
Communications systems and methods, POWs and, 142–43, 147–48, 149–50, 191–92, 237–38, 271, 379–80 (*see also specific prison camps*); tap code, 379–80
Communism, 358 (*see also specific countries, developments*); U.S. involvement in Southeast Asia and, 74–83
Congress, United States, 4, 77, 80, 82, 328
Connecticut Yankee in King Arthur's Court (Twain), 184
Conrad, Charles, Jr., 257
Cook, Bill, 309–10
Cooper, Ellen Stratton (sister), 46, 48–49, 54, 155–58, 217, 219–22, 245, 248, 249, 250, 308; and anti-war activities, 219–22, 258–63, 334–35; and brother's homecoming, 332, 334–35
Cooper, Richard (brother-in-law), 155, 157, 217, 245, 248, 250, 259

Corps of Cadets, 203
Costello, Charles, 53, 91–92
Crawford, Jeanne, 60
Crecca, Joseph, Jr., 166, 174, 195, 196, 197
C. Turner Joy, U.S.S., 4, 82
Culhaine, Marie, 52
Cu Loc (the "Zoo," NV POW camp), 110, 112, 119, 124, 141–42, 147–52, 165–66, 177

Daily Worker, 175
Davis, Edward, 305
Davis, Rennie, 172, 196, 240
Decker, Joe, 292
DELAG, 177
Dellinger, Dave, 169–71, 172–76, 381
Demonstrations, anti-war, 235, 256, 260–61, 273. *See also* Anti-war groups and movement; *specific groups, individuals*
Denton, Jeremiah A., Jr., 133, 254
DeSoto mission, 81, 82
Diem. *See* Ngo Dinh Diem
Dien Bien Phu, 29, 75, 76
Domino theory, 76
Donald, Myron Lee, 233
Doumer (Long Bien) Bridge, Hanoi, 22, 28, 115, 313
Dramesi, John, 237, 306
Duck, Bonnie, 225, 264
"Dum Dum" (NV POW interrogator), 96, 129, 130
Durup, Paul, 56–57, 308

East Germans, and POW interview and photos, 177–78, 192, 194
Egelson, Nicholas, 171–72, 175–76
Eisenhower (Dwight D.) administration, 75, 76, 77, 78, 293
Evans, Mae Rose, 224

Fall, Bernard B., 253
Fallaci, Oriana, 236
"Fink Release Program," 229
Flynn, John Peter, 271–72
Fonda, Jane, 298, 326, 345, 355, 383
Ford Motor Company, 354, 383
Foreign Languages Publishing House (Hanoi), 28

Four-Party Joint Military
Commission, 299
Fourth Allied POW Wing, 271–72
Foy, Mr. and Mrs. Tòm, 72, 88,
153, 154, 158, 159, 217, 224, 353
France: and Hanoi bombings,
276–77; and Indochina, 74–75,
116, 184, 346, 366
Frishman, Robert F., 239, 240–41,
245, 250, 251–52, 254, 257, 263,
264
Fulbright, William, 82

Galanti, Paul, 192
Gaylor, Noel A. M., 320
General Longstreet, U.S.S., 51
Geneva Conventions and pacts, 36,
37, 38, 78–79, 94, 137, 160, 193,
224, 255, 278
Georgetown University, 55, 57
German Democratic Republic (East
Germany), and POW interview
and photos, 177–78, 192, 194
Gia Lam airport, 98, 282–83, 299,
300, 313–16
Great Britain, 78–79
Green Berets. *See* Special Forces
Gruening, Ernest, 82
Guam, 287, 319, 320
Guarino, Larry, 142
Guy, Theodore, 237

Hainan Island, 4, 84
Haiphong, North Vietnam, 25, 27,
117, 276; mining of harbor, 275,
283
Halberstam, David, 77
Hamilton, Alexander, 202
Hancock, U.S.S., 3
Hanford, Calif., 16, 71, 84, 153
Hanoi, North Vietnam, 22–29, 77,
113 (*see also* Vietnam,
Democratic Republic of);
bombings of, 23–29, 94, 95,
98–99, 107ff., 116ff.; described,
23, 116, 276, 313; Government
House, 27; Hotel Metropole, 22,
27, 116, 117, 119, 132, 240;
Opera House, 28; and Paris peace
talks, final bombings, cease-fire,
and release of POWs, 276–81,
282–90, 292–94, 295, 299–300,

313ff.; POW camps in and near
(*see specific prison camps by
name*); Presidential Palace, 28,
117; Red River delta, 276
Harriman, W. Averell, 136–37, 155,
193, 208, 255, 288
Harris, Smitty, 379
Hayden, Thomas (Tom), 172, 195,
196–97, 298, 326
Hegdahl, Abe, 161, 162, 165, 195,
227, 246
Hegdahl, Douglas, 161–67, 195,
223, 231–34, 354; and Alice
Stratton, 226, 227, 241, 245–50,
263, 270; and daily prison camp
routine, 179ff.; described,
background, family, fall from
Canberra and capture of, 161–66,
167–69; and hunger strike, in
solitary confinement, 197, 231,
233–36; and interviews, 174–76,
177–78, 195–96; and POW
activity after release, 264, 266–70;
and press conference on treatment
of POWs, 251–52, 254, 257;
release from POW camp, 185;
186–89, 227ff., 245–47, 249–53;
and Stratton and resistance
methods in POW camps, 167,
168–69, 179–85, 186–89, 193,
195, 209, 227–41, 245–47,
249–50, 257, 305–7
Hegdahl, Edith, 162, 165, 195, 246
Heynowski, Walter, 176–77, 192
Hivner, James Otis, 305
Hoa Lo ("Hanoi Hilton," NV POW
camp), 23, 35, 183, 289–90;
Camp Unity, 270–73, 274, 301,
312; cease-fire and, 294;
communications network, 271,
379–80; effect of Ho Chi Minh's
death on, 209–10, 253–55;
Heartbreak Hotel section, 99,
105, 164, 274; interrogations and
torture at, 36–41, 91–100, 104–5,
110–11, 226; and release of
POWs, 301–10, 311ff.; resistance
by POWs in, 208, 209, 273
Hoang Tung, 28
Ho Chi Minh, 29, 74, 82, 109, 116,
117, 121, 162, 221, 227, 269, 275,
313; death of, 209, 253–54

Hon Me (island), 81
Hon Ngu (island), 81
Hoover, J. Edgar, 171
House Committee on Internal
   Security, 252
Hoyt, Thaddeus B., 210, 211–12
Hubbard, Ed, 174
Hubbell, John G., 254
Humphrey, Hubert H., 255, 259

Indochina, 116, 326 (see also
   specific countries, developments);
   background to U.S. involvement
   in, 74–83; France and (see under
   France)
International Commission of
   Control and Supervision, 299
International Control Commission
   (ICC), 23, 78–79, 98, 109, 118
Intrepid, U.S.S., 3

Jackson, James, 197
Japan (the Japanese), 78, 236
Javits, Jacob, 359
Jayroe, Julius, 169
Johnson, Edward R., 197
Johnson, Lyndon B. (Johnson
   administration): and U.S.
   involvement in Vietnam, 2, 3, 78,
   79–80, 82, 83, 170, 255, 258, 277,
   287, 293; and bombings, 24, 25,
   26, 82, 83, 109, 230, 287, 373;
   death of, 293; replaced by Nixon,
   255; and Tonkin Gulf Resolution,
   4, 82–83, 258
Just, Ward, 203, 204–5

Kasler, Jim, 306
Kennedy, Mrs. John F., 197
Kennedy (John F.) administration,
   77–78, 79
Kerrigan, Father, 308
Kim Seng, M.V., 285
Kisselstein, Al, 347–48
Kissinger, Henry, 256, 275, 278,
   279, 280, 281, 289, 303, 313; and
   cease-fire and release of POWs,
   292, 303, 313
Knightley, Phillip, 380
Knutson, Rodney, 344–45
Kobelev, Yevgeni, 146–47
Kopfman, Ted, 13, 328

Korean War, 74, 75, 76, 171, 230,
   317, 380
Krause, Ruth, 195

Laird, Melvin, 250–51
Lamar, Jim, 303, 307
Lang, Mr. (NV foreign press aide),
   113, 114, 115, 123
Laos, 79, 81, 84, 259
Larson, Gordon, 306
Le Duc Tho, 275, 278, 279, 280,
   289
Lemoore Naval Air Station, 71
Lexington, U.S.S., 3
Liberation magazine, 171
Life magazine, 113–14, 116, 119,
   135, 136, 144, 147, 153, 154–55,
   157–58, 159, 165, 173, 178,
   192–95, 206, 235
Lockwood, Lee, 113–19, 123–30,
   132–36, 154–55, 158, 369, 381
Lodge, Henry Cabot, 255, 256
López (Prensa Latina
   correspondent), 145–46
Loughran, Reverend Terrence, 339,
   350
Low, James, 230
Lucas, J. Anthony, 261–62

McCarthy (Senator Joseph) and
   McCarthyism, 56, 74, 76
McGovern, George, 279
McKeller, Edward, 98
MacKenzie, Barbara, 225
McNair, William, 329
McNamara, Robert, 25
Maddox, U.S.S., 4, 81–82
Madison, Thomas M., 328
Malcom, Andrew, 292
Malraux, André, 27
Mao Tse-tung, 74, 75
Marr family, 159
Martin, Murphy, 267–68, 269
Maugham, W. Somerset, 27
MEMO, 196
Methany, David, 228–29, 248
MIA (missing-in-action), families
   of, 210, 214, 215, 221, 222, 223,
   224; and POW/MIA movement,
   214, 221, 222, 224–26, 263, 264,
   268

Michigan, University of, 61, 65, 217, 265

Military service environment, professional, Code of Conduct and, 202–6ff.

Miller, Edison Wainright, 273, 382

Miller, William, 212

Miner, Michael, 298, 326, 383

Monroe Doctrine, 76

Moore, William G., Jr., 320

Morris, Bill, 265

Morrow, Gary, 348

Morse, Wayne, 82

Mullen, Jeanne Louise Riggins, 102, 105

Mullen, Richard Dean ("Moon"), 101–5, 106–7, 110–12, 119, 149–52, 166, 203, 273–74, 289–90; background, described, 101–2; capture of, 103–4, 110; interrogation and torture of, 104–5, 106–7, 110–12; release of, 305–6, 312

My Lai, 256

Nan Dinh, North Vietnam, 26, 29

Napalm, use of, 120, 121

National Council of Reconciliation and Concord, 278, 280

National League of Families (of American Prisoners and Missing in Southeast Asia), 210, 222–26, 252, 260, 263–66, 267, 268; formation of, 222, 224

National Liberation Front, 29, 77, 197, 256, 261. See also Vietcong

National Mobilization to End the War in Vietnam, 171

National Peace Action Coalition, 279

National Security Council, 74, 76

Neal, Roy, 341

Newburgh, N.Y., Oblates of Mary Immaculate at, 53, 54

New Runway, 189, 193

Newsweek magazine, 235

New York State, casualties in Vietnam War from, 292

New York Times, 22, 26–27, 155, 157, 175, 261, 292, 362

Ngo Dinh Diem, 76–77, 79, 366

Nguyen Phuong, 300, 314, 315

Nguyen Van Thieu, 256, 278, 279, 280

Nhan Dan (NV newspaper), 28

Nixon (Richard M.) administration, and Vietnam War, 255, 256, 258–61; and mining of Haiphong, 275; and Paris peace talks, final bombings, and cease-fire, 277, 279, 280, 283, 285–86, 293; and POWs, 259–61, 269, 300, 308, 334

North Vietnam. See Vietnam, Democratic Republic of

Oak Knoll Naval Hospital (Oakland, Calif.), 329–30, 331–33, 337–40, 341, 344–46, 347–48, 349

Officer Candidate School (Newport, R.I.), 55, 205

Omaha, Nebr., 67, 68, 70, 79

Operation Homecoming, 317–25, 326–40, 341–48

Operation Rolling Thunder, 24, 83

Operation 34A, 79–80, 81, 82

Oriskany, U.S.S., 3

Overly, Norris, 229

Palo Alto, Calif., 69–70, 72, 88, 153, 159, 213, 217, 222, 225, 321, 335–37, 338–40, 351, 353

Paris peace talks, 224, 236, 255, 258, 268–70, 277; renewed and final bombings, cease-fire, and release of POWs, 277–81, 282–90, 292–94, 295, 302

Parks, John, 7, 10, 11, 12, 14, 16, 17, 370, 371–72, 373

Paul VI, Pope, 285

Peace Committee of North Vietnam, 172

Peace groups and movement. See Anti-war groups and movement; Demonstrations; specific groups, individuals

Pentagon, 78, 132, 317; and bombing of North Vietnam, 80, 82

Pentagon Papers, The, 76, 77, 108–9

Perot, H. Ross, 268, 269

Perth Amboy (tugboat), 51

Pham Van Dong, 117, 133
Phosphorus bombs, use of, 120, 121
Phuc Yen airfield, 98
Phu Ly, North Vietnam, 26, 29
Pilots in Pajamas, 177–78
Pittman, Jack, 292, 293
Pittman, Maegene, 292
Pitzer, Daniel, 197
Plantation Gardens ("Country
    Club," NV POW camp), 166,
    167–68, 179–99; Pow
    communications system in,
    237–38; resistance and releases,
    227–41; Stratton and POW
    resistance methods in, 208–12,
    255
Pleiku, 82–83
Plumb, Joseph Charles, 209
Pnompenh, 197
Pompidou, Georges, 277
Posner, Joseph, 329
POW/MIA movement, 221,
    222–26, 309, 354. *See also*
    National League of Families
POWs (*see also specific
    developments, individuals, prison
    camps*): anti-war movement and
    (*see* Anti-war groups and
    movement); cease-fire, releases,
    and homecoming of, 188–89,
    227–41 *passim,* 276–81, 282–90,
    292ff., 299–300, 301–10, 311–16,
    317ff. (*see also specific aspects,
    developments, individuals*); Code
    of Conduct and, 151–52, 202–12,
    374–75 (*see also* Code of
    Conduct); and communications
    network and systems, 191–92,
    237–38, 271, 379–80 (*see also
    individual prison camps*);
    "confessions" and press
    conferences, 115, 118–31, 132–37
    (*see also specific individuals*);
    effect of Ho Chi Minh's death on
    treatment of, 210, 253–55; and
    food, 181, 186, 189, 198, 254,
    255, 286; Geneva agreements and,
    36, 37 (*see also* Geneva
    Conventions and pacts);
    hard-liners among, 206, 207–8,
    209, 210–12; isolation and
    boredom and, 180, 183; in

Korean War, 380; propaganda use
    of, 115, 118–31, 132–37, 209,
    210, 231–34, 236 (*see also
    specific developments, individuals,
    kinds*); resistance by, 150–51,
    173, 184, 191, 206–12ff., 255 (*see
    also specific developments,
    individuals, kinds, prison camps*);
    Son Tay raid on, 270–71;
    treatment of (beatings,
    harassment, torture), 91–100,
    103ff., 133ff., 168, 180, 183, 210,
    211, 237, 238, 250–53, 298, 323,
    344–46, 347, 355 (*see also
    Torture; specific aspects,
    individuals, kinds, prison camps*);
    United States government policy
    and revelations on treatment of,
    222–23, 224, 250–53; wives' and
    families' activity on behalf of,
    222–26 (*see also specific groups,
    individuals, kinds, movements*); in
    World War II, 51
Prisoners of war. *See* POWs

Quincy, Mass., 46, 48, 51, 52,
    262–63

"Rabbit, the" (POW interrogator),
    108, 120, 121, 131, 133, 227–28,
    236, 314–15
Rabinowitz, Ralph, 66
Radio Hanoi, 278
Red Cross, 193, 254, 264, 268
Reslie, William, 327
Risner, Robinson, 119, 303
Robertson, John, 62
Robertson, Margaret Jeanne
    Lobban, 62, 63, 64, 65, 67
Robertson, Martin Rindlaub, 62–63,
    64, 65, 68, 86, 355
Robertson, Philip, 62
Roman Catholic Church (Roman
    Catholicism), 4, 45, 46, 50, 52,
    62, 65, 76, 262–63, 339–40,
    342–43
Roosevelt, Franklin D., 74
Rowan, Stephen A., 380
Rumble, Wesley, L., 239, 240–41
Russell, Bertrand, and war crimes
    investigation and tribunal, 23,
    110, 120, 143, 170, 171

Russia. *See* Soviet Union

Saigon, 76, 77. *See also* South
   Vietnam
Salas, Bobby, 117, 123, 125, 130
Salisbury, Harrison E., 22, 23,
   26–27, 109
San Francisco, Calif., 60, 66, 222
San Francisco *Chronicle*, 225–26,
   342
San Lorenzo, Calif., 66
Scheumann, Gerhard, 177, 192, 312
Schoenbrun, David, 22
Schumaker, Robert H., 380
Segal, Erich, 269
Service academies, Code of Conduct
   and, 203–6
Seventh Fleet, U. S. Navy, 4, 81–82,
   281, 287
Shangri La, U.S.S., 3
Shields, Roger, 323
Shoup, Denny, 102–3
Shrike missiles, use of, 120, 377
Simon, Arthur, and Son Tay raid,
   270–71
Simon de Quirielle, François, 133,
   276
Sims, B. J., 87
Smith, Tom, 197–98, 228, 229
"Soft Soap Fairy" (NV prison camp
   administrator), 228–29, 230, 254
Song Coa (river), 11
Son Tay prison raid, 270–71
Southeast Asia, background to U.S.
   involvement in, 74–83. *See also
   specific countries, developments,
   events, individuals*
Southeast Asia Treaty Organization
   (SEATO), 76
South Vietnam, 2, 24, 256 (*see also*
   Saigon; Vietnam War; *specific
   developments, events, individuals,
   places*); background to U.S.
   involvement in, 76–83; and Paris
   peace talks and cease-fire, 278–79,
   280, 281; and POW releases,
   299–300
Soviet Union (Russia), 75, 79, 170,
   197, 283, 306
Special Forces (Green Berets), 78,
   256, 270
Stack, Peter, 225–26

Stackhouse, Charles D., 165, 166
Stafford, Hugh Allan, 236, 237–38
Stanford University, 69–70, 72
State Department, United States, 22,
   55, 75, 155, 170, 203, 208, 328
Stockdale, James B., 211–12, 223,
   382
Stockdale, Sybil, 222, 223, 224
Stockman, Hervey, 229–30, 237,
   239
"Straps and Bars" (NV prison camp
   torturer), 95, 104–5, 168
Stratton, Alice Marie Robertson
   (wife), 9–10, 13, 21, 60–73,
   153–54, 158–60, 194–95, 213–26,
   244, 245–50, 263–66, 274–75,
   321; described, background,
   family, 9–10, 60–73; and
   Hegdahl, 226, 227, 241, 245–50,
   263, 270; and husband's
   "confession," 153–54; and
   husband's release, homecoming,
   and readjustment, 296, 304–5,
   307–10, 321–24, 329–31, 335–40,
   343–44, 349–55, 356–62, 365;
   marriage and children, 9–10, 59,
   60–73; notified of husband's
   capture, 84–88; and POW
   activism, 220–26, 263–66
Stratton, Charles (brother), 46, 48,
   49, 50, 217, 249, 308, 332
Stratton, Charles (son), 9, 68, 70,
   71, 85, 216, 217, 218, 263, 266,
   275; and father's homecoming,
   308, 309, 310, 331, 338, 356–57,
   360, 366–67
Stratton, Charles Arthur (father),
   46–49, 50, 52, 217, 220, 262, 308,
   331–32, 355
Stratton, Ellen (sister). *See* Cooper,
   Ellen Stratton
Stratton, Mary Louise Hoare
   (mother), 46–47, 50, 156, 217,
   220, 262, 308, 331–32
Stratton, Michael Francis (son), 9,
   70, 71, 154, 216, 217, 275, 308,
   310, 331, 338, 349; and father's
   homecoming, 308, 310, 331, 338,
   349, 356–57, 360, 366–67
Stratton, Patrick Thomas (son), 9,
   70–71, 194, 215–16, 217, 218,
   226, 266, 275; and father's

homecoming, 308, 310, 331, 356–57, 358, 359, 360, 366–67
Stratton, Richard Allen, 4–15, 16–21, 22, 25, 30–35, 36–41, 45–59, 60–73, 74, 91–100, 167–95, 198–99; as an admiral's aide, 70; and aviation cadet training, 57–59; background, family, early education, 45–59; "Beak" as POW code name of, 237, 380; beatings and physical harassment in POW camps of, 41, 91–100, 105ff., 168, 210–11, 255, 257; and bowing incident, 123, 128–29, 130–31, 135, 137, 143, 147, 172, 173, 175, 185, 206, 208, 248, 321; and Code of Conduct, 203–12; capture of, 12–15, 16–21, 22, 30–35; and communications network and systems in prison camps, 211, 228, 237–38; "confession" of, 97–100, 107–10, 119–23, 132ff., 141ff., 154, 211, 307, 321, 344; as a controversial figure, 137, 261–62, 309, 321, 323; and daily prison camp routine, 179ff.; and Dellinger interview, 170–74, 175, 176; descriptions of, 4, 8–10, 48–50, 51, 53, 60–61, 63, 68, 69, 70–71, 205, 330, 332ff., 350ff.; and East Germans' interview, 177–78, 192, 194; effects of POW experiences on, 332–33, 344–48, 349–55, 356–62, 365–67; and final bombing of North Vietnam, cease-fire, and POW releases, 286, 287–88, 289–90; and Hegdahl (see Hegdahl, Douglas); interrogation and torture of, 36–41, 91–100, 105–10, 151–52; as a leader of Plantation Gardens POWs, 255; leaves for combat duty in Vietnam, 72–73; and lectures and education program in Hoa Lo prison, 290; Lockwood's interview and Life article and, 113–19; marriage, children, 9–10, 59, 60–73; medals and awards, 354; Mullen and, 101–2, 106–7, 110, 111, 112, 119, 150–52; ostracism of, in prison, 151–52, 207–9, 211–12, 321, 323; at

Plantation Gardens camp, 167–68, 179ff., 255; and POW/MIA activity after release, 354–55, 359; and press conferences after release and return home, 327–28, 341–43, 344–46; and press interview and "confession" as POW, 124–31, 132–37, 141–49, 170–74, 175, 176–78; reaction at home to his "confession," 153–60; reaction of wife and family to his POW confinement and treatment, 153ff., 213–26, 245–50, 258ff.; release, homecoming, and readjustment, 296, 301–10, 311–16, 317–25, 326–40, 341–48, 349, 356–62, 365–67; remains with Navy after his release, 352–53; and resistance in POW camps, 150, 206–12, 233, 236, 248, 255; and seminary training, 52–54; in solitary confinement, 190–92, 196, 198–99, 207; wife's reaction and readjustment to his release and homecoming, 296, 307–10, 321–24, 329–31, 335–40, 343–44, 349–55, 356–62, 365; written "confession" (verbatim text) of, 369–73
Students for a Democratic Society (SDS), 171–72, 252
Susini, Pierre, 276–77

Takman, John, 110, 143–44, 145, 146
Tass, 132, 147, 159, 283, 286
Taylor, Maxwell, 79
10th Aeromedical Evacuation Squadron, 314, 327
Tet holiday, 28, 145
Thailand, 81, 278, 281, 287
Thanh Hoa, North Vietnam, 10, 11, 16, 33, 34, 103, 164
Thieu, Nguyen Van, 256, 278, 279, 280
Thompson, Fred, 230
Thornberry, Otis, 292
Ticonderoga, U.S.S., 3–7, 10, 11, 16, 81–82, 84, 97, 98, 101, 102, 103, 119, 120, 126

Tonkin, Gulf of, 84–85; incidents and resolution, 4, 79, 81–83; Yankee Station, 4–15

Torture (charges, incidents, and issue), 91ff., 133, 298, 323, 344–46, 347 (see also under POWs; specific developments, individuals, prison camps); Code of Conduct and, 375

Tran Van Lam, 278

Travis Air Force Base, 327

Trident Missile project, 353

Truman (Harry S.) administration, 74, 75, 77, 293; and Truman Doctrine, 76

Turner Joy. See C. Turner Joy, U.S.S.

United States (see also specific administrations, agencies, etc.): and involvement in Vietnam, 74–83, 255–56, 258–61ff., 365–66 (see also Vietnam War; specific countries, developments, individuals); and Paris peace talks, renewed and final bombings, and cease-fire, 255–56, 276–81, 282–90, 291–94, 295; and release and return of POWs (see under POWs)

Van Dien air raid, 24, 119

Van Loan, Jack, 191–92, 198, 208–9

"Vegetable Vic" (NV prison torturer), 41, 91, 92, 95, 96, 121, 168

Vietcong (VC), 82–83, 84, 130, 299. See also National Liberation Front

Vietminh, 74–75, 76

Vietnam, Democratic Republic of (North Vietnam), 3–15, 16–21, 22 (see also Hanoi; specific developments, individuals, places); background to U.S. involvement in Vietnam and (see under United States; Vietnam War); bombings of, 3ff., 23–29,
31, 79, 80, 83 (see also specific places); Ho Chi Minh's death and, 253–54; and Paris peace talks, renewed and final bombings, and cease-fire, 276–81, 282–90, 291–94, 295; and POWs (see POWs; specific prison camps); and release of POWs, 299–300, 301ff.; Vietnamese Committee for Solidarity with the American People, 240

Vietnam-Poland Friendship School, bombing of, 24

Vietnam War, 4–15, 71–73, 74–83 (see also South Vietnam; Vietnam, Democratic Republic of); anti-war groups and movement and, 21 (see also Anti-war groups and movement); background to U.S. involvement in (see under United States); bombings and, 3ff., 23–29, 31 (see also specific places); and Paris peace talks, renewed and final bombings, and cease-fire, 255–56, 276–81, 282–90, 291–94, 295; and POWs (see POWs; specific individuals, prison camps)

Viets, Jack, 342

Vinh Son, 82

Voice of Vietnam radio (Hanoi Hannah), 179, 229

Vo Nguyen Giap, 286

Webb, Ron, 237–28

West Point, United States Military Academy at, 203

Wilber, Walter E., 273, 346, 382

Wilson, Dagmar, 195

Women's Strike for Peace, 195–96

World War II, 50–51

Xuan Thuy, 224

Zaio, Mary, 60

Ziegler, Ronald L., 283–84

Zinn, Howard, 229

Zumwalt, Elmo, 260

About the Author

Scott Blakey has been associate editor and a producer for "Newsroom" at KQED-TV in San Francisco, urban affairs reporter for the San Francisco *Chronicle,* and managing editor of the Concord (N.H.) *Daily Monitor.* Among his journalistic awards are two regional Emmys for *2251 Days,* a documentary on Captain Stratton and his family that was shown on PBS in 1974. Mr. Blakey, now a free-lance writer, lives in San Francisco with his wife and family. His previous book, *San Francisco,* with photographer Bernard Hermann, was published in 1975.